Michael F. Sadler

The Church Teacher's Manual of Christian Instruction

being the church catechism expanded and explained in question and answer - for the use of clergymen, parents, and teachers

Michael F. Sadler

The Church Teacher's Manual of Christian Instruction
being the church catechism expanded and explained in question and answer - for the use of clergymen, parents, and teachers

ISBN/EAN: 9783337260026

Printed in Europe, USA, Canada, Australia, Japan

Cover: Foto ©Lupo / pixelio.de

More available books at **www.hansebooks.com**

THE
CHURCH TEACHER'S MANUAL

OF

CHRISTIAN INSTRUCTION.

BEING THE CHURCH CATECHISM EXPANDED AND EXPLAINED IN QUESTION AND ANSWER.

FOR THE USE OF CLERGYMEN, PARENTS, AND TEACHERS.

BY

THE REV. M. F. SADLER,
PREBENDARY OF WELLS, AND RECTOR OF HONITON.

THIRD EDITION.

LONDON:
BELL & DALDY, YORK STREET, COVENT GARDEN.
1872.

LONDON: PRINTED BY WILLIAM CLOWES AND SONS, STAMFORD STREET
AND CHARING CROSS.

PREFACE.

THE twofold series of questions and answers on the Church Catechism, contained in the following pages, is the substance of many years' catechizing and teaching in Church, Confirmation Classes, and Schools.

It is designed as a help to the Clergy in catechizing in Church, and in the instruction of candidates for Confirmation, as well as a manual for teachers in Church Schools of all grades. It is published in the catechetical form, because the author believes that the majority of teachers require assistance in putting questions, just as much as the pupils require instruction in answering them.

The two sets of questions are intended to be used simultaneously as well as separately; the first set, containing the longer and more difficult questions, is intended for the more advanced scholars; and the second, or shorter, is not only a subordinate exercise on the higher questions for the same class of pupils, but also a distinct and independent form of instruction for the less advanced.

The longer Catechism, the author believes, will be found to 'go as deeply into the Theology of the Catechism as is needful for those who require to be instructed in such a formulary; whilst the second is, he trusts, as simple as possible without being childish.

The author would earnestly recommend those who use this book to read carefully both Catechisms before giving instruction, as the second is not, in all cases, a reproduction of the first in shorter and simpler questions. The longer contains many arguments which it would not be well to split up into short questions and answers for smaller children; and, on the other hand, the shorter Catechism contains many questions which have nothing strictly corresponding to them in the first or higher series of questions: in particular, the shorter Catechism contains more questions of a Liturgical character; that is, questions, the answers to which are taken from the words of the Prayer Book.

The author has endeavoured to make the answers, even of the longer Catechism, as short as possible. In most cases, in which this rule does not seem to be adhered to, it will be found, on examination, that the answers embody passages from Scripture, or from the Liturgy, which it would be impossible to shorten or break up.

This, however, does not apply to Section XXXII., "On the Scripture Proof of the Doctrine of the Trinity." The due examination of the proofs of this Great Mystery requires more the form of a treatise than of a Catechism, and the answers in that Section frequently embody a train of thought which cannot be expressed clearly in one or two short sentences. The same remark applies to the Sections on the Sacraments.

In preparing this work, the author has consulted at least fifty Catechisms, besides separate treatises on the Creed, the Lord's Prayer, the Ten Commandments, and the Sacraments.

The Sacrament of Baptism is twice dwelt upon: first, in Sections II., III., IV., where it is treated more simply, and with almost exclusive reference to the notice of it in the beginning of the Catechism; secondly, in Sections LIII., LIV., LV., where it is treated more deeply in connection with the general theory of Sacramental grace.

In treating of the Holy Communion, the order of the Catechism has been strictly adhered to, and, consequently, the first place given to the Commemoration, or Sacrificial aspect of the Eucharist, though in most Catechisms the Eucharist is considered primarily as a means of Communion, and only a very subordinate place given to the Sacrificial side of the Holy Rite.

A Catechism on Confirmation has been added, which is sold separately.

May He Who charged His Apostle first of all to feed the lambs of His Flock vouchsafe His blessing on this endeavour to carry out His Blessed Will.

NOTE.—The numerals in brackets at the end of many questions in the longer Catechism refer to the corresponding questions in the shorter.

THE CHURCH CATECHISM.

SECTION I.—THE CHRISTIAN NAME.

1. **WHAT IS YOUR NAME?**
   N. or M.
2. *Why is this the first question in the Catechism?*
   Because, at my Baptism, God's minister called me by this name when he said to me, "I baptize thee in the name of the Father, and of the Son, and of the Holy Ghost." (1-8)
3. *Is there any other reason why you should first of all be asked your name?*
   Yes; because certain promises and vows were then made in my name. (4)
4. *Is it well that you should be thus asked your name?*
   Yes; because it reminds me of my responsibility.
5. *How does it do this?*
   Because it reminds me that I, who am called by this name, must for myself renounce all the works of the devil: that I, who am called by this name, must for myself believe in God: that I, who am called by this name, must for myself do God's will. (11)
6. *Cannot any of these things be done for you?*
   No. I myself have been bought with the Blood of Christ to serve God, and I shall myself have to be judged at last for the deeds done in this my body. (8-12)
7. *Why do we hold the giving of a name to be so very solemn a matter that we make it a part of the Baptismal rite?*
   Because we find in the Scriptures that on particular occasions God Himself gave names to men, as when He sent His angel to call His Son by the name of Jesus. (Matt. i. 21.) [Also Abram, Abraham (Gen. xvii. 3-7); Jacob, Israel (Gen. xxxii. 28); Simon, Cephas (John i. 42); John the Baptist (Luke i. 13, 63).]

8. *Does Christ know you now by this name?*
   If I am one of His true sheep He does.
9. *Where do you learn this?*
   I read that "He calleth His own sheep by name;" and I read that He said, "I know my sheep, and am known of mine." (John x. 3, 14.)
10. WHO GAVE YOU THIS NAME?
    MY GODFATHERS AND GODMOTHERS IN MY BAPTISM, WHEREIN I WAS MADE A MEMBER OF CHRIST, THE CHILD OF GOD, AND AN INHERITOR OF THE KINGDOM OF HEAVEN.
11. *How came it that your God-parents gave you this name?*
    Because before the minister of Christ baptized me, he took me into his hands and said to my God-parents, "Name this child." (14) (15)
12. *Who presented you then to be baptized?*
    My Godfathers and Godmothers. (16-21)
13. *Did your parents present you?*
    They were not supposed to do so.
14. *Was this right?*
    Yes; because my God-parents represented the Church, in whose faith I was baptized.
15. *Were you not baptized in your parents' faith?*
    Not necessarily; for if my parents had not been believers in Christ, I could still have been baptized, if others undertook that I should be brought up in the faith.
16. *In what right then were you baptized?*
    In right of my redemption by the Blood of Christ.
17. *Are all redeemed by His Blood?*
    Yes; all the children of the first Adam are redeemed; that is, bought again, by the Blood of Christ, the Second Adam.
18. *Can you give any other reason why we should have God-parents?*
    Yes, by this Holy Custom five persons, rather than two only (the parents), are pledged to pray for, and instruct each child.
19. *Can you give another reason?*
    Yes. It is a custom which can be traced back almost to the times of the Apostles.
    [Tertullian, who flourished in the year 200, mentions it as if it were universally prevalent in his day.]

20. *But may not an old custom be a wrong one?*
 Yes; but it is more probable that it is a right one. A custom which can be traced to so early a date is far more likely to be right than wrong.

SHORTER CATECHISM.

1. *How many names has each child?*
 Two: a Christian name and a surname.
2. *Which name was given to you when you were baptized?*
 My Christian name.
3. *Can a child have more than one Christian name?*
 No: all his Christian names are reckoned as one.
4. *Why should you be asked your Christian name?*
 To remind me that I am a Christian child.
 [To remind me of my Christian privileges—of my Christian profession—of my responsibility.]
5. *What name do you receive from your parents?*
 My surname, *i.e.*, the name of my family.
 [NOTE. Surname. The name which one has over and above his Christian name. To explain it as sire-name, *i.e.*, the name of the sire, seems a mistake.]
6. *What name did you receive from the Church?*
 My Christian name.
7. *Why do you say that you received it from the Church?*
 Because the minister of the Church first named me by it.
8. *When did you receive your Christian name?*
 When I was christened, or made a Christian.
9. *Who are Christians?*
 The disciples, or scholars of Christ (Acts xi. 26).
10. *When then you are asked your Christian name, of whom should it remind you?*
 It should remind me of my Master.
11. *Of what else should it remind you?*
 Of my calling.
12. *Why should it do this?*
 Because as surely as I am called by a Christian name, so surely am I called to serve Christ.
13. *Why is your Christian name asked you in your Catechism?*
 Because the Catechism is for baptized persons only, and my Christian name is the name I received at my Baptism.
14. *By whom was your Christian name given to you?*
 By my godfathers and godmothers.
15. *When?* At my Baptism, or when I was christened.
16. *Why was it given to you then?*
 Because I was then brought into covenant with God.

17. *What is a covenant?*
    An agreement between two or more persons.
18. *What was then agreed upon between you and God?*
    God agreed to give me certain benefits, and I agreed to do certain duties.
19. *By whom did God make the agreement?*
    By the minister who baptized me.
20. *Through whom did you make the agreement?*
    Through my god-parents.
21. *Why are they called godfathers and godmothers?*
    Because they present us to be made children of God; and so, as our natural parents have brought us into our earthly family, so our god-parents have brought us into a heavenly family.
22. *What family is that?* The family of God.
23. *What are they called besides?* Sponsors and sureties.
24. *What is a sponsor?* One who answers in behalf of another.
25. *What is a surety?*
    One who undertakes that another shall do a thing.
26. *What is the duty of a god-parent or sponsor?*
    To see that the infant be taught, so soon as he shall be able to learn, what a solemn vow and promise has been made in his name.
27. *Is it right that a Christian name should be given at Baptism?*
    Yes; if we then enter into covenant with God.
28. *Can you give any reason from Scripture for this?*
    Yes, the Jews, the ancient people of God, received their names at their circumcision.
29. *What was circumcision?*
    The rite or ceremony by which they entered into covenant with God. (*See* Gen. xvii. 5, 6, 7.)
30. *Give two remarkable instances of persons receiving their names at their circumcision.*
    John the Baptist and our blessed Lord (Luke i. 59–63; ii. 21).
31. *What amongst us answers to circumcision?*
    Holy Baptism.
32. *When then should we receive our name?* At our Baptism.
33. *Can an unbaptized person have a Christian name?*
    Not one given to him in a Christian way.
    [In fact, such an one is named with no more religious dedication than a dumb animal.]
34. *To what church does St. Paul say that Christians have come?*
    To the church of the first-born, whose names are written in Heaven (Heb. xii. 23).
35. *What, then, should be our anxiety about our Christian name?*
    We should be, above all things, anxious that Christ should never blot it out of the book of life.

SECTION II.—MEMBERS OF CHRIST.

1. *What were you made in Holy Baptism?*
   In my Baptism I was made a member of Christ, the child of God, and an inheritor of the Kingdom of heaven. (1) (2)
2. *Are these three separate blessings?*
   No; the two latter are included under the first. I was made a child of God, and an inheritor of the Kingdom of heaven, because I was made a member of Christ.
3. *What do you mean by a member of Christ?*
   I mean a member of His Body, the Church. (2-6)
4. *In what sense is the Church the Body of Christ?*
   It is His mystical body. (7)
5. *Why do you call the Church His mystical body?*
   To distinguish it from His natural body.
6. *Why is it called a mystical body?*
   Because all the members of it are joined to Him as their head in some mysterious or supernatural way, which we cannot comprehend. (13-19)
7. *Do you believe that they are really joined to Him, though you do not understand how?*
   Yes; the Church is called in Scripture the *body* of Christ, and it is the nature of a body to be made up of a number of members, all joined to their head, and all receiving life from the head, and governed by it. (13)
8. *But is not all this what is called a figure, or a figurative way of speaking?*
   It may be a figure, but it is a figure used by God's Holy Spirit, and so must teach us something very real. (13-24)
9. *What must be implied by the use of such a figure?*
   That we are in some mysterious way as closely joined to Christ as the members or limbs of a body are joined to its head. (13-24)
10. *Where are you taught in Scripture that Christians are members of Christ?*
    In very many places, especially in the Epistles of St. Paul.

11. *Mention one of these places.*
"As the body is one, and hath many members, and all the members of that one body, being many, are one body: so also is Christ. For by one Spirit are we all baptized into one body. . . . Now ye are the body of Christ, and members in particular."—1 Cor. xii. 12, 27.

12. *Mention another.*
Ephes. i. 22. God hath given Christ to be "Head over all things to the Church, which is His body." Also, Col. i. 18 : "He is the head of the body, the Church."

13. *Is it of importance that we should believe and remember that we have been made members of Christ?*
Yes : it is of the greatest importance.

14. *Why?*
Because they who really believe such a thing must be kept from sin by the remembrance of it.

15. *How do you show this?*
First because the Apostle, speaking by the Holy Ghost, writes to the Corinthian Churches that they are to put away from them everything unholy and impure, because unholy actions would defile the members of Christ.
"Know ye not that your bodies are the members of Christ?... Know ye not that your body is the temple of the Holy Ghost which is in you; and ye are not your own? For ye are bought with a price; therefore glorify God in your body, and in your spirit, which are God's."—1 Cor. vi. 15, 19, 20. (32)

16. *What other Christian grace would the thought that you are a member of Christ work within you?*
The grace of Christian charity and sympathy.
[St. Paul, in 1 Cor. xii., draws attention to the need which the various members of the human frame have for one another's help, and applies all this to the mystical body of Christ in the words (v. 11-13), " God hath tempered the body together... that the members should have the same care one for another ; and whether one member suffer, all the members suffer with it ; and one member be honoured, all the members rejoice with it."] (35)

17. *Is there any other way in which we should be better Christians if we were ever to remember that we have been baptized into Christ's body?*
Yes ; St. Paul reminds the Roman Christians of it, in order that they might not think of themselves more highly than they ought to think, but think soberly. (Rom. xii. 3, 4, 5.) (34)

18. *Would the constant remembrance of this first Baptismal privilege have any other good effect?*
Yes ; it would make us truthful ; for St. Paul writes :

"Putting away lying, speak every man truth with his neighbour, for we are members one of another," *i. e.* in the body of Christ. (Ephes. iv. 25.) (33)

19. *What proof did our Saviour give from heaven that He held Himself and the members of His Church to be one [body]?*

When He appeared to Saul He said to him, "Saul, Saul, why persecutest thou me?" "I am Jesus, whom thou persecutest." (Acts ix. 4, 5.)

20. *What does this mean?*

That Saul, in persecuting the members of Christ's Church, had persecuted Christ Himself.

[This answer was given unprompted by a little child under ten in a National School. He seems to have grasped the truth as firmly as the great Saint (Augustine) who writes : " If thou lovest the Head, thou lovest also the members ; but if thou lovest not the members, neither lovest thou the Head. Dost thou not quake at the voice uttered by the Head from heaven on behalf of His members, ' Saul, Saul, why persecutest thou Me?' The persecutor of His members He calls His persecutor ; His lover, the lover of His members. Now what are His members, ye know, brethren? none other than the Church of Christ."] (39–44)

21. *In realising then this truth that we are members of Christ, what do we realise?*

The love of Christ to His people. (39–44)

22. *How does St. Paul set forth this?*

In the words, " Christ also loved the Church, and gave Himself for her (αὐτῆς) ; that He might sanctify and cleanse her with the washing of water by the word... so ought men to love their wives as their own bodies. No man ever yet hated his own flesh, but nourisheth and cherisheth it, even as the Lord the Church. For we are members of His body, of His flesh, and of His bones." (Ephes. v. 25–30.)

23. *Is not all this a strong reason why we should often call to mind our Baptism and its benefits?*

Yes. To forget it is to forget a great part of the love of Christ to His people.

24. *Is there any danger lest we should presume that we are members of Christ, and so safe if we continue in sin?*

No : men cannot presume upon any such a thing. Men

always fall into sin by forgetting their union with Christ; never by presuming upon it.

25. *Under what figure does our Lord set forth that we are members of His Body?*
    Under the figure of a vine and its branches.
    [John xv. 1–8. "I am the true vine... Abide in me... I am the vine; ye are the branches."] (44–53)

26. *What do you gather from these words of our Saviour?*
    I first of all gather, that we can be "in" Him, in some mysterious way, just as the branches of a vine are in the vine. (44–53)

27. *What next do you gather from these words?*
    I gather that all our power to do good works, pleasing to God, comes from Christ, just as the power of a vine-branch to bear fruit comes from its being a real part of the vine. (47–51)

28. *What lastly do you gather?*
    I gather that those who are grafted into Christ are not sure of continuing in Him to the end, but must strive and pray with all diligence that they may so continue. (51–53)

SHORTER CATECHISM.

1. *When you were baptized of Whom were you made a member?*
    I was made a member of Christ.
2. *Were you born a member of Christ?* No.
3. *What is a member?* A limb: a part of the body.
4. *Mention some members of your body?*
    The hands, the feet, the tongue.
5. *Were you made the hands or the feet of Christ in Baptism?* No.
6. *What then do you mean by saying that you were made a member of Christ?*
    I was made a member of His Church.
7. *What is His Church?*
    A company of people who believe in Him as the Son of God, and are baptized.
8. *When were you made one of these people?*
    At my Baptism.
9. *What is this company of people called?*
    The body of Christ.
10. *Who calls this company of people the body of Christ?*
    The Holy Spirit.

11. *Where does He so call them?*
    When He says, "Ye are the body of Christ" (1 Cor. xii. 27).
12. *Where else?*
    When He says that Christ is head over all things to the Church, which is His body (Ephes. i. 22, 23).
13. *If the Holy Spirit calls this company of people the body of Christ, what must it be?*
    It must really be in some wonderful way joined to Christ, as a human body is to its head.
14. *Of what is this company or Church of Christ made up?*
    • Of persons, *i.e.*, of men, women, and children.
15. *But are the limbs of our bodies persons?* No.
16. *How then can a number of persons be called a body?*
    Because they are all under one head.
17. *What do you mean by that?*
    That they are all directed or governed by one head.
18. *What part of your body directs or controls all the other members?*
    My head—the soul or spirit which is in my head.
19. *For your head to control or govern all the members of your body, what must there be?*
    There must be some connection between my head and the members of my body.
20. *What makes the connection between your head and the members of your body?*
    The nerves.
21. *If these nerves were cut or destroyed, what would take place?*
    My hands could not feel or work, and my feet could not walk.
22. *What would become of them?*
    They would wither, or be palsied, or paralysed.
23. *How then can our hands and feet do their work?*
    Because they are joined to the head.
24. *Is there anything like all this with respect to us and Christ?*
    Yes; or the Holy Spirit would not call us members of Christ.
25. *If the members of Christ's body, the Church, are joined to Him, what will they have?*
    They will have spiritual life.
26. *Give some mark of spiritual life.*
    Trying to serve and please God.
27. *Give another.* Loving one another.
28. *Give a third.* Praying to God.
29. *If a baptized person does not do any of these things, what have we reason to fear?*
    We have to fear that he is falling away from Christ (or ceasing to be a member of Christ).
30. *What ought baptized persons ever to remember?*
    That they have been made members of Christ.

31. *If we always remembered that we were members of Christ, what would it make us?*
    Holy and pure.
32. *What would it make us shun?*
    Every filthy defiling action (1 Cor. vi. 15, 18, 19).
33. *What besides would it make us?*
    Truthful (Ephes. iv. 25).
34. *What besides?* Sober-minded (Rom. xii. 3, 4, 5).
35. *What besides would it make us have?*
    A fellow-feeling for all Christians (1 Cor. xii.).
36. *After whose example?*
    After the example of Christ our Head.
37. *Does the head feel when the members are hurt?* Yes.
38. *Does Christ, our Head, feel, when we, His members, are hurt?*
    Yes.
39. *What words of His show this?*
    His words to Saul of Tarsus: Why persecutest thou me?
40. *Had Saul ever persecuted Christ Himself?* No.
41. *Whom had he persecuted?* The members of His Church.
42. *How did the Saviour regard this?*
    As if Saul had persecuted Him.
43. *To what does our Lord compare Himself and His Church?*
    To a vine and its branches (John xv. 1–10).
44. *Why do the branches of a vine bear fruit?*
    Because they are grafted into, or joined to, the vine itself.
45. *How comes this about?*
    Because, when they are rightly joined, the sap or goodness flows from the vine into them.
46. *Are all Christians then in Christ?*
    No: only those who bear fruit.
47. *What is the fruit that Christians bear?*
    The same fruit as Christ bore.
48. *Why?*
    Because He gives them of His nature (just as the vine gives of its nature to the branches).
49. *Mention some of these fruits.*
    Prayer, thankfulness, love or charity, patience.
50. *Why do some baptized Christians bear no fruit?*
    Because they do not keep united to Christ.
51. *What will become of them?* They will be cut off.
52. *What will be their doom at last?*
    They will be cast away and burned (John xv. 6).

SECTION III.—MEMBERS OF CHRIST BY BAPTISM.

1. *When were you thus made a member of Christ?*
    In my Baptism. (1–5)
2. *What took place when you were baptized?*
    The minister dipped me in water, or poured water upon me, "in the name of the Father, and of the Son, and of the Holy Ghost."
3. *But how could this make you a member of Christ?*
    Because it was ordained by Christ Himself for that purpose. (1–5)
4. *When did He ordain it?*
    When He said, "Go ye and teach all nations, baptizing them in the name of the Father, and of the Son, and of the Holy Ghost." (Matt. xxviii. 19.) And when He said, "He that believeth and is baptized shall be saved." (Mark xvi. 16.)
5. *On what occasion besides this did He set forth the necessity of Baptism?*
    When he said, "Except a man be born of water and of the Spirit, he cannot enter into the kingdom of God. (John iii. 5.) (12–15)
6. *What does the Kingdom of God mean here?*
    The Church of Christ.
7. *Why?*
    Because our Lord founded only one Society, which is sometimes called His Kingdom, and sometimes His Church.
8. *How do you know that our Lord alludes here to our admission into His Church?*
    Because when His Church was actually set up on the day of Pentecost men were admitted into it by Baptism. "What shall we do? Repent, and be baptized every one of you in the name of Jesus Christ for the remission of sins." (Acts ii. 37, 38.)
9. *But though these places tell us that Baptism is needful to salvation, they do not tell us that we are made members of Christ in it?*
    Salvation consists in union with Christ. If then Bap-

tism contributes to our salvation, it can only do so because in it we are united to Christ. (10, 11)

10. *But is it ever expressly said that we are made members of Christ in this rite?*

Yes. In Galatians iii. 26. "As many of you as have been baptized into Christ have put on Christ. There is neither Jew nor Greek . . . for ye are all one"—[*i. e.*, one body] in Christ Jesus.

[See also Rom. xii. 4, 5; 1 Corinth. xii. 12, 13; Ephes. iv. 4, 5, 25.]

11. *Is it anywhere else expressly declared?*

Yes. When St. Paul says, "By one Spirit are we all baptized into one body." (1 Corinth. xii. 13.)

12. *What does he mean by this?*

He means that though the ministers of the Church are many, the Spirit of Whom they are the instruments is One, and the Body into which they engraft men is one also.

13. *But can men be thus the instruments of the Spirit?*

They must be, if we are to receive any benefit in Baptism, for we do not baptize in our own power or name.

14. *But is it not hard to believe that men in flesh and blood can be the instruments of uniting us in the body of One at the right hand of God?*

Not if we remember that the Son of God came amongst us in flesh and blood, and ordained men in flesh and blood to act for Him as His ambassadors (John iv. 1, 2; xx. 21; Acts iii. 12; v. 4; ix. 34; 2 Corinth. ii. 10; iv. 7; v. 20); and ordained an outward organization of men in flesh and blood, and sanctified our very bodies, and will raise up our bodies at the last day.

SHORTER CATECHISM.

1. *When were you made a member of Christ?*
   In my Baptism.
2. *Who baptized you?* The Holy Spirit.
3. *By whose hands.* By the hands of the minister
4. *In whose name did the minister baptize you?*
   In the name of the Father, and of the Son, and of the Holy Ghost.

5. *By whose command?*
   By the command of Christ (Matt. xxviii. 19, 20; Mark xvi. 16; John iii. 5).
6. *For what purpose?*
   That I might be made a member of Christ.
7. *For what further purpose?*
   That I might be taught as a member of Christ.
8. *For what further purpose?*
   That I might live as a member of Christ.
9. *Why were you baptized so early?*
   Because I cannot be too soon made a member of Christ, and be taught to live as a member of Christ ought to live.*
10. *Is Baptism needful to salvation?* Yes.
11. *Why?*
    Because we are saved by being brought into the mystical body or Church of Christ.
12. *What is the Church of Christ called by our Lord?*
    The Kingdom of God.
13. *How must we enter into the Kingdom of God?*
    By being born of water and of the Spirit (John iii. 5).
14. *Does the minister bring us into the Kingdom of God?*
    No: God does this by the hands of the minister.
15. *Will all those brought into the Kingdom of God here be in the Kingdom of God at last?*
    No: our Lord says that some of the children of the kingdom shall be cast into outer darkness (Matt. viii. 12).

* This answer was also given unprompted by a child of about ten years of age.

SECTION IV.—INFANT BAPTISM.

1. *You were baptized when an infant, before you could understand what blessing you received: was this right?*
   Yes: assuredly it was right that I should be then baptized. (1-12)
2. *Why?*
   Because Christ is the second Adam.
3. *What has this to do with your Baptism as an infant?*
   I was baptized into Christ, the second Adam, in order that I might receive grace from Him to undo the evil I had received from the first Adam. (3-8)
4. *Was this reasonable?*
   Yes, it was reasonable; for if I received evil from the first Adam when I knew not what I received, why should I not receive good from the Second Adam, when I equally knew not what I received? (6-11)
5. *But is not faith required in each one of us before we can receive a blessing from Christ?*
   No: faith is only required in those who are old enough to believe for themselves.
6. *Show this from Scripture.*
   Our Lord laid His hands, to bless them, upon infants, who could not have then known Him, or expected to receive any blessing from Him. (13-18)
7. *But was this " Laying on of hands " by our Lord the same thing as Baptism?*
   It was the same thing as Baptism in this respect, that it was the outward visible sign of an inward grace or blessing. From such an one as our Lord, it must have conveyed some blessing. (18-22)
8. *Have you any other proof that Christ is willing to bless those who cannot exercise faith?*
   Yes. It is recorded that on several occasions Christ healed deaf and dumb persons and lunatics, and even those who, being possessed with evil spirits, opposed and rejected Him. (Matt. viii. 29, ix. 2; Mark vii. 32, ix. 17.)

9. *Does our Lord say anything respecting infants which would lead us to believe that He would make them members of His Body in Holy Baptism?*
    Yes: He says of infants, "Suffer little children to come unto me, and forbid them not;" and He also says of them, "Of such is the Kingdom of God." (Mark x. 13.) (13)
10. *But when He says, "Suffer little children to come unto me," may He not have meant, "Suffer them to come to me for instruction?"*
    He cannot then have meant any such thing, because the persons who were bringing the children were bringing them that He should lay His hands upon them, not that He should instruct them.
11. *What then do you learn from this?*
    That children may be brought to Him, and be blessed by Him in a rite of which they do not, at the time, understand the meaning. (14–22)
12. *What does He mean by saying, "Of such is the Kingdom of God?"*
    He probably means, "Of such is the Church of God."
13. *What, then, do you infer from these words of Christ?*
    That if the Church is composed of such as are like children, children themselves may of course belong to it, and so must be brought into it by Baptism.
14. *Have you any other reason for the Baptism of infants?*
    Yes: St. Peter says, "Repent, and be baptized every one of you in the name of Jesus Christ for the remission of sins, and ye shall receive the gift of the Holy Ghost; for the promise is to you, and to your children." (Acts ii. 38, 39.)
15. *How does this bear upon Infant Baptism?*
    We are baptized because of a promise, but this promise equally belongs to children, and so children, who have a right to the promise, have a right to the Baptism which seals the promise. (23–27)
16. *What promise, among others, must St. Peter have meant?*
    The promise in Isaiah: "I will pour my Spirit upon thy seed, and my blessing upon thine offspring; and they shall spring up as among the grass, as willows by the water-courses." (Isaiah xliv. 3, 4.)
17. *Have we any other reason for infant Baptism?*
    Yes, we read of whole households being baptized. (Acts xvii. 15, 33; 1 Corinth. i. 16.)

18. *But we have no proof that these households contained children.*

It is probable that they were mostly made up of children.

19. *Why do you suppose this?*

Because it is very unlikely that, if they had been made up of persons of full age, all these would at once have consented to be baptized into a despised religion.

20. *Can you give any other reason for Infant Baptism?*

The Jews were required to bring their children into covenant with God when they were infants [on the eighth day after their birth]. (26–29)

21. *Is this any law or rule for us?*

No; it is not a rule, but it is an assurance. (30–34)

22. *In what way?*

If God so cared for the children of Jews that he made them so early partakers of His covenant, and of its outward sign, much more will He provide for the children of Christians—that they should have a Sacrament to assure them of His good-will. (30–34)

23. *But how is it that we have no rule in the New Testament to baptize children on a particular day?*

Because the New Testament is not a book of laws or rules, but an account of the life of our Lord, and of the love it shows to all men.

24. *For what is it especially given to us?*

To excite our faith in the Only Begotten Son of God.

25. *What, then, does the Church show when she baptizes infants?*

She shows her faith in Jesus, as the same yesterday, to-day, and for ever.

26. *Repeat the words in which she would stir up this faith in us.*

"Doubt ye not, therefore, but earnestly believe, that He will likewise favourably receive this present infant: that He will embrace him with the arms of His mercy; that He will give him the kingdom of heaven and everlasting life"

SHORTER CATECHISM.

1. *When were you baptized?* When I was an infant.
2. *Why were you baptized when you were an infant?*
   Because I was born in sin as an infant.
3. *What were you born under?*
   I was born under a curse (Ephes. ii. 3).
4. *What were you baptized for?*
   That I might come under a blessing.
5. *Under what curse were you born?*
   I was born in sin (under the curse of sin).
6. *From whom did you receive this sin?* From my parents.
7. *From whom did they receive sin?* From their parents.
8. *From whom then have all received sin?* From Adam.
9. *What blessing did you receive at Baptism?*
   The blessing of being made a member of Christ.
10. *Why did you receive this blessing from Christ?*
    Because He is the second Adam.
11. *For what purpose did you receive it?*
    To undo the sin and curse I received from the first Adam.
12. *When you received this blessing from Christ in Baptism, did you know what you received?*
    No, I did not; just as I did not know that I received evil from the first Adam when I was born in sin.
13. *Do you think that Christ is willing that you should be brought to Him for a blessing?*
    Yes; He expressly said that He is when He said, "Suffer the little children to come unto Me, and forbid them not, for of such is the Kingdom of God" (Mark x. 14).
14. *How did these children come to Christ?*
    They were brought by others (by their parents).
15. *For what were they brought?*
    That Christ might bless them by laying His hands upon them.
16. *Did they understand the meaning of what Christ did to them?*
    No.
17. *Was it right for them to be brought to Christ?*
    Yes: because Christ can bless us before we understand the nature of the blessing we receive from Him.
18. *Did the disciples think this?*
    No: they thought that these children were too young to receive the laying on of Christ's hands.
19. *Did Christ praise or blame them for this?*
    He was much displeased.
20. *What did He do?*
    He took the children up in His arms, put His hands upon them, and blessed them.

21. *What does this outward gesture and deed show?*
    Christ's good will towards infants.
22. *What infants?*
    Any infants that can be brought to Him in Baptism.
23. *What blessing do we hope to receive in Baptism?*
    The Holy Spirit.
24. *Are infants capable of receiving this?* Yes.
25. *Is there any promise in the Old Testament that they should receive it?*
    Yes; Isaiah xliv. 3.
26. *With what does St. Peter connect this promise?*
    With Baptism (Acts ii. 38, 39).
27. *Into what family do we enter at Baptism?*
    Into the family of God.
28. *What is this entry into God's family called?* Adoption.
29. *When did the Israelites enter into the family of God?*
    At their circumcision.
30. *When a Jewish child was circumcised on his eighth day, did he understand into whose family he was brought?* No.
31. *Was his circumcision any advantage to him?* Yes.
32. *What was the advantage?*
    He was entitled to all the promises and blessings of the Jewish Covenant.
33. *How was he to be brought up?*
    As one who had been already brought into the family of God.
34. *What is all this to us who are Christians and not Jews?*
    It assures us that if God cared for the children of Jews, much more will He care for the children of Christians.
35. *What besides this does it teach us?*
    That children can receive the blessings of God's covenant before they understand its nature.
36. *Does this seem reasonable?*
    Yes: they receive a curse from the first Adam before they can understand the evil they receive; why should they not receive a blessing from Christ, the Second Adam, before they can understand the benefit they receive?

SECTION V.—CHILDREN OF GOD.

1. *What is the second blessing which you received in Holy Baptism?*
   I was made "the child of God." (1)
2. *Can you separate this benefit from the first; that you were made a member of Christ?*
   No: because I am made a member of Christ, I am the child of God. (1-9)
3. *How can this be?*
   Because, being a member of Christ, God looks upon me as in His Son, and so His child, because in the body of His Holy Child Jesus. (1-9)
4. *In what sense are you God's child?*
   By adoption.
   " God sent forth His Son, made of a woman .... that we might receive the adoption of sons." (Gal. iv. 4, 5.)
5. *Are the children of God by adoption necessarily obedient children?*
   No; some of them, like the Prodigal in the Parable, leave the house of their Father. (9-14)
6. *In how many senses are the children of men called children of God?*
   In four senses:
   (1) By creation.
   " Have we not all one Father? hath not one God created us?" (Mal. ii. 10.)
   " We are also his offspring." (Acts xvii. 28.)
   (2) By adoption.
   (*a*) Jews, in circumcision.
   " Who are Israelites, to whom pertaineth the adoption." (Rom. ix. 4.)
   " I have nourished and brought up children, and they have rebelled against me." (Isaiah i. 2.)
   (*b*) Christians, in Baptism.
   " Ye are all the children of God by faith in Christ Jesus. For as many of you as have been baptized into Christ have put on Christ. God sent forth His Son into the world, made of a woman, made under the law, that we might receive the adoption of sons: and because ye are sons, &c." (Gal. iii. 26; iv. 5, 6.)
   (3) By following the example of Christ.
   " Blessed are the peacemakers, for they shall be called the children of God. Love your enemies. Bless them that curse you; do good to them that hate you, and pray for them that despitefully use you, and persecute you, that ye may be the children of your Father which is in heaven." (Matt. v. 9, 44, 45.) (14-19)

(4) By the Resurrection.
"They which shall be accounted worthy to obtain that world, and the resurrection from the dead, neither marry, nor are given in marriage. Neither can they die any more; for they are equal unto the angels, and are the children of God, being the children of the Resurrection." (Luke xx. 35, 36.)

Also :
"He that overcometh shall inherit all things (*i. e.*, at the last day); and I will be his God, and he shall be my son." (Rev. xxi. 7.)

7. *What is the reason why so many are adopted into God's family in Baptism, and so few, apparently, are children of God in the way of following the example of Christ?*

Because that which they received at their Baptism does not abide or remain in them. (14)

8. *What ground have you for saying this?*

Our Lord's words, where he says,
"Abide in me, and I in you. . . . He that abideth in me, and I in him, the same bringeth forth much fruit." (John xv. 4, 5.)

Also St. John's words :
"Whosoever is born of God doth not commit sin, for his seed remaineth in him." (1 John iii. 9.)

9. *Does St. John when he says, " Whosoever is born of God doth not commit sin," mean all the baptized?*

No : only those who retain that connection with the second Adam, which was once begun in Baptism.

10. *Is there any connection between these several senses of the term " child," or " son " of God?*

Yes. We are born into this world in order that we may be brought into the family of God by adoption in Baptism.

We are brought into the family of God in Baptism, in order that we may walk in newness of life, and so be children of God by following the example of Christ.

And we follow His example, and live here as the faithful and loving children of God, in order that hereafter we may be raised up in the likeness of His own Son, and be the " children of God, being the children of the Resurrection."

SHORTER CATECHISM.

1. *What besides a Member of Christ were you made in Baptism?*
The child of God.
2. *How were you made a child of God.*
By being made a member of Christ.

3. *Were you born a child of God?* No.
4. *But did not God create you?* Yes.
5. *Why then did you require to be made God's child?*
    Because all mankind fell from God and became children of wrath.
6. *In whom did all men fall?*
    In Adam. (In the first Adam.)
7. *In whom are they restored to the favour of God?*
    In Christ. (In Christ, the second Adam.)
8. *If then we are in the favour of God, in whom must we be?*
    In Christ.
9. *If you are in Christ, how does God regard you?*
    As His child or son.
10. *Are all the children of God obedient children?* No.
11. *Give an example of one who was not obedient.*
    The Prodigal Son (Luke xv. 12).
12. *Can the children of God be rebellious?* (Isaiah i. 2.)
13. *Can the children of God provoke Him?* (Deut. xxxii. 19.)
14. *Do all baptized children continue true children of God?*
    No: only those who live as if they were baptized.
15. *If we continue the children of God, by whom must we be led?*
    By the Spirit of God.
16. *Into what will He lead us?*
    Into all goodness, righteousness, and truth (Ephes. v. 9).
17. *What must the children or sons of God be?*
    Without murmurings and disputings: blameless and harmless (Phil. ii. 14, 15).
18. *Whom does our Lord call the children of God?*
    The peace-makers (Matt. v. 9).
19. *Upon whom does a child depend?*
    Upon his father.
20. *Upon whom do the children of God depend?*
    Upon their Father in Heaven.
21. *How do we show our dependence upon Him?*
    By praying to Him.
22. *If you are God's child, what will He do for you?*
    He will love me and take care of me in body and soul.
23. *And what must you be towards God?*
    I must be religious, loving, and obedient.
24. *If you have disobeyed God, what must you do?*
    I must be sorry, and confess my sins and forsake them.
25. *Will God receive you if you return?* Yes.
    "Like as a father pitieth his own children, even so is the Lord merciful unto them that fear Him." (Psalm ciii. 13.)
26. *Because God has brought you into His family, what are you entitled to call Him?*
    Father.

27. *By whose power alone can you in heart call Him Father?*
    By the power of His Holy Spirit (Gal. iv. 6).
28. *When particularly do you call Him Father?*
    When I say the Lord's prayer.
29. *If you are God's true child, what else will He do for you?*
    He will correct or chastise me if I do wrong.
30. *Would you be His real child if He did not do this?*
    No: (Hebrews xii. 8).
31. *What will He do to correct you?*
    He will send grief, losses, misfortunes, sickness, and such things.
32. *Must you be cast down by these things?*
    No: we must look upon them as coming from a Father.
33. *If we are the children of God, who is our brother?*
    Jesus Christ (Rom. viii. 29).
34. *Are we worthy of such a brother?*
    No; and yet He is not ashamed to call us brethren (Heb. ii. 11).
35. *If we are members of Christ and children of God, who are our brethren?*
    All the members of the Church.
36. *What does St. Peter say respecting our duty in this respect?*
    We are to love one another with a pure heart fervently (1 Peter i. 22).
37. *What besides?* We are to love as brethren (1 Peter iii. 8).

SECTION VI.—INHERITORS OF THE KINGDOM OF HEAVEN.

1. *What is the third blessing of which you were made a partaker at your Baptism ?*
   I was made an inheritor of the Kingdom of heaven. (1–5)
2. *What is an inheritor ?*
   One who will in due time come into possession of a kingdom or an estate. (1–5)
3. *Is there any place in Scripture from which we gather that in Baptism we were made heirs or inheritors ?*
   Yes : St. Paul writes,
   "As many of you as have been baptized into Christ have put on Christ... Ye are all one in Christ Jesus; and if ye be Christ's, then are ye Abraham's seed, and heirs according to the promise." (Gal. iii. 27, 29.)
4. *Give another place.*
   "According to His mercy He saved us, by the washing of regeneration (bath of new birth, or font of new birth), and renewing of the Holy Ghost... That being justified by His grace, we should be made *heirs* according to the hope of eternal life." (Tit. iii. 5, 7.)
5. *Of what are Christians made heirs ?*
   Of a "Kingdom prepared for them from the foundation of the world." (Matt. xxv. 34.)
6. *What other account have we of it which shows its exceeding blessedness ?*
   It is a place prepared for us by no other than the eternal Son of God.
   "I go to prepare a place for you. . . . that where I am there ye may be also." (John xiv. 2, 3.)
   Also :
   "An inheritance incorruptible, undefiled, and that fadeth not away, reserved in heaven." (1 Peter i. 4.)
7. *Will all who are once made heirs enjoy this inheritance ?*
   No. According to our Saviour's own account of the judgment, those only will receive the Kingdom who have fed, or clothed, or otherwise succoured Christ in His poorer brethren. (Matt. xxv. 31–46.) According to St. Paul, it will be finally enjoyed by those who "By patient continuance in well-doing seek for glory, and honour, and immortality." (Rom. ii. 7.) [Esau, Heb. xii. 16, 17.] (6–13)

SHORTER CATECHISM.

1. *What is an inheritor?* An heir.
2. *Can children be heirs?* Yes; nothing is more common.
3. *Of what are Christians heirs?* (1 Peter i. 4.)
4. *If Christians are children of God, what must they be?*
    If children, then heirs (Rom. viii. 17).
5. *Why are Christians inheritors of the Kingdom of Heaven?*
    Because they are members of Christ and children of God.
6. *At what time are we made heirs?* At Baptism.
7. *Can you show this from Scripture?*
    Yes (Gal. iii. 27, 29 ; Titus iii. 5, 6, 7).
8. *Can an heir lose his inheritance?* Yes.
9. *Have we any instance of one losing it?*
    Yes : Esau (Heb. xii. 16, 17).
10. *But was not the blessing which Esau lost only a temporal one?*
    Perhaps so; but he is brought forward as a warning to us lest we lose an eternal blessing.
11. *What will exclude us from the everlasting inheritance?*
    Unbelief (John iii. 18) and unrighteousness (1 Cor. vi. 9)
12. *What else?* Selfishness (Matt. xxv. 41, 42, 43).
13. *What must we do in prospect of such an inheritance?*
    We must give all diligence to make it sure (2 Pet. i. 10).

SECTION VII.—RENOUNCING THE DEVIL.

1. *What did your Godfathers and Godmothers then for you?*
   They did promise and vow three things in my name: First, that I should renounce the devil and all his works, the pomps and vanity of this wicked world, and all the sinful lusts of the flesh; secondly, that I should believe all the articles of the Christian faith; and, thirdly, that I should keep God's holy will and commandments, and walk in the same all the days of my life.
2. *What was the first thing renounced in your name?*
   The devil and all his works. (1-8)
3. *Who is the devil?*
   He is the chief of the evil angels: of the angels which kept not their first estate. (Jude 6) (8-13)
4. *What do you mean by this?*
   I mean that God tried the angels as He tried man, by allowing some temptation to be presented to them. The evil angels yielded in the time of temptation, and became the irreconcilable enemies of God and all good.
5. *Is it reasonable to believe that there are angels?*
   Yes; it seems reasonable to believe that there are many orders of beings between ourselves and the Infinite and Eternal God.
6. *Is it reasonable to believe that there are evil angels?*
   Yes. It is reasonable to believe that these beings had their time of probation and trial, as mankind had; and if so, there is nothing unreasonable in supposing that some fell away under temptation as man did.
7. *Why in Baptism have you to renounce the devil and all his works?*
   Because in Baptism I was made a member of Him Who came amongst us that He might destroy the works of the devil. (1 John iii. 8) (13-15)
8. *What is the first work of Satan which you renounce?*
   Unbelief.
9. *Why do you call unbelief the first work of Satan?*

Because it was the evil work by which he got the better of our first parents.

10. *How was this?*

He tempted our first parents to disbelieve in God's goodness when he asked, "Yea, hath God said, ye shall not eat of all the trees of the garden?" (Insinuating that God was not so good as they thought.)

11. *And in any other words?*

Yes. He tempted them to disbelieve in God's severity and truth when he said to them, "Ye shall not surely die."

12. *Does he continue to use this temptation?*

Yes. It is, and always will be, his great weapon. He would keep us separate from God by making us disbelieve in His goodness; and he would make us think that God will not punish sin.

13. *What words does St. Paul use respecting this work of Satan?*

"The god of this world hath blinded the minds of them which believe not, lest the light of the glorious Gospel of Christ, who is the image of God, should shine unto them." (2 Corinth. iv. 4.)

14. *With what must we oppose this great work of Satan?*

With the work of God.

15. *What is that?*

Our Saviour says,

"This is the work of God, that ye believe on Him whom He hath sent.' (John vi. 29.)

16. *Does St. Paul teach us the same thing?*

Yes; where he says,

"Above all take the shield of faith, wherewith ye shall be able to quench all the fiery darts of the wicked [one]." (Ephes. vi. 16.)

17. *How should you do this?*

When I am tempted to commit sin, I must distinctly call to mind that God's own Son took our flesh, and died, and rose again, and is now at the right hand of God, to deliver me from sin, and in the strength of this I must pray to God for help.

18. *What works of darkness are often called the works of Satan?*

Lying and murder.

"He was a murderer from the beginning, and abode not in the truth, because there is no truth in him. When he speaketh a lie, he speaketh of his own: for he is a liar, and the father of it." (John viii. 44.)

Pride.

"Lest being lifted up with pride he fall into the condemnation of the devil. (1 Tim. iii. 6.)

RENOUNCING THE DEVIL. 27

9. *Has God given to us any other weapon wherewith to resist Satan?*
   Yes: the sword of the Spirit, which is the word of God. (Ephes. vi. 17.) (24–27)
10. *Give an example of one who resisted Satan with this sword.*
    Our blessed Saviour, when He was tempted, repelled each temptation by a word from Scripture. (Matt. iv. 4, 7, 10.)
11. *Give me an instance of the way in which you would use this sword.*
    If when I am tempted to tell a lie, I remember that our Lord says that lying is the work of His enemy and mine, then I thrust at Satan or his angel with the sword of the Spirit.
12. *What promise is there for those who perseveringly resist temptation?*
    "The God of peace shall bruise Satan under your feet shortly." (Rom. xvi. 20.)

SHORTER CATECHISM.

1. *What was promised in your name?*
   Three things; first, that I should, &c.
2. *Why in your name?*
   Because I was unable to promise them myself.
3. *Who promised these things in your name?*
4. *What did they first promise?*
5. *What did the minister demand of the god-parents?*
   "I demand therefore, dost thou, in the name of this child, renounce, &c."
6. *And what answer did they give?*
   I renounce them all.
7. *What do you mean by renouncing?*
   Determining to have nothing more to do with a thing.
8. *Why do you first renounce the devil?*
   Because he is the author of all evil.
   [Because he is the chief enemy of God and Christ.]
9. *Who is the devil?*
   The chief or prince of the evil spirits.
10. *How is he represented in Scripture?*
    As the God of this world (2 Cor. iv. 4); as the prince of this world (John xiv. 30).

11. *How besides?*
    As the ruler of the darkness of this world (Ephes. vi. 12).
12. *Who are his children?*
    All who wilfully continue in sin (John viii. 44; 1 John iii. 8.)
13. *Is it right that you should renounce Satan in Baptism?*
    Yes; if in Baptism I am made the child of God.
14. *Why?*
    Because I cannot be at once the child of God and of His enemy.
15. *What is the meaning of the word "Satan?"*
    An enemy. He is *the* enemy or adversary (Matt. xiii. 25, 28, 39).
16. *How does He show his enmity?*
    By tempting men to displease God—their best friend. He is the tempter.
17. *Whom did he tempt?*
    Eve (Gen. iii. 1-6); Cain (1 John iii. 12); David (1 Chron. xxi. 1); Job (by affliction, Job i. 12); Judas (John xiii. 2); Ananias (Acts v. 3).
18. *Whom did he assail by temptations?* Jesus Christ.
19. *What consolation have we from the thought that Jesus Christ was tempted by Satan?*
    This; that it is no sin to be tempted if we do not yield.
20. *What else?*
    That Christ having been tempted can feel for us when we are tempted (Heb. ii. 18).
21. *How besides does Satan show his enmity?*
    By accusing us after we have fallen.
22. *What name has he from this?*
    The very name of devil or accuser (Rev. xii. 10).
23. *To what does St. Peter compare him?*
    To a roaring lion walking about seeking whom he may devour (1 Peter v. 8).
24. *Is he irresistible?*
    No: we must resist him, and he will flee from us (James iv. 7).
25. *What does that mean?* He will cease to tempt us.
26. *With what sword must we resist him?*
    The sword of the Spirit, which is the word of God (Eph. vi. 17).
27. *Give an example of One who so resisted him.*
    Our blessed Lord (Matt. iv. 4, 7).
28. *With what shield must we resist him?*
    The shield of faith (Eph. vi. 16).
29. *How must we do this?*
    We must call to mind that we are redeemed by Jesus Christ from the power of Satan.

30. *For what purpose was our Lord made known?*
    That He might destroy the works of the devil (1 John iii. 8).
31. *Against what snare of Satan does our Lord warn careless hearers of the word?*
    Against his snatching it out of their hearts (Matt. xiii. 19).
32. *What was Satan at the first?* An angel of light.
33. *How did he fall?* By disobedience.
34. *What is his doom?* (Rev. xx. 10.)
35. *Who will share his doom?* (Matt. xxv. 41.)
36. *Is this ever brought forward as a warning to Christians?* (Jude 5, 6).

SECTION VIII.—THE WORLD.

1. *What next do you renounce?*
   I renounce the pomps and vanity of this wicked world.
2. *What is the world?*
   Human society.
   The men and women living in the world, especially those amongst whom I live. (2, 3, 4)
3. *Why is it here called " wicked?"*
   Because the greater part of those who live in it are not true Christians [not led by the Spirit of God]. (4)
4. *But is not the Christian religion the religion of the country in which we live?*
   It may be so; but still the greater part of people in it do not live as if they had been baptized into Christ, for they do not walk in newness of life. (4) (5)
5. *What is the effect of this?*
   The effect of this is that the spirit of the world, its principles, maxims, and opinions, are contrary to the Spirit of God.
6. *Do you renounce the world itself?*
   No: I renounce the pomps and vanity of this wicked world. (3)
7. *Why do you not renounce the world itself?*
   Because God has cast in my lot in the world, and I am not to leave it. (John xvii. 15; 1 Cor. v. 10; vii. 20.)
8. *Could you so leave the world as to avoid its temptations?*
   No; for wherever I was I should have temptations to pride and selfishness, and these are " of the world."
9. *What do you mean by the pomps of the world?*
   I mean worldly display, parade, and ostentation. (6)
10. *But may you not sometimes be obliged to take part in these?*
    Yes: it may sometimes be a duty; as, for instance, to bear a part in a military parade if I am a soldier; but I

must not seek for such things as means of personal display.

11. *How does the Holy Spirit teach us that we are to regard the world?*

"Love not the world," he says, "neither the things which are in the world: if any man love the world, the love of the Father is not in him: for all that is in the world, the lust of the flesh, the lust of the eyes, and the pride of life, is not of the Father, but of the world." (1 John ii. 15.)

12. *What besides the world are we not to love?*

The things in the world: the lust of the flesh, the lust of the eyes, and the pride of life.

13. *What does the Holy Spirit mean by these things?*

" He means all things around us, so far as they draw off our hearts from heaven, and make us to be in love with this present world." [Keble.]

14. *Mention some.*

"Money, things that are money's worth, beauty, dress, and fine clothes; skill and strength in bodily labour; the praise and honour and good opinion of men; satisfaction in being admired, and in feeling that we ought to be." [Keble.]

15. *Why are these things so hurtful?*

Because they make us love this present state of things in which such things are, and so prevent us from hoping for another state of things in which they will have passed away.

16. *How does the Holy Spirit by St. Paul teach us that we are to regard the world?*

He says that,

"They that rejoice [are to be] as though they rejoiced not; they that buy, as though they possessed not; and they that use this world, as not abusing it; for the fashion of this world passeth away." (1 Cor. vii. 30.)

17. *What injunction does St. Paul give respecting the world?*

" Be not conformed to this world." (Rom. xii. 2.)

18. *What does he mean by this?*

That we are not to be led by the opinions, or to follow the example of those around us, when they are contrary to the revealed will of God?

19. *Is the world the same to each one of us?*

No, we have each a different world; for the society which we live in and mix with is the world to us.

20. *Are we always then in danger from the evil influence of the world?*

Yes. The great mass of mankind, whether in high

or in low conditions, do not fear God; and so their lives and opinions and conversation have a continual tendency to lower the tone of religion, rather than to raise it.

21. *How do you commonly yield to the temptations of the world?*

By slavishly deferring to the opinions, or copying the fashions and frivolities of those in high places.

22. *How besides?*

By courting popularity.

23. *How besides?*

By laying myself out, or making it my business, to please men.

"If I yet pleased men, I should not be the servant of Christ." (Gal. i. 10.)

24. *How besides?*

By making those who live contrary to their Christian profession my companions or familiar friends.

"Now I have written unto you not to keep company, if any man that is called a brother be a fornicator, or covetous, or an idolater, or a railer, or an extortioner; with such an one no not to eat." (1 Cor. v. 11.)

25. *Are persons who have begun to be religious in danger from the world?*

Yes. Our Lord speaks of those who hear the word and receive it with joy, yet are offended by tribulation or persecution, *i.e.*, by the opposition of the world. (Matt. xiii. 20, 21.)

26. *Is there any other warning in the same parable against the deceits of the world?*

Yes. Our Blessed Lord speaks of him that receiveth seed among thorns as being one who heareth the word, and the care of this world, and the deceitfulness of riches, [and the lust of other things] choke the word, and he becometh unfruitful. (Matt. xiii. 22.)

27. *Is there any reason why you should renounce the pomps and vanity of this wicked world at your Baptism?*

Yes. I was then baptized into a Saviour Whom the world hated; Who refused all its pomps and vanities; Who overcame it by His Sufferings and Death, and Who will hereafter judge it.

28. *What does our Lord lead His true followers to expect?*

The opposition of the world.

"If ye were of the world, the world would love his own." (John xv. 19.)
"In the world ye shall have tribulation." (John xvi. 33.)

29. *How are we to overcome the world?*

By faith in the Son of God. "Who is he that overcometh the world, but he that believeth that Jesus is the Son of God?" (1 John v. 5.)

30. *How will this deliver us from the fear and love of the world?*

They cannot fear and love the world who believe that the world crucified its Maker; that He (Jesus, its Maker) overcame the world, not by its own weapons, but by Suffering and Death, and that He will hereafter judge it.

SHORTER CATECHISM.

1. *What do you next renounce?*
The pomps and vanity of this wicked world.
2. *What is the world to you?*
My companions. The people among whom I live.
3. *Are you to give up their acquaintance or society?*
No: but I am not to be led by their opinions, or fall into their ways when they are wrong.
4. *Why is the world wicked?*
Because the greater part of mankind do not fear or love God.
5. *Is this true of a Christian country?*
As far as we can see it is.
6. *What is the meaning of pomp?*
Outward show: grandeur: worldly distinctions.
7. *What is vanity?* It literally means emptiness.
8. *What is meant by the vanity of the world?*
The things of the world which worldly men eagerly pursue.
9. *Why are these called vanity?*
Because they give no real satisfaction to an immortal spirit, and so are like empty vessels.
10. *What place of God's word shows us the vanity of all earthly things?*
The things which are seen are temporal, but the things which are not seen are eternal (2 Cor. iv. 18).
11. *What other place?*
The fashion of this world passeth away (1 Cor. vii. 31).
12. *When are we overcome by the world?*
When we follow the leading of our friends and neighbours rather than the will of God.
13. *When besides?* When we love dress and finery and display.
14. *How besides?*
By covetous desires, *i.e.*, by continually thinking about how we are to become richer or more honourable.

15. *Give an example of one who perished because of his love of these things.*
   Balaam (2 Peter ii. 15).
16. *Are riches and honours dangerous to the soul?* Yes.
17. *Why?* Because they tend to make us satisfied with this world.
18. *Is there any other reason?*
   Yes. Because rich men are followed and flattered by the world.
19. *How is this dangerous?*
   Because its tendency is to make them think of themselves?
20. *Must a rich and honourable man be always a worldly man?*
   No: God's grace can save him from the love of the world.
21. *Give an example of one so saved.*
   Daniel (Daniel xii. 13); the three Holy Children (Daniel iii. 27, 30).
22. *Give other examples.*
   Abraham (Heb. xi. 8, 10); Joseph (Heb. xi. 22.); Joseph of Arimathæa (Luke xxiii. 50).
23. *Can a poor man be overcome by the world?*
   Yes: if he allows his companions, or neighbours, or employment, to make him forget God.
24. *What does St. Paul say respecting the world?*
   "Be not conformed to this world" (Rom. xii. 2).
25. *What does he mean by this?*
   Do not imitate the conduct of worldly people. Be not led astray by the opinions of godless people.
26. *What does St. James say respecting one who is the friend of the world?*
   That he is the enemy of God (James iv. 4).
27. *What does St. John say about one who loves the world?*
   That the love of the Father is not in him (1 John ii. 15).
28. *What does St. James say respecting true religion?*
   That one great part of it is "to keep ourselves unspotted from the world" (James i. 27).
29. *How are we to overcome the world?*
   By believing in Jesus Christ with all our hearts (1 John v. 5).

SECTION IX.—THE FLESH.

1. *What is the next thing which you renounced in your Baptism?*
   The sinful lusts of the flesh.
2. *What are sinful lusts?*
   Sinful or immoderate desires
3. *Are all the desires of the flesh sinful?*
   No.
4. *When do they become sinful?*
   When they exceed the purpose for which God planted them in us.
5. *Give an example.*
   Hunger, for instance, and thirst, are implanted in us by God to compel us to support nature by eating and drinking; but when we eat and drink immoderately, then these natural desires become gluttony and drunkenness. (4-8)
6. *How is it that our desires have become liable to be temptations to sin?*
   Through the fall. (3)
7. *What do we receive from the fall?*
   An evil nature.
8. *What is this nature called in Scripture?*
   The flesh : the natural man. (Gal. v. 17 ; 1 Cor. ii. 14.)
9. *What does our Lord say of this evil nature?*
   He says, "Out of the heart proceed evil thoughts, murders, adulteries, fornications, thefts, &c." (Matt. xv. 19.)
10. *What does St. Paul say respecting it?*
    He says, "I know that in me, that is, in my flesh, dwelleth no good thing." (Rom. vii. 18.)
    [He speaks also of the flesh lusting against the Spirit, and the Spirit against the flesh (Gal. v. 17) ; that he that soweth to the flesh, shall of the flesh reap corruption (Gal. vi. 7, 8) ; and says, that "we all had our conversation in times past in the lusts of our flesh, fulfilling the desires of the flesh and of the mind, and were by nature the children of wrath even as others." (Eph. ii. 3.)]
11. *What are the fruits or works of this flesh or evil nature?*
    "The works of the flesh are manifest, which are these : adultery, fornication, uncleanness, lasciviousness, idolatry, witchcraft, hatred, variance, emulations, wrath, strife, sedi-

tions, heresies, envyings, murders, drunkenness, revellings, and such like." (Gal. v. 19.) (8–14)

12. *Have we any similar list of these evil things?*
   Yes; in Coloss. iii. 5, 6, 7, 8.
13. *What very remarkably strong expressions are used with reference to our renouncing these evil lusts?*
   1. We are to mortify them.
   "Mortify therefore your members which are upon the earth, fornications, uncleanness," &c. (Col. iii. 5.)
   2. We are to crucify them.
   "They that are Christ's have crucified the flesh with its affections and lusts." (Gal. v. 24.)
14. *How are we to mortify these evil inclinations?*
   Through the Spirit.
   "If ye through the Spirit do mortify the deeds of the body ye shall live." (Rom. viii.) (14, 15)
15. *How through the Spirit are you to mortify them?*
   By praying for the assistance of the Spirit, and by relying on the help of the Spirit; and to this end using those means by which He strengthens and refreshes us, as Confirmation, the Eucharist, united prayer, &c.
16. *How besides?*
   By bringing our bodies into subjection by self-denial and fasting. (1 Cor. ix. 27.)
17. *Why at our Baptism should we renounce the sinful lusts of the flesh?*
   Because we are then baptized into Christ, and put on Christ, Who Himself suffered in the flesh for the sins which we have committed.
18. *For what further reason?*
   Because we are then made members of Him Who died unto sin, and liveth unto God.

SHORTER CATECHISM.

1. *What besides the pomps and vanities of the world do you renounce?*
   All the sinful lusts of the flesh.
2. *What are lusts?* Desires.
3. *How is it that our desires are so often sinful?*
   Because we are born in sin.
4. *When are lusts or desires sinful?*
   When we break God's law by indulging them.
5. *For instance, hunger is a natural or innocent desire—when does it become sinful?*

When we eat not to sustain nature but for eating's sake, it becomes the sin of gluttony.

6. *Mention another case.*
Drinking is natural and necessary, but excess in it leads to the sin of drunkenness.

7. *Mention a third.*
Sleep is needful for the refreshment of our bodies, but excess in it becomes sloth.

8. *What other carnal lusts do you renounce?*
All filthy and unclean thoughts, words, and deeds.

9. *Are these very wicked?* Yes; they are deadly sins.

10. *When filthy, or unclean, or sinful thoughts rise in your mind, what must you do?*
I must put them out with all my might and pray to God against them, and think of some good thing.

11. *Respecting filthy words, what are you bound to do?*
I am bound not only not to speak them, but not to listen to them.

12. *Does this part of your vow bind you to renounce any other sorts of sins?*
Yes: it binds me to renounce sins of temper.

13. *Show this.*
St. Paul speaks of hatred, variance, wrath, strife, envyings, as works of the flesh (along with adultery and fornication) in Gal. v. 19, 20, 21.

14. *If we do not fulfil this part of our baptismal vow, what will be the end?*
If ye live after the flesh ye shall die (Rom. viii. 13).

15. *Mention another similar declaration.*
He that soweth to his flesh shall of the flesh reap corruption (Gal. vi. 8).

16. *What do you mean by " sowing to the flesh?"*
Giving way to the sinful desires of the flesh.

17. *How shall they die who do so?*
They shall die eternally.

18. *Mention some persons who lived after the flesh (sowed to the flesh) and perished.*
The Israelites in the wilderness (1 Cor. x. 1-11).

19. *Are these any warning to Christians?*
Yes: St. Paul regards them as being so (1 Cor. x. 12).

20. *Mention one who fell under these temptations and afterwards repented.*
David.

21. *Mention one who successfully resisted the lusts of the flesh.*
Joseph (Gen. xxxix. 9).

22. *Mention one who lived after the flesh and was lost.*
The rich man in the Parable (Luke xvi. 19).

SECTION X.—BELIEF.

1. *What is the second thing that your Godfathers and Godmothers promised in your name?*
    That I should believe all the articles of the Christian faith.
2. *Why at your Baptism was this promised on your behalf?*
    Because I was then baptized into the name of the Ever Blessed Trinity, the Father, the Son, and the Holy Ghost.
3. *Does this oblige you to believe in the Trinity?*
    Yes. It would have been folly and blasphemy for me to have been baptized into a name which I did not believe represented the truth of God's nature.
4. *But is the belief in the Trinity the same as belief in all the Articles of the Christian faith?*
    Yes. Belief in the Trinity is the foundation of belief in all the Articles of the Creed. I could not truly believe in the Creed unless I believed in the Trinity.
5. *But as an infant could you believe in the Ever Blessed Trinity?*
    No; but I could be reckoned as a believer if, when I was brought to Baptism, others, such as sponsors, engaged that I should be brought up in the belief of the Trinity.
6. *Have you any Scripture warrant for supposing that our Lord reckons such children amongst believers?*
    Yes. He expressly says, "Whoso shall offend one of these little ones which believe in me, it were better for him that a millstone were hanged about his neck, and that he were drowned in the depth of the sea." (Matt. xviii. 6.)
    [The further exposition of the answer to this question comes under the Articles of the Christian faith, as set forth in the Apostles' Creed.]

SECTION XI.—OBEDIENCE.

1. *What is the third thing promised in your name?*
That I should keep God's holy will and commandments, and walk in the same all the days of my life.
2. *Why was this promised in your name when you were baptized?*
Because in Baptism I was made a member of Him Who did in all things the will of God.
3. *For what other reason?*
Because I was then made a partaker of the Holy Spirit, and so had strength vouchsafed to me to do God's holy will.
4. *Where is the will of God to be found?*
In the word of God.
5. *Who is commissioned by God to interpret this will to us, and apply it to our hearts and lives?*
The Church, through her ministers.
6. *What short summary have we of the will and commandments of God?*
The Ten Commandments.
[The further exposition of the answer to this question comes under the exposition of the Ten Commandments.]

SECTION XII.—THE CHRISTIAN RESOLVE.

1. Dost thou not think that thou art bound to believe, and to do as they have promised for thee?

    Yes, verily, and by God's help so I will; and I heartily thank our Heavenly Father that He hath called me to this state of salvation, through Jesus Christ our Saviour; and I pray unto God to give me His grace that I may continue in the same unto my life's end.

2. *Why are you bound to believe and to do what your sponsors promised for you?*

    Because I am God's creature, and so bound to believe what He has revealed, and to do what He has commanded.

3. *Independently then of your having sponsors, you are bound to believe the word, and to do the will, of God?*

    Yes. My Baptism, quite independently of the vows then made on my behalf, laid me under the greatest obligations to believe and live as a Christian.

4. *How did it do this?*

    Because in it I mystically and sacramentally died, was buried, and rose again with Christ, that I might walk in newness of life.

5. *Can you express this in other words?*

    Yes. I had then some portion of the virtue and power of Christ's Death and Resurrection Life made over to me, that I might live a Christian life.

6. *Where do you learn this?*

    I learn it from three statements of Holy Writ: Rom. vi. 1–6; Coloss. ii. 12; 1 Pet. iii. 21.

    [The teaching of these places will be fully drawn out in the latter part of this work on the Sacraments.]

7. *But you said that, as God's creature, you were bound to believe God's word and obey His will; does your Baptism add to this obligation?*

    Yes; because I was there and then transferred, from the state of being a mere creature of God, into the state of adoption into God's family; and I had then grace vouchsafed to me to live as one should live who is brought into such a family.

8. *You say that by God's help so you will. Why do you say " by God's help"?*
Because it is only by God's special grace or help that I can believe in Him aright, or sincerely obey Him. (5-8)

9. *Is the knowledge of all this a thing that should make you thankful?*
Yes. "I heartily thank our heavenly Father that He hath called me to this state of salvation."

10. *What is this state of salvation?*
It is being a member of Christ. (9-12)

11. *How has God called you to this state of salvation?*
By His Providence, which caused me to be born of Christian parents, who brought me in infancy to Holy Baptism. (12, 13)

12. *Is it right to call this baptismal state a state of salvation?*
Yes. St. Peter expressly says that,

"Baptism doth now save us (not the putting away of the filth of the flesh, but the answer of a good conscience towards God) by the resurrection of Jesus Christ." (1 Peter iii. 21.) St. Paul also says: "By His mercy He saved us, by the font of regeneration, and renewing of the Holy Ghost." (Titus iii. 5.) (16, 17)

13. *Does this state of salvation by union with Christ imply final salvation?*
Not necessarily, for, "I pray unto God to give me His grace, that I may continue in the same unto my life's end." (19-24)

14. *Have you any need to put up this prayer?*
Yes; the greatest need.

15. *But is it not often taught that, if once we are in the grace of God, we must continue in it?*
Not by those who know the Scriptures?

16. *But is it possible for those once really grafted into Christ to fall away?*
Our Lord treats it as possible when He says,

"If a man abide not in me, he is cast forth as a branch and is withered, and men gather them, and cast them into the fire, and they are burned." (John xv. 6.) (21-26)

17. *Does St. Paul treat it as possible?*
Yes: when he says, "Behold therefore the goodness and severity of God: on them which fell, severity;

but toward thee goodness, if thou continue in His goodness: otherwise thou also shalt be cut off." (Rom. xi. 22.)

18. *What example does St. Paul bring of those who were once brought into a state of salvation, and yet not finally saved?*
The Israelites in the wilderness. (1 Corinth. x. 1–10.)

19. *What does St. Jude say of these?*
That God saved the people of Israel, and yet destroyed them that believed not. (Jude 5.)

20. *What fearful example does St. Jude also mention?*
The angels who kept not their first estate. (Jude 6.)

SHORTER CATECHISM.

1. *When you answer this question in these words, what do you do?*
I ratify and confirm with my own lips the promises made in my name.

2. *Who alone heartily answer this question?*
Those who earnestly desire to live as true Christians.

3. *Why are you bound to believe and do as your sponsors have promised?*
Because I am bound to glorify God and save my soul.

4. *Is there any time appointed by the Church in which you can publicly confirm these vows in your own person?*
Yes: in Confirmation.

5. *Why do you say " By God's help"?*
Because without His help I can do nothing.

6. *Where do you learn this?*
From John xv. 5 : Without me ye can do nothing.

7. *From any other place?*
Yes ; from many. Rom. vii. 18 ; 2 Cor. iii. 5 ; Phil. ii. 13.

8. *Can you by His help believe and live as a Christian?*
Yes: St. Paul says "I can do all things through Christ which strengtheneth me" (Phil. iv. 13 ; also Luke i. 6).

9. *Into what state have you been called?*
A state of salvation.

10. *Why?* Because I have been made a member of Christ the Saviour.

11. *Who has called you?* Our Heavenly Father.

12. *How do you know that He has called you?*
Because I have been baptized, and because I am now being instructed in the Christian faith.

13. *Through whom were you called?*
Through Jesus Christ our Saviour.

14. *Is God desirous that you should be saved?*
   Yes: He is not willing that any should perish (2 Pet. iii. 9).
15. *But is He desirous that children should be saved?*
   Yes: His Son says, "It is not the will of your Father which is in Heaven that one of these little ones should perish" (Matt. xviii. 14).
16. *In what does this salvation consist?*
   In the forgiveness of my sins.
17. *In what else?*
   In the help of God's Spirit to make me holy.
18. *What return do you now make to God?*
   I heartily thank our Heavenly Father that, &c.
19. *Because you are now in a state of salvation, are you quite sure that you will be saved at last?*
   No: "I pray unto God to give me His grace that I may continue in the same unto my life's end."
20. *What does our Lord say respecting this "continuing"?*
   He that endureth to the end shall be saved (Matt. x. 22).
21. *Do the Apostles speak as if they thought that men would always continue as they have begun?*
   No (Rom. xi. 22; Heb. iii. 6-14).
22. *Against what do they perpetually warn Christians?*
   Against falling away (1 Cor. x. 12; Heb. vi. 6).
23. *What are they afraid that their converts may resist?*
   The grace of God (2 Cor. vi. 1; Heb. xii. 15).
24. *Do the Apostles regard those who have once believed as sure of salvation?*
   No (1 Tim. v. 12).
25. *Does our Lord speak of those once forgiven as sure of salvation?*
   No (Matt. xviii. 32, 34, 35).
26. *What then should be our care?* (2 Pet. i. 5-11.)

SECTION XIII.—THE FAITH.

1. *What was the second thing which was promised in your name at your Baptism?*
   That I should believe all the articles of the Christian faith. (1) (2)
2. *What is faith?*
   Believing anything to be true.
3. *Has this word more than one meaning in Holy Scripture?*
   Yes. It has two meanings. (3-6)
4. *What are they?*
   It first means that power, or faculty, or virtue in the soul or spirit, which believes a thing to be true on God's word.
   It means, secondly, that body of truth which God gives to us to be believed by us. (In which latter case it is usually designated "the faith.")
5. *Give an instance of the first of these meanings.*
   It means the first in the words,
   "Without faith it is impossible to please God; for he that cometh to God must believe that He is, and that He is a rewarder of them that diligently seek Him." (Heb. xi. 6.) [Also, "Now abideth faith, hope, and charity, these three, but the greatest of these is charity." (1 Cor. xiii. 13.) Also Luke xvii. 5; Acts vi. 5, &c.]
6. *Give an instance of the second.*
   One Lord, one Faith, one Baptism. (Ephes. iv. 5.)
   [Also, "Holding the mystery of the faith in a pure conscience." (1 Tim. iii. 9.) "Let us hold fast the profession of our faith without wavering.' (Heb. x. 23.) "Ye should earnestly contend for the faith." (Jude 3.) "Thou holdest fast My name, and hast not denied My faith." (Rev. ii. 13.) "In latter times some shall depart from the faith—they have erred from the faith." (1 Tim. iv. 1; vi. 10.) (6-9)
7. *Do we find this latter sense in the Catechism?*
   Yes. In the words, "Secondly, that I should believe all the articles of the Christian faith"

8. *What do you gather from these places?*
    I gather that God not only demands faith from us, but that that faith should accept and embrace a certain definite body of truth called "The faith once delivered to the Saints." (Jude 3.)
9. *Is it reasonable that we should believe in this faith?*
    Yes. If God reveals any truth to us, it is most reasonable that we should believe and accept it as an act of submission to Him Who created us, and Who redeemed us at such a cost.
0. *But do we not all believe in the Bible: and is not this sufficient?*
    No, it is not; because many profess to believe in the Bible, and reject or explain away the principal truths contained in it.
1. *Is there any other reason?*
    Yes; because the Bible contains an immense number of facts, some of which are immeasurably more important than others.
2. *Give an instance.*
    We read in one part of the New Testament of the Sufferings and Death of our Saviour Christ; and in another a very full account of the voyage and shipwreck of St. Paul: both these are parts of the same Bible, and yet no one in his senses would hold the latter to be of anything like the importance of the former.
3. *How is it that we hold one fact of the Bible to be infinitely more important than another?*
    Because we hold "the faith once for all delivered to the saints."
4. *But do not some true Christians among us think lightly of the Creeds of the Church?*
    Yes; but these men owe all their right views of God and Christ to the influence which in past ages men who held the Creeds have exercised upon the Church.
5. *Do the Scripture writers themselves witness to the existence of a definite body of truth, in all respects answering to our Apostles', or Nicene Creed?*
    Yes; in very many places. (10–17)
6. *Mention some.*
    St. Paul, in Romans vi. 17, speaks of a form of doctrine delivered to the Roman Christians; and in 2 Tim. i. 13, he speaks of this being embodied in some "form of sound

words" which he bids St. Timothy "hold fast;" and this was also called a profession of faith : for he writes to the Hebrews to "hold fast the profession of their faith." (Heb. x. 23.) (10–17)

17. *What is this called?*

It is called The Faith : "Contend earnestly for the faith once delivered to the saints." It is declared to be "one," *i.e.*, one and the same everywhere, just as Baptism is one : "One Lord, one faith, one Baptism." (Ephes. iv.)

[We are all to come in the unity of the faith to a perfect man. (Ephes. iv. 13.) St. Paul preached this faith (Gal. i. 23) ; he exhorted men to continue in it. (Acts xiv. 22.) Ministers are expected to hold the mystery of this faith. (1 Tim. iii. 9.) Others denied this faith, and in later times men will depart from it. (1 Tim. v. 8 ; iv. 1.)]

18. *But does this faith, or body of truth, in all respects answer to the Apostles' Creed?*

We have several distinct proofs that it does. (18–27)

19. *Give one.*

We find that St. Paul, in four places at least, mentions particularly the Gospel which he preached, and in each case we find that his Gospel was expressed in the form of an article of the Creed.

20. *Mention these places.*

In 1 Cor. xv. 1–8, St. Paul declares that the Gospel which he preached, and by which his converts were saved, was, first of all, that "Christ died for our sins according to the Scriptures, and that He was buried, and that He rose again the third day :" that is, three articles of the Apostles' Creed.

21. *Mention a second.*

In 2 Tim. ii. 8, we read,

"Remember that Jesus Christ, of the seed of David, was raised from the dead according to my Gospel."

22. *Mention a third.*

In Rom. ii. 16, St. Paul declares that the coming of Christ to judge men (which is an article of the Creed) is according to his Gospel.

23. *Mention a fourth.*

St. Paul, in the opening verses of his Epistle to the Romans, speaks of the Gospel as being "Concerning His Son Jesus Christ our Lord, which was made of the seed of David according to the flesh, and declared to be the

Son of God with power ... by the resurrection from the dead." In other words, the Incarnation and the Resurrection of Jesus.

24. *What do you gather from these places?*
That the Apostolic Christians possessed a short summary of the great truths of our redemption virtually the same as our Apostles' Creed. (18–27)

25. *What must have been the form of this?*
It must have been in an historical form, setting forth facts rather than doctrines or internal feelings.

26. *Are there any other reasons for believing that the primitive Gospel was in this historical form?*
Yes. The four narratives of the Life, Death, and Resurrection of Christ have been from the first called The Four Gospels. The author of the second Gospel (St. Mark) gives this very name to his account, where he calls it "The Gospel of Jesus Christ, the Son of God." (Mark i. 1.)

27. *Have we any other reason for believing that the original teaching was in the historical form?*
Yes; St. Luke, in the Preface to his Gospel, tells us that he wrote it to confirm one Theophilus in the certainty of the things in which he had been instructed (or catechized).

28. *What does this prove?*
That Theophilus must have been instructed or catechized in the facts of the Incarnation, Birth, Life, Death, Burial, Resurrection, and Ascension of Jesus Christ, because St. Luke's Gospel is occupied with nothing but these things.

29. *Is the form of the Gospel which we have in the four Gospels, and in the Creeds of the Church, most calculated to draw out our faith and love?*
Yes; we may be sure that it is; or it would not have been chosen by God.

30. *Do we use the Creed in the public worship of God?*
Yes.

31. *How can we do this? Is it a prayer, or a thanksgiving?*
No; we use it as an act of faith. (30–32)

32. *Is it needful that we should use acts of faith?*
Yes. St. Paul tells us so when he says, "With the heart man believeth unto righteousness, and with the mouth confession is made unto salvation." (Rom. x. 10.)

33. *What had St. Paul just said that we must confess with the mouth, and believe in the heart?*

He had said, "If thou shalt confess with thy mouth the Lord Jesus, and shalt believe in thine heart that God hath raised Him from the dead, thou shalt be saved." (Rom. x. 9.)

34. *How must we confess with our mouth the Lord Jesus?*

If we are to confess Him according to the Scriptures, we must confess him as the Only-begotten Son of God; as Incarnate, as Crucified, Dead, Buried, Risen again, Ascended, and now sitting at the Right Hand of God.

35. *But may not all this be said lifelessly and formally?*

Yes, it may; but this does not undo the fact that if we are to be guided by Scripture we must confess Christ after this form, rather than after any other.

36. *What then must be our care in this matter?*

We must take care that we do not say such a confession lifelessly and formally.

37. *How are we, using the words of the Creeds, to make confession unto salvation?*

We are first of all to say it remembering that we say it in the presence of God, Who searcheth the hearts, and requires both the belief of our hearts and the acknowledgments of our lips.

38. *How besides?*

We are to say over each article, remembering that each one is the statement of the love of God to a lost world, and to ourselves as living in the world.

39. *How besides?*

We are to say it remembering that in bygone days our fathers in the faith held to the truths it sets forth, through tortures and death. (32-37)

40. *What then is our duty with respect to the Creed?*

We must pray for faith that we may realize each statement which it contains, and we must take pains to understand of how much grace and love each article is the assurance. (42-46)

41. *But would it not be better to substitute for the Creed some more particular declaration that Christ died for us [for me], or a declaration in which we profess to appropriate to ourselves the merits of His Death?*

No; assuredly it would not be better for each soul to separate itself from its fellow-souls in any such a way. The

Apostles almost invariably speak of Christ dying for us: for all men, for sinners, for man, for the world.

2. *But would it not be well to have some more distinct declaration that we have no merits of our own, or that we are justified by faith; or that we are saved when we believe?*

No; it would not be well; for all such statements more or less imply that we are saved by believing in an idea, rather than in a person. We are saved not by believing that we have no merits, or that we are justified by faith; but, according to St. Paul (1 Cor. xv. 1–4), by believing that Christ died for our sins; that He was buried, and that He rose again, and all this by the will and appointment of God the Father, Who raised Him from the dead.

3. *But would it not be better to say that we are saved by "coming to Christ?"*

No: coming to Christ is the direct consequence of our truly believing in Him. Just as it is said, "He that cometh to God must believe that He is,"—so with respect to "coming to Christ:" when we believe that He is what He is set forth to be in the Scriptures, then we come to Him, or rather to the Father through Him. (John xiv. 6; Ephes. ii. 18; Heb. vii. 25.)

4. *How can we come to Christ?*

In prayer, and in the Sacraments.

5. *You said that the faith was one: what is this one faith sometimes called?*

The Catholic faith.

6. *Why?*

Because it is, and has been from the beginning, the belief of the Catholic Church.

SHORTER CATECHISM.

1. *When you were baptized what, in the second place, did the minister demand of your god-parents in your name?*

Dost thou believe in God, the Father Almighty, &c.

2. *What did your sponsors answer to this demand?*

All this I steadfastly believe.

3. *What is this belief of yours called?* Faith.

4. *Where must it be if you are to be saved?* In my heart.

5. *What proof from Scripture have you of this?*
   "With the heart man believeth unto righteousness" (Rom. x. 10).
6. *What have you to believe with the heart?*
   The Faith once delivered to the Saints.
7. *Does the Scripture make any difference between faith and the faith?*
   Yes. Faith is that in us which makes us believe. The faith is the truth which we believe.
8. *What do the Scriptures call this truth?*
   The faith of the Gospel (Phil. i. 27).
9. *What besides?* The common faith (Titus i. 4).
10. *Why do they call it the common faith?*
    Because it is the truth held in common by all.
11. *It must then be one throughout the Church.*
    Yes: it is expressly said that there is "one faith" (Ephes. iv. 5).
12. *What is our duty respecting it?*
    We are to hold fast the profession of it (Heb. x. 23).
13. *What besides?*
    We are to continue in, and to be established in, the faith (Acts xiv. 22; xvi. 5).
14. *What besides?* We are to contend earnestly for it (Jude 3).
15. *What should we fear respecting the faith?*
    We are to fear lest we deny it (1 Tim. v. 8); lest we err from it (1 Tim. vi. 10, 21); lest we depart from it (1 Tim. iv. 1).
16. *How are we to hold it?*
    We are to hold the mystery of the faith in a pure conscience (1 Tim. iii. 9).
17. *Where does the Church direct us to look for this faith?*
    In the articles of our Belief.
18. *What is this form of sound words called?*
    The Apostles' Creed.
19. *Why?*
    Because it is the simplest form of *the* Faith which the Apostles believed and preached.
20. *Can you prove this from the writings of the Apostles?*
    Yes: St. Paul expressly declares that the Gospel which he preached consisted of three things, all which we find in the Creed.
21. *What are these three things?*
    That Christ died for our sins according to the Scriptures, that He was buried, and that He rose again the third day, according to the Scriptures (1 Cor. xv. 1-4).
22. *Have you any other proof that the Creed embodied the Gospel?*
    Yes: St. Paul declared expressly that the judgment by Christ at the last day, which is an article of the Creed, is "according to his Gospel" (Rom. ii. 16).

. *Have you any other proof?*
Yes: St. Paul bids Timothy remember that the Resurrection of Jesus (*i.e.* an article of the Creed) was "according to his Gospel" (2 Tim. ii. 8).
. *Have you any other proof?*
Yes: in the very beginning of the Epistle to the Romans, St. Paul writes as if the Gospel consisted in the three facts that Christ was the Son of God, that He became incarnate, and that He rose from the dead (Rom. i. 1-4).
. *Have we any proof that this faith or Gospel was in a form of words?*
Yes: St. Paul bids Timothy hold fast the "form of sound words" which he had heard of him (2 Tim. i. 13).
. *Have we any other proof?*
Yes: he speaks of a "form of doctrine" delivered to the Roman Christians (Rom. vi. 17).
. *What is the simplest form conceivable of this faith?*
The Apostles' Creed.
. *Shall we be saved by the mere saying of it?*
No: we must believe with all our hearts.
. *But do not almost all professing Christians believe the facts mentioned in it?*
They believe them, but not as things in which they have at present any real concern.
. *How must you then believe them?*
I must believe them as things especially revealed by the great and Eternal God.
. *How besides?*
I must believe them as all of them showing the love of God to us sinful creatures.
. *How besides?*
I must believe them as things which God requires me both to believe and to acknowledge if I am to be saved.
. *Where in Scripture do you find that God requires you to acknowledge the faith?*
Rom. x. 9. "If thou shalt confess with thy mouth the Lord Jesus, and shalt believe in thine heart that God hath raised Him from the dead, thou shalt be saved."
. *Where besides?*
Let us hold fast the *profession* of our faith without wavering (Heb. x. 23).
. *Was it always so easy to confess the faith of Christ as it is now?*
No, by no means.
. *What, for many hundred years, were those in danger of who confessed the faith of Christ?*
Tortures and death.
. *What were those who suffered for the faith called?* Confessors.

38. *What were those called who chose to die rather than to deny the faith?*
    Martyrs.
39. *Are these Martyrs ever mentioned in Scripture?*
    Yes: Acts xxii. 20; Rev. vi. 9.
40. *For what did they suffer death?*
    Because they would not deny the faith.
41. *But did they die for the Creed?*
    They died for the faith of which the articles in the Creed are the oldest and simplest statements.
42. *Should we be able to die for the faith if God were to call upon us to do so?*
    If He gives us His Almighty grace we should.
43. *But since God has not as yet called us to this, what is our duty now?*
    To live to the faith.
44. *How do we do this?*
    By living as if we believed our Creed to be true.
    [By living as if we believed that God our Father always sees us, that Jesus Christ has died to deliver us from sin, and that we must live for ever after death.]
45. *Can we believe that the things in the Creed are true, and yet not be saved?*
    Yes: we read, "The devils believe and tremble" (James ii. 19).
46. *Can we believe to the saving of our souls without the grace or help of God?*
    No: faith is the gift of God (Eph. ii. 8; Phil. i. 29).
47. *What then should we do?*
    We should pray to God for faith.
48. *Mention the prayer of one who asked for faith.*
    Lord, I believe, help thou mine unbelief (Mark ix. 24).
49. *What was the prayer of the Apostles?*
    "Increase our faith" (Luke xvii. 5).

SECTION XIV.—GOD THE FATHER ALMIGHTY.

1. *Rehearse the Articles of thy belief.*
 I believe in God the Father Almighty, Maker of heaven and earth, and in Jesus Christ, &c.
2. *What is the first Article of the Christian faith?*
 "I believe in God the Father Almighty, Maker of heaven and earth." (3–5)
3. *Why do we call God, the Father?*
 Because He is the Father of One only begotten Son. (6–8)
4. *Is this the first reason why we should acknowledge Him to be the Father?*
 Yes, unquestionably. By His very nature He is, and always has been the Father, because He is, by His very nature, the Father of One only Son. (9–13)
 [" God, then, though He is in an improper sense the Father of many things, yet, by nature, and in truth, is Father of One only, the Only begotten Son, our Lord Jesus Christ: not becoming so in course of time, but being from everlasting the Father of the Only Begotten; not first without Son, and then becoming a Father, by a change of purpose; but before all substance and all intelligence, before times, and all ages, hath God the prerogative of Father, and more honoured in this than in all the rest." (St. Cyril, of Jerusalem, page 80, Oxford Translation.)]
5. *Was there ever a time when God the Father was not a Father?*
 No. He begat One only Son, "before all worlds," *i. e.*, from all eternity.
6. *Is not this a very mysterious truth?*
 Yes, it is; but it is not more mysterious than any other truth which God reveals to us respecting Himself. It is not more mysterious than His eternal existence, or His perfect knowledge of all things, past, present, and to come.
7. *Was God always thus known and revealed as the Father?*

No; He was not clearly revealed as the Father till His only begotten Son came amongst us and "declared" His name. (14-18)

8. *How know you this?*

Because it is written, "The only-begotten Son, who is in the bosom of the Father, He hath declared Him" (John i. 18): and our Lord says to His Father, "I have manifested Thy *name* unto the men which thou gavest me out of the world:" and again, "I have declared unto them Thy name." (John xvii. 6, 26.)

9. *But was He not known as the Father in the times of the Old Testament?*

He was known as the Father of all men by creation, and as the Father of the Jews by His having adopted them into His family; but it was naturally reserved to His only begotten Son to make Him fully known as by His very nature the Father. (17-20)

10. *Why do you say that it was naturally reserved to His only begotten, to make Him known as the Father?*

Because one is not a father unless he has begotten a son: so, till His Son was revealed, God Himself could not be realized as a true Father.

11. *By what name did God reveal Himself to the Jews?*

By His name Jehovah.

12. *Does this mean the same as the Father?*

No; it simply means one who is, *i. e.*, the self-existent Being. "I am that I am." (21-24)

13. *When you confess in your Creed, " I believe in God the Father," do you more particularly mean to confess Him as the author of your being?*

No; assuredly not.

14. *Why?*

Because, though He is the author of my being, yet if I am to have everlasting life I must believe in Him, and confess Him as the Sender of Jesus Christ His Son to save me, according to Christ's own words, "He that heareth my word, and believeth on Him that sent me, hath everlasting life." (John v. 24.)

15. *Have you any other Scriptural reason?*

Yes. If with my heart I am to believe unto righteousness, I must believe in God as He Who raised up His Son from the dead, as the Apostle tells me. (Rom. x. 9.)

16. *Can you give any other reason?*

GOD THE FATHER ALMIGHTY.

Yes. St. Paul tells us that we are justified when we believe on Him that raised up Jesus our Lord from the dead, *i. e.*, on God the Father. (Rom. iv. 23, 24.)

17. *Does any other Apostle witness to the same truth?*

Yes; St. Peter says that God "raised Him from the dead and gave Him glory, that our faith and hope might be in God." (1 Pet. i. 21.)

18. *But are we not to believe in God as the God Who made us?*

Yes; but even in this we must not separate Him from His Son, for He made us by His Son; as St. John says, "All things were made by Him" (*i. e.*, the Eternal Word, or Son); and St. Paul says, "By Him (God the Son), were all things created, visible and invisible." (Col. i. 16.)

19. *When, then, you say "I believe in God," do you merely mean to acknowledge a Supreme Being, just as Mahometans or Theists may acknowledge a Supreme Being?*

No. I mean to assert that the Supreme Being, or Eternal God, is not what this or that man may think Him to be, but He is the Eternal God, revealed by Jesus Christ as His Father from all eternity. (24-27)

20. *What besides do you profess to believe respecting God the Father Almighty?*

That He is the Maker of heaven and earth.

21. *Express this in other words.*

I believe that all the visible and invisible universe, the heavenly bodies, and the earth, and all things in it, did not exist from everlasting, but were called into being by God.

22. *What besides must you believe, if you believe this?*

I must believe that all the life and order and beauty which there is in the visible universe did not proceed out of that universe itself, but came from Him Who made it.

23. *Does the profession of your belief in God as the Maker of heaven and earth require you to believe in any particular theory of Creation?*

No: it only requires me to believe that in whatever way all things were brought into being, it was by His sole wisdom and power.

[For instance, it does *not* require me to deny that the living creatures upon the earth were brought to their present state of perfection by some such process as that which is called "natural selection;" but it *does* require me to acknowledge that this natural selection (if such a thing there be) was planned by the wisdom of God, and that every single stage in its progress was ordered and controlled by His Almighty Power.]

24. *What does the Nicene Creed add to these words of the Apostles' Creed?*

That God is the Maker "of all things, visible and invisible."

25. *What do the things invisible refer to?*

The world or worlds of angels, or the spiritual, unseen, and (as we call it) supernatural world.

26. *Why were these words inserted in the Creed?*

Because many ancient heretics believed that some of the angelic natures were not created by the God revealed to us in the Scriptures.

27. *Why did they entertain so monstrous an opinion?*

In order to account for the origin of evil.

28. *Did God create the sin and evil that is in the world?*

No.

29. *How then did it arise?*

As far as we can gather from Scripture, it arose out of the free will with which God had endowed angels and men, and the trial or probation which, in His wisdom, He saw fit to allow them to undergo.

30. *Can we explain this?*

No: it is the deepest of all mysteries.

SHORTER CATECHISM.

1. *What do you mean by rehearse?* Repeat.

2. *In whom do you first profess that you believe?*

In God the Father Almighty.

3. *Why do you first profess your belief in God the Father?*

Because He is the first person in the Godhead.

4. *But in order to be saved, must you not believe in Jesus Christ?*

Yes; but I could not believe that Jesus is the Son of God unless I believe that there is a God, and that He has a Son.

5. *Show that belief in God must be before all other belief.*

Our Lord says, "Ye believe in God, believe also in me' (John xiv. 1).

6. *Who is the God in Whom you believe?*

The Father of our Lord Jesus Christ (Eph. iii. 14).

7. *But is He not the Creator of heaven and earth?*
   Yes; but "before all worlds" He was the Father.
8. *Why?*
   Because He has been from everlasting the Father of an only Son.
9. *Is this the first and principal reason why you call God the Father?*
   Yes: it is by far the most important reason.
10. *But is He not the Father of men and angels?*
    Yes; but not by nature: He created them.
11. *Of whom is He the Father by His very nature?*
    Of God the Son.
12. *Was there ever a time when He was not the Father?* No.
13. *Was there ever a time when He had no Son?* No.
14. *Is it important that we should thus believe in the name of the Father?*
    Yes: because it is the name by which Christ made Him known to us (John i. 18; xvii. 6, 26).
15. *How do we know that God is the Father?*
    Because we know that He has an only Son.
16. *Can we know it in any other way?* No.
17. *Did God reveal this name to the Jews?* No.
18. *But is He not in some places of the Old Testament called the Father?*
    Not in the sense in which our Lord reveals Him as the Father.
19. *How did He reveal Himself to the Jews as a Father?*
    As their Father by adoption.
20. *Is this ever asserted in Scripture?*
    Yes: St. Paul says that to the Israelites pertained (or belonged) the adoption (Rom. ix. 4).
21. *By what name did He reveal Himself to the Israelites?*
    By the name Jehovah.
22. *Does this mean the same as Father?* No.
23. *What does it mean?*
    It means, "I am from everlasting to everlasting."
24. *Who only can believe in God as the Father?*
    Christians: those who believe that Jesus is the Son of God.
25. *Why do they only believe in God the Father?*
    Because they only believe that He has a true Son.
26. *Do the Mahometans believe in the same God as we do?* No.
27. *Why not?*
    Because the God in Whom they believe has no Son.
28. *What is God the Father?* He is Almighty.
29. *What is that?* He is able to do all things.
30. *Can He do what is wrong or sinful?*
    No; because it is contrary to His goodness and truth.

31. *What proof has He given of His Almighty power?*
    He has made heaven and earth.
32. *Does this include the angels?*
    Yes: He is the Maker of all things, visible and invisible.
33. *By whom did He make all things?* By His Son.
34. *Give a proof of this from Scripture.*
    All things were made by Him (Jesus Christ the Word), and without Him was not anything made that was made (John i. 2).
35. *How are we to honour God the Father?*
    By honouring the Son (John v. 23).
36. *Cannot we honour the Father without acknowledging the Son?*
    No:"whosoever denieth the Son the same hath not the Father" (1 John ii. 23).
37. How must we come to God the Father?
    Through the Son (John xiv. 6).
38. *How must we pray to God the Father?*
    We must pray to Him in the name of His Son (John xvi. 23).

SECTION XV.—THE NAME OF JESUS.

1. *What is the second article of the Christian faith?*
 I believe in Jesus Christ, His only Son, our Lord.
2. *Who is Jesus Christ?*
 The only Son of God, the Redeemer and Saviour of the world. (2)
3. *Who gave to Him the name of Jesus?*
 God sent His angel to give Him this name before He was conceived in the womb. (Luke ii. 21.) (10, 11, 12)
4. *Was there any reason why He should be called by this name?*
 Yes; it was given to Him because of the Salvation which He came into the world to accomplish: as the angel said to St. Joseph, "Thou shalt call His name Jesus, for He shall save His people from their sins." (Matt. i. 21.) (3-9)
5. *Does the name of Jesus then signify Saviour?*
 It rather means, " Jehovah, our Saviour," or " Jehovah is salvation."
 [Oshea would be Saviour. Jehoshua, contracted into Joshua (and in Greek, Jesus), means Jehovah our Saviour, the first syllable being the Hebrew Jah.] (13)
6. *In what respect does He save from sin?*
 He saves us from the guilt, the defilement, the power, and the punishment of sin.
 [He saves, for instance, the drunkard from his drunkenness, the thief from his dishonesty, the covetous man from his covetous desires; and if there be any other form of evil, He saves us from its power here and its punishment hereafter.] (14-17)
7. *What is ever to be remembered respecting the import of this His saving name?*
 That it was given to Him because He saves His people *from* their sins, and not *in* them.
8. *But cannot He save His people in sin?*
 No; that would not be salvation, because sin itself is that which keeps us separate from God, and must by its very nature destroy us. (12-16)

9. *How do we honour the name of Jesus?*
   Outwardly: by making some sign of reverence, such as bowing the head or knee when we hear it named. Inwardly: by pleading with His Father the saving power of His Name. (17, 18)

SHORTER CATECHISM.

1. *After God the Father, in Whom do you say that you believe?*
   In Jesus Christ His only Son our Lord.
2. *Whose Son is Christ?*
   He is the only Son of God.
3. *What name has He?* The name of Jesus.
4. *Was any other person called by this name?*
   Yes: Joshua, or Jesus, the son of Nun (Heb. iv. 8).
5. *What is there remarkable about Joshua?*
   He subdued the enemies of Israel, and led them into the land of promise.
6. *Of whom is Joshua, or Jesus, then a type?*
   Of Jesus, Who subdues our enemies and Who leads us into heaven.
7. *Were any other persons called by this name?*
   Yes: Joshua, the High Priest (Haggai i. 14).
8. *What then was this name among the Jews?*
   It was a name given to men.
9. *How then could the name of a man be given to the Son of God?*
   Because He was made man.
10. *Who gave to our Lord this name of Jesus?* God.
11. *By whom?* By the angel Gabriel.
12. *Why was this particular name given to Him?*
    Because He was to save His people from their sins (Matt. i. 21).
13. *What then does the name mean?*
    Jehovah is salvation.
14. *From what does He save us?*
    From our enemies.
15. *What are our enemies?*
    Our sins—our evil lusts, our wicked hearts.
16. *From whom, above all, does He save us?* From Satan.
17. *Is His name a name of great honour?*
    Yes: it is the name which is above every name (Phil. ii. 9).
18. *How then are we to show it honour?*
    At the name of Jesus every knee shall bow.

SECTION XVI.—THE CHRIST, OR MESSIAH.

1. *What do we mean by the name Christ?*
We mean the anointed One—the Messiah.
2. *Is this title especially claimed for Him?*
Yes. St. Peter says, "Let all the house of Israel know assuredly that God hath made that same Jesus whom ye have crucified both Lord and Christ." Acts ii. 36. [For St. Paul, *see* Acts ix. 22.] (1-6)
3. *Is there any reason for such importance being attached to His right to this title of Christ?*
Yes. The Prophets of the Old Testament led the Jews to expect that One called the Christ should come to save men.
4. *Give instances.*
David speaks of the rulers taking counsel against the Lord and against his Christ. (Psalm ii. 2., Daniel speaks of Messiah being cut off, but not for Himself. (Dan. ix. 26.) Isaiah speaks of One anointed to preach good tidings to the meek. (Isa. lxi. 1.)
5. *What public persons were set apart by anointing?*
Prophets (1 Kings xix. 16); priests (Levit. viii. 12); and kings (1 Sam. x. 1 ; 1 Sam. xvi. 13 ; 1 Kings i. 39). (7-11)
6. *With what was our blessed Lord anointed?*
With the Holy Ghost at His Baptism. (Acts x. 38.) (12-14)
7. *To what offices was He anointed?*
To those of Prophet, Priest, and King.
8. *What is the duty or work of a Prophet?*
To make known the express will of God. [Thus saith the Lord.] (18-20)
9. *Our Lord, then, does not speak as a Prophet only when He foretells the destruction of Jerusalem?*
No : in every discourse He claims to speak in God's name, and to set forth God's word and will. (John v. 43 ; xiv. 24.) (20-25)
10. *Did our Lord cease to act as a Prophet when He left this world?*
No : He expressly promises that when He should leave

this world He would yet continue to speak by the mouths of His Apostles : "He that heareth you, heareth me." (Luke x. 16.) " I have many things to say unto you, but ye cannot bear them now ... The Spirit shall not speak of Himself." (John xvi. 12, 13.) St. Paul also speaks of Christ speaking in him. (2 Cor. xiii. 3.) (24)

11. *Our Lord, you said, was anointed to be a priest : what were the functions or duties of a priest ?*

To offer sacrifices and intercessions on behalf of the people to God, and to bless the people from God. [In God's name.] (25–28)

12. *Who is the first person mentioned as a priest in the Scriptures ?*

Melchizedec.

" And Melchizedec, king of Salem, brought forth bread and wine, and he was the priest of the Most High God," &c. (Gen. xiv. 18—21.)

13. *Does this bear upon the Priesthood of Christ ?*

Yes. Our Lord is a Priest for ever, after the order of Melchizedec, rather than after the order or type of Aaron. (Ps. cx. 4.) (34)

14. *When did our Lord exercise the office of a Priest ?*

When He gave His Body to be broken, and His Blood to be shed for many for the remission of sins. (Matthew xxvi. 26, 27.)

When by His own blood He entered in once into the Holy Place, having obtained eternal redemption for us. (Hebrews ix. 11, 12.) (30–34)

15. *But He is a Priest for ever : how does He now exercise His Priesthood ?*

By His perpetual intercession in heaven He offers up the prayers and Eucharists of His Church to God, and He blesses His Church with all spiritual blessings from God. (34–36)

16. *Does He bless us as a priest only by Himself, or by means of others ?*

In both ways. He blesses us from God secretly, as He sees fit, and He also blesses us through the ministers of His Church.

[He it is Who really baptizes us through His ministers ; He confirms when the Bishop confirms ; He absolves through the mouth of the priest, and He feeds us through His ministers with His Body and Blood in the Eucharist.] (37–40)

17. *But does He ever tell us that He exercises His Priesthood by the hands or mouths of His ministers?*

Yes; over and over again. He says respecting His ministers, "He that receiveth you receiveth me." (Matth. x. 40.) And again, "As my Father hath sent me, even so send I you; whose soever sins ye remit, they are remitted unto them." (John xx. 21, 23.) And again: "Whatsoever ye shall loose on earth, shall be loosed in heaven." (Matth. xviii. 18.) (39–44)

18. *Are there any other instances?*

Yes. St. Paul says, when he excommunicates a certain offender, that he does it in the name and by the power of Jesus Christ (1 Cor. v. 4); and when he absolves him, it is by the same. (2 Cor. ii. 10.)

[Jesus also, we read, baptized by the hands of His disciples (John iv. 1, 2); and fed the multitude by their hands. (Matt. xiv. 19.)] (44, 45)

19. *How must we honour Christ as our Priest?*

By firmly believing that by "His one oblation of Himself once offered He made a full, perfect, and sufficient sacrifice, oblation, and satisfaction for the sins of the whole world." (47)

20. *How besides?*

By coming boldly to the throne of grace through Him. (Heb. iv. 14, 15, 16.) (46)

21. *How besides?*

By expecting that, as an ever-present Priest, He will bless us by the ministers, and through the means of grace, which He has appointed.

22. *Do we honour Him as the only Priest by denying that His ministers are priests?*

No: by doing so we deny the truth of His word and promise, and we deny His sovereignty.

23. *How is this?*

We deny the truth and perpetual application of the promise, "Lo I am with you always even unto the end of the world." We deny also His ever-present power and authority to work through any instruments He chooses.

24. *But is not our Saviour the one only Priest?*

Yes; in the sense in which He is the one only Bishop, and the one only Pastor: but as there are Bishops and Pastors acting under Him in His name, in exercising oversight and pastoral care, so there are priests acting in His name, to convey the atonement made by His one offering of Himself. (48, 49)

25. *What other office is He anointed to bear?*
That of King: as He said to the High Priest, "Thou sayest that I am a King" (John xviii. 37): and He accepted the testimony of Nathaniel, "Thou art the Son of God; Thou art the King of Israel." (John i. 49.) (50)

26. *Did the prophets foretell that He should be thus a King?*
Yes: in Psalm ii.: "I have set my King upon my Holy hill of Sion." Also by Jeremiah xxiii. 5: "A King shall reign and prosper," who shall be "the Lord our Righteousness." Also by the angel (Luke i. 32, 33); and in the Revelation xix. 16: "King of Kings, and Lord of Lords."

27. *What is the extent of His kingly power?*
It is unbounded; for He says, "All power is given unto me in heaven and in earth." (Matt. xxviii. 18.)

28. *How do we honour Him as King?*
1. By obeying His word.
2. By submitting to all the dispensations of His Providence, for as Mediator He now orders all things.
3. By regarding Him as the fountain of all true honour and so seeking honour from Him alone.

29. *How besides?*
By offering Him free will offerings of our substance. The Magi offered to Him, when in His cradle, gold, frankincense, and myrrh, as He that was born King. (Matt. ii. 11.)

30. *Do we elsewhere learn the duty of offering to Him as a King?*
Yes; we learn from His own lips that at the last day He, *as the King*, will say to them on His right hand, "Come, ye blessed, for I was an hungred, and ye gave me meat;" accounting what was done to His brethren as done to Himself. (Matt. xxv. 34, 35.)

SHORTER CATECHISM.

1. *Has our blessed Saviour a title?* Yes.
2. *What is it?* He is Christ—the Christ.
3. *What does this word mean?*
It means anointed—the anointed One.
4. *To what language does this sacred name belong?*
To the Greek.

THE CHRIST, OR MESSIAH.

5. *What is the name Christ in the Hebrew language?* Messiah.
6. *What is it to be anointed?*
   To be set apart to a sacred office by the pouring of oil upon the head.
7. *Who in old times were anointed?*
   Prophets, priests, and kings.
8. *Give an instance of a prophet being anointed.*
   Elisha (1 Kings xix. 16).
9. *Give an instance of a priest.* Aaron (Levit. viii. 12).
10. *Give instances of kings.*
    Saul (1 Sam. x. 1) ; David (1 Sam. xvi. 13).
11. *With what oil were priests anointed?* Exod. xxx. 22.
12. *With What was our Saviour anointed?* Acts x. 38.
13. *When?* At His Baptism.
14. *By whom?* By God the Father.
15. *To what sacred offices was our Lord anointed?*
    To those of prophet, priest, and king.
16. *By whom was our Lord foretold as the Christ or Messiah?*
    By Daniel (Dan. ix. 25); by David (Ps. ii. 2); by Isaiah (lxi. 1).
17. *Do Christians partake of Christ's anointing?*
    Yes (1 John ii. 20, 27).
18. *What is the office of a prophet?* To declare the will of God.
19. *Is it not to declare future events?*
    That is only a part of the office of a prophet.
20. *When did our Lord act as a prophet?*
    Whenever He taught the people or His disciples.
21. *As a prophet did He foretell future events?*
    Yes : His own crucifixion.
22. *What besides did He foretell?*
    The destruction of Jerusalem.
23. *What besides?* His own second coming.
24. *Does He teach as a prophet now that He is in Heaven?*
    Yes : He speaks by His Spirit.
25. *To what office besides that of a prophet is our Lord anointed?*
    To that of a priest.
26. *What is the duty of a priest?*
    To offer sacrifices.
27. *Where do you find the offering of sacrifices ordained?*
    In Levit. i. ii. iii. iv. xvi.
28. *What other duty belonged to the priest?*
    He interceded for the people (Numb. xvi. 46).
29. *What further duty belonged to the priest?*
    He blessed the people in God's name (Numb. vi. 23).
30. *Does our Lord, as our Priest, do all these things?* Yes.
31. *What sacrifice did He offer?* Himself.
32. *On what altar?* On the cross.

33. *What was the effect of His sacrifice?*
    It made atonement (or satisfaction) for all sin.
34. *Is our Lord a priest now?* Yes: He is a priest for ever.
35. *How is this?* He ever liveth to make intercession.
36. *As a priest does He bless?*
    Yes: all blessings come from God through Him.
37. *Does He ever bless His people through others?*
    Yes: through His ministers.
38. *Does this prevent His being the one priest?* No.
39. *Why not?*
    Because His ministers act only in His Name and by His Power.
40. *Give an instance of this.*
    When a minister baptizes, he baptizes only in the Name and by the Power of Christ.
41. *Give another.*
    When a bishop confirms, he confirms only in the Name and by the Power of Christ.
42. *Give another.*
    When a priest celebrates the Lord's Supper, he does it in the Name and by the Power of Christ.
43. *What does our Lord say of His ministers?*
    As my Father hath sent Me, even so send I you. Whose soever sins ye remit they are remitted (John xx. 22).
44. *Give an instance of a minister acting in the name of Christ.*
    St. Paul, in absolving the Corinthian sinner (2 Cor. ii. 10).
45. *Give an instance of a minister blessing in Christ's name in the Eucharist.*
    "The cup of blessing which we bless, is it not the communion of the blood of Christ?" (1 Cor. x. 16).
46. *If Christ is our priest what must we do?*
    We must ask His intercession.
47. *What else?*
    We must rely on His atoning sacrifice.
48. *In what sense is Christ the only priest?*
    He alone has reconciled mankind to God by His sacrifice.
49. *In what sense are His ordained ministers priests?*
    He has commissioned them to apply to us the atonement He alone has made.
50. *What besides is Christ anointed to be?* A King.
51. *Of whom is He said to be the king?* Of Israel (John i. 49).
52. *Did He ever reign over the Jews like an earthly king?* No.
53. *How then is He King of Israel?*
    He reigns over the true Israel, the Israel of God—His Church.
54. *What two kings were types of Christ as a King?*
    David and Solomon.

55. *How was David a type of Christ as our king?*
    He was a warlike king, who won his throne by subduing his enemies.
56. *How was Solomon a type of Christ?*
    As a king ruling God's people in peace (the Prince of Peace).
57. *Under what name does Ezekiel prophesy of our Lord as King?*
    Under the name of David?
58. *What Psalms are written of our Lord as King?*
    Psalms ii. xxiv. xlv. lxxii. cx.
59. *How long will His reign last?* For ever (Luke i. 33).
60. *If we are to be His true subjects, where must He reign*
    In our hearts.
61. *Amongst whom does He rule?*
    Amongst His enemies (Psalm cx. 2).
62. *Who are His enemies?*
    The same as our enemies—the world, the flesh, and the devil
63. *What enemies has Christ within us?*
    Our evil lusts and passion.
64. *How must we chiefly honour Him as King?*
    By resisting them, and by doing His will.

SECTION XVII.—GOD'S ONLY SON.

1. *What further do you profess to believe concerning Jesus Christ?*
   That Jesus Christ is God's only Son, *i. e.*, His only begotten Son.
2. *Is the word " only begotten " ever expressed in the Apostles' Creed?*
   Yes. In the Baptismal Service the minister demands of the God-parents, "Dost thou believe in Jesus Christ, His only begotten Son?"
3. *Was there ever a time when God had no Son?*
   No: God is by His very nature the Father, and so must have a true Son from all eternity.
4. *How is this article of the Apostles' Creed expressed in the Nicene Creed?*
   "I believe . . . in one Lord Jesus Christ, the only begotten Son of God, begotten of His Father before all worlds." (5–9)
5. *Is there any direct proof in Scripture that He was begotten before all worlds?*
   Yes: "In the beginning was the Word, and the Word was with God; . . . all things were made by Him." Also St. Paul tells us that, "He is before all things" (Col. i. 17); and, "By Him [Jesus Christ] God made the worlds." (Heb. i. 2; also John xvii. 5.) (1-12)
6. *If Christ be thus the only begotten Son of God, must He be God?*
   Yes: as a son of man partakes of his father's nature, and is truly man, so the only begotten Son of God must partake of His Father's nature, and be truly God. (10–13)
7. *Does our Lord ever assert this?*
   Yes; when He says that God was His (*i. e.*, His own proper—ἴδιος) Father, making Himself equal with God. (John v. 18.) (14–26)
8. *Is it essential that we should believe in Him as the only begotten Son of God?*
   Yes; our Lord Himself says, "He that believeth not is condemned already, because he hath not believed in the name of the only begotten Son of God" (John iii. 18)

—*i.e.* hath not believed that He is what His name of "only begotten Son" implies.

9. *What other reason have we for confessing this great truth?*
By confessing it we honour the love of the Father. "For God so loved the world that He gave His only begotten Son." (John iii. 16; 1 John iv. 10.) (26)

10. *Is there any other reason?*
Yes: unless we believe that, being the only begotten, He is truly God, we cannot believe in His redemption, for God challenges the work of redemption or salvation as His work.

11. *How are we to honour Him as the Son of God?*
All men are to honour the Son, even as they honour the Father. (John v. 23.) (25, 26)

12. *In what ways?*
By believing in Him. "Ye believe in God, believe also in me." (John xiv. 1.)
By worshipping Him as the Son of God, equal in nature and glory with God, as we do in the Services of the Church.

SHORTER CATECHISM.

1. *Whose Son is Jesus Christ?* He is the Son of God.
2. *Are we not sons of God?* Yes; but Jesus is God's only Son.
3. *How is Jesus God's Son?* By nature.
4. *In what sense is Jesus God's Son?*
In the same sense as each one of us is the son of his father.
5. *How is this expressed in the Nicene Creed?*
Jesus is there said to be "the only begotten Son of God."
6. *When was He begotten?* Before all worlds.
7. *What does that mean?* From all eternity; from everlasting.
8. *Was there ever a time in which there was no Son of God?* No.
9. *What then has God always been?*
He has always been a Father—the Father.
10. *If the Father is God, what must His true and only Son be?*
He must be God also.
11. *Why?* Because a true son partakes of his father's nature.
12. *If the father is a human being, of what nature is his true son?*
Of the human nature.

13. *If the Father is the Divine Being, of what nature must His Son be?*
    Of the One Divine Nature.
14. *Does our blessed Lord ever claim to have the same Divine nature as God His Father has?*
    Yes: when He says, "I and my Father are one" (John x. 30).
15. *What must He mean by this?*
    That He and His Father are one in Godhead.
16. *Are they one in power also?*
    Yes: Christ says, What things soever the Father doeth, these also doeth the Son likewise (John v. 19).
17. *Is the Son equal to the Father?*
    He must be equal in nature, otherwise He would not be His Son.
18. *But is not a father always superior to a son?*
    Never in point of nature.
19. *How can a father be above his son?*
    Only in authority or station.
20. *Is the eternal Son then equal in nature to His Father?* Yes.
21. *Was He ever heard to assert this?*
    Yes: John v. 18.
22. *Who heard Him claim to be the same as God?*
    The Jews; His enemies
23. *What did they do?* They sought to slay Him.
24. *What would our Lord have done if He had not been God?*
    He would have told them that He was not; but He did not.
25. *What did He proceed to say?*
    That all men should honour the Son even as they honour the Father (John v. 23).
26. *If we refused Divine honour to the Son, whom should we dishonour?*
    We should dishonour the Father, for Christ Himself tells us that "he that honoureth not the Son, honoureth not the Father" (John v. 23).

SECTION XVIII.—OUR LORD.

1. *What further do we believe respecting Jesus Christ?*
That He is our Lord. (1)
2. *By whom is this Divine Name given to Him?*
By St. Thomas, where he says to him, "My Lord and my God" (John xx. 28) ; and by the Angel, who says that St. John the Baptist shall "turn many of the children of Israel to the Lord their God, for He shall go before Him in the spirit and power of Elias." (Luke i. 17.) (7, 8)
3. *Before whom did St. John the Baptist go?*
Before Jesus Christ, to prepare His way. (8)
4. *In what sense must the word "Lord" be used in these places?*
In the sense that Jesus is the Lord Jehovah, as partaking with His Father of the uncreated nature. [It is consequently a translation of the Hebrew word Jehovah.] (1–8)
5. *Is the term "Lord" given to Christ in any other sense?*
Yes : as man He is Lord of all ; which Lordship He receives from His Father, as St. Peter says : "God hath made that same Jesus whom ye have crucified both Lord and Christ." (Acts ii. 36.)
6. *Is it needful that we should confess this Lordship of Christ?*
Every tongue is to confess that Jesus Christ is Lord to the glory of God the Father. (Phil. ii. 11.)
7. *How are we to acknowledge this Lordship of Christ?*
By ever remembering and confessing His absolute property in us. (Rom. xiv. 8, 9.) "Whether we live, we live unto the Lord, or whether we die, we die unto the Lord : whether we live, therefore, or die, we are the Lord's. For to this end Christ both died and rose and revived, that He might be Lord both of the dead and living." (9–14)

SHORTER CATECHISM.

1. *What is the only Son of God to us?* He is our Lord.
2. *How many senses has the word Lord?* Two.
3. *What is the first?*
   The first is Lord, as meaning the Eternal God.
4. *Is this ever applied to Christ?*
   Yes, in the Prophet Jeremiah (xxiii. 6), "The LORD our righteousness."
5. *In any other place?*
   Yes, in Malachi iii. 1, He is called the LORD, whose way John the Baptist was sent to prepare.
6. *Of what Hebrew word does this word Lord seem a translation?*
   Of the word Jehovah.
7. *Where is this word Lord in this sense given to Jesus in the New Testament?*
   By St. Thomas, in John xx. 28.
8. *By whom besides?* By the angel Gabriel, in Luke i. 16.
9. *In what other sense is this word Lord applied to Jesus?*
   In the sense of His being the Governor, Master, and Possessor of us and of all things.
10. *Give an instance of the word Lord being applied to Him in this sense.*
    God hath made that same Jesus whom ye have crucified both Lord and Christ (Acts ii. 36).
11. *Why did Jesus require to be made Lord by His Father?*
    Because He was man, and so must have His dominion given to Him by God the Father (Phil. ii. 11).
12. *How must we honour Christ as Lord?*
    By ever acknowledging Him as our Master. By ever remembering that we have been bought by Him.
13. *What price did He pay that He might possess us as our Lord?*
    His own Blood (Acts xx. 28).
14. *Is this His title in Heaven?*
    Lord of Lords (Rev. xix. 16).

SECTION XIX.—CONCEIVED BY THE HOLY GHOST, BORN OF THE VIRGIN MARY.

1. *What further do we profess respecting Jesus Christ?*
   That God's only Son, our Lord, was conceived by the Holy Ghost, born of the Virgin Mary.
2. *What word is used to express this in the Nicene Creed?*
   He was incarnate. [The only begotten Son of God ... Who for us men, and for our salvation, came down from heaven, and was incarnate by the Holy Ghost of the Virgin Mary, and was made man.] (1–6)
3. *Does this mean that He ceased to be God, and was changed into man?*
   No, not for a moment. It means that He laid aside for a time His Divine glory, and having assumed the nature of man, He was born and grew up, and spoke, and acted, and suffered as a man.
4. *What place has the Incarnation in the New Testament?*
   The very first place; for it is the first thing revealed in each of the four Gospels, and the first thing taught in such Epistles as those to the Romans and Hebrews. (4)
5. *How is it revealed in St. Matthew's Gospel?*
   In the words of the angel to Joseph : " Thou Son of David, fear not to take unto thee Mary thy wife, for that which is conceived in her is of the Holy Ghost, and she shall bring forth a son, and thou shalt call his name Jesus." (Matt. i. 20.)
6. *But does this imply that God should be incarnate?*
   All this was done to fulfil a prophecy that a virgin should bring forth a Son, Who should be Emmanuel—God with us. (Matt. i. 23.) (8–10)
7. *How is the Incarnation revealed in St. John's Gospel?*
   At its very commencement, in the words, " In the beginning was the Word, and the Word was with God, and the Word was God. And the Word was made flesh, and dwelt amongst us." (John i. 1–14.) (11–14)
8. *When was the Word made flesh?*
   When, in the words of St. Luke, The Holy Ghost

came upon the Virgin, and the power of the Highest overshadowed her, and therefore that Holy Thing which was born of her was called the Son of God. (Luke i. 35.)

9. *If Christ is the Son of God, and also the Son of Man, is He two persons?*

No: He has two whole and perfect natures, the Godhead and manhood, in one Person. (16–19)

10. *Can you show from the Scriptures that He was regarded as God and man in one person?*

Yes: when He was brought into the world in weakness and humiliation, He yet received, by God's command, the worship of angels and men. (Matt. ii. 11; Heb. i. 6.) [The frankincense offered by the wise men being an offering as to God.]

"Incense doth their God disclose."—Hymns A. and M. 59.

11. *What other proof can you give?*

When sitting with Nicodemus in a room at night, He speaks of Himself as "He that came down from heaven, even the Son of Man which is in heaven" (John iii. 13); and though not fifty years old, He says, "Before Abraham was, I am." (John viii. 58.)

12. *What other proof?*

When St. Thomas was assured that He had risen in the same body which had been crucified, he confessed His Divine nature in the words, "My Lord and my God." (John xx. 28.) (20)

13. *Then was God in very deed amongst us?*

Yes. When men saw Jesus, they saw God; when men heard Him speak, they heard God speak; when men handled Him, they handled of the Word of life (1 John i. 1); when men crucified Him, they crucified the Lord of Glory (1 Cor. ii. 8).

14. *But are we required to believe and confess a truth so exceedingly deep and mysterious?*

Yes, we are required, because it is the way in which God gave His Son for our salvation.

15. *How was this?*

As long as Christ was in the glory of His Father, He could not be "given," but He took a nature in which He could be "given" to suffer death, and this nature He assumed when He was conceived by the Holy Ghost, and born of the Virgin Mary.

16. *Of whom was our Lord born?*
 Of the Virgin Mary. (24-27)
17. *Of what family was she?*
 Of the family of David ; for St. Paul says that He was made of the seed of David according to the flesh. (Rom. i. 3.) (28-33)
18. *What were the words in which the angel Gabriel announced to her the exceeding honour which God had vouchsafed to her?*
 " Hail, thou art highly favoured ; the Lord is with thee : blessed art thou among women." (Luke i. 28.)
 [Also Elizabeth, filled with the Holy Ghost, said, " Blessed art thou among women, and blessed is the fruit of thy womb : and whence is this to me, that the mother of my Lord should come to me ?" (Luke i. 42-43.)]
19. *In what condition was our Blessed Lord born?*
 He was born in an extremely low and poor condition ; for on account of the poverty of His parents He was born in a stable and laid in a manger.
20. *Did He continue in this condition?*
 Yes. He had not where to lay His head (Matt. viii. 20) ; and certain women ministered unto Him of their substance (Luke viii. 3).
21. *Had our Lord a human soul, or was His Divine nature in the place of a human thinking soul?*
 He had a sinless human soul, for we read of His saying, " My soul is exceeding sorrowful." (Matt. xxvi. 38.) We read of Him rejoicing in spirit. (Luke x. 21.) We read of Him, as regards His human soul or spirit, increasing in wisdom as His body increased in stature. (Luke ii. 52.)
22. *For what great reasons did our Lord come amongst us in the flesh?*
 That He might suffer for us in the flesh.
 That He might feed us with the spiritual food of His flesh and blood. (John vi. 53.)
 That we might be one flesh with Him ; bone of His bone, and flesh of His flesh. (Ephes. v. 30, 31, 32.)

SHORTER CATECHISM.

1. *How did the Son of God come amongst us?*
 He was conceived by the Holy Ghost, and born of the Virgin Mary.

2. *Who was conceived by the Holy Ghost, and born of the Virgin Mary?* The Son of God.
3. *Why did this take place?* That He might become man.
4. *Show from the Scriptures that He was conceived by the Holy Ghost.*
   Matthew i. 20; Luke i. 35.
5. *What does this mean?*
   That His human nature (His Body and Soul) was prepared for Him by the Holy Ghost.
6. *How does St. Paul express this truth?*
   That God's Son was made of the seed of David, according to the flesh (Rom. i. 3).
7. *How elsewhere does St. Paul describe it?*
   Jesus Christ, who, being in the form of God, thought it not robbery to be equal with God, but made Himself of no reputation, and took upon Him the form of a servant; and was made in the likeness of men, and being found in fashion as a man, He humbled Himself (Phil. ii. 7).
8. *Because then the Son of God was conceived by the Holy Ghost, what was He?*
   He was God and Man. The God-Man.
9. *What name of our Lord teaches us this?*
   His name of Emmanuel, *i.e.*, God with us.
10. *What does this signify?*
    That God is with us as one of ourselves. That God personally dwells amongst men.
11. *By what one word is this coming of God's Son among us as a man described?*
    By the word "Incarnation."
12. *What does this word mean?*
    The flesh-taking. The assuming of a body of flesh.
13. *Is it ever said that God's Son took our flesh?*
    Yes: "The word was made flesh" (John i. 14).
14. *Who is the Word here?* The Eternal Son of God.
15. *Why did God's Son take our flesh?*
    That He might give it for the life of the world.
16. *Are there two persons in Christ?* No.
17. *But did you not say that He is God and Man?*
    Yes: He has two natures, but only one person.
18. *Was He always the same person?*
    Yes: He is from eternity the Son of God.
19. *Does He ever tell us this in very startling words?*
    Yes · He said, "Before Abraham was, I am" (John viii. 58).
20. *What did He suffer Himself to be called?*
    Lord and God (John xx. 28).
21. *What did He do before He came amongst us?*
    He made the worlds (John i. 3).

BORN OF THE VIRGIN MARY.

22. *What does His coming amongst us show?*
    The love of God. [God so loved the world, &c., John iii. 16.]
23. *Because He was conceived by the Holy Ghost, from what was He free?* From all stain of sin. From original, or birth sin.
24. *What was the earliest prophecy of His coming amongst us?*
    The prophecy of the seed of the woman bruising the serpent's head (Gen. iii. 15).
25. *Why was He the seed of the woman?*
    Because He was born of the Virgin Mary.
26. *Had He no earthly Father?* No.
27. *Who then was St. Joseph?* His foster-father.
28. *Of what family were both Joseph and Mary?*
    Of the family of David.
29. *Why?*
    To fulfil the prophecies that the Messiah should be the Son of David.
30. *Of what tribe was our Lord?* Of the tribe of Judah.
31. *To fulfil what prophecy?* That of the Shiloh (Gen. xlix. 10).
32. *In what city was He born?* Bethlehem.
33. *To fulfil what prophecy?* Micah v. 2.
34. *What did our Lord call Himself?* The Son of Man.
35. *Why was he made the Son of Man?*
    That we might be made the sons of God (Gal. iv. 4, 5).

SECTION XX.—SUFFERED UNDER PONTIUS PILATE, WAS CRUCIFIED.

1. *What is the next thing in which you profess your belief?*
   I believe in Jesus, God's only Son, our Lord, who suffered under Pontius Pilate, was crucified, dead, and buried.
2. *How is it that no notice is taken in the Creed of the years between our Lord's birth and His crucifixion?*
   Because our Lord took our nature in order that He might suffer and die for us. [He took our flesh in order that He might give that flesh for the life of the world.]
3. *But did He not live in order that He might set us an example of Godly life?*
   Yes: but the great object of His Incarnation was that He might die for our sins, and rise again to impart to us of His Risen Life.
4. *Did He suffer before He suffered under Pontius Pilate?*
   Yes; all His life he was "a man of sorrows, and acquainted with grief." (Isaiah liii. 3.) (4, 5)
5. *Mention some of the things which He suffered during His lifetime?*
   Poverty. "Had not where to lay His head." (Matt. viii. 20.)
   Contempt. (Luke xvi. 14; John viii. 48.)
   Rejection by His own people. (John i. 11; Luke xix. 41.)
   Unbelief of His chosen disciples. (Matt. xvii. 17.)
   Temptations of Satan. (Heb. ii. 18.) (6–14)
   Disappointment. (John v. 40.)
   Weariness. (John iv. 6.)
   Hunger. (Matt. iv. 2.)
S. *What are the sufferings in which we express our belief?*
   Those which ended in His death.
   His betrayal. (John xiii. 21.) His agony and bloody sweat. (Luke xxii. 44.) His apprehension as if He were a malefactor. (Matt. xxvi. 55.) His desertion by all His disciples. (Matt. xxvi. 56.) The insults from the chief priests and their menials. (John xviii. 22; Matt. xxvi. 67; Mark xiv. 65; Luke xxii. 63, 65.) His denial by Peter.

(Matt. xxvi. 69, 75.) The insults He suffered at the hands of Herod. (Luke xxiii. 8–12.) His mock trial before Pilate. His being scourged (John xix. 1); crowned with thorns (Matt. xxvii. 29); spitted on and mocked (Matt. xxvii. 30, 31). (14–37)

7. *But what was the last suffering which we expressly mention in this confession of our faith ?*
His Crucifixion. (38)

8. *Describe this horrible form of death.*
It has been thus described by Bishop Beveridge—
"A straight piece of timber being set fast in the ground, with a cross-beam towards the upper part of it, His hands were fastened with nails, the one to the one side and the other to the other side of the [said] cross-beam, and His feet to the straight timber that stood in the ground, His body being partially sustained or held up by a little piece of wood that jutted out for that purpose about the middle of the upright timber. In this most painful and ignominious posture He hung for several hours together."

9. *Was it written in prophecy that the Messiah was to suffer such a death as this ?*
Yes ; in the Twenty-second Psalm. (39–47)

10. *What sufferings that our Lord endured when He was crucified are there set forth ?*
Nearly all.
  1. The wounds in His hands and feet. "They pierced my hands and my feet." (Psalm xxii. 17.)
  2. The parting of His garments. (Verse 18.)
  3. Agony as if He were on the rack. "All my bones are out of joint." (Verse 14.)
  4. Total loss of strength. (Verses 14, 15.)
  5. Burning thirst. "My tongue cleaveth to my gums." (Verse 15.)
  6. The taunts and revilings of a mob of His enemies. (Verses 6, 7, 12, 13, 17.) (39–47)

11. *What types of this death were there in the Old Testament ?*
Isaac carrying the wood on which he was to be sacrificed. (Gen. xxii. 6, 7, 9.)
The brazen serpent lifted on a pole. (Num. xxi. 8.) Compare John iii. 14. (48–50)

12. *Had our Lord Himself said that He must be crucified ?*
Yes ; He said, "They shall condemn Him to death,

and shall deliver Him to the Gentiles, to mock, and to scourge, and to crucify." (Matt. xx. 18, 19.) And He said, "I, if I be lifted up, will draw all men unto Me." (John xii. 32 : also viii. 28.)

13. *How came it to pass that He suffered a Gentile form of death ?*

Because the sceptre had departed from Judah, and a Roman governor had the sole power of life and death. ["It is not lawful for us [the Jews] to put any man to death." (John xviii. 31.)] (51–57)

14. *Is there any reason why the name of Pontius Pilate should be mentioned in the Creed ?*

Yes : it assures us of the particular time in which Christ redeemed us, for Pilate is a name mentioned in profane history as a Procurator in the reign of Tiberius Cæsar.

["As the Son of God, by His determinate counsel, was sent into the world to die in the fulness of time, so it concerns the Church to be assured of the time in which He died."—*Bp. Pearson.*

"Christ, the founder of that name [of Christians] was put to death as a criminal by Pontius Pilate, Procurator of Judæa, in the reign of Tiberius."—*Tacitus' Annals*, xv. 44.] (58)

15. *What was the termination of our Lord's sufferings on the cross ?*

He died. "Was crucified, DEAD."

16. *Was our blessed Lord's life taken from Him ?*

No; it is expressly said, both by Himself and His Evangelists, that He surrendered it Himself. His dying was an act of His own. "I lay down my life." (John x. 15-18.) "Into Thy hands I commend my Spirit." (Luke xxiii. 46.)

17. *For what purpose did Christ die ?*

That we might have forgiveness of sin, and be restored to the favour of God. (59–62)

18. *Show this from the Scriptures.*

He is the propitiation for our sins ; and not for ours only, but for the sins of the whole world. (1 John ii. 2.)

He Himself bare our sins in His own body on the tree. (1 Peter ii. 24.)

"The Lord hath laid on Him the iniquity of us all." (Isaiah liii. 6.)

"When thou shalt make His soul an offering for sin."
(Isaiah liii. 10.)
"Whom God hath set forth to be a propitiation through faith in His blood." (Rom. iii. 25.)
"Christ was once offered to bear the sins of many." (Heb. ix. 28.) "We are sanctified through the offering of the body of Christ once for all." (Heb. x. 10.) (59-62)

19. *What are all these ways of speaking?*
They are all sacrificial terms or ways of speaking ; *i. e.*, they describe the efficacy of the death of Christ in the same terms in which God described the efficacy of the Jewish sacrifices. (63-74)

20. *But could the blood of bulls and of goats take away sin?*
Not of itself. The Jewish sacrifices could only atone because they set forth before God our Lord's sacrifice.

21. *What then do we learn from these Jewish sacrifices setting forth Christ's death?*
We learn that as the Jewish sacrifices cleansed and restored the worshippers in an imperfect manner (Levit. xvi. 33), much more must the sacrifice of the Eternal Son cleanse our consciences from dead works to serve the living God. (65-74)

22. *Does our Lord claim for His Blood this sacrificial power?*
Yes ; where He says, when He instituted the Eucharist, "This is my blood of the new covenant, which is shed for many for the remission of sins." (Matt. xxvi. 28.)

23. *For whom did our Lord die?*
For all men. For the whole world. (1 Tim. ii. 6 ; 1 Tim. iv. 10 ; 1 John ii. 2.) (73-79)

24. *What book of God's word seems especially to have been written to set forth the sacrificial nature and efficacy of the death of Christ?*
The Epistle to the Hebrews.

25. *How must we glorify Christ for having offered up Himself upon the cross for us?*
By relying with all our hearts on the efficacy of His death.

26. *How besides?*
By ever remembering that He has bought us with His Blood, so that we are not our own. (1 Cor. vi. 19, 20.) (80-83)

27. *How besides?*
By constantly receiving the Holy Eucharist as His own solemn commemoration of His death. [Do this in remembrance of me. As often as ye eat this bread, and drink this cup, ye do shew the Lord's death till He come. (1 Cor. xi. 20, 26.)] (83-85)

28. *What other lessons do the Scripture writers teach from the Crucifixion of Christ?*
   1. That as He was crucified for us, so must we crucify our carnal lusts (Gal. v. 24), by denying our wills, and bringing our bodies into subjection.
   2. That we should have the same mind which was in Him Who, being in the form of God, yet became obedient unto death, even the death of the cross. (Phil. ii. 8.)
   3. That we should pass our lives in godly fear. (1 Peter i. 17, 18.)
   4. That we should be patient under injuries. (1 Peter ii. 21.)
   5. That we should love one another. (1 John iv. 16.)

29. *Whose love is shown in the sufferings and death of Christ?*
The love of the Father, as well as of the Son. (John iii. 16; Rom. v. 8; viii. 32.)

30. *Can we divide between the love of the Father and that of the Son in this matter of our Redemption?*
No; not for a moment. Christ says, "I and my Father are one." (John x. 30.) Also, "He that hath seen me hath seen the Father." (xiv. 9.)

31. *What sign do we receive in token that we are to believe in and to follow a crucified Saviour?*
We are signed in Baptism with the sign of the Cross, in token that, "Hereafter we shall not be ashamed to confess the faith of Christ Crucified," &c.

SHORTER CATECHISM.

1. *Who suffered under Pontius Pilate?*
God's only Son, our Lord.
2. *But did you not say that He was God—how then could He suffer?*
Because He had taken a nature which could suffer?
3. *But was He not sinless, and is not suffering the penalty of sin?*
Yes: but He suffered for our sins, not for His own.

4. *Were His sufferings under Pontius Pilate the first thing which He suffered?*
   No: His whole life was a suffering life.
5. *What, on account of His suffering life, was He called in prophecy?*
   A man of sorrows, and acquainted with grief.
6. *What did He suffer throughout His whole Life?* Poverty.
7. *Had Christ any place which He could call His home?*
   No: "Foxes have holes, and the birds of the air have nests, but the Son of man hath not where to lay His head" (Matt. viii. 20).
8. *Did Christ ever weep?*
   Yes: He wept over Jerusalem.
9. *Why did He thus weep?*
   Because He sorrowed for the unbelief of His countrymen.
10. *Why did this give Him sorrow?*
    Because He knew that if they would not believe in Him they would die in their sins.
11. *Did He weep on any other occasion?*
    Yes, at the grave of Lazarus. He wept through compassion when He saw others weep.
12. *Did He suffer anything from Satan?*
    Yes: He "suffered being tempted" (Heb. ii. 18).
13. *Did He suffer anything from His disciples?*
    Yes: from their unbelief.
14. *What sufferings are particularly mentioned in the Creed?*
    Those He suffered under Pontius Pilate.
15. *Is our faith particularly directed to these sufferings?* Yes.
16. *By whom?* By Himself (Matt. xvi. 21; xx. 18, 19).
17. *By whom in prophecy?*
    By David, in Psalm xxii.; by Isaiah, in ch. liii.; by Daniel ix. 26.
18. *By whom was our Lord betrayed?* By Judas.
19. *Was this foretold in prophecy?*
    Yes: in Zachariah xi. 12.
20. *In what did our Lord's betrayal consist?*
    In Judas telling the chief priest where He could be found, that they might seize Him when alone in the absence of the multitude.
21. *Did the thought of this oppress Him?* Yes (John xiii. 21).
22. *How did the near prospect of His sufferings affect Him?*
    It wrung from Him His agony and bloody sweat.
23. *What was the first indignity He endured?*
    He was apprehended as if He had been a malefactor, with swords and staves (Matt. xxvi. 55).
24. *Before whom was our Lord first taken?* Before Annas (John xviii. 13).
25. *To whom did Annas send Him?* To Caiaphas (John xviii. 24).

26. *What indignities and insults did He suffer in the hall of Caiaphas?*
   He was smitten and buffeted (John xviii. 22; Matthew xxvi. 67, 68.
27. *Did His friends and disciples stand by Him under all this?*
   No: they forsook Him (Matt. xxvi. 56).
28. *How did the foremost among them treat Him?*
   He denied Him (Matt. xxvi. 70).
29. *Before whom was He now taken?* Before Pilate.
30. *Why did not the chief priests punish Him?*
   Because He must be delivered to the Gentiles. It was not lawful for the Jews to put any man to death (John xviii. 31).
31. *To whom did Pilate send Him?* To Herod (Luke xxiii. 7).
32. *What did He suffer before Herod?* Luke xxiii. 11.
33. *To whom was He at last sent?* To Pilate.
34. *What did He suffer before Pilate?* Scourging.
35. *Was this expressly mentioned in prophecy?* Yes (Isaiah l. 6).
36. *What else did He suffer?*
   He was crowned with thorns (John xix. 2).
37. *What other indignity?* He was spit upon (Isaiah l. 6).
38. *And what was the end?* He was crucified.
39. *Was this particular punishment foretold?*
   Yes: the sufferings foretold in Psalm xxii. can be all endured together under no other form of death.
40. *What are the sufferings described in this Psalm?*
   They are the sufferings of one "lifted up" to die.
41. *How is this?*
   They are the sufferings of one who dies in public with his enemies raging around him (ver. 6, 7, 12, 13, 17).
42. *What other sufferings are there depicted?*
   The sufferings of one who has his hands and feet pierced (ver. 17).
43. *What other sufferings?*
   Of one whose bones are racked and stand out (ver. 14).
44. *What suffering beside?*
   Exhaustion and burning thirst (ver. 14, 15).
45. *Would one dying of stoning complain thus?* No.
46. *Would one dying in battle complain thus?* No.
47. *Or in prison?* No.
48. *Did our Lord bear His cross on the way to His crucifixion?*
   At first He did (John xix. 17).
49. *Was any type fulfilled by this?*
   Yes: Isaac bearing the wood (Gen. xxii. 6).
50. *Was any other type fulfilled in the death of our Lord?*
   Yes: as the serpent was lifted up, so was He (John iii. 14).
51. *Under whom did He suffer crucifixion?*
   Under Pontius Pilate.

52. *Who was this Pontius Pilate?* The Roman governor.
53. *How came it that a foreign governor had power to order the crucifixion?*
    Because the sceptre, *i.e.,* the supreme power, had departed from Judah (Gen. xlix. 10).
54. *Did he desire to crucify our Lord?*
    No: he declared Him to be innocent (John xix. 6, 12).
55. *Who then urged him to crucify Jesus?* The chief priests.
56. *With what threat?* John xix. 12.
57. *What then was Pilate's sin?*
    Selfish cowardice and godless fear of men.
58. *Why is Pilate's name mentioned in the Creed?*
    To mark the time when our Lord suffered.
59. *Mention in the words of the prophet Isaiah the purpose for which Christ died?*
    To make His soul an offering for sin, and to bear the sin of many (Isaiah liii. 10, 12).
60. *For what purpose did He Himself say that His blood was to be shed?*
    For the remission of sins (Matt. xxvi. 28).
61. *What other word is used respecting His death?*
    That it is a propitiation (Rom. iii. 25; 1 John ii. 2).
62. *What in the Epistle to the Hebrews is said of Christ's death?*
    That He was offered to bear the sins of many (ix. 28).
63. *What are all these ways of speaking called?*
    They are called sacrificial.
64. *Why?*
    Because they are the ways of speaking used throughout the Old Testament, to describe the benefits derived from the Jewish sacrifices.
65. *What did the Jewish sacrifices make?* Atonement.
66. *What is atonement?* It is the act of making people at one.
67. *What other name is consequently given to it?*
    Reconciliation.
68. *Show that the Jewish sacrifices made atonement.*
    Exod. xxix. 36; Levit. i. 4; iv. 20.
69. *Was there a real atonement through such sacrifices?*
    It is not possible that the blood of bulls and of goats should take away sins (Heb. x. 4).
70. *How is their efficacy described?*
    They only sanctified to the purifying of the flesh (Heb. ix. 13).
71. *What good did they do then?*
    They restored the sinner to the congregation of Israel.
72. *How is the effect of the blood of Christ described?*
    It purges or purifies the conscience (Heb. ix. 14).

73. *What is the blood of Christ said to do for us?*
    It is said to cleanse us (1 John i. 7), to wash us from sin (Rev. i. 5).
74. *What is the meaning of all these ways of speaking?*
    They all mean that through the death of Christ, *i.e.*, His blood shedding, God forgives us.
75. *Do they mean anything besides this?*
    Yes: they signify that because of Christ's death we are brought back into the favour of God.
76. *Have they any further meaning still?*
    Yes: they mean that because of Christ's death we have power given to us to die to sin, and to live to God.
77. *How was it that Jesus could shed blood of such power?*
    Because He was at once God and man.
78. *For whom did He shed His blood?* For all men (1 John ii. 2).
79. *What did He make by giving Himself?* A ransom for all.
80. *What other name is given to this ransoming?*
    It is called Redemption, *i.e.*, buying again those taken captive.
81. *If we are ransomed or redeemed, to whom do we belong?*
    To Him Who redeemed us, Jesus Christ (Acts xx. 28; 1 Cor. vi. 20).
82. *How are we to show our gratitude for all this?*
    By loving Him (2 Cor. v. 14, 15).
83. *How do we show our love?*
    By keeping His commandments (John xiv. 15).
84. *Can we love Him if we do not strive to keep His commandments?*
    No (John xiv. 23, 24).
85. *What commandment must we keep in particular commemoration of His death?*
    Do this in remembrance of me.

SECTION XXI.—BURIED.

1. *What further do we profess to believe respecting Jesus?*
That the only Son of God, Who was crucified and died, was "buried." (1–6)
2. *Is it an essential part of the faith to confess that our Lord was buried?*
St. Paul says that his Gospel, which he preached, was that Christ died for our sins, AND THAT HE WAS BURIED. (I Cor. xv. 3, 4.) *See* also Acts xiii. 29. (7)
3. *What intimations were there in the Old Testament that the Messiah should be buried?*
"My flesh shall rest in hope." (Psalm xvi. 9.)
Also Jonah, as a type of our Lord. (Matt. xii. 40.) (10–12)
4. *What honours were paid to our Lord's Body?*
Nicodemus "brought a mixture of myrrh and aloes . . Then took they the body of Jesus, and wound it in the linen clothes with the spices." (John xix. 39.) "The women also which came with Him from Galilee . . . . prepared spices and ointments." (Luke xxiii. 56.) (2, 3)
5. *Would our Lord's Body have ever corrupted?*
No : He whom God raised again saw no corruption. (Acts xiii. 37.) (10)
6. *What do we learn from the honour paid to our Lord's Body?*
That it is well pleasing to God to honour the bodies of the faithful.
7. *Did our Lord ever intimate that such care for His Body was an act of piety, well pleasing to Him?*
Yes : when He commended the act of the woman who poured the contents of the box of ointment on His head. "She did it for my burial." (Matt. xxvi. 12.) (11, 12)
8. *Have baptized persons any peculiar interest in our Lord's Burial?*
Yes. St. Paul twice asserts that we are buried with Him in Baptism, that we may walk in newness of life. (Rom. vi. 4 ; Col. ii. 12.) (13, 14, 15.)

SHORTER CATECHISM.

1. *Did our Saviour's dead Body hang long upon the cross?*
   No: it was taken down the same day and buried.
2. *By whom?* By Joseph of Arimathæa (Matt. xxvii. 57).
3. *Who assisted Him in this good work?*
   Nicodemus (John xix. 39).
4. *Was it the custom among the Romans to bury those who had been crucified?*
   No: the bodies of crucified persons frequently hung on the cross till they were corrupted and dissolved.
5. *Who desired that our Lord should be taken down?*
   The Jews (John xix. 31).
6. *What precautions were taken respecting His body?*
   Matt. xxvii. 63.
7. *Is the burial of Christ ever mentioned as a part of the Gospel?*
   Yes; by St. Paul (Acts xiii. 29; 1 Cor. xv. 4).
8. *What type was fulfilled in the state of our Lord's body when it was laid in the tomb?*
   The Paschal Lamb, a bone of which was not broken (John xix. 36).
9. *What prophecy was also fulfilled?* Zec. xii. 10; John xix. 37.
10. *What prophecy was fulfilled by the state of our Lord's body whilst it continued in the tomb?*
    That His flesh should not see corruption (Ps. xvi. 10).
11. *Does our Lord ever allude to His own burial?*
    Yes: He cites that which happened to Jonah as a type of it.
12. *Does He elsewhere allude to it?* Yes (Matt. xxvi. 12).
13. *Are we in the use of any means of grace "buried with Christ?"*
    Yes: in Baptism (Rom. vi. 4; Col. ii. 12).
14. *How must baptized persons be afterwards buried with Him?*
    By continually mortifying all their evil and corrupt affections (Collect for Easter Eve).
15. *What then will the Christian's grave be?*
    It will be the gate through which he passes to his joyful resurrection (Collect for Easter Eve).

SECTION XXII.—HE DESCENDED INTO HELL.

1. *What became of the soul of Christ, after its separation from the body?*
He descended into hell, *i. e.*, into Hades, the unseen place; the receptacle of departed spirits. (1-7)
2. *What do we know of this place?*
We know nothing of it, except that the souls of the righteous are in rest and bliss in one part of it, separated by an impassable gulf from the abodes of the wicked. (Luke xvi. 22, 23, 26.) (8, 9, 10)
3. *But did not the souls of righteous men who died before the time of Christ ascend at once into heaven?*
No. An Apostle says that such a saint as David is not yet ascended into the heavens. (Acts ii. 34.)
4. *The soul of Christ then did not ascend into heaven when He died?*
No: He Himself says, after His Resurrection and before His Ascension, "I am not yet ascended to my Father." (John xx. 17.)
5. *What Scripture proof have we of our Lord's descent into hell?*
The express words of the Apostle that David, being a prophet, spake of the Resurrection of Christ, that "His soul was not left in hell, neither did His flesh see corruption." (Acts ii. 31.) (11, 12)
6. *Is there any other place?*
Yes. St. Paul says, "Now that He ascended, what is it but that He also descended first into the lower parts of the earth?" (Ephes. iv. 9.)
[The lower parts of the earth here cannot mean a tomb hewn out of a rock, on an elevated piece of ground, such as was our Lord's tomb. Again: the Apostle joins this *descent* with an *ascent* far above all heavens; which latter requires something more by way of contrast than a mere laying of the unconscious body in a tomb on the surface of the earth. As the *ascent* was a personal act, so must the *descent* be also a personal act.]
7. *Is there any other place?*

We read (1 Peter iii. 19) that our Lord was "put to death in the flesh, but quickened in the Spirit, by which He went and preached to the spirits in prison, which sometimes were disobedient." (14, 15, 16)

8. *But is not this a difficult place of Scripture?*
It may be difficult to understand why St. Peter mentions these particular spirits, but the allusion to the disembodied Spirit of our Lord, going and preaching to some spirits then in prison, *i.e.*, descending into the unseen place, or Hades, is as plain as possible.

9. *Does it seem needful to confess the descent into hell?*
Yes : by doing so we profess to believe that our Lord, being perfect man, had a reasonable soul or spirit, which, like our souls or spirits, could exist, and move, and act though separated from the body ; and that He actually died as man dies, for human death consists in the passing away of the soul into the unseen place. (19, 20, 21)

SHORTER CATECHISM.

1. *What is the next article of the Creed?*
He descended into hell.
2. *What does hell mean here?* The place of departed spirits.
3. *What is the original word in the New Testament?* Hades.
4. *What does the word mean?*
It means simply the unseen place.
5. *How many words are there in the Greek Testament for our word Hell?*
Two : Hades and Gehenna.
6. *What does the latter signify?*
The place of eternal punishment.
7. *Did our Lord descend into the latter?* No.
8. *Into how many parts does Hades seem to be divided?*
Into two.
9. *What are they?*
The abode of the righteous, and that of the wicked.
10. *Is there any division between them?*
Yes : a great gulf, which none can pass (Luke xvi. 26).
11. *How many places of Scripture prove the descent of our Lord into hell?*
Three (Acts ii. 31 ; Ephes. iv. 9.; 1 Pet. iii. 18, 19, 20).
12. *Can hell mean the grave?*
No : because our Lord's body was in the grave, and His soul which left it must have been somewhere else.

HE DESCENDED INTO HELL.

13. *On what day was our Lord crucified?* On Good Friday.
14. *During what day then was He in the unseen place?*
    During the whole of Saturday, *i.e.*, Easter Eve.
15. *What did He do during this time?* 1 Peter iii. 19.
16. *Has our Lord dominion over the unseen world?*
    Yes: it is expressly said, "That at the name of Jesus every knee should bow, of things in heaven, and things in earth, and things *under the earth*" (Phil. ii. 10).
17. *Does this latter place mean Hades, or the unseen world?*
    Yes: if we compare it with Ephes. iv. 9, we see that it must mean Hades.
18. *What other place shows that our Lord has all power over the unseen world?*
    "I am He that liveth, and was dead, and behold I am alive for evermore, and have the keys of death and of hell (Hades)" (Rev. i. 18).
19. *Why should we confess that our Lord went down into hell?*
    To show that our Lord had a true reasonable soul or spirit.
20. *How does the descent into hell show this?*
    Because His soul underwent all that the souls of His brethren undergo.
21. *How does our Lord's triumph over hell appear?*
    He came forth out of it as a conqueror.

SECTION XXIII.—THE THIRD DAY HE ROSE AGAIN FROM THE DEAD.

1. *What further do we profess to believe in respecting Jesus?*
   That the third day He rose again from the dead.
2. *What do you mean by this?*
   I mean that the same Soul of Jesus which descended into the place of departed spirits, came back again, and reanimated the same Body Which had been crucified, and was dead and buried. (1, 2)
3. *Mention some proofs that our Lord had really risen in the same body.*
   He was seen by ten of the Apostles at once on the day of His Resurrection; then, eight days after, by the eleven; and on the shores of the sea of Galilee by five, and, according to St. Paul, by five hundred brethren at once in Galilee, where His followers were most numerous, and His Person the best known. (3–7)
4. *Mention two other proofs.*
   He ate and drank with them after His Resurrection (Luke xxiv. 43; John xxi. 9–16); and He invited them to handle Him. "Behold my hands and my feet that it is I myself; handle me and see, for a spirit hath not flesh and bones as ye see me have." (Luke xxiv. 39.) (6–20)
5. *Were the Apostles ready to believe that He had risen?*
   No: they all apparently doubted, till they had seen Him for themselves: He had to reprove them sharply for their unbelief. (Matt. xxviii. 17; Mark xvi. 11, 13, 14; Luke xxiv. 25.)
6. *What does this prove to us?*
   That they were not credulous persons who would be led away by any idle report, but that at first they sinned deeply on the side of unbelief.
7. *Is the belief in the Resurrection of Jesus a necessary part of the faith?*
   Yes; if we are to be guided by the Scriptures, it is the most necessary of all.
8. *Give some proofs.*

When an apostle is chosen, it is that he should be a witness of the Resurrection. (Acts i. 22.)

The united testimony of the Apostles is described in the words, "With great power gave the Apostles witness of the resurrection of the Lord Jesus." (Acts iv. 33.)

St. Paul says: "If Christ be not risen, then is our preaching vain, and your faith is vain" (1 Cor. xv. 14); and the one thing which he bids St. Timothy especially to remember, is that "Jesus Christ, of the seed of David, was raised from the dead according to his Gospel." (2 Tim. ii. 8.)

9. *Why should the Apostles put the Resurrection of our Lord into so exalted a place?*

Because the Resurrection of Jesus is God's own sign, seal, and assurance of the truth of all the Gospel of Jesus. (21–24)

10. *Give some proof of this.*

St. Paul tells us that the Gospel of God is concerning His Son Jesus Christ. . . Who was declared to be the Son of God with power, by the Resurrection from the dead. (Rom. i. 1–4.) (21–24)

11. *Give another proof.*

When the Jews demanded of our Lord a sign of His authority, He said, "Destroy this temple, and in three days I will raise it up; but He spake of the temple of His body." (John ii. 19–21.)

12. *Does the Resurrection prove that our Lord was God?*

Yes. St. Thomas, when he was assured that our Lord had risen in the same body in which He was crucified, exclaimed, "My Lord and my God." (John xx. 28.)

19. *What reason had he for thus confessing Christ to be God?*

Because he had heard our Lord claim to be equal with God; and St. Thomas was sure that if Christ had not really been what He claimed to be, God would not have raised Him from the dead. (24, 25)

14. *How does the Resurrection prove the efficacy of the death of Christ?*

He died to atone for our sins; and because He had actually atoned for them, He rose from the dead.

15. *Can you show this more fully?*

Yes. Death is the penalty which we all owe for our sins. But He, who had no sins of His own, died for our sins; and because He had fully borne our penalty, death could have no more dominion over Him. He had exhausted the curse, and so He rose from the dead in token that it was exhausted. (26–32)

16. *Is it then through the Resurrection of Christ that forgiveness is preached?*

So St. Paul says. He whom God raised again saw no corruption. Be it known unto you THEREFORE, brethren, that through this man is preached unto you the forgiveness of sins. (Acts xiii. 37, 38.) (28–33)

17. *But is not forgiveness of sins connected in Scripture with Baptism?*

Yes: but as St. Paul twice assures us, it is because we are buried with Christ in Baptism, wherein also we are risen with Him through the faith of the operation of God. (Rom. vi. 1–5; Coloss. ii. 12.) St. Peter also says that we are saved in Baptism [if we have the answer of a good conscience towards God] by the Resurrection of Jesus Christ. (1 Pet. iii.) (35–40)

18. *If Christ be not raised, what are the Sacraments?*

In that case mere delusive forms; for then we should be baptized into a Resurrection which never took place, and be fed with a Body Which has no existence.

19. *Does St. Paul distinguish between the benefit which we receive from the Death of Christ, and that which we receive from His Resurrection?*

Yes: He says we are reconciled to God by His Death, and shall be saved by His Resurrection. "If when we were enemies we were reconciled to God by the death of His Son, much more, being reconciled, we shall be saved by His life." (Rom. v. 10.)

20. *What means he by this?*

He means that we are saved from sin and death by the power of Christ's risen Life, a share in which is given to each Christian in Baptism. (35–42)

21. *How do we know that he means this?*

Because in the very next chapter He speaks of our being baptized that we should walk in newness of life; and so are to reckon ourselves dead unto sin, but alive unto God, through Jesus Christ our Lord. (vi. 11.) (39, 40)

22. *How are we to reckon ourselves then alive to God?*

By ever remembering that a share in Christ's Risen Life has been made over to us; by praying to God that it may be continued in us, and by prayerfully partaking in Holy Eucharist of the Living Bread for the support of that Life. (40)

23. *Of what other article of the faith is the Resurrection of Christ the assurance?*
    That He will judge the quick and the dead.
    God " Hath appointed a day, in the which He will judge the world in righteousness by that man whom He hath ordained; whereof He hath given assurance unto all men, in that He hath raised Him from the dead." (Acts xvii. 31.) (43-47)

24. *What other article of the Gospel or Creed is assured by the Resurrection?*
    The Resurrection of the body.
    " Now is Christ risen from the dead, and become the firstfruits of them that slept. For since by man came death, by man came also the resurrection of the dead. For as in Adam all die, even so in Christ shall all be made alive." (1 Cor. xv. 20. 21. Also Rom. viii. 11; 2 Cor. iv. 13, 14.) (47-52)

25. *The Resurrection, then, is a pledge of the truth of all that can be called the Gospel?*
    Yes: St. Paul says: "The promise which was made unto the fathers, God hath fulfilled the same unto us their children, in that He hath raised up Jesus again." (Acts xiii. 32, 33.)

26. *What Person of the Ever-blessed Trinity raised up our Saviour?*
    Each Person.
    God the Father. (Acts ii. 24.)
    God the Son raised Himself. (John ii. 19.)
    God the Holy Ghost. (Rom. viii. 11.) (52-54)

27. *Was the body of our Blessed Lord in any respect changed at His Resurrection?*
    Yes: it had become a spiritual body; *i.e.*, a body with the powers and properties of a spirit, for it came through the closed doors, and vanished and reappeared as we suppose a spirit has power to do. (55-62)
    [It has been said that our Lord's Body, before His Resurrection, had the same powers, for He walked on the water; but He gave the same power of walking on the water to Simon Peter, who had a body in nothing differing from ours.]

28. *On what day did He rise again?*
    On the third day after His death; *i.e.*, on the first day of the week: on Easter Day.

SHORTER CATECHISM.

1. *What next do you profess that you believe in respecting Jesus?*
   That the third day He rose again from the dead.
2. *Who rose again from the dead?*
   The Son of God, Who had been crucified for us, and had died and been buried.
3. *In what body did He rise again?*
   In the same Body Which had been crucified.
4. *How was it known to be the same Body?*
   Because it had all the marks which it had received when it was crucified.
5. *What were these?*
   The prints of the nails in the hands and feet (Luke xxiv. 39), and the wound of the spear (John xx. 27).
6. *To whom did our Lord appear?*
   To those who knew Him best before His crucifixion.
7. *Did they expect His Resurrection?* No.
8. *Ought they to have expected it?*
   Yes: He distinctly told them that He would rise again.
9. *How many times did our Lord appear after His Resurrection and before His Ascension?*
   About eleven appearances are recorded.
10. *What was the first of these?*
    That to Mary Magdalene (Mark xvi. 9; John xx. 14).
11. *What seems to have been the second?*
    To the other women (Matt. xxviii. 9).
12. *What was the third?*
    To the two disciples on the way to Emmaus (Luke xxiv. 31).
13. *What was the fourth?* That to St. Peter (Luke xxiv. 34).
14. *What appears to have been the fifth?*
    To the Apostles; Thomas, however, being absent (Luke xxiv. 33-46; John xx. 20).
15. *What the sixth?*
    To the eleven, eight days after (John xx. 26).
16. *What the seventh?*
    To Peter, Thomas, Nathaniel, and others at the shore of the sea of Galilee (John xxi. 1, 2).
17. *What was the eighth?*
    To the eleven, on a mountain in Galilee (Matt. xxviii. 16).
18. *Were there any appearances of which we do not know the time?*
    Yes, two, mentioned by St. Paul; one to James, one to five hundred brethren (1 Cor. xv. 6, 7).
19. *And what was the last?*
    When at the time of the Ascension He led them to Bethany (Luke xxiv. 50).

20. *Were these all the appearances?*
   No: in all probability there were many more, for "He was seen of the Apostles forty days," and nearly half of the appearances mentioned were on the first day.
21. *Did He appear to all the people?*
   No: only "to witnesses chosen before of God" (Acts x. 41).
22. *To what were the Apostles especially chosen to bear witness?*
   To His Resurrection (John xv. 27; Acts i. 22).
23. *Why is it said that they are witnesses of His Resurrection rather than of His death?*
   Because His Resurrection assures us that He made a full atonement for all our sins by His death.
24. *How does it assure us of this?*
   His Resurrection proves that He was the only begotten Son of God.
25. *Show this from Scripture.*
   He was "declared to be the Son of God with power, according to the Spirit of holiness, by the Resurrection from the dead" (Rom. i. 4).
26. *How does this show the atoning power of His death?*
   If the true and only Son of God died for us He could not die in vain.
27. *For what purpose did He die?* To make atonement for sin.
28. *If then He rose again, what does His Resurrection prove?*
   That our sins have been all atoned for by Him.
29. *If then Christ be not risen, in what state are we?*
   We are yet in our sins (1 Cor. xv. 17).
30. *But if Christ be risen, are we yet in our sins?*
   If we are, it is through our own fault.
31. *Why?* Because He rose again to deliver us from sin.
32. *In what words are we taught this?*
   In the words, He was raised again for our justification (Rom. iv. 25).
33. *What does this mean?*
   It means, that He rose again that we might have both pardon for sin and power to forsake sin.
34. *What else is said in Scripture respecting the power of Christ's resurrection?*
   St. Paul earnestly desires to know the power of our Lord's Resurrection (Phil. iii. 10).
35. *Why does He so earnestly desire to know this?*
   Because we are saved by Christ's Life (Rom. v. 10).
36. *How can we be saved by Christ's life?*
   Because He has power to give us of His Life.
37. *What life?*
   His Resurrection Life. The Life that He received when He rose again.

38. *When is this first given to us?* In Holy Baptism.
39. *How do we know this?*
    Because St. Paul twice asserts it (Rom. vi. 1-4; Col. ii. 12).
40. *What must the baptized do?*
    They must reckon themselves alive unto God through Jesus Christ our Lord (Rom. vi. 11).
41. *But have we this life if we do not believe in Christ?*
    No, assuredly not: unless we believe in Christ we have no hope in Him or no life from Him.
42. *What, if we would be saved, are we to believe respecting Christ?*
    If thou shalt . . . . believe in thine heart that God hath raised Him from the dead thou shalt be saved (Rom. x. 9).
43. *If Christ be raised from the dead shall we see Him again?*
    Yes: at the last day.
44. *What will He do then?*
    He will judge the quick and the dead.
45. *Has His own Resurrection anything to do with this?*
    Yes: it is an assurance to us that we shall be judged by Him (Acts xvii. 31).
46. *Why is it this?*
    The Resurrection is the proof that God will fulfil all His promises.
47. *But has God promised to judge men by His Son?*
    Yes: He has committed all judgment to the Son (John v. 22).
48. *In what will men rise again to be judged?*
    In their bodies.
49. *How will their bodies be raised?*
    By the power of Christ's risen Body.
50. *How do you know that?*
    Because He says, "I am the Resurrection and the Life" (John xi. 25).
51. *Does this mean that men will rise again because of His Resurrection?*
    Yes: the Apostle says, "As in Adam all die, even so in Christ shall all be made alive" (1 Cor. xv. 22).
52. *What then was Christ raised up to be?*
    To be the second Adam—the second Head of all men.
53. *Who raised Him?* God, the Father (Gal. i. 1).
54. *But did He ever say that He would raise Himself?*
    Yes (John ii. 19, 20, 21).
55. *Are these sayings at all contrary one to the other?*
    No (John v. 19, 20, 21).
56. *In what state was our Lord's Body raised?*
    In that of a spiritual body.
57. *What is that?*
    A body which can move and act as a spirit does.

58. *In what respects did our Lord's Body show this power?*
   It passed through the doors whilst they were closed (John xx. 19).
59. *In what other respects?*
   It vanished and reappeared at will (Luke xxiv. 31, 36).
60. *But could it have done all these things and yet be a body like our bodies?*
   Yes: it was a body like ours, for the Apostles felt and handled Him.
61. *Is all this a mere matter of curiosity or speculation?*
   No: we are above all things interested in it.
62. *Why?*
   Because our vile bodies will be fashioned like unto His glorious Body (Phil. iii. 21).
63. *Have we any other assurance of this?* Yes (1 John iii. 2).

SECTION XXIV.—HE ASCENDED INTO HEAVEN, AND SITTETH ON THE RIGHT HAND OF GOD THE FATHER ALMIGHTY.

1. *What is the next article of our Faith?*
That Jesus Christ ascended into heaven.
2. *How is the Ascension described?*
"And He led them out as far as to Bethany, and He lifted up His hands and blessed them. And it came to pass, while He blessed them, He was parted from them, and carried up into heaven." (Luke xxiv. 50, 51.) (1–6)
3. *When He ascended, did He suddenly disappear or vanish as a spirit might?*
No: He rose up above the earth, and whilst the Apostles gazed after Him, a cloud received Him out of their sight.
4. *Where is He now?*
He now sits at the right hand of God. (7–18)
5. *What does the expression "At the right hand of God" mean?*
The most exalted place in the universe. (7–18)
6. *How is this exaltation described?*
"[God set Christ]at His own right hand in the heavenly places, far above all principality, and power, and might, and dominion, and every name that is named, not only in this world, but also in that which is to come, and hath put all things under His feet." (Ephes. i. 20–22.)
7. *But if our Lord was one with the Father, how was it that He needed to be exalted by the Father?*
Because He had emptied Himself of His glory, and had taken the manhood into such union with His Godhead, that as man He needed to be glorified by His Father with the glory which He had with Him before the world was. (John xvii. 5.) (19)
8. *For what great purpose of salvation was Christ set at the right hand of God?*
To appear as our great High Priest in the presence of God for us. (Heb. ix. 11–24.)
9. *What part of the Jewish Ritual typified our Lord's entrance into heaven?*
The entrance of the High Priest once a year into the Holy of Holies. "Into the second [tabernacle] went the

High Priest alone once every year, not without blood . . But Christ being come an High Priest of good things to come . . . by His own blood He entered in once into the Holy Place, having obtained eternal redemption for us." (Heb. ix. 7, 11, 12.) (21, 22, 23)

10. *But did He not cease to act as a priest when He had completed our atonement on the Cross?*

No: He exercises in heaven an unchangeable Priesthood of intercession, for He is a Priest *for ever* after the order of Melchizedec. (Heb. vii. 21-26) (23-25)

11. *How does He act in doing this?*

We cannot *understand* how He acts, for it is a transaction betwixt Himself and His Father in the mysterious communion of the Ever Blessed Trinity, but we *believe* it.

12. *Has God revealed anything which may help us to realize the perpetual intercession of Christ?*

Yes: we read that there is in the heaven of heavens a Lamb as it had been slain (Rev. v. 6); and, though this was a vision, yet the reality of it must be that Christ appears in heaven as if He had been crucified, marked with the wounds which He had received when His Blood was shed for the remission of sins. (26)

13. *But did He not offer Himself once for all; and can He repeat His sacrifice upon the Cross?*

No: He cannot repeat His one sacrifice, so far as the pain and death He endured are concerned, but if He be a priest [and we know that He is a priest for ever] He must have something to offer. (Heb. viii. 3)

14. *What, then, does He offer?*

He offers Himself as the Head of His Body, the Church; and in doing this He necessarily offers His people, their hearts, and lives, and services in Himself; as the living members of Himself, their Head.

15. *Have we here on earth any means of joining ourselves in this His act of intercessory priesthood?*

Yes; as He presents the memorials of His death in heaven, so we, in the Holy Eucharist, join in His commemorative act, for as often as we eat this bread, and drink this cup, we show forth His death till He come. (1 Cor. xi. 26.) (26–34)

16. *Is there any other reason in the nature of the Eucharist why we, in devoutly receiving it, should join in His act of intercession?*

Yes. The Holy Spirit says by St. Paul : "We being many are one bread and one body, for we are all partakers of that one bread." (1 Cor. x. 17.) If by partaking of that bread we are members of the Body of Christ, we are members of That which He is ever presenting to God. (26–34) (See note B. page 318)

17. *But does He not appear in the presence of God in His glorified Body ?*
Yes ; but that Body in an ineffable way contains His mystical body : according to the words of the Apostle, "He hath raised us up together, and made us sit together in heavenly places in Christ Jesus." (Ephes. ii. 6.) (34)

18. *What does the intercession of Jesus Christ embrace ?*
Everything ; for He says, "Whatsoever ye shall ask in my name, that will I do." (John xiv. 13.)

19. *Does sin deprive us of the benefits of Christ's Intercession ?*
Not if we repent of it : "If any man sin, we have an advocate with the Father." (1 John ii. 1.)

20. *For what purposes of grace did Christ ascend into heaven ?*
For five.
1. To receive the glory which He had with the Father before the world was. (John xvii. 5.)
2. To appear in heaven as our High Priest. (Heb. iv. 14.)
3. To send down the Holy Ghost. (John xvi. 7.)
4. To rule over all things on our behalf. (Ephes. i. 22.)
5. To prepare a place for us. (John xiv. 2.)

21. *How then are we to honour the Ascension of Christ ?*
By coming to God through Him. (Heb. iv. 16 ; vii. 25.)
By setting our affections where He is on the right hand of God. (Col. iii. 2.)

SHORTER CATECHISM.

1. *What do we next profess to believe respecting Jesus Christ ?*
That He ascended into heaven.
2. *On what day did He ascend ?* On the fortieth day after Easter.
3. *In whose sight did He ascend ?* In the sight of the Apostles.

4. *In what body did He ascend?*
    In the body which He had taken for our sakes.
5. *What was He doing when He began to ascend?*
    He was blessing the Apostles (Luke xxiv. 51).
6. *How many accounts are there of His Ascension?*
    Two: one in Luke xxiv., one in Acts i.
7. *Into what place did He ascend?* Into heaven.
8. *What is heaven?*
    The place where God manifests His especial presence.
9. *Why must heaven be a place?*
    Because the glorified Body of our Lord is there.
10. *What holy man was a type of Christ in the manner of His removal from this world?* Elijah.
11. *How does the Church show her belief that Elijah's translation is a type of our Lord's Ascension?*
    By reading the account of it as one of the lessons on Ascension Day (2 Kings ii.).
12. *What prophecies have we in the Old Testament of the Ascension of Christ?*
    One especially in the 68th Psalm, "Thou hast gone up on high, Thou hast led captivity captive, and received gifts for men."
13. *Whose assurance have we that this refers to Christ's Ascension?*
    That of St. Paul in Ephes. iv. 8, 9, 10.
14. *In what other Psalm is the Ascension foretold?*
    In the 24th: "Lift up your heads, O ye gates; and be ye lift up, ye everlasting doors, and the King of glory shall come in."
15. *To what place in heaven did our Lord ascend?*
    To the highest and most honourable of all.
16. *How is it described in the Creed?*
    As the right hand of God.
17. *What Old Testament saint was a type of Him as regards His exaltation?* Joseph.
18. *In what especial manner is Joseph's exaltation a type of Christ?*
    In that he was exalted to be the Saviour of his brethren (Gen. xlv. 7).
19. *What prayer of Christ's was answered in His exaltation to the right hand of God?*
    The prayer: "Now, O Father, glorify Thou me with Thine own self, with the glory which I had with Thee before the world was" (John xvii. 5).
20. *What prophecy was fulfilled when Christ took His seat at the right hand of God?*
    The prophecy in the 110th Psalm: "The Lord said unto my Lord, sit Thou on my right hand until I make Thine enemies Thy footstool."
21. *What office does Christ discharge in heaven for us?*
    That of our Great High Priest.

22. *Had the Old Dispensation any type of this?*
    Yes: the High Priest entering the Holy of Holies.
23. *Has Christ ceased to be a priest?*
    No: He is a priest for ever after the order of Melchizedec.
24. *Has Christ yet to atone for our sins?* No (Heb. x. 12).
25. *In what respect then does He act as our High Priest?*
    By His perpetual intercession.
26. *How may we humbly suppose that He acts in this?*
    By pleading His sufferings and death; and presenting the memorial of them before God.
27. *How can we join with Him in this?* By the Holy Eucharist.
28. *Why?* Because in it we "shew forth His death."
29. *Before whom?*
    Before God the Father, as He is now doing.
30. *What has our Lord to offer to God?*
    Himself, as the Head of His Church, His Redeemed Body.
31. *Does the Eucharist enable us to join in this?*
    Yes: it is the Communion or partaking of His Body.
32. *What else?*
    It is the token and pledge of our continuance in the Church.
33. *What word of Scripture have you for this?*
    We being many are one bread and one body [*i.e.*, the Body of Christ], for we are all partakers of that one bread (1 Cor. x. 17).
34. *But does our Lord offer His Church to God?*
    Yes: in presenting Himself before His Father, He presents the Church, of which He is the Head.
35. *In what other capacity did our Lord ascend into Heaven?*
    As our Forerunner.
36. *Of what promise of His is this a pledge?*
    Where I am there ye shall be also (John xiv. 3).
37. *In what words is this expressed by St. Paul?*
    He hath "made us sit together in heavenly places in Christ Jesus" (Ephes. ii. 6).
38. *What power is now exercised by Christ?*
    All power (Matt. xxviii. 18).
39. *On whose behalf?* On behalf of the Church (Ephes. i. 22).
40. *Till what time?*
    Till the end of the Mediatorial Kingdom (1 Cor. xv. 24).
41. *When will this be?* (1 Cor. xv. 25.)
42. *Of what was our Lord's exaltation the reward?*
    Of His humiliation (Phil. ii. 8, 9).
43. *What does the Church teach us to pray for with respect to the Ascension of Christ into Heaven?*
    That we may in heart and mind thither ascend, and with Him continually dwell (Collect for Ascension Day).
44. *Where in Scripture is this laid upon us?* (Col. iii. 1, 2).

SECTION XXV.—FROM THENCE HE SHALL COME TO JUDGE THE QUICK AND THE DEAD.

1. *Will Christ always remain seated at the right hand of God?*
   No: from thence He will come to judge the quick and the dead.
2. *When will He come?*
   He will come on a day known only to His Father: "Of that day and hour knoweth no man; no, not the angels of heaven, but my Father only." (Matt. xxiv. 36.) (1-7)
3. *But though the time of the second coming be thus unknown to us, have we any duty respecting it?*
   Yes: Christ lays it upon His people in the most solemn and earnest manner, that they are to watch for His coming:
   "The Son of Man is as a man taking a far journey, who left his house, and gave authority to his servants, and to every man his work, and commanded the porter to watch. Watch therefore, for ye know not when the master of the house cometh, &c." (Mark xiii. 34-37.)
   Again: Luke xii. 40, and particularly Luke xxi. 36:
   "Watch ye therefore, and pray always, that ye may be accounted worthy to escape all these things that shall come to pass, and to stand before the Son of man." (Luke xxi. 36.) (10-15)
4. *But were not such warnings intended to prepare Christians for the destruction of Jerusalem?*
   No: they are particularly distinguished from the warnings respecting the destruction of Jerusalem. We have a warning respecting this latter visitation in this same discourse, in the words, "Let them which are in Judæa flee to the mountains." (Luke xxi. 21.)
5. *Do the Apostles teach the same?*
   Yes; there is nothing which they insist upon more. St. Paul, for instance, says, "Our conversation is in heaven; from whence also we look for the Saviour, the Lord Jesus Christ, who shall change our vile body," &c. (Phil. iii. 20. See also 1 Cor. i. 7; 1 Thess. i. 9, 10; iii. 13; iv. 17; v. 1-9; Titus ii. 13; Heb. ix. 28; James v. 8; 2 Pet. iii. 10-12; Rev. xvi. 15.)
6. *But are not all these meant to prepare us for the day of death?*

No : we are not to look for a day in which we shall leave this world, but for a day in which Christ will return to judge the world.

7. *Do we not fulfil these commands by watching against Satan, or against the evil of our own hearts?*

No ; we have to watch not only against an enemy, but for a friend (2 Tim. iv. 8) ; for a bridegroom (Matt. xxv. 1, 5, 10, 13) ; for a Redeemer from death and corruption (Luke xxi. 28) ; and for a just, yet most merciful Judge (1 Cor. iv. 5).

8. *What thought will be ever present in those who thus look for Christ's second coming?*

They will regard the present state of things as doomed, and liable to come to a sudden end at any moment.

9. *How does St. Paul describe the state of mind, with respect to this world, of those who look for Christ's second coming?*

"The time is short: it remaineth, that both they that have wives be as though they had none; and they that weep, as though they wept not; and they that rejoice, as though they rejoiced not; and they that buy, as though they possessed not; and they that use this world, as not abusing it: for the fashion of this world passeth away." (1 Cor. vii. 29.)

10. *But would not preparation for death have the same effect on the soul as looking for the day of Christ?*

No : assuredly not. They who look for the coming of Christ will have far less respect for a world which they believe may come to an end at any moment.

11. *But did not the Apostles look for the second Advent in their own lifetime; and were they not mistaken in so doing?*

The Apostles did so look ; and in doing this they fulfilled the will of God in looking for a day which He has purposely kept secret, in order that all men may look for it, and live as if His Son was ever at hand. (26, 27)

12. *Do our Lord or His Apostles speak of any signs by which the Church may know that Christ's coming is at hand?*

Yes : distress of nations and perplexity, men's hearts failing them for fear, the powers of heaven shaken, iniquity abounding, love growing cold, the faith nearly extinct, the sign of the Son of Man in heaven (Luke xxi. 25, 26, 27 ; Matt. xxiv. 12) ; and the revelation of the Antichrist (2 Thess. ii. 8-13).

13. *Who will the Antichrist be?*

He will be a person to whom Satan will be allowed to

give such power as man has never yet possessed, to tempt and draw men from the faith. (30–34)

14. *Can the Antichrist of St. Paul be explained as being a long series of Popes?*
It is quite impossible so to explain St. Paul's prophecy of the Antichrist, for, according to him, the Antichrist will possess Satanic power to draw after him all the wicked of the earth, which no one pretends to say that the Popes have done or will do.

15. *What will our Saviour come again to do?*
He will come to judge the quick and the dead, *i. e.*, all men. (36–40)

16. *Does this mean that He will judge His true people?*
Yes; He will judge Apostles even : for St. Paul saith, " He that judgeth me is the Lord." (1 Cor. iv. 4.) He says again, " We shall all stand before the judgment-seat of Christ, that every one of us may receive the things done in his body." (2 Cor. v. 10. Also 1 Peter iv. 17.)

17. *But do not some men profess to have an assurance of salvation which will render any judgment in their case a mere form?*
If they profess to have this, they profess to have a thing which the Apostle St. Paul repudiated in his own case, for he counts not himself to have attained to the resurrection of the just (Phil. iii. 11, 12, 13) ; and he kept under his body, lest he should be a castaway (1 Cor. ix. 27) ; and he bids us to judge nothing before the time till the Lord come (1 Cor. iv. 5). (41–43)

18. *How shall we be judged?* According to our works.
" The Son of Man shall come in the glory of His Father with His angels, and then shall He reward every man according to his works." (Matt. xvi. 27.) (45–50.)

19. *Is this asserted elsewhere in Scripture?*
Yes ; no truth is more insisted upon, both by Christ and by His Apostles. Christ says that all that " are in the graves shall hear His voice, and shall come forth ; they that have done good, to the resurrection of life ; and they that have done evil, to the resurrection of damnation." (John v. 29.)

20. *But is not the teaching of St. Paul supposed by some to set this aside?*
Only by those who fail to realise or see what he teaches ; for he says that God " will render to every man according to his deeds. To them that by patient con-

tinuance in well-doing seek for glory, honour and immortality, eternal life." (Rom. ii. 7.) (43, 44)

21. *What parables of our Lord teach us this truth?*
The Parable of the Talents (Matt. xxv. 14), and of the Pounds (Luke xix. 11–26).

In this latter parable, the servant who had increased the one pound committed unto him to ten, is made ruler over ten cities; he who had increased his pound to five, over five cities.

22. *Do any other very solemn words of our Lord assure us of this truth?*
Yes: He tells us that at the last day He will say to those on His right hand, "Come, ye blessed children of my Father, inherit the kingdom prepared for you before the foundation of the world: for I was an hungred, and ye gave me meat," &c. (Matt. xxv. 34.)

23. *But will the Judge take account of outward actions only?*
No; He will bring every secret thought into judgment. "I am He that searcheth the hearts and reins, and I will give to every one of you according to your works" (Rev. ii. 23) [*i.e.*, judged by my knowledge of your hearts]. Also 1 Cor. iv. 5. (50, 51)

24. *What besides our works and thoughts will come into judgment?*
All our words; for Christ says, "But I say unto you, that every idle word that men shall speak, they shall give account thereof in the day of judgment." (Matt. xii. 36.) (52)

25. *In judging us according to our deeds, will He only take into account what we have actually done?*
No: He will take into account all our opportunities—what we might have done and have neglected to do. [*See* the "Talents" and the "Pounds," Matt. xxv. 14, and Luke xix. 20–27. Also, "Depart, ye cursed, for I was an hungred, and ye gave me no meat." (Matt. xxv. 42.)]

26. *What other things will Christ take into account, in order that He may pronounce a most just judgment?*
Our knowledge of God and of our duty.
[The servant who knew his Lord's will. (Luke xii. 47.)]

27. *But shall we not be judged according to our faith?*
No: our faith itself must be judged, as to whether it be a dead or a living faith, for faith without works is dead.

28. *But if we are to be judged according to all that we have done or left undone, what room is there for the grace of God?*

The grace of God is given to us for this express purpose, that, " denying ungodliness and worldly lusts, we should live soberly, righteously, and godly in this present world." (Titus ii. 12.)

29. *But are we not saved by faith?*

Yes ; but faith is given to us to save us from sin, and to be within us the seed of all things well pleasing to God. (*See* Parable of the Sower, Matt. xiii. 18-24.) The very Saviour in Whom we believe assures us most solemnly that He will judge us according to our words and works.

SHORTER CATECHISM.

1. *What is the next article of the Faith?*
From thence He shall come to judge the quick and the dead.
2. *Who will come?*
Jesus Chrst, the Son of God, Who was conceived by the Holy Ghost, born Of the Virgin Mary, and Who suffered under Pontius Pilate.
3. *From whence will He come?* From the right hand of God.
4. *How will He come?*
In great glory. In His own glory, and the glory of His Father, and of the holy angels (Luke ix. 26).
5. *When will He come?* At the last day.
6. *When will that be?*
It is a day known only to God (Matt. xxiv. 36).
7. *Who first foretold His second coming to judgment?*
Enoch (Jude 14).
8. *Have we any other intimation of it in the Old Testament?*
Yes : Psalm l. 1-6 ; Isaiah xxx. 27, 28 ; Daniel vii. 9, 22 ; xii.; Malachi iv.
9. *When our Lord left this world, what promise of His return was given?*
"'This same Jesus, which is taken up from you into Heaven, shall so come in like manner as ye have seen Him go into Heaven " (Acts i. 11).
10. *Did our Lord ever foretell His second coming?*
Yes : repeatedly.
11. *To what especially does He liken it?*
To the coming of a thief in the night (Matt. xxiv. 43, 44 ; Luke xii. 39, 40).

12. *To what besides?*
    To the flood overtaking the ungodly (Matt. xxiv. 37).
13. *To what besides?*
    To the sudden coming of destruction on Sodom (Luke xvii. 28-30).
14. *To what besides?*
    To the springing of a snare or trap (Luke xxi. 35).
15. *To what besides?*
    To the flash of lightning (Matt. xxiv. 27).
16. *What do all these similitudes show?*
    The secret approach and suddenness of the second Advent.
17. *What besides?*
    That the world will be unprepared for Christ's coming.
18. *What then is our especial duty with respect to the second coming of Christ?*
    We are to be watching for it, or rather for Him.
19. *What are our Lord's words respecting this?*
    "Watch ye therefore, and pray always, that ye may be accounted worthy to escape those things that shall come to pass, and to stand before the Son of Man" (Luke xxi. 36).
20. *Are all thus to watch?*
    Yes: He says, "What I say unto you I say unto all—watch" (Mark xiii. 37).
21. *Is this watching or looking for Christ a necessary state of mind?*
    Yes, if we are to believe the Scriptures, none more so.
22. *What parable of our Lord shows its necessity?*
    The Parable of the Ten Virgins (Matt. xxv. 1-13).
23. *Why were the five foolish virgins shut out?*
    Because they were not ready to meet the Bridegroom.
24. *What words of St. Paul show the necessity of this watching?*
    Many; especially 1 Cor. vii. 29; 1 Thess. i. 10; Heb. ix. 28.
25. *Why has God kept the day of His Son's return so secret?*
    That all men may watch for it.
26. *Did the Apostles look for it?*
    Yes: they expected it in their own time.
27. *What does this show?*
    That they had the mind about it which God desired them to have.
28. *Did Christ ever intimate that His coming might be long delayed?*
    Yes; He speaks of the evil servant saying in his heart, my Lord delayeth His coming (Matt. xxiv. 48).
29. *Will this be any excuse for those who do not look for Christ's return?*
    No: we are to watch even though it be delayed till "the morning" (Mark xiii. 35).
30. *Who will be revealed before the coming of Christ?* The Antichrist.
31. *What does St. Paul call him?*
    The man of sin. The wicked or lawless one (2 Thess. ii. 3-13).

32. *What does St. John say that the spirit of Antichrist consists in?*
   The denial of the Incarnation (1 John iv. 3).
33. *What then will the Antichrist in all probability be?*
   Some infidel power.
34. *If we constantly looked for the coming of Christ, what should we do?*
   We should purify ourselves, even as He is pure (1 John iii. 2, 3).
35. *How does St. Peter express this?*
   Seeing that ye look for such things, be diligent that ye may be found of Him in peace, *without spot*, and blameless (2 Peter iii. 14).
36. *For what purpose will Christ come again?*
   To judge the quick and the dead.
37. *Who are the quick?*
   Those whom He will find alive when He comes.
38. *What will happen to the quick?*
   They will be changed (1 Cor. xv. 51, 52).
39. *What will happen to the dead?*
   They shall hear the voice of the Son of Man, and come forth (John v. 28, 29).
40. *Whom will Christ judge?*
   All men. Before Him will be gathered all nations (Matt. xxv. 32). He will judge the world in righteousness (Acts xvii. 31).
41. *But are not some persons saved now?*
   Yes: we must be saved now from sin, but this will not prevent us from being judged by Christ at last.
42. *But do not some persons say that they are assured of their salvation?*
   If they mean that, no matter what their future lives, they must be acquitted by the Judge at last, they speak wrongly and perversely.
43. *Do the Apostles themselves ever profess that they are thus delivered from a future judgment?*
   No, never. St. Paul says, He that judgeth me is the Lord (1 Cor. iv. 4).
44. *Does he repeat this statement?*
   Yes, where he says, "We must all appear before the judgment seat of Christ, that every one may receive the things done in His body, according to that He hath done" (2 Cor. v. 10).
45. *What one thing do we learn from every mention of the judgment in the Scriptures?*
   That all men will be judged according to their works.
46. *What is the first testimony to this?*
   That of the Judge Himself, in His own account of what He will do at the judgment (Matt. xxv. 31-45).

47. *Does He elsewhere assure us of this?*
Yes: where He says that "all they that are in the graves shall hear His voice, and come forth; they that have done good to the resurrection of life," &c. (John v. 29).
48. *Have we any other description of the general judgment?*
Yes; in Rev. xx., latter part.
49. *Have we the same truth stated there?*
Yes; "the dead were judged out of those things which were written in the books according to their works" (Rev. xx. 12).
50. *Will our outward actions only be judged?*
No: God will bring every work into judgment, with every secret thing (Eccles. xii. 14).
51. *What other evidence is there of this?*
The declaration of the Apostle, "God shall judge the secrets of men by Jesus Christ" (Rom. ii. 16; also 1 Cor. iv. 5).
52. *Will account be taken of words?* Yes (Matt. xii. 36).
53. *Will then the sins which we have sincerely repented of be remembered against us?*
No (Ezekiel xxxiii. 16).
54. *What does an Apostle say respecting this?*
Repent ye therefore and be converted, that your sins may be blotted out (Acts iii. 19).
55. *What Person of the Trinity will judge us?* God the Son.
56. *How do we know this?*
Because Christ says, "The Father judgeth no man, but hath committed all judgment unto the Son" (John v. 22).
57. *We shall be judged then by that Person of the Godhead who took our nature?* Yes.
58. *Is this a consolation to us?*
Yes: we shall be judged by Him Who knows our nature, for He has experienced its temptations.
59. *What will the judgment of Christ be?*
Most just and yet most merciful (Acts xvii. 31; Rom. ii. 11).
60. *What then should be our conduct in view of such a judgment?*
We should give all diligence to make our calling and election sure, &c. (2 Peter i. 10, 11).
61. *What besides?*
We should make the most of what has been committed to us (Parables of the Talents and the Pounds, Matt. xxv. 14; Luke xix. 12).
62. *What should be our prayer in prospect of such a judgment?*
We believe that Thou shalt come to be our judge; we therefore pray Thee help Thy servants whom Thou hast redeemed with Thy precious blood (also Psalm xix. 12, 13, 14, 15).
63. *What Collect of the Church?*
O God, whose blessed Son was manifested, &c. (Sixth after Epiphany).

SECTION XXVI.—THE HOLY GHOST.

1. *What is the next article of the Creed?*
   I believe in the Holy Ghost. (1-3)
2. *What do you believe respecting the Holy Ghost?*
   I believe, in the words of the Nicene Creed, that He is "the Lord," and that He is "the Giver of Life." I believe that "He proceedeth from the Father and the Son, and that with the Father and the Son together He is worshipped and glorified;" and that "He spake by the prophets." (4-7)
3. *Can you show that the Holy Ghost is to be believed in as God?*
   Yes: they who lied to the Holy Ghost are said to have lied to God. (Acts v. 3, 4.) They who are born of the Spirit are also born of God. (John iii. 6; compared with 1 John v. 4.) They who are taught by the Holy Ghost are "taught of God." (John vi. 45; compared with 1 Cor. ii. 13.) The temples of the Holy Ghost are the temples of God. (1 Cor. iii. 16; compared with vi. 19.) The prophets, when inspired by the Holy Ghost, were inspired by God. (2 Tim. iii. 16; compared with 2 Peter i. 21. (8, 9)
4. *What further proof can you give?*
   We are baptized into His Name equally with that of the Father and of the Son; and since Baptism is a most solemn dedication to God, we could not be thus dedicated to Him if He were not God. (10-13)
5. *When you say in the Nicene Creed that He is the "Lord" and "Giver of Life," do you mean that He is the Lord of Life only?*
   No: I mean that He is the Lord God, and that He is also the "Giver of Life," for it is His work, as the Third Person, to make the Church partake of the life of God and of Christ. (14, 15)
6. *What word do we use to denote the way in which the Holy Ghost exists in the Godhead?*
   We say that He *proceeds:* "He proceedeth from the Father and the Son." (16, 17)

7. *Do we know what this means?*
   No; but we use the word because we find it employed in Scripture to denote the way in which the Spirit exists, as distinguished from the way in which the Son exists. The Son is "begotten;" the Holy Ghost "proceeds." (18, 19)
8. *But in John xv. 26, the text in which He is said to proceed, we are told that He "proceedeth from the Father;" why do we say that He proceeds from the Son also?*
   Because we must compare one part of Scripture with another, and by doing so we find that in many places the Spirit is called the Spirit of the Son. [The Scriptures set forth the relation of the Spirit to the Son ... in the very same language in which they set forth the relation of the Spirit to the Father.—Bp. Harold Browne on Article v.] (20–23)
9. *Mention some proofs.*
   The Son breathed on the disciples when He said, "Receive ye the Holy Ghost." As breath proceeds from the body of a man, so the Divine Spirit proceeds from Jesus. Thus the Spirit is called the Spirit of the Son (Gal. iv. 6); the Spirit of Christ (Rom. viii. 9; Phil. i. 19); and St. Peter, speaking of His operation in the Prophets of the Old Testament, speaks of the Spirit of Christ in them. (1 Pet. i. 11.) (20–23)
10. *Why is He called the Holy Spirit?*
    Because His is eternal and uncreated holiness, and because it is His particular office to sanctify or make us holy.
11. *Can we give any reason why the Third Person in the ever Blessed Trinity is called "the Spirit," seeing that each Person in the Trinity is a Spirit?*
    It may be because He did not become incarnate, as the Son of God became incarnate. (24–28)
12. *But if He be the Spirit of God, can He be a distinct person in the Godhead; the spirit of a man not being distinct in person from the man himself?*
    We have the same reason for believing that the Holy Ghost is a person as we have for believing that the Father and the Son are persons.
13. *Can you give some Scripture proofs?*
    Our Lord promises to send *another* Comforter; and so, because *another*, distinct from Him in person. Again,

we are baptized into the name of the Holy Ghost, as well as into that of the Father and the Son ; and St. Paul invokes benediction from Him equally with the Father and the Son ; which things would have no meaning if He were not personally distinct from the Father and the Son. (John xiv. 16 ; Matt. xxviii. 19 ; 2 Cor. xiii. 14.) (28-32)

14. *Are there any other proofs ?*

Yes : all the things which can be said of a distinct living person are said of Him. He is said, for instance, to hear (John xvi. 13) ; to speak (John xvi. 13) ; to receive (John xvi. 14) ; to testify (John xv. 26). He is also said to intercede (Rom. viii. 26) ; to be grieved (Ephes. iv. 30) ; and to have despite done to Him (Heb. x. 29) ; and to be sinned against.

15. *How is the peculiar work of the Holy Spirit described in the Nicene Creed and in the Catechism?*

In the Nicene Creed he is said to be the " Giver of Life ;" in the Catechism, to " sanctify " the elect people of God. (32-37)

16. *Are these the same work ?*

Yes : because His great work is to make us partakers of the fruits of redemption by our Lord Jesus Christ, and this is to make us partakers of life and holiness. (32-37)

17. *In making us thus partakers of Redemption, does the Holy Spirit work in only one way : that is, in converting and enlightening our souls ?*

No : He works in many ways. The Apostle tells us that " there are diversities of gifts, but the same Spirit " (1 Cor. xii. 4, 8, 9, 10) ; and some of these, such as gifts of healing and of miracles, have to do with the body as well as with the soul.

18. *What is the first work of the Holy Spirit on record?*

At the time of the creation, He moved upon the face of the waters. (38-40)

19. *What is the first work ascribed to Him in the New Testament?*

The Incarnation of the Eternal Son : *i. e.*, that holy human nature which the Son of God assumed was created and prepared for Him by the Holy Ghost. (40-43)

20. *Was this what many would call a spiritual work?*

No, for it was a work in the body of the Blessed Virgin.

21. *What other operations of the Holy Spirit are mentioned?*

He co-operated, in some mysterious way, in every stage of the work of Redemption ; for at our Lord's Baptism He was anointed with the Spirit to be the Christ ; at His Crucifixion, He, *through the eternal Spirit*, offered Himself to God (Heb. ix. 14) ; and by the Spirit He was raised from the dead (Rom. viii. 11). (44–46)

22. *What further work of salvation is now wrought by the Spirit?*

It is He through Whom Christ is present in the Church ; as we learn from Christ's words, " I will not leave you comfortless ; I will come to you " (John xiv. 18) : but He came by and in the Spirit.

23. *What, above all, shows the importance of this gift of the Holy Ghost?*

That in order that He (the Spirit) might come to us, Christ went away : " If I go not away, the Comforter will not come unto you ; but if I depart, I will send Him unto you." (John xvi. 7.) (47, 48)

24. *Into how many classes may the works of the Holy Spirit be divided?*

Into two.
1. Those on behalf of the Church, the body of Christ.
2. Those on behalf of each individual soul.

25. *What are His works on behalf of the Church?*

The Inspiration of the Scriptures. He spake by the Prophets. (2 Tim. iii. 16 ; 2 Pet. i. 21; Acts xxviii. 25.)

And He spake by the Evangelists and Apostles. (John xiv. 26 ; xvi. 13 ; Mark xiii. 11.) (50–53)

26. *What other works does the Spirit work for us in the Catholic Church?*

The ministry of the Church, and its governing, ordaining, absolving, and teaching powers are His gifts. (54–62)

27. *Show that the government of the Church is His gift.*

The Apostles were, during the whole of the times of the New Testament, the governors of the Church ; and Christ is expressly said to have given them, as well as the Prophets, Evangelists, and pastors, as gifts of the Spirit. (Eph. iv. 11, 12.) Governments are especially included in a list of the works of the Spirit in 1 Cor. xii. 28.

28. *Show that all ordaining powers are from the Spirit.*

St. Paul speaks of the Holy Ghost having made the Ephesian elders overseers of the Church of Christ (Acts xx. 28) ; and when SS. Paul and Barnabas were ordained, it is recorded that the Holy Ghost said, "Separate me Barnabas and Saul for the work whereunto I have called them." (Acts xiii. 2.) (54–62)

29. *Show that all absolving power comes from the Spirit.*

Our Saviour Himself, when He gave to the Apostles power to remit sins, gave it in connection with the Holy Ghost: "He breathed on them, and said unto them, 'Receive ye the Holy Ghost: whose soever sins ye remit, they are remitted unto them.'" (John xx. 22, 23.)

30. *Show that all teaching power is the gift of the Spirit.*

Pastors and teachers are the gifts of Christ at His ascension; that is, when He sent down the Holy Ghost. (Eph. iv. 8–12.) Again, the spirit of wisdom and the spirit of knowledge are mentioned as the first of the gifts of the Spirit. (1 Cor. xii. 8.) (54–62)

31. *What are the gifts or works of the Holy Spirit on the individual soul?*

It is through Him that we are regenerated in Holy Baptism, according to our Lord's words: "Except a man be born again (of water and of the Spirit) he cannot enter into the kingdom of God." (John iii. 3, 5.) Again, "By one Spirit are we all baptized into one body." (1 Cor. xii. 13.) (63–70)

32. *What is this Regeneration?*

It is the gift of a principle of good from the Second Adam, to undo the principle of evil we have received from the first Adam.

33. *But is this the first gift of the Holy Spirit?*

It is the first, if, in our infancy, we were brought to Christian Baptism. If we have been brought up as heathen, we must first be converted to the Christian faith, which we cannot be without the Holy Spirit working in us.

[*See* particularly, for the action of the Holy Spirit before Baptism, Acts x. 47.] (63–70)

34. *What is the next work of the Holy Spirit upon the Baptized?*

He is given to them to make them profit by Christian teaching and instruction. For instance, He shows us of the things of Christ, and brings to our remembrance Christ's words. (John xiv. 26; 1 John ii. 20.) He sheds abroad the love of God in our hearts. (Rom. v. 5.) He helps our weakness in prayer. (Rom. viii. 26; Eph. vi. 18;

Jude 20.) In a word, all that tends to the internal illumination and sanctification of the soul is His work. (71-78)

35. *At what time ought young Christians especially to look for and pray for the Spirit?*

At Confirmation. (Acts viii. 17; Acts xix. 6.) (79, 80)

36. *What other most important work of the Holy Spirit must follow up His gift in Confirmation?*

He must feed us in Holy Communion with the body and blood of Christ, for it is through Him that the elements are consecrated; and through Him we "so eat the flesh and drink the blood of the Son of Man, that our sinful bodies are made clean by His Body, and our souls washed through His most precious Blood." (81-87)

37. *But have you not omitted one work which is often considered His one work, i. e., His work in conversion?*

Yes; I purposely omitted it, because they who have received grace in Baptism, and have been brought up in the nurture and admonition of the Lord, ought not to need conversion.

38. *What is conversion?*

Conversion is turning from sin, and turning to God; and men are not to fall into sin and forsake God, in order that they may be afterwards turned or converted. (88, 89)

39. *But if they do thus turn from God, is not conversion a needful work of the Spirit?*

Unquestionably; conversion, or rather, the repentance unto life which includes it, and of which it is but a part, is, of course, a work of the Spirit. (88-90)

40. *What are the fruits of the Spirit?*

"The fruits of the Spirit are love, joy, peace, long-suffering, gentleness, goodness, faith, meekness, temperance." (Gal. v. 22.)

And again—

"The fruit of the Spirit is in all goodness, and righteousness, and truth." (Eph. v. 9.) (93-95)

41. *What will be the last and crowning work of the Holy Ghost?*

He will raise up our bodies at the last day. (Rom. viii. 11.)

42. *What does our Saviour call the Holy Spirit?*

The promise of the Father. (St. Luke xxiv. 49.) (96-100)

43. *Where was He promised?*

All through the Old Testament (Prov. i. 23; Isa. xliv.

3 ; Ezek. xxxvi. 27 ; Joel ii. 28) ; and especially by our Lord : " He shall give you another Comforter, that He may abide with you for ever." (John xiv. 16.)

44. *But was not He given all through the Dispensation of the Old Testament?*
Not for the same wonderful purposes of grace for which He has been given under the New.

45. *When was the Holy Spirit given in fulfilment of these promises?*
On the day of Pentecost. (105-109)

46. *Is the Holy Ghost still given?*
Yes : He is given when He comes with His illuminating and sanctifying grace into each particular soul. (95-100)

47. *Does the Holy Spirit always continue in those to whom He has been once given?*
We dare not say so, with all the solemn warnings in Scripture respecting grieving (Eph. iv. 30), resisting (Acts vii. 51), quenching (1 Thess. v. 19), doing despite to (Heb. x. 29) the Spirit ; and especially since God has taught us to pray, " Take not Thy Holy Spirit from us " (Psalm li. 11). (101-104)

48. *Is this grieving the Holy Spirit the same as the unpardonable sin?*
No. The sin against the Holy Ghost seems to be the ascribing the works of Christ to the power of the devil. (Mark iii. 29, 30.) (110-114)

49. *In what measure is the Holy Spirit given to the Church?*
In most abundant measure. (Tit. iii. 6.) All the baptized are throughout the New Testament addressed as, in some sort, partakers of the Spirit, and so responsible for God's grace.

50. *Do the Apostles seem to regard such an idea as dangerous?*
No ; on the contrary, they always assume that there is danger lest men forget that God has given to them some gift of His Spirit : in fact, lest they forget their dedication to God by His Spirit in Holy Baptism.

[*See* especially 1 Cor. vi. 19 : " Know ye not that your body is the temple of the Holy Ghost which is in you ?" Also, Eph. iv. 30 ; 1 Thess. iv. 7, 8 ; 2 Peter i. 9.] (115-118)

SHORTER CATECHISM.

1. *In Whom do you next profess your belief?*
   I believe in the Holy Ghost.
2. *What does the word "Ghost" mean?* Spirit.
3. *Who is the Holy Ghost?* The Third Person in the Trinity.
4. *What do you believe respecting Him?*
   I believe that He is the Lord.
5. *Where do you confess this?*
   In the Nicene Creed, when I say, "I believe in the Holy Ghost, the Lord [and giver of Life"].
6. *What else do you confess that you believe respecting Him?*
   That He is "the Giver of Life."
7. *But is not God both "the Lord" and "the Giver of Life?"*
   The Holy Ghost is God.
8. *How do you prove this from Scripture?*
   Because He is called God in the place where Ananias, who lied to the Holy Ghost, is said to have lied to God (Acts v. 3, 4).
9. *What further proof?*
   He is called the Lord (2 Cor. iii. 17).
10. *How besides can you show that He is God?*
    We are dedicated to Him in Holy Baptism.
11. *How is this?*
    Because we are then baptized into His Name.
12. *What are we then made?* His temples.
13. *And because of this what are we?*
    The temples of God (1 Cor. iii. 16).
14. *Of what life is He especially the giver?* Of Spiritual life.
15. *Of what life does He make us to partake?*
    Of the Life of God and of Christ.
16. *Is the Holy Spirit a Son of God?*
    No: God has one only begotten Son.
17. *How then does He exist?*
    He proceeds from the Father and from the Son.
18. *Do you know what this procession is?*
    No: it is one of the deepest things of God.
19. *Why then do you use a word which you do not understand?*
    Because it is the word used in Scripture.
20. *From Whom does the Spirit proceed?*
    From the Father and the Son.
21. *Did Christ ever do a thing which seems to show that the Holy Spirit proceeds from Him?*
    Yes: when He breathed on the disciples and said, "Receive ye the Holy Ghost" (John xx. 22).

THE HOLY GHOST.

22. *Of Whom is the Holy Ghost called the Spirit?*
    He is called the Spirit of Christ as well as of God.
23. *Where?* Particularly in Gal. iv. 6, and 1 Pet. i. 11.
24. *Did the Holy Spirit ever become incarnate?* No.
25. *Was He ever seen?*
    Yes: He was seen in a bodily shape like a dove when our Lord was baptized (Luke iii. 22).
26. *Why did He assume a bodily shape?*
    To show that He was given to our Lord in all His fulness.
27. *Why did He assume this particular form of a dove?*
    Because He is the Spirit of love, and of meekness and gentleness (Gal. v. 22, 23).
28. *Is He a separate person in the Godhead?* Yes.
29. *What proof is there of this?*
    Our Lord calls Him "another Comforter" (John xiv. 16).
30. *Can you give any other proof?*
    Yes: we are baptized into His Name, and so dedicated to Him.
31. *How does this show that He is a person?*
    We cannot be baptized into the name of a lifeless thing or dedicated to an unthinking thing.
32. *If the Holy Ghost be the "Giver of Life," what do we receive from Him?* Life.
33. *What life?* The life of the soul, or spiritual life.
34. *In what does this life consist?* In holiness and righteousness.
35. *From what death then does He deliver us?*
    From the death of sin.
36. *What is to be made holy called?* To be sanctified.
37. *What does the Holy Spirit give us to make us holy?*
    Life from Christ (Colos. iii. 4).
38. *Where is mention first made of the Holy Spirit?*
    In the very beginning of the Bible we read, "The Spirit of God moved upon the face of the waters."
39. *Of what has this been always considered a type?*
    Of His work in Holy Baptism.
40. *Was this work in creation His greatest work?* No.
41. *What was the greatest work of the Spirit.*
    The Incarnation of our Lord Jesus Christ.
42. *Did He bring this about?*
    Yes: so we read in the first page of the New Testament (Matt. i. 20).
43. *Do we confess that we believe this?*
    Yes: when we say that we believe that our Lord was "conceived by the Holy Ghost."
44. *Was then the work of the Holy Spirit necessary to our Redemption?*
    Yes: to every part of it.

45. *Did then the Holy Ghost redeem us?*
    No: but He enabled our Saviour to redeem us.
46. *How did He do this?*
    It was by Him that our Saviour was anointed to be our Prophet, Priest, and King.
47. *Why did our Saviour leave this world?*
    He tells us that it was that the Comforter, *i.e.*, the Holy Ghost, might come (John xvi. 7).
48. *What do we gather from this?*
    The exceeding value of the gift of the Holy Ghost.
49. *What great gift do we owe to the Holy Spirit?*
    The Holy Scriptures.
50. *Do we ever confess this in our Creed?*
    Yes: when we say that the Holy Ghost "spake by the Prophets."
51. *What is the gift by which men were enabled to write the Scriptures called?*
    It is called Inspiration. "All Scripture," the Apostle says, "is given by Inspiration of God" (2 Tim. iii. 16).
52. *How is this Inspiration described by one who felt it?*
    Holy men spake as they were moved by the Holy Ghost (2 Peter i. 21).
53. *For what purpose were the inspired writers moved by the Holy Ghost?*
    To make men wise unto salvation through faith which is in Christ Jesus (2 Tim. iii. 15).
54. *What other gift do we owe to the Holy Spirit?*
    The ministry of the Church.
55. *Show this from Scripture?*
    St. Paul tells us that Apostles, prophets, evangelists, pastors, and teachers, are His gifts (Eph. iv. 11).
56. *Does he anywhere else teach us the same?*
    Yes: when he speaks to the Ephesian elders as having been made overseers over the flock of Christ by the Holy Ghost (Acts xx. 28).
57. *By whom was St. Paul called to the ministry?*
    By the Holy Ghost (Acts xiii. 2).
58. *By what was he set apart to the ministry?*
    By the laying on of hands—in ordination (Acts xiii. 3).
59. *What is given by the laying on of hands in ordination?*
    Gifts of the Spirit, to enable ministers to work the work of Christ.
60. *What is the duty of ministers in respect of these gifts?*
    To stir up by prayer the gift of God given them in ordination (2 Tim i. 6).
61. *How must ministers keep this gift?*
    By the same Holy Spirit (2 Tim. i. 14).

62. *What then is our especial duty as regards the ministers of Christ's Church?*
   To pray for them.
63. *When were you baptized?* When I was an infant.
64. *What were you then made?* A member of Christ.
65. *Who made you a member of Christ?* The Holy Spirit.
66. *How do you know this?*
   Because I read, "By one Spirit are we all baptized into one body" (1 Cor. xii. 13).
67. *Did you then receive the Holy Spirit in Baptism?* Yes.
68. *How do you know this?* From Acts ii. 38, 39.
69. *How besides?*
   All baptized Christians are throughout the Scriptures assumed to have had the Spirit given to them.
70. *But if they do not live as Christians, is it not a sign that they have never had the Spirit?*
   No: it is rather a sign that they are grieving and quenching Him.
71. *Is the Holy Spirit only given you in Baptism?*
   No: I am taught by the Church to pray that I may "daily be renewed by God's Holy Spirit"(Collect for Christmas Day).
72. *How does He renew us?* By striving with us (Gen. vi. 3).
73. *How besides?*
   By convincing or convicting us of sin (John xvi. 9).
74. *How besides?*
   By showing to us the things of Christ, such as His Incarnation and Sacrifice for sin (John xvi. 14).
75. *How besides?*
   By shedding abroad the love of God in our hearts (Rom. v. 5).
76. *When do we especially pray for this?*
   In the Collect for purity (Cleanse the thoughts of our hearts by the Inspiration of thy Holy Spirit, that we may perfectly love Thee).
77. *What other blessings do we receive from Him?*
   Comfort. He is often called the Comforter.
78. *What other blessing?* Help in prayer (Eph. vi. 18).
79. *What particular rite was ordained that in it we might receive the Holy Spirit?*
   Confirmation, or the laying on of hands.
80. *What then should we do when we are preparing to be confirmed?*
   We should pray very earnestly that we may receive God's Holy Spirit when we are confirmed.
81. *Can we receive the Holy Communion to our salvation without the Holy Spirit?* No.
82. *What does He do for us in the Holy Communion?*
   He prepares us to receive it aright, *i.e.*, in faith and prayer.

83. *What besides?*
    He feeds us with the body and blood of Christ in it.
84. *What besides?*
    He consecrates the elements so that through them we partake of the Body and Blood of Christ.
85. *Does the Church teach this?*
    Yes: when she says that we "spiritually eat the flesh of Christ."
86. *What does "spiritually" mean?*
    By the power and grace of God's Holy Spirit.
87. *Give then, in one word, what the Spirit enables us to do?*
    He enables us to "discern the Lord's body" 1 Cor. xi. 29).
88. *If we fall into sin or forgetfulness of God, is there any work of the Spirit of God yet granted to us?*
    Yes: He sometimes renews us by repentance.
89. *Is repentance His gift?*
    Yes: our Saviour says that He convinces or convicts men of sin.
90. *Can wilful sinners count upon His renewing them to repentance?*
    No.
91. *By Whom do we come to God?*
    By the Spirit, through the Son (Eph. ii. 18).
92. *What wonderful knowledge do we receive through the Spirit?*
    We know "the things which God hath prepared for them that love Him. The things which are freely given to us of God" (1 Cor. ii. 9, 12).
93. *What are the gifts of the Spirit?* 1 Cor. xii. 8, 9, 10.
94. *What are the fruits of the Spirit?* Gal. v. 22.
95. *What promise does Christ give respecting the Holy Spirit?*
    That God will give Him to them that ask for Him (Luke xi. 13).
96. *Do we in Church claim from Christ the fulfilment of this promise?*
    Yes; very often.
97. *Mention one place.*
    When we say Amen to the prayer at the end of the Absolution: "Wherefore let us beseech Him to grant us true repentance and His Holy Spirit."
98. *Mention another.*
    When we pray God in the Litany to "endue us with the grace of His Holy Spirit to amend our lives according to His Holy Word."
99. *Mention another.* In the Prayer for the clergy and people.
100. *Mention another.*
    The Collect for purity at the beginning of the Communion Service

101. *What prayer respecting the abiding of God's Spirit in us are we taught to use?*
  Take not thy Holy Spirit from us.
102. *Where is this prayer to be found?*
  In the 51st Psalm.
103. *Are we taught in Scripture that we can resist God's Spirit?*
  Yes; very often (Acts vii. 51; Eph. iv. 30).
104. *What does God say respecting this?*
  My Spirit shall not always strive (Gen. vi. 3).
105. *When was the Holy Spirit sent down?*
  On the day of Pentecost.
106. *What was the sign of His presence?*
  Cloven tongues as of fire sat upon the Apostles (Acts ii. 3, 4).
107. *What wondrous gift did He bestow upon them?*
  The gift of tongues.
108. *What prophecies were fulfilled on that day?*
  Psalm lxviii. 18; Joel ii. 28.
109. *What fruits of His immediately appeared in men's lives?*
  Acts ii. 44-47.
110. *Is there any sin which cannot be forgiven?*
  Yes: the sin against the Holy Ghost, or the blasphemy against the Holy Ghost.
111. *What is this sin?*
  It is ascribing the works of the Spirit of God to the spirit of evil.
112. *Who committed it, or were in danger of doing so?*
  Mark iii. 29, 30.
113. *Does not Satan tempt religious persons to fear that they have committed this sin?*
  Yes: very often.
114. *What is a sign that they have not?*
  Their desire for forgiveness, or their deep concern for having sinned at all.
115. *Is the Holy Spirit given to only a few in the Church, or to all?*
  The Scripture says, The manifestation of the Spirit is given to every man to profit withal (1 Cor. xii. 7).
116. *Is this stated but once?*
  No: it is repeatedly stated. "We have been all made to drink into one Spirit" (1 Cor. xii. 13; Tit. iii. 6).
117. *What then should we all consider ourselves?*
  We should consider ourselves as each one of us answerable for some degree of grace (Matt. xxv. 15).
118. *And what should we do in the face of this?*
  We should "Work out our salvation with fear and trembling, for it is God that worketh in us" (Phil. ii. 13).

SECTION XXVII.—THE HOLY CATHOLIC CHURCH.

1. *In what do you next profess your belief?*
   In the Holy Catholic Church.
2. *Why does this profession come next to that of your faith in the Holy Ghost?*
   Because the formation of the Holy Catholic Church was the first work of the Holy Spirit when He was sent down from heaven.
3. *What is the word used in the New Testament for this word Church, and what does it mean?*
   It is " Ecclesia," and simply means any assembly called out for some particular purpose.
4. *Is this an appropriate name for the Christian body of believers?*
   Yes ; because the Church was originally called out of the world, and its members have always, at their entrance into the Church, renounced all that is evil in the world.
5. *What is the Holy Catholic Church?*
   A body or society of persons united under Christ as their head.
   [" Head over all things to the Church, which is His body." (Eph. i. 22.) " We, being many, are one body in Christ." (Rom. xii. 5.) " Ye are the body of Christ, and members in particular." (1 Cor. xii. 27.)] (1–5)
6. *What is this body sometimes called?*
   It is called Christ's mystical body, to show that all the members are united to the Head, and to one another, not by a natural, but by a supernatural or mysterious union. (Eph. v. 30–33.) (6–10)
7. *What other name is given by our Lord to the Church?*
   He calls it the kingdom of God when He says, " Except a man be born of water and of the Spirit, he cannot enter into the kingdom of God ;" and when in various parables He likens it to a field in which the Son of Man sowed good seed, to a grain of mustard-seed, and to a net cast into the sea, and gathering of every kind. (Matt. xiii. 24, 31, 47.) (10, 11, 14, 15)

8. *Is any other figure used to describe the Church?*
   Yes: it is called the house of God, having as its stones men and women who believe in Christ. (1 Tim. iii. 15; 1 Peter ii. 5.)
9. *Does our Lord ever use this figure?*
   Yes; when He says, " Upon this rock (*i. e.*, the belief that He is the Christ, the Son of the living God) I will *build* my Church." (Matt. xvi. 18.)
10. *What similitude does our Lord use to teach us the nature of His Church?*
    He describes it as a vine, of which He is the trunk or stem, and His people the branches. (John xv. 1.) (12, 13)
11. *You say that you believe in the Holy Catholic Church: what do you mean by Catholic?*
    I mean universal, for it is designed by God to gather into itself all nations (Matt. xxviii. 19), as distinguished from the Jewish Church, which was intended for but one nation.
12. *Do not some say that there are two Catholic Churches, a visible and an invisible?*
    If they so speak, they go contrary to every account of the Church which we have in Scripture.
13. *Show that the descriptions of the Church which we have in Scripture teach us that it must be, by its very nature, a visible body.*
    When the Holy Spirit by St. Paul describes it as a *body*, He implies that it is, by its very nature, a visible organization; for it is the nature of a body to be visible, as it is the nature of a spirit to be invisible.
    [The figure of the kingdom teaches the same; for it is the nature of a kingdom to be visible in the king, and the officers under him, and the people. A " house " also is built of visible stones, and so the " house of God," the Church, is composed of visible men.]
14. *What has led men to say that there are two Churches, the visible and the invisible?*
    The fact that the Church contains both godly and ungodly members. Men cannot understand that the Church of Christ should be thus a mixed body, and so they imagine an invisible Church containing only the good. (14–21)
15. *Is this Scriptural?*
    No: our Lord speaks of His Church, or Kingdom, as a

net cast into the sea, and gathering of every kind, good and bad, and not to be separated till the end ; and He also compares it to a vine on some branches of which there is no fruit, which God will in time cast away. (20–27)

16. *Mention another proof.*

The Apostles write their Epistles to members of the One Church. They remind all to whom they write that they have all been grafted into this one body ; and yet they warn some as being in danger of falling from Christ. (Rom. xi. 17–22 ; 1 Cor. vi. 19, 20 ; x. 1–10.)

17. *What then would you say of Christians who fall into sin ?*

That they are unhealthy members of the one Body ; unfruitful branches of the one Vine ; self-willed subjects of the one kingdom ; and so are in danger of being cut off. (John xv. 2, 6 ; Rom. xi. 22.) (26–28)

18. *Would you deny them, then, to be members of the true Church ?*

No ; I should rather deny that they are true members of the Church.

19. *But is it not dangerous to teach that the Church is a mixed body ?*

No ; it cannot be dangerous, because it is the teaching invariably adopted by Christ and His apostles.

20. *But will not careless persons deem themselves secure if they are taught that they are, or have been, in the Holy Catholic Church?*

Not if they are taught what Christ teaches when He says, "Every branch in me that beareth not fruit, God taketh away." (John xv. 2.)

21. *Had the Apostles any fear of teaching all professing Christians that they were in the Church?*

No ; so far from this, they seemed afraid lest professing Christians should forget it, and so forget the obligations to be holy under which they were by being members of the Church.

22. *Why is the Church called Holy ?*

The Church is called Holy because she is sanctified by the merits of Christ, applied to her through the sacraments, and because of the perpetual presence of the Holy Spirit within her.

"Christ loved the Church, and gave Himself for her'; that He might sanctify and cleanse her with the washing of water by the word." (Eph. v. 26. Also 1 Cor. x. 16. 17 ; xii. 12, 13.) (28–34)

23. *Give an account of the founding of the Church.*

"Then (*i. e.*, on the Day of Pentecost), they that gladly received his (St. Peter's) word were baptized, and the same day there were added unto them about three thousand souls ; and they continued steadfastly in the Apostles' doctrine, and in (their) fellowship, and in (the) breaking of bread, and in (the) prayers." (Acts ii. 41.) (35-42)

24. *What are the marks of the Church here mentioned?*
Four—
1. Receiving, and continuing in, the Apostles' doctrine.
2. Abiding in the Apostles' fellowship.
3. Receiving the two Sacraments of Baptism and Holy Communion.
4. Continuing steadfastly in (the) prayers.

25. *What is the doctrine of the Apostles?*
The doctrine or teaching of the Incarnation, and Birth, Life, Death, Burial, Resurrection, and Ascension of Jesus Christ, the Son of God, together with the sending of the Holy Ghost, the setting up of the Church, and the institution of the Sacraments, and other means of grace. (43-54)

26. *What form did this doctrine of the Apostles take?*
Invariably the historical form, as it is embodied in the Creeds. (50-53)

27. *How do we know that the doctrine of the Apostles took this form?*
Because it appears in this form in the sermons of St. Peter and St. Paul (Acts ii. and xiii.) ; and because when St. Paul mentions in any place of his Epistles the "Gospel" which he preached, we find that it is always expressed in almost the very words of some article of the Creed.

28. *Have we any other proof?*
Yes ; we gather from Luke i. 3, 4, that the earliest Christians were instructed in such records as those of St. Luke's Gospel, *i. e.*, in historical accounts of the Birth, Life, Miracles, Sufferings, Crucifixion and Resurrection of Jesus.

[It seems to be a particular mark of the Church, as distinguished from non-Catholic bodies, to set forth this form of doctrine. The most corrupt branches (or those which we account the most corrupt) adhere to it ; whilst even established non-Catholic bodies, such as the Kirk of Scotland, have thrust it aside for some, in their eyes, more evangelical form. The doctrine of the Apostles, in its historical form, is the basis of the Church year, which

K

all Catholic bodies instinctively adhere to, and which the sects as instinctively repudiate.]

29. *But was not Justification by faith the leading truth which constituted the apostolic Gospel or teaching?*

No; it was impossible that it should have been so. Faith, by its very nature, must have some object, that is, some person, or fact or truth on which to rest; and that object was always the person of Christ, as set forth in the Evangelical narrative.

30. *But did not the Apostles, before all things, call on men to rest on the finished work of Christ?*

No; we have no instance of their preaching taking any such form; whereas we have multitudes of instances of their preaching taking the form in which it is now enshrined in the Creed.

31. *What is the Apostles' fellowship?*

It is the union of Christians in one body or organization, under the direction and government of the Apostles. (54-58)

32. *But were not the Apostles removed by death?*

Yes; but the Saviour had promised that He would be with them "alway, even unto the end of the world;" that is, He would be with those who would take their place in the superintendence of the Church. (Matt. xxviii. 20.)

33. *What form did the fellowship of the Apostles assume?*

That of an organized body, in which the Apostles and ministers appointed by them were the means by which the whole body was joined to the Head.

34. *Where do we read this?*

In the words of St. Paul. "The Head, from which all the body by joints and bands having nourishment ministered, and knit together, increaseth with the increase of God." (Col. ii. 19.) (*See* also "the Vine and the branches" in John xv. 1-6.)

35. *What were these joints and bands?*

Evidently the Apostles and other ministers of the Church. (Eph. iv. 11-17.) (60-62)

36. *What kind of government was the Apostolic?*

It was episcopal; for the various Christian congregations were not independent of one another, and did not govern one another; but were governed by the Apostles, being, to the very end of the New Testament times, under their oversight. (62-67)

37. *Have we any proof that this was to continue?*
   Yes: the Apostles, when they died, committed the oversight of the Church, not to synods or committees, but to individuals, who succeeded them in all their powers of teaching, superintending, and ordaining. (62-67)
38. *Was there any other superintendence of the Church?*
   No: there was no other for above fifteen hundred years. (68-71)
39. *What other mark of the Church have we?*
   The reception of Sacraments. Baptism: "They that gladly received His word were baptized"; and the Lord's Supper: "They continued steadfastly in...the breaking of bread." (Acts ii. 41, 42.)
40. *When does our Lord ordain Baptism as the entrance into His Church?*
   When He says, "Except a man be born of water and of the Spirit, he cannot enter into the kingdom of God." (John iii. 5.) (43-45)
41. *Why must He here allude to Baptism?*
   Because when by His authority His Church or kingdom was actually set up on the day of Pentecost, men were introduced into it by Baptism.
   [Again (1 Cor. xii. 13), "By one Spirit we are all baptized into one body;" (Eph. v. 26), "Christ sanctifies and cleanses His Church with the washing of water by the word"]
42. *What Sacrament besides Baptism did the Pentecostal Christians receive?*
   The Holy Communion, or, as it is there called, "The Breaking of Bread." (72-74)
43. *Had Christ ever promised that this should be a means of union with Himself?*
   Yes; where He said, "He that eateth my flesh, and drinketh my blood, dwelleth in me, and I in him." (John vi. 56.) (75-79)
44. *When did He address the disciples as thus in Him?*
   Not till He had given to them His Body and Blood in Holy Communion; then He addressed them as in Himself the true vine. (John xv. 4, 5, 7.)
45. *Have we any further proof that Holy Communion is the means of our continuing in the body of Christ?*
   Yes: "We being many are one bread, and one body (the body of Christ): for we are all partakers of that one bread." (1 Cor. x. 17.) (75-79)

46. *What is the fourth mark of the Church?*
    They continued steadfastly in "the prayers," *i. e.*, the public prayers of the Church. (80-83)
47. *Has the Church always ordained public prayers?*
    Yes; she has always had (at least) the weekly celebration of the Eucharist, and she has always enjoined daily prayers.
48. *Has the Church always used the same prayers?*
    The Catholic Church has always used certain prayers (with others, of course), such as the Lord's Prayer, certain hymns found in Scripture, and the entire Psalter, and above all, certain acts of devotion common to all her Communion offices, such as the Sursum Corda, the angelic Hymn (Holy, Holy, Holy), and the repetition of our Lord's words in the prayer of Consecration in the Eucharist. (82-85)
49. *Has the Church Catholic any one visible head on earth?*
    No: her Head is in Heaven. "God hath given Him (Christ) to be Head over all things to the Church which is His body." (Ephes. i. 22, 23.) (88)
50. *But must not a visible body have a visible Head?*
    No: the Head may be concealed for a while, just as the Head of a kingdom may be hidden from the gaze of men, and yet order all in the kingdom. (88-92)
51. *You said that the Church must be, by its very nature, a visible body; are then all its members visible?*
    No: by far the greater part are invisible to us, because they are in the unseen state.
52. *But are these to be reckoned as part of the Church?*
    Yes. The Apostle writes to Christians, members of the visible Church: "Ye are come to Mount Zion, the city of the living God ... and to the spirits of just men made perfect." (Heb. xii. 22.)
53. *What do you gather from this?*
    I gather that, if the Church have the greater part of her members now in the unseen state, she may also have a Head Who, as yet, withdraws Himself from our sight, though He is present in spirit and in power.
54. *Do the Apostles ever recognise one of their number as the visible head of the Church, so that all Christians must have fellowship with him, if they are to have fellowship with the Head?*
    No; there is not the smallest trace of such an opinion

in their writings, or in the writings of any of the early fathers of the Church. (94-97)

55. *Do the Scripture writers ever recognise any local Church —as, for instance, the Church of Rome—as having a right to impose its name or decrees on the whole Church ?*

No; they recognise no such authority in any Church. If any Church could have had such authority, it would have been the Church of Jerusalem, for this Church was first founded by the Apostles.

56. *Can, then, the Church of Rome be called the mother and mistress of all Churches ?*

No ; in no sense consistent with the teaching of Scripture or history can she be so called. (97, 98)

57. *What branch of the Catholic Church furnishes to us English Christians the means of union with the Holy Catholic Church ?*

The Church of England. (100)

58. *Has she the same outward marks of the Church as the Church of the Apostolic times ?*

Yes ; all of them. (101)

59. *Show that she continues steadfastly in the Apostles' doctrine.*

She continues steadfastly in the Apostles' doctrine or teaching, for she sets forth with the utmost prominence the objective facts of the Incarnation, Life, Death, Resurrection, and Ascension of the Eternal Son. (102-106)

60. *How does she continue in the Apostolic fellowship ?*

She is governed by a ministry derived by succession from the Apostolic, as writers of the Roman obedience even have allowed. (107, 108)

61. *Does she continue in " the breaking of Bread," and in the Prayers ?*

Yes ; she ordains an Eucharistic service for each Sunday and holiday, and she imposes the offering of daily prayers on all her ministers, and in her Communion and other offices she has retained all the leading features of the most ancient services. (109-115)

62. *In all this account of the Church and her privileges, do you not put the Church into the place of Christ ?*

No, not for a moment ; for if the promise of Christ yet holds good, He is with His Church in all which she ministers in His name.

["Lo I am with you alway." (Mat. xxviii. 20.) Also Mat. xviii. 20; 2 Cor. ii. 10; Heb. xii. 22, 24; Rev. i. 13.]

63. *Show this more fully.*

It is He Who baptizes by the hands of His ministers when they baptize. (John iv. 1, 2.) It is He Who ratifies their absolutions. (2 Cor. ii. 10.) It is He Who feeds us through their hands with His Body and Blood. (Matt. xiv. 19, comp. with 1 Cor. x. 16.)

64. *What, then, will keep us from putting the Church and her sacraments into the place of Christ?*

Striving with all faith and prayer to realize that the promises of Christ still hold good, that He is ever with, and in, His Church by His Spirit.

65. *But do we not put the ministers of the Church in some sense between ourselves and Christ?*

We have not put them, but Christ has when He said, "As my Father sent me, so send I you; whose soever sins ye remit, they are remitted unto them" (John xx. 21); and when His Spirit inspires St. Paul to say, "We are ambassadors for Christ, as though God did beseech you by us." (2 Cor. v. 20.)

66. *In what sense then are ministers between us and Christ?*

In the sense in which a nerve is between the head and any limb of our bodies, according to the Holy Spirit's own illustration: "The Head, from which the whole body by joints and bands [*i. e.*, by its nerves and arteries] having nourishment ministered, and knit together, increaseth with the increase of God." (Col. ii. 19.)

SHORTER CATECHISM.

1. *What is the next article of your Christian faith?*
   I believe in .... the Holy Catholic Church.
2. *What have you to do with the Holy Catholic Church?*
   I was grafted into it when I was baptized. [Seeing now, dearly beloved, that this child is .... grafted into the body of Christ's Church.]
3. *But were you not made in baptism a member of Christ?*
   Yes: because Christ is the Head of the Church, and we are members of His body.

THE HOLY CATHOLIC CHURCH.

4. *Because then you were made a member of the Church, you were made a member of Christ?*
    Rather, by being made a member of Christ I was made a member of the Church.
5. *Of what is the Church composed?*
    Of men, women, and children, who are baptized into Christ and continue to believe in Him.
6. *The Church, then, is not Christ's natural body?*
    No: His natural body is at the right hand of God.
7. *Why then is it called His body at all?*
    Because as each of our bodies is joined to its head, and directed and guided by its head, so is the Church in and under Christ.
8. *Can we understand the way in which the members of the Church are all joined in one body to Christ?*
    No: they are joined in some mysterious way far above our comprehension.
9. *What is the Church called because of this, its mysterious nature?*
    Christ's mystical body.
10. *What does our Lord call His Church?*
    The kingdom of Heaven. The kingdom of God.
11. *Why?* Because it is under Him as its King.
12. *To what does our Lord compare Himself and His Church?*
    To a vine and its branches (John xv. 1-10).
13. *Why does He use this figure?*
    To show us that as the branches are joined to the vine, so is His Church joined to Him.
14. *When our Lord likens His Church to a kingdom, does He mean that all the people in it will be His faithful subjects?*
    No: He particularly warns us to the contrary.
15. *Where does He so warn us?*
    When He compares His Church to a net cast into the sea, and gathering good and bad fish (Matt. xiii. 47).
16. *Where besides does He warn us of this?*
    When He compares His Church or Kingdom to a field sown with wheat and tares (Matt. xiii. 24).
17. *When our Lord likens His Church to a vine and its branches, does He mean that all the branches are fruitful?*
    No: He says "every branch in me that beareth not fruit, God taketh away" (John xv. 2).
18. *Has Christ then two kingdoms, one of good only, the other of good and bad?*
    No: He Himself tells us that His kingdom is mixed, containing good and bad.
19. *Can there be two vines—one of fruitful branches, the other of unfruitful?*

No: He tells us that there are both sorts of branches in the one Vine.

20. *Are there two bodies?*
No: The Spirit says, "There is one body" (Eph. iv. 4).

21. *Are there two or more Catholic Churches?*
No: Christ speaks of but one Church, one Vine, one Kingdom.

22. *What then must the Church be?* It must be visible.

23. *Why?*
Because it is of the very nature of an organized body to be visible.

24. *Is it right to call the good members (true believers) the invisible Church?* No.

25. *Why?*
Because by so doing we deny what Christ Himself says about His Church (that it is a mixed body).

26. *Will all that are in the Church be saved at last?* No.

27. *Who will be saved?*
Only those who make their calling and election sure (2 Peter i. 10).

28. *Are all the members of the Church called?*
Yes: throughout the New Testament all the members of the Church are addressed as called.

29. *What are they called to be?* Holy (1 Peter i. 15).

30. *Are all the members of the Church truly holy?* No.

31. *Why not?*
Because they do not walk worthy of the calling wherewith they are called (Eph. iv. 1–4).

32. *In what sense then is the Catholic Church holy?*
Because Christ, her Head, is holy, and because all her members are dedicated to God.

33. *In what other sense?*
Because she possesses all the means of making men truly holy.

34. *What are these means?*
The Word of God and the Sacraments.

35. *When was the Church founded or set up?*
On the day of Pentecost.

36. *What day do we commonly call that?* Whitsunday.

37. *Why is it called Pentecost?*
Because it is the fiftieth day after Easter. Pentecost meaning fifty.

38. *By whom was the Church founded?*
By Christ, through the Holy Spirit.

39. *Were any men employed as instruments?*
Yes: the Apostles.

40. *By what were men called into the Church?*
By the preaching of the Apostles.

41. *What was the especial subject of their preaching?*
    Salvation by Christ the Son of God.
42. *Had Christ ever promised that His Church should be built on this?*
    Yes : when He says, " on this rock (*i.e.*, the confession that I am the Christ, the Son of the living God) I will build my Church" (Matt. xvi. 18).
43. *By what were those who obeyed this calling admitted into the Church?*
    By Baptism.
44. *Why?*
    Because Christ had said, "Except a man be born of water and of the Spirit, he cannot enter into the kingdom of God" (John iii. 5).
45. *Had Christ said anything else about the necessity of Baptism?*
    Yes : His last words were, "Go ye and teach all nations, baptizing them in the name of the Father, and of the Son, and of the Holy Ghost" (Matt. xxviii. 19).
46. *Did those who were baptized receive further instruction?* Yes.
47. *How do you know this?*
    They continued steadfastly in the Apostles' doctrine.
48. *What was the Apostles' doctrine about?* About Jesus Christ.
49. *What respecting Him?*
    His Godhead, Incarnation, Life, Death, Resurrection, Ascension, and His sending the Holy Ghost.
50. *What then would this teaching most resemble?*
    The articles of the Creed.
51. *But were they only taught the bare facts?*
    No : they were taught, of course, how all these facts had to do with our salvation.
52. *But was not the Apostles' doctrine the Gospel?*
    Yes : and so it mainly consisted of such teaching respecting Christ as we find in the four Gospels (see also 1 Cor. xv. 1-6).
53. *But was not the Apostles' teaching principally about faith?*
    No, certainly not ; it was all about the Person Jesus Christ, in Whom we are to have faith.
54. *Were those persons who thus continued in the Apostles' doctrine under any rule or guidance?*
    Yes : they continued steadfastly in the Apostles' fellowship.
55. *What does this mean?*
    It means that they did not split up into many independent bodies, but all continued in the same society.
56. *Who were at the head of this society?* The Apostles.
57. *Were some under one Apostle and some under another?*
    No : the Apostles all acted together as one man.
58. *Did the Apostles always continue in Jerusalem?* No.

THE HOLY CATHOLIC CHURCH.

59. *Under whom did the first Christians in Jerusalem continue after their departure in their fellowship?*
They continued under the presidency of St. James, the first Bishop of Jerusalem.

60. *But were there not Christians soon in all parts of the world?* Yes.

61. *Were these all in one fellowship?*
Yes: they all continued under the control and oversight of the Apostle who converted them.

62. *Give instances.*
The Galatian, Ephesian, Philippian, and Thessalonian Christians continued in the fellowship and under the oversight of St. Paul as long as he lived.

63. *When he died did this fellowship continue?*
Yes: after his death the Christians converted by him continued under the control of the men whom he appointed.

64. *Did the other Apostles take the same means to continue this fellowship as St. Paul did?*
Yes: history tells us that they did.

65. *Why should the Apostles take steps to continue this oversight even after their deaths, and not leave the Churches to govern themselves as they pleased?*
Because they believed that God intended the Church to be one body or society, and not many different bodies or sects.

66. *But would it not have been sufficient if they had all believed the same things?*
No: the Holy Spirit tells us that there is one BODY as well as one *spirit* and one *faith* (Eph. iv. 4).

67. *What does that mean?*
That there is one outward society or organization as well as one inward belief.

68. *Has this oversight and fellowship continued to our times?* Yes.

69. *Have we reason from our Lord's words to believe that it will continue to the end?*
Yes: He said to the Apostles when He gave them their commission to baptize and to teach, "Lo I am with you alway, even unto the end of the world" (Matt. xxviii. 20).

70. *But did He not foresee when He said this that the Apostles would be removed by death long before His second coming?*
Yes: and so His words mean that He will be with those who take their places till He returns.

71. *What order of ministers has the Church always considered to be in the place of the Apostles?*
The Bishops of the Catholic Church.

72. *What Sacrament besides Baptism did the members of the earliest Church receive?*
The Lord's Supper, or Holy Communion.

73. *What is it here called?* The breaking of bread.
74. *Why has it this name?*
    Because our blessed Lord solemnly brake the bread in token that His body would be broken on the cross.
75. *For what purpose did the early Church receive continually this Sacrament?*
    That they might receive the Body and Blood of Christ.
76. *For what particular end?* That they might be united to Christ.
77. *How does our Lord express this?*
    He that eateth my flesh and drinketh my blood dwelleth in Me and I in him (John vi. 56).
78. *If they were thus united to Christ, to whom also were they united?*
    To one another. "We being many are one body in Christ, and every one members one of another" (Rom. xii. 5).
79. *Does the Holy Spirit ever connect this with the Eucharist?*
    Yes: when He says by St. Paul, "We being many are one bread and one body, for we are all partakers of that one bread" (1 Cor. x. 17).
80. *In what besides the Holy Communion did the early Church continue?*
    In the prayers.
81. *Does this mean that they were constant in private prayer only?*
    No.
82. *What does it mean then?*
    That they continued steadfastly in the daily prayers of the Church.
83. *How do we know this?*
    Because the word is not "prayer" but "the prayers," *i.e.,* the stated prayers of the Church.
84. *What has always formed a large part of the daily worship of the Church?*
    The Psalter or Psalms of David.
85. *What besides?*
    The Lord's Prayer, the Hymns, such as the Magnificat, found in the New Testament, and parts of the Communion Service.
86. *Is the Church of Christ only in this world?*
    No: by far the greater part of it is in the unseen world.
87. *What do we sometimes call the members of the Church in the unseen world?*
    The Invisible Church.
88. *Where is the Head of the Church?*
    In Heaven, at the right hand of God.
89. *But should not the visible Church on earth have a visible head?*
    No: just as the greater part of her members are out of our sight, so is the Head.

90. *Is this any disadvantage to the Church?*
   No: because the Head is everywhere and always present.
91. *How do you know this?*
   Because of His promise: "Lo I am with you alway, even unto the end of the world" (Matt. xxviii. 20).
92. *Any other promise?*
   "Where two or three are gathered together in My Name, there am I in the midst of them" (Matt. xviii. 20).
93. *Would it be well that one man should be considered the Head of the Church?*
   No: it would hinder our realizing that there is one supreme ever-present Head.
94. *Is there any Head of the Church except Jesus Christ recognized in Scripture?*
   None whatsoever.
95. *Is any one of the Apostles recognized as the Infallible Head of his brethren?* No.
96. *Is it ever hinted that to abide in the Apostolic fellowship Christians are to have communion with one Apostle—say St. Peter?*
   No.
97. *Did the Primitive Church ever recognize one bishop as the head and sovereign of all bishops?*
   No: it never for a moment allowed any such pretensions.
98. *Which Church was first founded and organized?*
   The Church of Jerusalem.
99. *Has the Catholic Church any branches?* Yes.
100. *With what branch of the Catholic Church have we to do?*
   With the Church of England.
101. *How do we know that the Church of England is a branch of the Catholic Church?*
   Because she has all the marks of it.
102. *What is the first mark?*
   She abides "in the Apostles' doctrine."
103. *How does she do this?*
   She teaches first, and more than all else, the truths respecting Jesus Christ, as they are set forth in the Creeds.
104. *What are these truths?*
   The Godhead, Incarnation, Life, Death, Resurrection, Ascension, Intercession, and second coming of Christ.
105. *How does she set forth these prominently?*
   By the use of the Creeds in her daily and other services.
106. *How besides?*
   By keeping the great festivals and observing the Christian year as the Catholic Church has ever done.
107. *What other mark of the Church has she?*
   She continues in the Apostolic "fellowship."

THE HOLY CATHOLIC CHURCH. 141

108. *How does she do this?*
 She hands down the succession of bishops, and continues under their rule and oversight.
109. *What other mark has she?*
 She continues steadfastly in " the breaking of bread."
110. *What does this mean?*
 She ordains the constant and frequent celebration of the Lord's Supper.
111. *How often?*
 Once a week at the least, *i.e.*, on every Sunday and on all Saints' days.
112. *In what besides this does our branch of the Church continue?*
 In "the Prayers."
113. *How does she do this?*
 She ordains a daily offering of prayer, praise, and thanksgiving.
114. *Did the early Christians attend public prayers daily?*
 Yes: Acts ii. 46; iii. 1.
115. *But do not many, both ministers and people, neglect this?*
 Yes: but this does not undo the fact that the Church has ordained it.
116. *What is our duty to the Church of Christ?*
 We should pray earnestly for it.
117. *What especially should we ask God for on its behalf?*
 That God would cleanse and defend it (Collect for 16th Sunday after Trinity).
118. *What besides should we ask God for on its behalf?*
 For its peace, and the healing of its divisions.
119. *In what words do we continually ask God for this?*
 In the words that " all who profess and call themselves Christians may be led into the way of truth, and hold the faith in Unity of Spirit, *in the bond of peace*, and in righteousness of life."
120. *In what words in the Communion Office?*
 " Grant that all who profess Thy Holy Name may agree in the truth of Thy Holy Word, and live in unity and godly love."

SECTION XXVIII.—THE COMMUNION OF SAINTS.

1. *What is the next article of the Creed?*
   The Communion of Saints. (1, 2)
2. *What do you mean by Saints?*
   Holy or dedicated persons—persons set apart for the service of God. (3-4)
3. *Are, then, all who have been dedicated to God in Baptism Saints?*
   Throughout the Old Testament the word "Saint," or "Holy," is applied to all the Israelites, as dedicated to God in circumcision; and throughout the New the title is given to all who are baptized into the body of Christ. (Deut. vii. 6; xiv. 2, 21; Acts ix. 13, 32, 41.) (5)
4. *Has this word any further meaning?*
   Yes; it is often used to denote those persons who abide in the grace of their first dedication, or are restored to it and become truly holy in heart. (6)
5. *What must it mean in this article of the Creed?*
   The latter; because none can have true communion in the things of God except those who know and serve God. (7-10)
6. *What does this "Communion" mean?*
   It means—
   1. Intercourse.
   2. Sharing with one another in certain blessings.
7. *With whom have the true Saints intercourse?*
   With each person in the Ever Blessed Trinity. Truly our fellowship is with the Father, and with His Son Jesus Christ. (1 John i. 3.) "The fellowship of the Holy Ghost" is "with them." (2 Cor. xiii. 14; Phil. ii. 1.) (11-13)
8. *How do they exercise this intercourse?*
   By prayer, praise, and thanksgiving at all times, but especially in the Eucharist, and in the prayers of the Church.
9. *With whom, besides, have true Saints communion?*
   With one another. "If we walk in the light, as He is

in the light, we have fellowship one with another."(1 John i. 7.) (14-16)
10. *But can truly holy persons only have this fellowship?*
Only the holy can have intercourse with one another in the things of God.
11. *How do the true Saints have this intercourse or communion with one another?*
By Christian converse. By praying together and for one another. By taking the Holy Communion together. By assisting one another in spiritual and temporal matters. (18-29)
12. *Show that Christian conversation is the duty of the Saints.*
" Teaching and admonishing one another in psalms and hymns and spiritual songs." (Col. iii. 16.) Again : " Warn them that are unruly, comfort the feeble-minded, support the weak, be patient towards all men." (1 Thess. v. 14. Also Rom. xiv. 19; xv. 1, 2; 2 Cor. i. 4.)
13. *But are not these things the especial duty of the clergy?*
They may be; but if a layman realizes the Communion of Saints, he will endeavour by his godly conversation to edify those around him. (17)
14. *Show that prayers for one another are a part of this Communion.*
" Pray for us, that the word of the Lord may have free course, and be glorified." (2 Thess. iii. 1.) " Pray one for another." (James v. 16.) (18-20)
15. *Show that Holy Communion is a part of the Communion of Saints.*
" We being many are one bread, and one body; for we are all partakers of that one bread." (1 Cor. x. 17.) (21-23)
16. *Show that the Communion of Saints implies mutual help in temporal matters?*
" They sold their possessions and goods, and parted them unto all men as every man had need." (Acts ii. 45; 2 Cor. viii., ix., *passim.* Also, Rom. xii. 13; Gal. ii. 10; vi. 2, 6; Eph. iv. 28.) (24-29)
17. *But you said that Communion also meant sharing in certain blessings: in what blessings have all Saints a share?*
In all the blessings of the Christian Covenant. " All things," St. Paul tells Christians, "are yours; whether Paul, or Apollos, or Cephas (*i.e.*, all the gifts and labours of ministers), or life, or death, or things present, or

things to come; all are yours; and ye are Christ's, and Christ is God's." (1 Cor. iii. 21–23. Also, Eph. iv. 4–6.)

18. *Does the Communion of Saints embrace only those now living in this world?*

By no means. We have fellowship with the holy angels, and with the spirits of those who have departed hence in the Lord. (30–40)

19. *How can you show this?*

I find that St. Paul writes to Christians living in this world, and yet liable to fall away, that they have "Come to the Mount Zion, the city of the living God, the heavenly Jerusalem, and to an innumerable company of angels .. and to the spirits of just men made perfect." (Heb. xii. 22–26.) (33)

20. *Have we any assurance from an angel that he holds himself to belong to the same communion?*

Yes; on two separate occasions an angel said to St. John, "I am thy fellow-servant, and of thy brethren that have the testimony of Jesus." (Rev. xix. 10; xxii. 9.) (31)

21. *Does St. Paul seem to recognise this communion with the angels?*

Yes; he says to St. Timothy, "I charge thee before God, and the Lord Jesus Christ, and the elect angels." (1 Tim. v. 21.) He could scarcely do this unless he believed that angels were present, though invisible, and so could witness as to whether St. Timothy kept the charge. (*See* also Phil. iii. 20.)

22. *What else is there in the way of communion between us and the angels?*

In some mysterious way they are brought nearer to God through the mediation of Christ, according to the words of the Apostle: "In the name of Jesus every knee shall bow, of things in heaven." (Phil. ii. 10.) And his other words: "By Him (Jesus Christ) to reconcile all things unto Himself: by Him, I say, whether they be things on earth, or things in heaven." (Col. i. 20.) (36–37)

23. *In what consists our communion or fellowship with the angels?*

They assist us by their ministrations. We join with them in worship and praise. (34–40)

24. *Where do we read that they assist us?*

They are "all ministering spirits sent forth to minister for them who shall be heirs of salvation." (Heb. i. 14.

See also Gen. xix. 16 ; xxxii. 1, 2, 24 ; Psalm xxxiv. 7 ; xci. 11 ; ciii. 20, 21 ; Dan. iii. 28 ; vi. 22 ; Matt. xviii. 10 ; Luke i. 19 ; Acts xii. 7 ; xxvii. 23.) (38-40)

25. *When do we join with them in praise and worship ?*
More particularly in the Holy Eucharist, where we say, " Therefore with angels and archangels, and with all the company of heaven . . . Holy, Holy, Holy."

26. *Is it lawful to worship them ?*
No ; they expressly repudiate it : " See thou do it not ; I am thy fellow-servant . . . worship God." (Rev. xix. 10.) (35)

27. *Have we fellowship with the departed Saints ?*
Yes : "we are come . . . to the general assembly and church of the first-born . . . and to the spirits of just men made perfect." (Heb. xii. 23.) (41)

28. *What fellowship have we with them ?*
We have fellowship in hope and in prayer.

29. *What common hope have we with them ?*
The hope of the second coming and the consummation. St. Paul himself speaks of receiving his crown " at that day," *i. e.*, the day of the second advent of Christ. (2 Tim. iv. 8.)

30. *What fellowship in prayer have we ?*
They pray for us. We pray for their rest, and the perfecting of their bliss.

31. *How do we know that they pray for us ?*
We read of the souls of the martyrs under the altar crying to God for vengeance on their persecutors. Now, if they so prayed for vengeance upon the wicked, we may be sure that they would pray for grace upon the righteous. (Rev. vi. 10.)

32. *When do we pray for the perfecting of their bliss ?*
When we pray " that we, with all those that are departed in the true faith of Thy holy Name, may have our perfect consummation and bliss, both in body and soul, in Thine eternal and everlasting glory." (Burial Service.)

33. *Are such prayers scriptural ?*
Yes : St. Paul prays for Onesiphorus, " The Lord grant unto him that he may find mercy of the Lord in that day." (2 Tim. i. 18. By comparing this place with 2 Tim. iv. 19, it is evident that Onesiphorus was not alive. The prayer is, in substance, exactly what all the prayers in the early Liturgies for the faithful departed are.)

L

34. *Does this imply that the state of those after death can be altered?*
   No : life is the time of probation. We shall receive at the judgment for the deeds done in the body ; and between the souls of the saved and the lost there is an impassable gulf.
35. *How besides do we recognise the communion of Saints?*
   By keeping the days of certain great Saints, such as the Apostles, and St. John the Baptist, and the Blessed Virgin.
36. *Is it lawful to invoke the aid of the Saints?*
   There is no instance of such invocation in Scripture ; and the records of the early Church are altogether silent upon such a practice.

SHORTER CATECHISM.

1. *What great privilege belongs to the Catholic Church?*
   The communion of Saints.
2. *What do you mean by communion?*
   "Sharing in," or "having part in," something.
3. *What is the meaning of the word Saint?*   Holy person.
4. *How are Christians made holy?*
   By being dedicated to God. By keeping themselves from every evil thing.
5. *Is a baptized child holy?*
   Yes : because it has been dedicated to God.
6. *But as it grows up will it continue holy?*
   Only if it remembers its first dedication, and puts away from it all sin and evil.
7. *What persons can have communion, or a share in, the things of Christ?*
   Only the truly good and holy.
8. *Ought all in the Church to be thus holy and faithful?*
   Yes : because the promises of grace are given to all in the Church.
9. *What place of Scripture shows this?*
   Having therefore these promises, dearly beloved, let us cleanse ourselves from all filthiness of flesh and spirit (2 Cor. vii. 1).
10. *Can we realize the blessings in which the Saints partake unless we are doing this?*   No.

THE COMMUNION OF SAINTS.

11. *What is the first blessing in which the Saints partake?*
    They have converse with God in prayer.
12. *In what besides do they have part?*
    They have part in the Intercession of Christ (John xv. 7, 10).
13. *In what besides?*
    They have the fellowship or communion of the Spirit (2 Cor. xiii. 14).
14. *In what besides?*
    They have fellowship with one another (1 John i. 7).
15. *How do they show this?*
    They speak to one another about the things of God.
16. *How must they walk who can hope truly to have this fellowship?*
    If we walk in the light as He is in the light, we have fellowship one with another (1 John i. 7).
17. *Is speaking about holy things the duty of the clergy only?*
    No: Malachi speaks of those who fear the Lord speaking often one to another (Mal. iii. 16; Col. iii. 16).
18. *In what do the Saints have communion?*
    In mutual prayer. In prayer one for another (James v. 16).
19. *Are the prayers of the Saints needful for the well-being of the Church?*
    Yes: even a man like St. Paul felt that he could not do without them (2 Thess. iii. 1).
20. *For whom will those who believe in the communion of Saints especially pray?*
    For the bishops and other ministers of the Church.
21. *By what ordinance more especially are the Saints assured that they have part in the communion of Saints?*
    By the Holy Communion.
22. *Show this from Scripture.*
    "We being many are one bread and one body, for we are all partakers of that one bread"(1 Cor. x. 17).
23. *How do we recognise this in our Communion Office?*
    In the second post-Communion Prayer: "We most heartily thank Thee that Thou . . . dost assure us thereby . . . that we are very members incorporate in the mystical body of Thy Son."
24. *In what outward way do Christians show that they realize this communion of Saints?*
    By contributing to the relief of one another's necessities.
25. *Give instances of this from Scripture.* Acts ii. 44, 45; iv. 34, 35
26. *Give another instance.* Rom. xv. 25, 29.
27. *Give some precepts for this.*
    Rom. xii. 13; Gal. vi. 10; Heb. vi. 10.
28. *Did St. Paul himself ever partake of this fruit of the communion of Saints?*
    Yes: Phil. iv. 15.

29. *What promise did he give them in return for this?*
    My God shall supply all your need, &c. (Phil. iv. 19).
30. *With whom besides the good and holy in this world have true Saints fellowship?* With the holy angels.
31. *What do the holy angels profess themselves to be?*
    Our fellow-servants (Rev. xxii. 9).
32. *Have we any proof that the angels, though invisible, are present with us?*
    Yes: Elijah and his servant (2 Kings vi. 15-17).
33. *Have we any communion or fellowship with them?*
    Yes: we have "come to an innumerable company of angels" (Heb. xii. 22).
34. *What do the angels do for us?*
    They guard and assist us secretly in numberless ways. "He shall give his angels charge over thee to keep thee in ALL thy ways" (Psalm xci. 11).
35. *May we offer them worship?*
    No: they expressly refuse it, and bid us worship God (Rev. xxii. 10).
36. *In what have we communion with them?*
    In worship. All things in heaven and earth, and under the earth, worship in the same Name—the Name of Jesus (Phil. ii. 10).
37. *In what else?*
    In the merits and mediation of Christ, for we read that *all* things in Heaven as well as on earth are reconciled unto God by Jesus Christ (Col. i. 20).
38. *What are the angels called with respect to what they do for us?*
    Ministering spirits sent forth to minister unto them that shall be heirs of salvation (Heb. i. 14).
39. *To whom especially were they sent to minister?*
    To our Lord (Matt. iv. 11; Luke xxii. 43).
40. *To which of His servants were they sent to minister?*
    To St. Peter (Acts xii. 7); to St. Paul (Acts xxvii. 23); to St. John (Rev. xxi. 9).
41. *With whom in the unseen world, besides the angels, have we fellowship?* With the departed Saints.
42. *How do you prove this from Scripture?*
    From Heb. xii. 23, where it is said that we have "come to the spirits of just men made perfect."
43. *In what especially have we fellowship with the departed?* In hope.
44. *In hope of what?*
    In hope of the second coming, and the consummation of their bliss.
45. *But have not the saints already received their crown?*
    No: the crown will be given even to a Saint like St. Paul in *that* day, *i.e*, the day of Christ's appearing (2 Tim. iv. 8).

46. *But are they not now in glory?*
   The Apostle says, "When Christ, who is our Life, shall appear, then shall ye also appear with Him in glory" (Col. iii. 4).
47. *Do the Saints and our departed friends pray for us?*
   We humbly hope and trust that they do.
48. *Do we pray for them?*
   The Church, in her earliest Liturgies, has always prayed for their rest and the consummation of their bliss.
49. *But will not God in His own time perfect their bliss?*
   Yes: but what He wills to do, He wills also that we should pray Him to do.
50. *Do we pray that God would change the state of the departed?*
   No.
51. *Do we pray for souls departed as being in purgatory?* No.
52. *Do we ask the Saints to pray for us?* No.
53. *In what prayer especially do we ask for the consummation of their bliss?*
   In the words, "that we, with all those that are departed in the true faith," &c. (Burial Service.)
54. *In what prayer do we pray that we may follow their example?*
   In the Collect for All Saints' Day.

SECTION XXIX.—THE FORGIVENESS OF SINS.

1. *What is the next article of the Christian faith?*
I believe in . . . the forgiveness of sins. (1)
2. *What is sin?*
The transgression of the law of God. (2-8)
3. *Is this law the ten commandments, or the moral precepts of the Bible only?*
No. The law of God is, above all, the law of the Spirit of life in Christ Jesus. (Rom. viii. 2.) (2-8)
4. *What law is this?*
It is faith in Christ Jesus, and includes everything which a true faith in Christ would lead us to observe and do; such as to receive the Sacraments, and to abide in the unity of the Church.
5. *To what body of men is promised the forgiveness of sins?*
To the members of the Holy Catholic Church. (1)
6. *Why?*
Because its Baptism is for the remission of sins, its ministers are the ministers of reconciliation, and in its Eucharist we partake of the Blood shed for the remission of sins. (Acts ii. 38; 2 Cor. ii. 10; v. 18; Matt. xxvi. 28.)
7. *Are all sins the same?*
No; some sins are of a far more deadly and defiling character than others. (Eph. v. 5; Col. iii. 5, 6.) (8-12)
8. *Give an illustration of what you mean.*
Allowing one's thoughts to wander in prayer, or neglecting prayer at stated times, are both very wrong, but they are not in the sight of God like adultery, or fornication, or blasphemy, or covetousness.
9. *What sins are forgiven?*
All sins. It is written that "the blood of Christ cleanseth from all sin" (1 John i. 7); and our Lord says that all sin shall be forgiven except the blasphemy against the Holy Ghost. (Matt. xii. 31, 32.)
10. *Why cannot this be forgiven?*
Because it is the worst form of the denial of the Divine

Person and Mission of Jesus, and shuts out the persons who thus sin from ever asking for forgiveness.

11. *If men go on in impenitence, can they count upon receiving forgiveness?*

No. God may either cut them off in their sins, or so withhold His grace that they cannot repent.

12. *How can an infinitely holy God forgive sins so unreservedly?*

Because He gave His only Son to be on the Cross, " a full, perfect, and sufficient sacrifice, oblation, and satisfaction for the sins of the whole world." (23-28)

13. *How is the virtue of this sacrifice for sin made over to each one?*

First, in Holy Baptism : " Repent and be baptized every one of you in the name of Jesus Christ for the remission of sins." (Acts ii. 38.) " Arise and be baptized, and wash away thy sins." (Acts xxii. 16; also Mark xvi. 15, 16.) (28)

14. *Is then a man forgiven who comes to Baptism in impenitency?*

No : the Apostle says, *Repent*, and be baptized.

15. *When after Baptism is our sin remitted?*

On our repentance and confession to God.

"I said, I will confess my sins unto the Lord, and so Thou forgavest the wickedness of my sin." (Psalm xxxii. 6.)

" If we confess our sins, He is faithful and just to forgive us our sins.' (1 John i. 9.) (29, 30)

16. *What besides repentance must we have?*

We must have an unfeigned faith in God's Holy Gospel ; that is, we must believe with all our hearts that God sent His Son into the world to suffer for our sins, and raised Him from the dead in token that our sins were fully atoned for by His sufferings. (31)

17. *Is there any difficulty in believing this?*

Not if we realise the doctrine of the Incarnation ; for if the Eternal Son Himself assumed our nature, and died to atone for sin, sin must be indeed fully atoned for. (32-35)

18. *But is it not said that the pride of our natural hearts prevents all of us at first from accepting a free salvation through Jesus Christ?*

Such pride can only exist in those who very inadequately, if at all, realize the Eternal Godhead and Incarnation of Jesus. (34-38)

19. *How is this?*
   To those who realize that the Eternal Word took our nature to bestow salvation upon us, that salvation can only appear as a free gift, for no merits of ours could possibly draw down from heaven such a Person, or make us entitled, by way of right, to any part in Him. (34-40)
20. *What, then, is the great antidote to self-righteousness in all its forms?*
   A right apprehension of the Catholic faith?
21. *But is there any confession to man needful?*
   Yes; when our sins have been public, or known to others, we must take to ourselves the shame of acknowledging them to others.
22. *Is any other confession to man imperative?*
   Yes: when by our sin we have injured another, we must confess to him that we have wronged him, and ask his forgiveness, and be willing to make all the reparation in our power.
23. *Is it well that we should ever confess to a minister of the Church?*
   At times it is.
24. *Is this recognised in the Prayer Book?*
   Yes; in the words: "Let him come to me, or to some other discreet and learned minister of God's word, and open his grief, that by the ministry of God's holy word, he may receive the benefit of absolution," &c. And in the "Visitation of the Sick" we have this rubric: "Here shall the sick person be moved to make a special confession of his sins, if he feel his conscience troubled with any weighty matter."
25. *Should you gather from this that our branch of the Church considers that confession to the priest ought to be systematic—as, for instance, at seasons such as Easter; or so often in the year or month—or only occasional?*
   Only occasional.
26. *Are there any directions respecting confession to a minister in Scripture?*
   Yes; we have the people coming to John the Baptist "confessing their sins." We read also that at Ephesus, under the preaching of Paul, "many came and confessed and shewed their deeds." (Acts xix. 18.)
27. *Does this seem part of a systematic practice of confession at stated intervals?*

No ; there was no such system in the Church till many centuries after the times of the Apostles.

28. *But the Apostle St. James says, " Confess your faults one to another;" why should we confess particularly to a minister ?*
On principles of common sense : for, first of all, a minister of Christ being one whose business is the saving and oversight of souls, is most likely to guide us aright ; and, secondly, the ministers of Christ are the commissioned ministers of reconciliation, who have the power of absolution committed to them. On both these grounds they are the natural recipients of such confessions as the Church encourages.

[Let those who object to all confession to a priest, as Romish, consider the words of Bishop Latimer, who, of all men, cannot be taxed with leanings Romeward. Speaking of confession, he says, " But to speak of right and true confession, I would to God it were kept in England ; for it is a good thing. And those which find themselves grieved in conscience might go to a learned man, and there fetch of him comfort of the word of God, and so to come to a quiet conscience : which is better and more to be regarded than all the riches of the world ; and surely it grieveth me much that such confessions are not kept in England." (Sermon xl. p. 180. 'Remains :' Parker Society.)

Again, Bishop Ridley writes : " Confession unto the minister, which is able to instruct, correct and inform the weak, wounded, and ignorant conscience, indeed I ever thought might do much good in Christ's congregation, and so I assure you I think even at this day." (From a letter to one West. 'Works :' Parker Society, p. 338.) Again, Arbp. Usher : " Be it therefore known unto him, that no kind of confession, either public or private, is disallowed by us that is in any way requisite for the due execution of that ancient power of the keys which Christ bestowed on the Church." (From 'Answer to a Jesuit.' Cambridge reprint, p. 75.)]

29. *Are there any outward means for making over to the penitent sinner, after Baptism, the merits of Christ's death ?*
There are two : Absolution and Holy Communion.

30. *When does our Lord give authority to absolve ?*
In the words, " Whose soever sins ye remit, they are remitted unto them ; and whose soever sins ye retain,

they are retained." (John xx. 23.) And again: "Whatsoever ye shall bind on earth, shall be bound in heaven; and whatsoever ye shall loose on earth, shall be loosed in heaven." (Matt. xviii. 18. Also xvi. 19.) (45–49)

31. *Do we find any minister exercising this power?*
Yes; St. Paul exercises both binding and loosing in the case of a great sinner in the Corinthian Church. He binds, *i. e.*, excommunicates him; or, what is more, lays it on the Corinthian Church to do so, in 1 Cor. v. 4, 5; and he speaks of having loosed, or absolved him, in 2 Cor. ii. 10.

32. *Can any one forgive sins but God only?*
No: God only can forgive sins; but as He is a Sovereign, He can make over His remission to the sinner in any way He chooses. (50)

33. *Can any minister remit the sins of an impenitent man?*
No: God the Father Himself, consistently with His own declaration, will not do so. (50–52)

34. *When our Lord absolved the man sick of the palsy from his sins, did He do it as God or as man?*
As man; for He says expressly that He did it as the Son of Man upon earth; *i. e.*, with power which He had received from God. (Mark ii. 5-10.) (55–62)

35. *Did any persons cavil at the exercise of this power on the part of our Lord?*
Yes; the Pharisees did: they assumed to have more regard for the honour of God than Christ Himself had. They asked, "Who can forgive sins, but God only?" (55–66)

36. *What does this teach us?*
That it is no sign of a spiritual mind to object to the powers which Christ has lodged in His Church for the consolation of sinners. (55–69)

37. *How is the exercise of this power, which Christ has lodged in His Church, claimed in the Prayer Book?*
In three forms of absolution :—
   1. In the daily Service.
   2. In the Communion Service.
   3. In the Service for the Visitation of the Sick. (68, 69)

38. *Repeat this latter form.*
"Our Lord Jesus Christ, who hath left power to His Church to absolve all sinners who truly repent and believe in Him, of His great mercy forgive thee thine offences: and by His authority committed to me I absolve thee

from all thy sins, in the name of the Father, and of the Son, and of the Holy Ghost."

39. *What is recognized in this form?*
    1. That our Lord Jesus Christ hath left a power of absolution in His Church.
    2. That this power is for the benefit of those who truly repent.
    3. That the ratification of any exercise of this power is reserved to Himself.
    4. That it is exercised by His authority, and in the Name of the Holy Trinity.

40. *What do we by the use of such a formula?*
    We honour the word and promises of Christ Himself, and confess our belief in their ever-abiding application.

41. *In what other Sacrament is forgiveness assured to the baptized if they truly repent and believe?*
    In the Holy Eucharist; for the partaking of the bread and cup is, in a heavenly and spiritual way, the partaking of the Body broken and Blood shed for the remission of sins. (70, 71)
    This function of the Eucharist is very distinctly recognized in the earliest Liturgies. In the Clementine: "That all who partake of it may be confirmed in godliness, may receive remission of their sins, may be delivered," &c. In St. James': "That they may be, to those who partake of them, for remission of sins, and for eternal life." In St. Mark's: "That they may be to all of us who participate in them, for faith, for sobriety . . . for the remission of sins." In St. Chrysostom's: "So that they may be to them who participate, for purification of soul, forgiveness of sins," &c.

42. *But could not God extend forgiveness to us without the intervention of any outward means?*
    Certainly He could; but though He can dispense with them Himself, He has bound the use of them upon us.

43. *But does God never extend forgiveness except through Church ordinances or sacraments?*
    God forbid that we should say so: but if we are to speak of forgiveness, we must speak of it as it is set forth in Scripture; and in some places of Scripture it is expressly connected with Baptism (Acts ii. 38; xxii. 16; Eph. v. 26), and also with the exercise of Absolution by the ministers of the Church. (Matt. xvi. 19; xviii. 18;

John xx. 23; 1 Cor. v. 3-5; 2 Cor. ii. 10; James v. 14, 15.)

44. *What is the forgiveness of sins as to its extent?*
It is the fullest possible, for it comprehends the remission of guilt, and the complete restoration of the soul to the favour of God. (Parable of Prodigal Son, Luke xv. 11–32; especially verses 22, 23.) (72–75)

45. *Is the exercise of forgiveness on God's part unconditional?*
It is perfectly unconditional, so far as merit is concerned. We neither have done nor can do anything to deserve it.

46. *But has Christ laid down any conditions, in addition to repentance and faith, which we must fulfil before we can receive forgiveness?*
Yes; we must forgive those who have offended or injured us. Christ says, "If ye forgive men their trespasses, your heavenly Father will also forgive you; but if ye forgive not men their trespasses, neither will your heavenly Father forgive your trespasses." (Matt. vi. 14.) (78-81)

47. *Does our Lord ever tell us that the sentence of forgiveness may be reversed?*
Yes; in the Parable of "The Unmerciful Servant."
"Shouldest thou not have had compassion on thy fellow-servant, even as I had pity on thee? And his lord was wroth, and delivered him to the tormentors, till he should pay all that was due to him. So likewise shall my heavenly Father do also unto you, if ye from your hearts forgive not every one his brethren their trespasses." (Matt. xviii. 33–35.)

48. *But do not you think that to mention these conditions, or needful states of mind, is to fetter the freeness of the offer of forgiveness?*
No matter whether it seems to do so or not, we must obey God rather than men, and say on this matter what Christ our Redeemer and Judge has said. (78–81)

SHORTER CATECHISM.

1. *What great privilege belongs to the Catholic Church?*
The forgiveness of sins.
2. *What is sin?* Disobedience to God.
3. *What does St. John call it?* The transgression of the law (1 John iii. 4).

4. *What law is this?*
   Any command or precept which God has given to us to observe and do.
5. *What does St. John include under sin?*
   All unrighteousness (1 John v. 17).
6. *Mention by name some sins.*
   Idolatry, blasphemy, disobedience to parents, lying, murder, theft.
7. *But these are outward acts; mention any sin committed in the heart.*
   Malice, envy, evil thoughts, covetousness, or evil desires, and, above all, unbelief.
8. *Is all sin displeasing to God?*
   Yes: St. Paul says, "The wrath of God is revealed from Heaven against all ungodliness and unrighteousness of men, who hold the truth in unrighteousness" (Rom. i. 18).
9. *Are some sins more displeasing to God than others?*
   Yes: some sins are called in the Bible deadly sins, or sins unto death.
10. *Where in Scripture are some of these mentioned?*
    In Colos. iii. 5, 6.
11. *Does St. John make this distinction?*
    Yes: He speaks of a sin unto death, and of men who sin not unto death (1 John v. 16, 17).
12. *Can we sin in any way and not displease God?*
    No: he that offends against God's law in one point is guilty of all (James ii. 10).
13. *What is the very first declaration of forgiveness under the Gospel?*
    "Repent and be baptized every one of you in the name of Jesus Christ for the remission of sins" (Acts ii. 38).
14. *What does this show?*
    That in order to have forgiveness we must be brought into the body of Christ.
15. *What is the body of Christ?* The Church of Christ.
16. *When were you brought into the Church or body of Christ?*
    In Baptism, when I was an infant.
17. *But had you any sin in you?*
    Yes: I had a sinful nature; I was born in sin.
18. *What is this sin called?* Original sin.
19. *What was the effect of your Baptism?*
    The guilt of my birth sin was cleansed, and I was made a child of grace.
20. *Have you committed sin since your Baptism?*
    Yes: in many things we offend all (James iii. 2).
21. *What should you do when you have in any way offended God?*
    I should seek forgiveness from Him.

22. *Is He ready to forgive?*
   Yes: David says, Thou, Lord, art good and ready to forgive (Ps. lxxxvi. 5).
23. *For whose sake will God forgive you?*
   For the sake of Jesus Christ.
24. *How can God forgive sins for His sake?*
   Because Jesus Christ made upon the cross an atonement for all our sins.
25. *Mention this in the words of Scripture.*
   He is the propitiation for our sins, and not for ours only, but for the sins of the whole world (1 John ii. 2).
26. *Mention it in other words.*
   Christ was once offered to bear the sins of many (Heb. ix. 28).
27. *Mention it in other words.*
   In whom we have redemption through His Blood, the forgiveness of sins (Eph. i. 7).
28. *How then was it that St. Peter said, Repent and be baptized in the name of Jesus Christ for the remission of sins?*
   It could only be because God has ordained certain outward means in the use of which He makes over to us the forgiveness or reconciliation which Christ has obtained for us.
29. *What must we do before we can expect forgiveness from God?*
   We must repent.
30. *How must we show our repentance?*
   By confessing our sins to God.
31. *What else must we do?*
   We must believe that Jesus Christ, the Son of God, bore all our sins in His own body on the tree.
32. *Is there any difficulty in believing this?*
   Not if we believe in the Scriptures at all.
33. *Why?* Because it is so often asserted in the Scriptures.
34. *But is it not often said that men have a great difficulty in submitting to receive forgiveness and salvation through Christ?*
   There is no difficulty about it if we believe in the Incarnation.
35. *Explain this.*
   If God's only begotten Son shed His Blood for us, that Blood cannot but save us from sin.
36. *But will not the natural pride of our hearts prevent us from accepting forgiveness through the Blood of Christ?*
   Not if we believe that He is both God and man.
37. *What have we then first to believe in respecting Jesus?*
   That He is God manifest in the flesh.
38. *If we believe this, can we have the least difficulty about receiving forgiveness as a gift?*
   Of course not, if, that is, we really desire deliverance from sin.

THE FORGIVENESS OF SINS.

39. *Does God forgive us freely?*
    Yes; most freely. I forgave thee all that debt because thou desiredst me (Matt. xviii. 32).
40. *Have we then to do any good work in order to purchase forgiveness?*
    No: by grace we are saved through faith, and that not of ourselves, it is the gift of God (Eph. ii. 8).
41. *Does God then forgive our sins without looking into the state of our heart?*
    No: we must earnestly desire to be free from the guilt and power of sin (Ps. lxvi. 18).
42. *What besides this must we have?*
    We must receive in submissive faith all that God reveals to us respecting His Son.
43. *Is there any merit in this?*
    No: but unless we have this state of heart, we are not in a condition to be forgiven.
44. *Has God left us in His Church any assurances of His forgiveness?*
    Yes: Absolution and the Sacraments.
45. *Did Christ ever give His ministers power to absolve?*
    Yes: on three occasions.
46. *Where are these recorded?*
    In Matt. xvi. 19; in Matt. xviii. 18; and in John xx. 23.
47. *Repeat the last.*
    "Whose soever sins ye remit, they are remitted unto them; and whose soever sins ye retain, they are retained."
48. *To whom were these wonderful words spoken?* To the Apostles.
49. *To the Apostles alone?*
    No: to the Apostles as the representatives of all future ministers or priests of the Church.
50. *Can these ministers or priests absolve by their own power?*
    No: no one has ever imagined that they could.
51. *Can they absolve impenitent or unbelieving persons?*
    No: God Himself has engaged not to do so.
52. *Why do they absolve or remit sins?*
    Because God has commissioned them so to do.
53. *If they put from them all power to absolve in any circumstance, what would they do?*
    They would set aside a part of their Master's commission.
54. *How do we honour Christ's words?*
    By believing that they will continue in force till He comes again (Matt. xxviii. 20).
55. *Did Christ ever claim to absolve?* Yes.
56. *Did He claim this power as God or as man?* As man.
57. *On whose authority then did He act?* On that of His Father.
58. *Did any persons object to this absolving power which He claimed?*
    Yes: the Pharisees.

59. *On what grounds?*
   On the ground that God only can forgive sin.
60. *But was not this a right principle?*
   Yes: but they used it wrongly.
61. *How?*
   They would take away all power on God's part to act through others.
62. *Does God act through our fellow-men?*
   Yes: in everything in religion.
63. *Can you give an instance?*
   Yes: He converts us through the preaching of our fellow-men.
64. *Can you give another?*
   Yes: He baptizes us by the hands of our fellow-men.
65. *Can you give another?*
   Yes: He feeds us in the Holy Communion with the True Bread by the hands of our fellow-men.
66. *How can men presume to do such things as these?*
   Because God has commissioned them so to do.
67. *Is absolution a thing resembling the administration of Baptism or the Holy Communion?*
   Yes: in this, that in all three God acts through His ministers.
68. *Do the ministers of the Church claim these powers?*
   Yes: they would not be ministers of the Church if they willingly set aside any ordinance which God has appointed for the salvation or consolation of sinners.
69. *Which is the greater presumption, to claim to absolve sinners in God's name, or to refuse to do so?*
   To refuse; because in such a case we should presume to pronounce some of the most remarkable words of Christ unmeaning and unnecessary.
70. *Have we any assurance of forgiveness in the Lord's Supper?* Yes.
71. *How is this?*
   Because in it we receive in a heavenly and spiritual way the "blood of the New Covenant shed for many for the remission of sins" (Matt. xxvi. 28).
72. *Are all sins forgiven?* Yes: all sins that can be repented of.
73. *Is it safe then to go on offending God?* No.
74. *Why?*
   Because sin persisted in hardens the heart, so as to make repentance, humanly speaking, impossible.
75. *Why do you say humanly speaking?*
   Because nothing is out of the power of Almighty grace.
76. *What will those do whose sins are forgiven?*
   They will love God much (Luke vii. 47).
77. *How will they show their love?*
   By keeping Christ's commandments (John xiv. 15, 23, 24).

78. *Through whose merits do we receive forgiveness?*
 Through the sole merits of Christ.
79. *Has our Lord limited forgiveness to any persons?*
 Yes : in very express terms.
80. *To whom has He limited the receiving of forgiveness?*
 To those who forgive others.
81. *Where has He expressed this limitation?*
 In four places, at least: Matt. vi. 14, 15; xviii. 35; Mark xi. 26; Luke vi. 37.

SECTION XXX.—THE RESURRECTION OF THE BODY.

1. *What is the next article of your Creed?*
   The Resurrection of the Body. (1–3)
2. *What do you mean by the Resurrection of the Body?*
   I mean the reunion of the spirit with the same body from which it was separated in death. (4, 5)
3. *Is it needful to believe that we shall be raised up in the same body?*
   Yes; if our Resurrection is to be in accordance with the type and pattern of our blessed Lord's Resurrection, Who was raised in the same Body in which He had been crucified. (6–7)
4. *Is there any other reason why the same body should be raised?*
   Yes; in order that we may receive in the body hereafter, according to the deeds which we have done in the body here.
5. *Is it not a hard thing to believe that we shall rise again in these same bodies?*
   Not if we believe in the Omniscience and Almighty Power of God, who has His eye upon every particle of the substance of our bodies, and can bring all together again at any moment. (8)
6. *Has God given to us anything in nature which may help us to believe in the Resurrection of the Body?*
   Yes; there is a sort of Resurrection every year, from the death or torpor of winter to the life and beauty of spring and summer; and the seed sown in the ground, whose body decays whilst its germ shoots forth into life, is a type of our Resurrection.
7. *Can these or any other illustrations explain the way in which God will bring about the Resurrection of the body?*
   No; it will take place by an act of the same miraculous power by which our Lord raised Himself from the dead. (Rom. viii. 11.)
8. *What will our bodies be at the Resurrection?*

Spiritual bodies, raised up after the likeness of Christ's risen Body, which though as a Body it could be seen and handled, yet could assume at will the properties of a spirit. (26–31)

9. *Mention some of these properties.*
It passed through the closed doors. It vanished and reappeared as we might suppose a spirit would do. It was only recognised when its Owner willed. It ascended up through the air into heaven. (Luke xxiv. 31, 39, 51; John xx. 20.) (30, 31)

10. *How does St. Paul speak of the contrast between the body which now is, and that which shall be?*
" It is sown in corruption, it is raised in incorruption; it is sown in dishonour, it is raised in glory; it is sown in weakness, it is raised in power; it is sown a natural body, it is raised a spiritual body." (1 Cor. xv. 42, 43.) (27–35)

11. *What does our Lord say respecting the Resurrection state?*
" They which shall be accounted worthy to obtain that world, and the resurrection from the dead, neither marry, nor are given in marriage; neither can they die any more; for they are equal unto the angels" (or as the angels, Matt. xxii. 30). (Luke xx. 35, 36.)

12. *Is the Resurrection of the Body an essential part of the Gospel?*
Yes; it is intimately connected with the belief in Christ Himself. In one place (Acts iv. 2) we read, The Apostles "preached through Jesus the Resurrection from the dead." In another (Acts xvii. 18), St. Paul preached unto the Athenians, "Jesus and the Resurrection." Again, St. Paul says, "If there be no Resurrection of the dead, then is Christ not risen; and if Christ be not risen, then is our preaching vain." (1 Cor. xv. 13.) (9–21)

13. *But does it not seem sufficient to believe in the Resurrection of the soul to spiritual life?*
No; St. Paul said of two men who said that the Resurrection was past already—that is, who believed only in the resurrection of the soul—that they overthrew the faith. (2 Tim. ii. 18.)

14. *Did the heathen believe in the Resurrection?*
No; some of them believed in the immortality of the soul; but none, that we are aware of, in the Resurrection of the body.

15. *Did the Jews believe in the Resurrection of the Body?*
   Yes; in Christ's time all except the Sadducees believed in it. Martha, we read, said to our Lord, "I know that he (Lazarus) shall rise again in the Resurrection at the Last Day." (John xi. 24.) (16–20)

16. *Was the Resurrection revealed in the Old Testament?*
   Yes; Daniel writes, "Many of them that sleep in the dust shall awake." (xii. 2.) Again, Job says, "I know that my Redeemer liveth .. though after my skin worms destroy this body, yet in my flesh shall I see God." (Job xix. 26.)
   Also in the vision of dry bones in Ezekiel, the bones are clothed again with flesh. (xxxvii. 8.) (16–20)

17. *How many Resurrections seem to be revealed in Scripture?*
   Two. The first, a Resurrection of the true saints: the second, of all men. (36–38)

18. *What is said of those who will attain to the first?*
   "Blessed and holy is he that hath part in the first resurrection." (Rev. xx. 6.)

19. *Are there any other allusions to this?*
   Yes; St. Paul speaks of the dead in Christ rising first (1 Thess. iv. 16); and he also uses the words, "If by any means I might attain to the Resurrection from the dead" (ἐξανάστασιν τῶν νεκρῶν). (Phil. iii. 11.)

20. *He seems then to consider the attaining to this Resurrection a matter of difficulty?*
   Yes; undoubtedly; and so also does our Lord when He uses such words as, "They that shall be accounted worthy to obtain ... the resurrection from the dead." (Luke xx. 35.) (35–38)

21. *What Sacrament is a pledge to us of our Resurrection?*
   Baptism: for it is written, "If we have been planted together (or with Him; evidently referring, as the context shows, to Holy Baptism), in the likeness of His death, we shall be also in the likeness of His Resurrection." (Rom. vi. 4, 5, 6.) (39–42)

22. *Upon what does our Blessed Lord make our Resurrection through Him to depend?*
   Upon our eating His Flesh, and drinking His Blood; for He says, "Whoso eateth my flesh and drinketh my blood hath eternal life, and I will raise him up at the last day." (John vi. 54.) (43, 44)

23. *But will not all men, whether they have been united to Christ or not, be raised again?*
Yes; but those in Christ will be raised through grace, because they have Him in them Who is Himself the Resurrection. "I am the Resurrection." (John xi. 25.) Also, "Every man (will be raised) in his own order; Christ the firstfruits; afterwards they that are Christ's at His coming." (1 Cor. xv. 23.) Also Rom. viii. 11: "He that raised Christ from the dead shall also quicken your mortal bodies by His Spirit that dwelleth in you."

24. *How then will the wicked be raised?*
By the power of God only, in order that they may receive the just recompence of their deeds.

25. *If the bodies of Christians will thus be raised, how should we regard them?*
As holy; and so keep them from all defilement of sin, and bury them after death with all honour and solemnity in ground set apart for such a purpose. (45)

26. *What is our duty in the prospect of such a Resurrection?*
To mortify our evil lusts.
"When Christ, who is our life, shall appear, then shall ye also appear with Him in glory. *Mortify therefore* your members which are upon the earth; fornication, uncleanness, inordinate affection, evil concupiscence, and covetousness, which is idolatry." (Col. iii. 4, 5.)

27. *What is our prayer in prospect of such a Resurrection?*
"We meekly beseech Thee, O Father, to raise us from the death of sin unto the life of righteousness, that when we shall depart this life we may rest in Him,[as our hope is this our brother doth],and that at the general Resurrection in the last day we may be found acceptable in Thy sight." (Burial Service.)

SHORTER CATECHISM.

1. *What, after the forgiveness of sins, do we profess to believe in?*
   The Resurrection of the Body.
2. *What do you mean by Resurrection?* Rising again.
3. *How is the word mostly used?*
   As meaning a rising again from the dead.
4. *What rises again?* The body.
5. *What body?* The same body which died
6. *Must it be the same body?* Yes.
7. *Why?*

Because Christ's Resurrection is the pattern of ours, and He rose again in the same body.

8. *How can the same body be raised again?*
By the Almighty power of God.

9. *Has God given to us any assurance that He will exert this power?*
Yes: He tells us by the word of His own Son that all that are in the graves shall hear His voice, and shall come forth (John v. 28, 29).

10. *Where besides this have we any assurance in our Lord's own words?*
When He was about to raise Lazarus, He said, "I am the Resurrection, and the Life" (John xi. 25).

11. *What other assurances have we?*
The preaching of all the Apostles, for they preached through Jesus the Resurrection from the dead (Acts iv. 2).

12. *Mention another instance.*
St. Paul at Athens preached Jesus and the Resurrection (Acts xvii. 18).

13. *Is the Resurrection a part of the Gospel?*
Yes: so necessary a part of it that St. Paul says, "If the dead rise not, then is not Christ raised" (1 Cor. xv. 16).

14. *In what remarkable passage of Scripture is the Resurrection from the dead most fully explained?*   1 Cor. xv.

15. *Where is the greater part of this chapter read?*
In the Burial Service of the Church.

16. *What Old Testament saint believed in the Resurrection?*
Abraham (Heb. xi. 19).

17. *What other saint of old expressed His belief in it?*
Job (xix. 25, 26, 27).

18. *Can you mention another instance of an Old Testament saint believing in it?*
Yes; David. "Thou wilt not leave my soul in hell, neither wilt Thou suffer Thine Holy One to see corruption" (Ps. xvi. 10; also xlix. 15).

19. *What remarkable vision of the Resurrection have we in an Old Testament Prophet?*
The vision of dry bones clothed with flesh (Ezekiel xxxvii.).

20. *Does Isaiah seem to confess it?*
Yes: "Thy dead men shall live, together with my dead body shall they arise" (Isaiah xxvi. 19).

21. *What does St. Paul say respecting the importance of this doctrine?*
That it is one of the first principles of the doctrine of Christ (Heb. vi. 2).

22. *But must not our souls be raised to life?*
Yes: if they are dead or asleep in sin (Eph. v. 14).

23. *Where do we pray for this?*

THE RESURRECTION OF THE BODY. 167

When we pray in the Burial Service, "We meekly beseech Thee, O Father, to raise us from the death of sin unto the life of righteousness."

24. *Is it sufficient to believe in this?*
No: if we are true believers we must believe in the Resurrection of the Body.

25. *Why?* Because God and Christ so very expressly assert it.

26. *Will our risen bodies be the same as our present bodies?*
They will be the same, because each man's particular body will be raised.

27. *Will they be raised up in the same condition?*
No: they will be raised up spiritual bodies.

28. *What does this mean?*
Bodies that are endowed with the powers of spirits.

29. *Do we understand how a body can be at once bodily and spiritual?*
No: but we take God at His word when He says by St. Paul, "There is a natural body and there is a spiritual body" (1 Cor. xv. 44).

30. *What do we suppose one of the properties of a spirit to be?*
That it can move through all obstacles.

31. *But can the Resurrection body do this?*
Our Lord's body could, and we know that "He shall change our vile body, that it may be fashioned like unto His glorious body" (Phil. iii. 21).

32. *What other properties will our future bodies have?*
They will be incorruptible and immortal (1 Cor. xv. 53).

33. *What other property will they have?*
They will be glorious (1 Cor. xv. 43; Phil. iii. 21).

34. *What other property?*
Power. They will be raised in power.

35. *To what does our Lord liken those who will attain to a blessed Resurrection?*
They will be like unto the angels (Matt. xxii. 30; Luke xx. 35, 36).

36. *Will all men rise at the same time?*
Scripture tells us that the dead in Christ shall rise first.

37. *What is this called?* The First Resurrection (Rev. xx. 6).

38. *Will a part in this be the privilege of all, or only of some?*
Apparently only of some— of those who know Christ, and the power of His Resurrection, and the fellowship of His sufferings (Phil. iii. 10)].

39. *Is there any connection between Baptism and our Resurrection?*
Yes: St. Paul twice asserts that we are buried and raised again with Christ in Holy Baptism (Rom. vi. 1-4; Col. ii. 12).

40. *But is this a pledge of our Resurrection?*
Yes: St. Paul seems to assert it when He says, "If we have

been planted together in the likeness of His death, we shall be also in the likeness of His Resurrection" (Rom. vi. 5).

41. *To whom is Baptism a pledge of this?*
   To those only in whom Baptism has its proper permanent effect.

42. *What is that?* Walking in newness of life.

43. *Is there any connection between the faithful receiving of the Lord's Supper and our Resurrection?*
   Yes: our Lord says, "He that eateth my flesh and drinketh my blood, hath everlasting life, and I will raise him up at the last day" (John vi. 54).

44. *Is there any recognition of this in our Communion Office?*
   Yes: when the minister says to each communicant, "The body of our Lord Jesus Christ, which was given for thee, preserve thy body .... unto everlasting life."

45. *If our bodies are thus to rise again, how should we regard them?*
   As holy, and so we should keep them from all sinful defilement.

46. *How should we regard the departure of true Christians?*
   As only a brief separation; for we read, "if we believe that Jesus died and rose again, even so them also which sleep in Jesus will God bring with Him" (1 Thess. iv. 13, 14).

47. *How should we regard death?*
   As the gate of our joyful resurrection (Collect for Easter Eve)

SECTION XXXI.—THE LIFE EVERLASTING.

1. *What is the last article in the Creed?*
   I believe in . . . the Life Everlasting. (1–5)
2. *How does our Saviour describe Life Eternal?*
   "This is life eternal, that they may know Thee the only true God, and Jesus Christ, whom Thou hast sent." (John xvii. 3.) (21–23)
3. *Is this the Life Eternal, or everlasting, in which we profess our belief?*
   It is the beginning or foundation of it: it is its first stage. (21–23)
4. *In what stage of it do we particularly profess our belief?*
   In that on which we shall enter after the Resurrection and the Judgment. (5–8)
5. *How is the happiness of this state described?*
   As being inconceivably great; for it will be sharing in the joy of Christ Himself: "Enter thou into the joy of thy Lord." (Matt. xxv. 21.) Also, "Eye hath not seen, nor ear heard," &c. (1 Cor. ii. 9.) Also Rev. vii. 16, 17: "They shall hunger no more," &c. (10, 11)
6. *What will be the crowning blessedness of the Saints?*
   That they shall see God.
   "Blessed are the pure in heart, for they shall see God." (Matt. v. 8.)
   "When He shall appear we shall be like Him, for we shall see Him as He is." (1 John iii. 2.)
   It is also said—
   "They shall see His face." (Rev. xxii. 4.)
7. *What is this blessedness called by Divines?*
   The Beatific Vision.
8. *What is Eternal Life called?*
   The gift of God (Rom. vi. 23), because none deserve it; but all who receive it, receive it by an act of grace in and through Jesus Christ, and by His Spirit. (6–9)
9. *But is this gift given irrespectively of our dispositions and conduct?*
   No: our Blessed Lord says, "My sheep hear my voice, and I know them, and they follow me: and I give unto

them eternal life." (John x. 27.)   He gives eternal life to those who hear, and follow Him.

10. *What will be the doom of the wicked?*
Our most merciful Lord speaks of it as everlasting punishment (Matt. xxv. 46); and as the gnawings of a never-dying worm. (Mark ix. 44.)   (12, 13)

11. *Who will experience this dreadful doom?*
The finally impenitent. They who have wilfully, knowingly, and deliberately rejected the calls of God. (14, 15)

12. *Will there be degrees in the blessedness of the righteous?*
Yes; our Lord says that in His Father's house there are many mansions (John xiv. 2); and St. Paul compares future glory to "one star differing from another star in glory." (1 Cor. xv. 41.) Also Luke xix. 17, 19: Ten cities; five cities. (16, 17)

13. *Will there be degrees in future punishment?*
Yes; some will be beaten with many, some with few stripes. (Luke xii. 47, 48.)

14. *If we really believe in the Life Everlasting, what shall we do?*
We shall lay hold upon the hope set before us in Jesus Christ. (Heb. vi. 18.)
We shall abide in Him. (1 John ii. 28.)
We shall eat His Flesh and drink His Blood, knowing that he who doeth this hath eternal life. (John vi. 54.)
We shall give all diligence to make our calling and election sure ... for so an entrance shall be ministered unto us abundantly into the Everlasting Kingdom of our Lord and Saviour Jesus Christ. (2 Peter i. 10, 11.)

SHORTER CATECHISM.

1. *What is the last great truth in which we profess to believe?*
The Life Everlasting.
2. *How is this expressed in the Creed in the Baptismal Service?*
Everlasting life after death.
3. *How in the Nicene Creed?*
I believe in .... the Life of the world to come.
4. *How in the Creed of St. Athanasius?*
They that have done good shall go into life everlasting, and they that have done evil into everlasting fire.
5. *Is this life everlasting the same as the immortality of the soul?*

No : it is the joint life of soul and body after the day of the Resurrection.
6. *Whose gift is this everlasting life?*
It is the gift of God and of Christ.
7. *Where is God said to give it?*
The gift of God is eternal Life through Jesus Christ our Lord (Rom. vi. 23).
8. *To whom does Christ give it?*
To His sheep who hear His voice, and whom He knows, and who follow Him (John x. 27).
9. *To whom does St. Paul say that God will grant eternal life?*
To them who by patient continuance in well doing. seek for glory, honour, and immortality (Rom. ii. 7).
10. *Where is the happiness of this life described?* (Rev. xxi., xxii.).
11. *Can it be understood by us?*
St. Paul says, "Eye hath not seen, nor ear heard, neither have entered into the heart of man, the things which God hath prepared for them that love Him" (1 Cor. ii. 9).
12. *Will all at last enjoy this life?*
No : our Lord speaks of those who "shall go away into everlasting punishment" (Matt. xxv. 46).
13. *Where else is this terrible doom declared?*
"The fearful, and the unbelieving, and the abominable, and murderers, and whoremongers, and sorcerers, and idolaters, and all liars, shall have their part in the lake which burneth with fire and brimstone : which is the second death" (Rev. xxi. 8).
14. *But are not all sins now forgiven?*
Yes, to those who repent and believe the Gospel.
15. *Who then are these who will be thus destroyed?*
Those who have deliberately continued in sin and refused the remedy set forth in the Gospel.
16. *Will all the righteous have the same reward?*
No : it is expressly said that every man shall receive his own reward according to his own labour (1 Cor. iii. 8).
17. *What does St. John exhort with respect to this?*
"Look to yourselves, that we lose not those things which we have wrought, but that we receive a full reward" (2 John 8).
18. *What does our Lord say respecting those that inherit life?*
"He that heareth My word, and believeth on Him that sent Me, hath everlasting life" (John v. 24).
19. *What does our Lord mean by this hearing of His word?*
He means, of course, humbly believing, and abiding in, His word.
20. *How do you know this?*
Because He says afterwards, "If a man *keep* my saying, he shall never see death" (John viii. 51).

21. *What is eternal life?*
"This is life eternal, that they may know Thee, the only true God, and Jesus Christ whom Thou hast sent" (John xvii. 3).
22. *Where is eternal life?*
"Your life is hid with Christ in God" (Col. iii. 3).
23. *Who is eternal Life?*
"I am the Resurrection and the Life" (John xi. 25). "I am the Way, the Truth, and the Life" (John xiv. 6). "Christ, who is our Life" (Col. iii. 4).

SECTION XXXII.—SCRIPTURE PROOF OF THE DOCTRINE OF THE TRINITY.

1. WHAT DOST THOU CHIEFLY LEARN IN THESE ARTICLES OF THY BELIEF?
 FIRST, I LEARN TO BELIEVE IN GOD THE FATHER, WHO HATH MADE ME, AND ALL THE WORLD.
 SECONDLY, IN GOD THE SON, WHO HATH REDEEMED ME AND ALL MANKIND.
 THIRDLY, IN GOD THE HOLY GHOST, WHO SANCTIFIETH ME AND ALL THE ELECT PEOPLE OF GOD.
2. *Do you believe in three Gods?*
 No; I believe that "there is but One living and true God;" but I believe also that, " in unity of this Godhead, there be Three Persons, of one substance, power and eternity: the Father, the Son, and the Holy Ghost."
3. *How is it that you believe that there are three Persons in the one Godhead?*
 Because in the same Scriptures which reveal to us that there is but One God, all that can be said of the one true God is said of Three Persons, and not of One only.
4. *How, in the Scriptures, does God distinguish Himself from all His creatures?*
 In four ways:
 (1) He calls Himself by certain names.
 (2) He claims certain attributes as belonging to Himself alone.
 (3) He declares that He alone can do certain works.
 (4) And he demands from His creatures certain worship to be given to Him alone.
5. *By what names does God call himself?*
 By the names of Lord and God especially, and also by such names as Lord of Hosts, Most High, Holy One of Israel, King of Israel.
 "I am the Lord thy God, who brought thee out of the land of Egypt." (Exod. xx. 2.)
 " The Most High dwelleth not in temples made with hands." (Acts vii. 48.)
 " The Lord of Hosts is with us." (Ps. xlvi. 11.)
 " I am the Lord thy God, the Holy One of Israel." (Isaiah xliii. 3.)
 " Thus saith the Lord, the King of Israel." (Isaiah xliv. 6.)

6. *Are these names given to only One Divine Person?*
No; they are all given to Him Who is called the Only Begotten Son, or Word of God.

"In the beginning was the Word, and the Word was with God, and the Word was God." (John i. 1.)
"Thomas answered and said unto Him (Jesus), my Lord and my God." (John xx. 28.)
"Christ came, who is over all, God blessed for ever." (Rom. ix. 5.)
"Our great God and Saviour (or the great God and Saviour of us) Jesus Christ." (Titus ii. 13.)
"Many of the children of Israel shall He turn to the Lord their God, and He shall go before Him (the Lord God) in the spirit and power of Elias." (Luke i. 17.)

[This is said of Christ's forerunner, who went before Christ, not before the Father] (5-13)

7. *Are such terms as Lord of Hosts, the Highest, the King of Israel, ascribed to our Lord Jesus Christ?*
If we compare the Old Testament with the New, we find that they are.

Isaiah vi. 5 : "Mine eyes have seen the King, the Lord of Hosts," compared with John xii. 40, 41, shows that the prophet saw the glory of the eternal Son.

In Isaiah xliv. 6, God is called the King of Israel ; and in John i. 49, we find that Christ permits this title of God to be given to Himself.

John the Baptist is called the Prophet of the Highest, because he goes "before the face of the Lord to prepare His way ;" but he prepared the way of the Lord Jesus. (Luke i. 76, compared with John iii. 28.)

8. *Do the Jewish Prophets ascribe these Divine names to the Messiah?*
Yes : David speaks of God saying to the Messiah, "Thy throne, O God, is for ever and ever." (Ps. xlv. 6.) Isaiah prophesies of the birth of a Child Who should be called "The mighty God." (Isa. ix. 6.) Jeremiah, of a King reigning upon the earth Who should be called "The Lord our Righteousness." (Jer. xxiii. 6.)

9. *Can you show that the incommunicable attributes of the One True God are ascribed to the Son?*
Yes ; the attribute of Eternity is ascribed to the Son where it is said that, "He was in the beginning with God" (John i. 2) ; and where it is said of Him that His "goings forth have been from old, of everlasting" (Mic. v. 2). He claims it for himself when He says, "Before Abraham was, I am" (John viii. 58) ; and when He says,

"I am Alpha and Omega, the beginning and the end, the first and the last" (Rev. xxii. 13). (14-18)

10. *Does this latter expression imply eternal existence?*
Yes; God claims it for Himself when He says, "Thus saith the Lord the King of Israel, and His Redeemer the Lord of Hosts; I am the first, and I am the last." (Is. xliv. 6.)

11. *What other attribute of Godhead does Christ claim?*
Omniscience; for He claims to know the Father, as the Father knows Him. (Matt. xi. 27; also John x. 15.) He claims to do what only the omniscient God can do, to search the hearts (Rev. ii. 23, compared with Jer. xi. 20; xvii. 10); and He suffers His servant to address Him as knowing all things. (John xxi. 17; also Matt. ix. 4; xii. 25, compared with Acts xv. 8). (28)

12. *What further attribute of Godhead does Christ claim?*
Omnipresence.
"Where two or three are gathered together in My name, there am I in the midst of them." (Matt. xviii. 20.) He engages to be always with His Apostles and their successors, wheresoever they should plant His Church (Matt. xxviii. 20); and Christians in all parts of the world are addressed as "in" Christ, just as they are "in" God. (1 Thess. i. 1; 2 Thess. i. 1.) (19-23)

13. *What further attribute of Deity does Christ claim?*
Omnipotence, or Almighty power. He Himself claims to do all that God does when He says, "Whatsoever things He (the Father) doeth, these also doeth the Son likewise. (John v. 19.) Again, "The Father loveth the Son, and hath given all things into His hand." (John iii. 35.) Again, He engages to do all that is asked in His name. (John xiv. 13.) Again, it is said that by Him all things subsist (Col. i. 17); and that He (Christ) upholds all things by the word of His power (Heb. i. 3). (27)

14. *Is Christ ever said to perform certain works which God claims to Himself as His special works?*
Yes: God claims to Himself the sole power of creating, redeeming, sanctifying, saving the soul, raising the dead, and judging all men; and all these things are said to be the especial works of Christ also.

Thus Creation: "All things were made by Him, and without Him was not anything made that was made." (John i. 2.)

Redemption is throughout the Old Testament ascribed to God ; and in the New Testament the whole is ascribed to our Lord Jesus Christ. (Rev. v. 9 ; Gal. iii. 13.)

Salvation is throughout the New Testament ascribed to Christ and to God, as it were, indiscriminately. The very name of Jesus is given to Him because He saves His people from their sins. (Matt. i. 21.) (In the short Epistle to Titus, the term Saviour is applied to God three times, and to Christ three times.)

Again, God is said to raise the dead (2 Cor. i. 9) ; and Christ is the Resurrection. (John vi. 54. xi. 25.)

God is the Judge of all (Heb. xii. 23), and yet Christ will come to judge the quick and the dead. (29–35)

15. *Is the worship and Divine honour due to the One True God given also to Christ?*

Yes : He himself says that "all men are to honour the Son even as they honour the Father." (John v. 23.) He prays, " Now, O Father, glorify Thou me with Thine own self with the glory which I had with Thee before the world was." (John xvii. 5.) And so we find that " at " or " in " the name of Jesus every knee should bow, of things in heaven, and things on earth, and things under the earth ; and that every tongue should confess that Jesus Christ is Lord. (Phil. ii. 10, 11.) (36–43)

16. *What Divine worship was actually accorded to Him ?*

When God brought in the First-Begotten into the world, He said, " Let all the angels of God worship Him." (Heb. i. 6.) When He was an infant just born, the Magi offered to Him frankincense as God. (Matt. ii. 11.) The children in the temple shouted Hosanna to His praise, and when asked to rebuke them, He significantly replied that if they held their peace the very stones would cry out. (Matt. xxi. 9 ; Luke xix. 40.) And in a vision of the Book of Revelation, Blessing and glory, and honour and power, are ascribed to Him along with the Father, and this by the whole creation. (Rev. v. 13.) (36–43)

17. *What other remarkable acts of worship are accorded to Him?*

We are baptized into His name, as well as into the name of the Father and the Holy Ghost, and so are solemnly dedicated to Him as well as to the Father ; and continually throughout the Epistles grace is invoked conjointly from Him and from His Father. (40, 41)

18. *But have not some said that these places are few, in comparison with those in which worship is directed to the Father?*

Of course they are comparatively few; and for this reason that in Scripture the Son is chiefly set forth as the Mediator between us and God; and so, as a rule, we come to God through Him, and beseech the Father in His name; but at times we must accord to Him (as we do in the Litany) direct worship, or we should not honour Him as we honour the Father.

19. *What further proof can you give of the Godhead of Christ?*

"All things that the Father hath are His." (John xvi. 15.) And so we find that—

The people of God are His people. (Compare 1 Pet. ii. 10, with Matt. i. 21.)

The Church of God is His Church. (Acts xx. 28; 1 Tim. iii. 15.)

The servants of God are His servants. (1 Pet. ii. 16, compared with 2 Pet. i. 1.)

The ambassadors of God are His ambassadors. (Gal. i. 15, compared with 2 Cor. v. 18, 20.)

The angels of God are His angels. (Matt. xiii. 41.)

20. *Do not all these things imply that He is equal in nature to His Father?*

Yes; and that is what is expressly asserted in the Scriptures, where it is said that "being in the form of God, He thought it not robbery (rather, a thing to be tenaciously held to) to be equal with God, but made Himself of no reputation." (Phil. ii. 6.) (43–45)

21. *But is not a son necessarily inferior to his father?*

Never in nature. It is the glory of a father to beget a son with the same nature and perfections as those which he possesses.

22. *Is this natural equality of a son to his father ever alluded to in Scripture with especial reference to our Lord?*

Yes: when Christ said that God was His own Father (ἴδιον), the Jews took up stones to stone Him, because (as the Evangelist implies) by the very fact of His saying that God was His own Father, He made Himself equal with God. (John v. 18.)

23. *But is not a son in some sense subordinate to his father?*

In the family he is; and there is a certain priority in the Father as the Father recognised in Scripture, so that the Father is said to send the Son, and to give the Son, and to glorify the Son with the glory which He had with the Father; but this implies equality of nature.

24. *So far for the Godhead of the Son; but are the same Divine names, attributes, and actions ascribed in Scripture to the Holy Ghost?*

Yes: He is called the Lord in one place of Scripture (2 Cor. iii. 17), and God in many other passages; as where Ananias, in lying to Him, is said not to have lied unto men, but unto God (Acts v. 3, 4); and Christians, because He is dwelling in them, are the temples of God. (1 Cor. iii. 16.) (46, 47)

[See, under Article of the Creed, "I believe in the Holy Ghost," p. 113.]

25. *What attributes of God are ascribed to Him?*

Eternity: He is called the Eternal Spirit. (Heb. ix. 14.)

Omniscience: for He is said to know the things of God, as the human spirit knows the things of a man. (1 Cor. ii. 11.)

Omnipresence: for the Psalmist asks, "Whither shall I go from Thy Spirit?" (Ps. cxxxix. 7.)

Omnipotence: for all the works of Christ are ascribed to His power. (Matt. xii. 28; John xiv. 12.)

[The "greater" works mentioned in the latter passage are those which the Apostles would do because of the coming of the Holy Ghost.] (47-50)

26. *Do we rely upon these as the principal proofs of His Godhead?*

By no means: His essential Godhead, and equality in nature with the Father and the Son, is shown by His place in the economy of Redemption. (51-56)

27. *Explain what you mean by this.*

It was He Who, speaking by the Prophets, prepared the way for the reception of the Redemption of Christ.

It was He Who brought about the Incarnation Itself, for He created in the womb of the Virgin, of her substance, an undefiled human nature, which the Eternal Son assumed, and the Holy Ghost brought about this union. (51-53)

28. *How is this expressed in the Scriptures?*

"The Holy Ghost shall come upon thee, and the power of the Highest shall overshadow thee: therefore also that

DOCTRINE OF THE TRINITY.

Holy Thing which shall be born of thee shall be called the Son of God." (Luke i. 35.) [So that our Lord, as regards His human nature, was the Son of God through His Conception by the Holy Ghost.]

29. *In what further way did the Holy Ghost co-operate in the work of Redemption ?*

At His Baptism our Lord was anointed by the Spirit to be the Messiah or Christ, as He Himself witnesses by quoting as applying to Himself the words of Isaiah, "The Spirit of the Lord is upon me, because He hath anointed me," &c. (Luke iv. 18.) (54)

30. *But could not our Blessed Lord have done all His work by His own unaided power and wisdom ?*

Humanly speaking He could ; but He emptied Himself of His glory, and did His mighty works, and even taught His disciples (Acts i. 2), through the power of that Spirit by Whom we also are enabled to work the works of God.

31. *Did the Holy Spirit co-operate in the final act of Redemption ?*

Yes : " Through the Eternal Spirit (Christ) offered Himself without spot to God " (Heb. ix. 14) ; and by the same Spirit He was raised from the dead. (Rom. i. 4 ; viii. 11.) (55)

32. *How does the Holy Spirit now work ?*

He guides into all truth. He takes of the things of Christ and shows them to the soul (John xvi. 13, 14) ; through Him Christians are born of God (John iii. 5) ; grafted into the body of Christ (1 Cor. xii. 13) ; washed, sanctified, and justified (1 Cor. vi. 11) ; and by His power their bodies will be raised again at the last day. (Rom. viii. 11.)

Everything in the Church—its powers, offices, graces—are all ascribed to Him. (Eph. iv. 1-12.) He gives to one the word of wisdom ; to another the word of knowledge, &c.; and as the conclusion of all it is said, "All these worketh that one and the selfsame Spirit, dividing to every man severally as He will." (1 Cor. xii. 11.)

33. *What, then, is the great proof of the Godhead of the Spirit of God?*

The Godhead of Christ ; for it is impossible for us to believe that He by Whose operation the Eternal Son became Incarnate, and so became as to His human nature the Son of God, that He through Whom the human nature of the Eternal Son was sanctified to work the work of Redemption, that He Who mysteriously co-operated in every stage of that work, and by Whose power it is now applied to those who are saved, is less than God.

34. *What, then, will most help us to realize the Godhead of the Blessed Spirit?*

We shall most fully realize the Godhead of the Holy Spirit when we realize the greatness of each part of the work of Christ.

35. *Show this more particularly.*

The more we realize the stupendous mystery of the Incarnation, the more we shall give glory to the Spirit Who brought it about.

The more we realize the Divine character of the teaching of Christ, the more we shall give glory to that Spirit, without Whom Christ taught nothing.

The more we realize the Divine nature of the work which Christ did, and yet does for us, as Prophet, Priest, and King, the more we shall give glory to that Spirit by Whom He was anointed to bear these offices of love towards us.

The more we realize the power of Christ's Death and Resurrection, the more we shall realize the Godhead of Him by Whom He offered Himself, and by Whom He was raised again.

The more we realize the perpetual presence of Christ in the Church, the more we shall honour that Spirit by Whom He is now present.

36. *There can be nothing, then, more certain than the truth of the Godhead of the Spirit?*

Nothing can be more certain to the man who truly believes in the Divine nature of the Eternal Son, and the Divine character of the work which He came to do.

37. *Does the history of the Church confirm this view?*

Yes: the Godhead of the Holy Ghost has been ever held and confessed by those who held and confessed the Godhead of the Son; and by consequence, rejected by those who rejected the Godhead of the Son. In fact, it seems impossible for those who hold the truth of the Scriptures, and believe that the Holy Spirit is a person, to doubt His Godhead.

38. *You before showed me your grounds for believing the*

Personality of the Blessed Spirit; can you recapitulate the proof as it appears in Scripture?

Every mark of distinct personal existence is ascribed to Him.

We are baptized into His name as well as into that of the Father and the Son. (Matt. xxviii. 19.)

Grace is invoked from Him as well as from the Father and the Son. (2 Cor. xiii. 14.)

He is promised as *another* Comforter. (John xiv. 16.)

As One Who shall guide, and teach, and receive of the things of Christ, and show them. (John xvi. 13, 14.)

He will not come unless Christ departs. If Christ depart He will send Him. (John xvi. 7.)

He convinces or reproves. (John xvi. 8.) He commands. (Acts xiii. 2.) He forbids. (Acts xvi. 6.) He works as He will. (1 Cor. xii. 11.) He is grieved. (Eph. iv. 30.) He makes intercession. (Rom. viii. 27.)

39. *Seeing, then, that the three Divine Persons are thus set forth separately, as Each doing the work of God, are they ever joined together as performing Divine acts, or receiving Divine honour?*

Yes: we are baptized into the name of the Father, and of the Son, and of the Holy Ghost. The grace of the Lord Jesus, the love of God, and the communion of the Holy Ghost are invoked upon Christians. (2 Cor. xiii. 14.)

The voice of the Father is heard, and the Holy Ghost descends like a dove upon the head of Christ at His Baptism. (Matt. iii. 16.)

Christ associates the three Persons together when He says: "The Comforter, which is the Holy Ghost, whom the Father will send in my name, He shall teach you all things." (John xiv. 26.)

Through Christ we have access by one Spirit unto the Father. (Eph. ii. 18.)

Christians are "elect according to the foreknowledge of God the Father, through sanctification of the Spirit, unto obedience and sprinkling of the Blood of Jesus Christ." (1 Peter i. 2.) And according to St. Jude, Christians are to "pray in the Holy Ghost," to "keep themselves in the love of God," and to "look for the mercy of our Lord Jesus Christ unto eternal life." (Jude 20, 21.)

40. *But have you not omitted the striking passage about the three Heavenly Witnesses?* (1 John v. 7.)

I have omitted it, because it is not to be found in the oldest and best manuscripts and versions; but it contains what is absolutely true, for there *are* Three who bear record (and do much more than bear record) in heaven, the Father, the Word, and the Holy Ghost; and we believe that these Three are One."

41. *But has it not been said that the Persons in the Trinity are three manifestations or characters of but One Person?*

If this be so, then the last and most perfect Revelation of God's will gratuitously misleads us in the matter of the very nature of the Supreme God.

42. *How does this appear?*

The Holy Scriptures, in ascribing Divine attributes and actions to a Father and a Son, have gone as far as possible in the way of marking the personal distinction between the Two.

43. *Can you show this more fully?*

Yes; in this way: If the Scriptures had ascribed Divine attributes to a Creator and a Redeemer, without making any further distinction, then it might have been said that they meant but one person bearing two offices; but such terms as Father and Son are not names of offices, but names implying the relationship of different persons to one another; the mere mention of a Father implying a Son distinct from Himself; and the mention of a Son implying the (in some sense) separate existence of a Father.

44. *Is this personal distinction between His Father and Himself, as Father and Son, ever insisted upon by our Saviour?*

Yes; very distinctly indeed, where He says: "It is also written in your law that the testimony of two men is true. I am one that bear witness of myself, and the Father that sent me beareth witness of me." And He had just before this said: "I am not alone, but I and the Father that sent me." (John viii. 16, 17, 18.)

45. *Do you remember any other words of our Lord in which He sets forth the personal distinction between the Persons in the Godhead?*

Yes: "I will pray the Father, and He shall give you another Comforter, that He may abide with you for ever." (John xiv. 16.)

46. *Is not the doctrine of the Trinity in Unity an incomprehensible mystery?*

Yes; it is an unsearchable mystery; but so is every other thing which can be said of an infinite and eternal Being, as God is.

47. *Show this with respect to other attributes of God which are acknowledged by all.*

His Omnipresence and Eternity. We can form no conception of the mode in which a Being exists Who is Himself wholly present in every part of the vast universe which He has created, just as we cannot comprehend an Existence which has no beginning.

48. *The mysterious nature, then, of the Doctrine of the Trinity is no argument against its truth?*

No : the mysterious nature of this doctrine, though it is no positive proof of its truth, is an argument in its favour so far as this, that it accords with the incomprehensible character of every other attribute which belongs to the Godhead.

49. *Why is it necessary that Christians should hold the truth of the Ever-Blessed Trinity?*

Because we are baptized into the Name of the Trinity, and it is above all things necessary that we should know and confess the meaning and significance of the Name of Father, Son, and Holy Ghost, in Which we are baptized.

50. *Is there any other reason?*

Yes. Unless we apprehend the doctrine of the Trinity, we cannot apprehend the truth of God; for God is set forth in Scripture as One, and yet all that can be said of God is in Scripture said of Three, and not of One only.

51. *But is there not, in this mysterious matter, a danger of speculating beyond what is revealed?*

Not in this our day : the danger now is of coming far short of what is revealed. In speaking, for instance, of the glory of the Eternal Son, it is impossible to go beyond such statements as, " The Word was God." " All things were made by Him." " He said that God was His Father, making Himself equal with God." " I and the Father are one." " Who, being in the form of God, thought it not robbery to be equal with God." The doctrine of the Trinity, as contained in the Creeds of the Church, teaches us how we are to give to these statements their full meaning, and yet hold that God is One.

52. *Is there any other reason why we should hold the doctrine of the Trinity?*
Yes. Unless we believe in the Ever-Blessed Trinity, we cannot realize that " God is love."

53. *Why so?*
Because, if God had no Son Who was in His bosom from all eternity, and no Spirit proceeding from Him, then He only began to love when He created angels and men ; but if He be a Trinity in Unity, then He has loved from all eternity : for from everlasting the Father has loved the Son ; and the Father and the Son have from everlasting loved the Holy Ghost ; and the Holy Ghost has loved the Father and the Son.

SHORTER CATECHISM.

1. *What dost thou chiefly learn by these articles of thy Belief?*
First, I learn to believe in God the Father, &c.
2. *What name is given by the Church to the Father, the Son, and the Holy Ghost?*
The name of the Trinity. The Ever-Blessed Trinity.
3. *What is each Person in the Ever-Blessed Trinity?*
God and Lord.
4. *Are there then three Gods or three Lords?*
No:"we are forbidden by the Catholic religion to say, There be three Gods or three Lords."
5. *Who is the Second Person in the Trinity?*
God the Son—the Eternal Son of God—Jesus Christ.
6. *What is the name given to Him in the first verses of St. John's Gospel?*
The Word.
7. *What does St. John say of the Word?*
In the beginning was the Word, and the Word was with God, and the Word was God (John i. 1).
8. *Did the Word, or Son of God, always remain in glory in Heaven?*
No : " For us men, and for our salvation, He came down from Heaven."
9. *How does St. John express this?*
The Word was made flesh, and dwelt among us (John i. 14).
10. *Does this mean that our Lord is not now God?*
No : He was called by St. Thomas, one of his Apostles, Lord and God (John xx. 28).

11. *Did He reprove St. Thomas for so addressing Him?*
   On the contrary; He said to Him, "Thou hast believed."
   [Because thou hast seen Me thou hast believed.]
12. *Does St. Paul ever call our Lord " God?"*
   Yes: in Rom. ix. 5.
13. *Does St. John ever call our Lord God?* Yes: (1 John v. 20).
14. *What other proof have we that our Lord is God?*
   He says things which only God can say.
15. *Mention one of these things.*
   He says, "I am Alpha and Omega, the beginning and the end, the first and the last" (Rev. xxii. 13).
16. *What does He mean by saying this?*
   He means that He is from everlasting to everlasting.
17. *Who alone can be from everlasting to everlasting?*
   The one true God.
18. *Why then can Jesus say this?*
   Because He is one God with the Father and the Spirit.
19. *Mention another thing which Jesus said.*
   "Where two or three are gathered together in My Name, there am I in the midst of them" (Matt. xviii. 20).
20. *What does He mean by this?*
   That He is in every place at once.
21. *What name do we give to this power of being in every place at once?*
   Omnipresence.
22. *To whom does this power of being in every place belong?*
   To the one true God.
23. *How then can Jesus be in every place?*
   Because He is with the Father, and the Spirit, the one God.
24. *What do we call such a thing as omnipresence?*
   We call it an attribute of God.
25. *What do you mean by an attribute?*
   Something which we say of God. Something which we say that God is.
26. *What do we say of God?*
   We say that He is eternal, that He is present everywhere or omnipresent, that He is all-wise or omniscient, and all-mighty or omnipotent.
27. *Does Jesus Christ ever claim to be omnipotent?*
   Yes: when He says, "What things soever He (the Father) doeth, these also doeth the Son likewise" (John v. 19).
28. *Does Christ ever claim to be omniscient or all-knowing?*
   Yes: when He allows St. Peter to say to Him, Lord, Thou knowest all things (John xxi. 17).
29. *Mention three great works which God alone, because He is Almighty (or omnipotent), can do.*

He alone creates. He sustains or upholds all things. He raises the dead.

30. *Is it ever said that the Son of God has the power to create?*
Yes: He created all things (John i. 3; Heb. i. 2).

31. *Is it ever said that the Son of God has the power to uphold all things?*
Yes: by Him all things consist (Col. i. 17). He upholds all things by the word of His power (Heb. i. 3).

32. *Is it ever said that the Son of God has power to raise the dead?*
Yes: He Himself claims to do so (John vi. 54).

33. *What two other works are ascribed to God alone?*
To judge all men (God is the Judge), and to save sinners. Besides me there is no Saviour (Isaiah xliii. 11).

34. *Does it belong to Christ to judge?*
Yes: "The Father judgeth no man, but hath committed all judgment unto the Son" (John v. 22).

35. *Does it belong to Christ to save?*
Yes: His name was given to Him because He saves His people from their sins (Matt. i. 21).

36. *If Christ then is called "Lord" and "God," and does all these things which God only can do, ought He to be honoured as God?*
Yes: "All men should honour the Son even as they honour the Father" (John v. 23).

37. *Are we then ever to worship Him?*
Yes, or we should not honour Him as we honour the Father.

38. *Give instances of angels worshipping Christ.*
Heb. i. 6; Rev. v. 13.

39. *Give instances of men worshipping Him.*
The Magi (Matt. ii. 11). The holy women on the day of the Resurrection (Matt. xxviii. 9). The Apostles (Luke xxiv. 52). St. Stephen (Acts vii. 59).

40. *How in addition to this is He honoured as God?*
We are baptized into His Name.

41. *What does this imply?*
That we are dedicated to Him as God.

42. *Where does the Church worship Him as God?*
In the Gloria Patri; in the Te Deum; in the Litany; in the Prayer of St. Chrysostom; and in several Collects.

43. *If then He is called Lord and God, and does all that God does, and receives the worship due to God, is He inferior to God?*
No: "He thought it not robbery to be equal with God" (Phil. ii. 6).

44. *But is He not the true and only Son of God?*
Yes: and so He must be equal in nature to His Father (John v. 18).

DOCTRINE OF THE TRINITY. 187

45. *Do we dishonour the Father by giving Divine honour to His Son?*
No: unless we did so we should not honour God the Father (John v. 23).
46. *Is the Holy Ghost called God in Scripture?*
Yes: in Acts v. 3, 4.
47. *Is He ever called Lord?* Yes: (2 Cor. iii. 17).
48. *Is He ever said to be eternal?* Yes: (Heb. ix. 14).
49. *Is He ever said to be omniscient, or to know all things?*
Yes: (1 Cor. ii. 10).
50. *Is He ever said to be omnipresent?*
Yes: "Whither shall I go from Thy Spirit?" (Ps. cxxxix. 6).
51. *What work of God did He bring about?*
The greatest work of God that has been revealed to us.
52. *What is that?* The Incarnation of the Son of God.
53. *Was this the work of the Holy Ghost?*
Yes: (Matt. i. 20; Luke i. 35).
54. *By Whom did our Lord become the Christ?*
By the Holy Ghost, by whom He was *anointed*.
55. *By Whom did He offer Himself a sacrifice for sins?*
Through the Eternal Spirit.
56. *Whom must the Holy Ghost be if He does these things?*
He must be God, one with the Father and the Son.
57. *Why, particularly, are we to honour Him as God?*
Because we are baptized in His Name, and so dedicated to Him.
58. *What work of the Holy Spirit is especially mentioned in the Nicene Creed?* He spake by the Prophets.
59. *When the Prophets spake in God's Name, how did they begin?*
With the words, "Thus saith the Lord."
60. *If then they spoke by the Holy Ghost, what must He be?*
The Lord God.
61. *If then all these things can be said of the Son and of the Holy Ghost as well as of the Father, what is our duty?*
We must worship One God in Trinity, and Trinity in Unity.
62. *Can we do this without the help of God's grace?*
No: God has given to us grace by the confession of a true faith to acknowledge the glory of the Eternal Trinity (Collect for Trinity Sunday).
63. *How must we come to God?*
Through Christ, by the Spirit. We must come to God, the First Person, through the Second, by the Third.
64. *How do we worship and glorify the Trinity in Unity in the services of the Church?*
In the Gloria Patri; in the Gloria in Excelsis ("Glory be to God on high"); in the Litany; in the confession of the Creeds, especially the Creed of St. Athanasius.

SECTION XXXIII.—THE PREFACE TO THE COMMANDMENTS.

1. You said that your Godfathers and Godmothers did promise for you, that you should keep God's Commandments. Tell me how many there be?
   Ten.
2. Which be they?
   The same which God spake in the twentieth chapter of Exodus, saying, I am the Lord thy God, Who brought thee out of the Land of Egypt, out of the house of bondage.
3. *When did your Godparents promise for you that you should keep God's commandments?*
   When, at my Baptism, I was brought under the New Covenant. (7–13)
4. *What is one part of that covenant?*
   "I will put my laws into their minds, and write them in their hearts, and I will be to them a God, and they shall be to me a people." (Heb. viii. 10.) (13–17)
5. *If, then, at your Baptism you entered into the New Covenant, what did you receive?*
   Grace from God to do His Holy will; for I was then buried and raised again with Christ, that I might walk in newness of life. (Rom. vi. 1–4.) (14–18)
6. *How must you stir up this grace within you?*
   By calling upon God in prayer; by ever remembering my dedication to God, and by using all means of grace which He has given to me. (19–21)
7. *How does our Lord sum up the commandments?*
   In two, viz., "Thou shalt love the Lord thy God with all thy heart, and with all thy soul, and with all thy mind;" and "Thou shalt love thy neighbour as thyself." (Matt. xxii. 37.)
8. *If, then, we break any one commandment, what do we show?*
   Our want of love to God. (22, 23)
9. *If, then, Christ has summed up all the commandments in these two, why do we say that there are ten?*

Because, though our duty can be all summed up in one word, yet the ways of performing it are manifold.
10. *Are these commandments binding upon Christians?*
    Yes. 1. Because they have been confirmed by Christ and His Apostles.
    2. And also because they express that natural law which God has written in the hearts of even the heathen. (Rom. ii. 15.) (23–27)
11. *When did our Lord confirm their authority?*
    When He said : " If thou wilt enter into life, keep the commandments." (Matt. xix. 17, 18, 19.)
    [Also throughout the Sermon on the Mount, particularly when He says, "Whosoever shall do and teach them, the same shall be called great in the kingdom of heaven" (Matt. v. 19); and when He denounces the guilt of the Scribes and Pharisees in making void God's law by their tradition (Matt. xv. 6).] (25–27)
12. *But was not St. Paul inspired to say that we are not under the law, but under grace?*
    Yes : we are not under the law as the means of our justification in God's sight; but the very grace which we receive is given to us to enable us to fulfil the law. According to St. Paul's own words, " God sent His own Son in the likeness of sinful flesh . . . that the righteousness of the law might be fulfilled in us, who walk not after the flesh, but after the Spirit." (Rom. viii. 3.) (29–36)
13. *But is this righteousness the keeping of the ten commandments?*
    It must be. The ten commandments, as spiritually expounded by our Saviour, are the moral law, and God has given us no other.
14. *On what ground did God bid the children of Israel keep the ten commandments?*
    On the ground that He was the Lord their God, Who had brought them out of the land of Egypt; out of the house of bondage.
15. *Does this apply to us?*
    Yes ; with tenfold force ; for God redeemed the Israelites from temporal subjection, whereas He has redeemed us from sin by the humiliation and death of His Only Begotten Son. (30–37)
16. *Are the ten commandments ever classified or divided?*
    Yes ; into two tables. The first containing the

first four commandments, on the love of God; and the second the last six, on the love of our neighbour.

17. *Where has the Church given to us the spiritual meaning of these two tables?*

She has given to us the spiritual meaning of the commandments of the first table in the "Duty towards God;" and the spiritual meaning of the commandments of the second table in the "Duty towards my Neighbour." (44-47.)

18. WHAT IS YOUR DUTY TOWARDS GOD?

MY DUTY TOWARDS GOD IS TO BELIEVE IN HIM, TO FEAR HIM, AND TO LOVE HIM WITH ALL MY HEART, WITH ALL MY MIND, WITH ALL MY SOUL, AND WITH ALL MY STRENGTH; TO WORSHIP HIM, TO GIVE HIM THANKS, TO PUT MY WHOLE TRUST IN HIM, TO CALL UPON HIM, TO HONOUR HIS HOLY NAME, AND HIS WORD, AND TO SERVE HIM TRULY ALL THE DAYS OF MY LIFE.

SHORTER CATECHISM.

1. *What was the third thing which your Godparents promised in your name?*
That I should keep God's holy will and commandments.
2. *How many commandments are there?* Ten.
3. *Where in Scripture are they to be found?* Exod. xx.
4. *Is there any other place where they are to be found?*
Yes (Deut. v. 6-21).
5. *Who gave the ten commandments at the first?*
God Himself (Deut. v. 4).
6. *To whom did He give them?* To His people Israel.
7. *Did He give them to those who heard His voice or to all?*
To all His people in every age (Deut. v. 3).
8. *When did each Israelite become one of the people of God?*
At his circumcision, when he was eight days old.
9. *What is now the Israel of God?* The Church of God.
10. *When did you become a member of the Church?* At my Baptism.
11. *Into what did you enter then?* Into covenant with God.
12. *What covenant?* The new covenant.
13. *What is the difference between the two covenants?*
The old covenant had no grace annexed to it; but under the new we have grace given to us. [We are hereby made the children of grace.]
14. *What does God give us grace to do?* To do His will.

15. *Where do we read this?*
   Where St. Paul (quoting Jeremiah) writes: "I will put my laws into their minds, and write them in their hearts" (Heb. viii. 10).
16. *Is this grace given to us in Baptism?*
   Yes: in some degree it is given, or St. Paul would not write that we are baptized in order that we might walk in newness of life (Rom. vi. 4).
17. *But how is it that so many Christians do not keep God's law?*
   Because they fall from grace.
18. *Is this certain?*
   We find that the Apostles, when they hear of baptized Christians sinning, always assume that they sin against grace.
19. *What must we do then?*
   We must always remember that we have been made members of Christ.
20. *What besides must we do?*
   We must pray to God through Christ that we may have more grace.
21. *What besides?* We must use the means of grace.
22. *Can you give the meaning of the commandments in one word?*
   Yes: in the one word "love."
23. *Does our Lord ever sum up the meaning of the commandments so?*
   Yes: when He says that the first and great commandment is, Thou shalt love the Lord thy God with all thy heart; and the second, Thou shalt love thy neighbour as thyself. (Matt. xxii. 37.)
24. *Must we, who are Christians, keep the Commandments?* Yes.
25. *Why?* Because our Lord Jesus Christ requires us so to do.
26. *Where does He so require us?*
   When He says: "If thou wilt enter into life, keep the commandments" (Matt. xix. 17).
27. *Shall we enter Heaven because we keep God's law?* No.
28. *Why?* Because we are saved by Jesus Christ.
29. *Why then must we keep God's law?*
   Because Jesus Christ saved us from sin, which is the transgression of God's law.
30. *What is salvation?*
   Deliverance from sin, and doing the will of God.
31. *But is not salvation being taken to Heaven?*
   No: unless we had God's law in our hearts we could not be happy in Heaven.
32. *Where is this meaning of Salvation expressed in Scripture?*
   In the well-known words: "That we being delivered out of the hand of our enemies, might serve Him without fear, in holiness and righteousness before Him" (Luke i. 74, 75).
33. *But has not Christ fulfilled the law for us?*
   Not in the sense of excusing us from fulfilling it ourselves.

34. *But is He not our Righteousness?*
   Yes; and so because He is in us as our Righteousness, we must be righteous.
35. *How can this be?* By the power of His Spirit within us.
36. *For what purpose does St. Paul say that God sent His Son?*
   "That the righteousness of the law might be fulfilled in us" (Rom., viii. 4).
37. *Before God gave the Israelites His law, what did He tell them?*
   What He had done for them.
38. *In what words?*
   "I am the Lord thy God, Who brought thee out of the land of Egypt, out of the house of bondage."
39. *Has God done anything like this for us?*
   Yes: He has done a far greater thing.
40. *What is that?* He has redeemed us from the bondage of sin.
41. *How?* By the Death of His Son.
42. *How do we know that we have part in this Redemption?*
   Because we have been baptized into His Church.
43. *Because of this, how are we to walk?* In newness of life.
44. *What is the rule of this new life?* The commandments.
45. *How interpreted?* Interpreted in their full spiritual meaning.
46. *Where in the Scriptures do we find their spiritual meaning set forth?*
   In the Sermon on the Mount.
47. *Is it drawn out in the Catechism?*
   Yes: in the "duty towards God" and the "duty towards our neighbour."

SECTION XXXIV.—THE FIRST COMMANDMENT.

1. *What is the first commandment?*
   THOU SHALT HAVE NONE OTHER GODS BUT ME.
2. *Who is this God Who claims our sole worship?*
   The God into Whose Name we have been baptized. The Father, the Son, and the Holy Ghost. (9, 10)
3. *Is this commandment kept by us if we merely hold that there is but one God?*
   No; we must take the One true God to be our God, and think of Him, and live to Him as the Maker of all things and the Redeemer and Judge of all men.
4. *What part of our " duty towards God" teaches what God requires of us in this first commandment?*
   "My duty towards God is to believe in Him, to fear Him, and to love Him with all my heart, with all my mind, with all my soul, and with all my strength."
5. *What state of mind, then, is enforced by this first commandment?*
   Godliness. (7, 8)
6. *What must we have within us if we would have this state of mind?*
   Faith. We must believe in God; Who He is, and what He has done for us. (9–14)
7. *Why are we called upon first of all to believe in God?*
   Because unless we believe in Him, we cannot fear or love Him, or come to Him in prayer [as the Apostle says, "He that cometh to God must believe that He is." (Heb. xi. 6.)]
8. *In what consists the open violation of this first commandment?*
   In worshipping other Gods, as the heathen do. (3–6)
9. *But cannot the heathen worship the same Supreme Being as we worship, under a different name?*
   No: the God Whom we worship has revealed Himself as the Father of Jesus Christ. (11–14)
10. *Can a Deist who professes to believe in one Supreme Being, but rejects the record which God has given of His Son, keep this commandment?*

No; there is no being in the unseen world answering to the God of the Deist. (11-14)

11. Can a Mahometan believe in the one living and true God?

No; the Mahometan profession is that God cannot have One Only Begotten Son, which the One True God has. (11-15)

12. How is this commandment set at nought amongst us?

By those who deny the personal existence of God,—that He is One Who loves, and hears, and sees, and has created all men, and will hereafter judge us all. (16-34)

13. Are there those amongst us who seem to deny the personal existence of God?

Yes; those who say that some unconscious powers of nature, such as natural selection, could of themselves, apart from the superintending Providence of God, bring all things into being, and continue them in well-being.

14. What does our Lord say respecting God's Providence?

That it orders all things. God clothes the grass of the field (Matt. vi. 30); feeds the fowls of the air (Luke xii. 24); orders the term of their lives (Matt. x. 29); and numbers the hairs of our heads. (Matt. x. 30.) (16-34)

15. What further state of mind must we have towards God?

We must fear Him.

16. What is the fear of God?

It is a perpetual sense of the presence of a Good and Holy God.

17. In what solemn words does our Lord bind upon us the fear of God?

In the words, "I will forewarn you [my friends] whom ye shall fear: fear Him, who after He hath killed hath power to cast into hell; yea, I say unto you, fear Him." (Luke xii. 5.) (16-34)

18. But does not St. John say that perfect love casteth out fear?

Perfect love casts out all slavish fear; or, as the Apostle explains it, all fear that hath torment (1 John iv. 18); but love itself must deepen the fear of offending One Whom we perfectly love and honour. (16-34)

19. Is the fear of God consistent with the comforts of religion?

Yes; we read of the earliest Christians, that "walking

in the fear of the Lord, and in the comfort of the Holy Ghost, they were multiplied." (Acts ix. 31.) (37, 38)

20. *What state of mind, in addition to faith and fear, must we have towards God.*

We are to love Him with all our heart, mind, soul, and strength. (39-40)

21. *What kind of love is this love of God in us?*

It is, first of all, a holy love, and so is inseparably bound up with the true fear of God: we cannot love God with a holy love unless we fear Him.

It is, secondly, a filial love: God hath sent forth the Spirit of His Son into our hearts, crying, Abba, Father. (Gal. iv. 6.)

22. *In what way is the love of God to be shown?*

In the one way of keeping His commandments; for Christ says: "He that hath my commandments, and keepeth them, he it is that loveth me." (John xiv. 21.) And St. John saith: "This is the love of God, that we keep His commandments." (1 John v. 3.) (44, 45)

23. *Are we to understand by this that we may keep merely the letter of the ten commandments?*

No: we are to understand by it obedience to every intimation of God's will; as that we should believe in His Son, receive the Sacraments of His Church, and forgive injuries.

24. *Is it safe to take the emotions of the soul towards God as signs of the love of God?*

No: our Lord asks, "Why call ye me Lord, Lord, and do not the things which I say?" And many profess to be moved by the love of God, who go directly contrary to His express will in some things which He has clearly revealed.

25. *But can we take correct outward conduct as a proof of the love of God?*

No. Love is a state of the soul or spirit.

26. *How are we to strive to have the love of God in us?*

By continual meditation on the love of God towards us in our Redemption by His Son: by earnest prayer, and by devoutly frequenting the Holy Eucharist, which is the pledge of God's love.

SHORTER CATECHISM

1. *Repeat the first commandment.*
   Thou shalt have none other Gods but me.
2. *What does this commandment forbid?*
   That I should have any other God except the one true God.
3. *Have mankind been under any temptation to break this command?*
   Yes: the vast majority of mankind are now breaking it.
4. *How?* By worshipping false gods.
5. *How does St. Paul say that idolatry became so prevalent?*
   Because men did not like to retain God (*i.e.* the true God) in their knowledge (Rom. i. 28).
6. *How did God punish the heathen for this?*
   He gave them over to a reprobate mind (Rom. i. 28).
7. *What does this commandment enjoin?*
   To take the true God for our God.
8. *How are we to do this?*
   We are to believe in Him, to fear Him, and to love Him, with all our heart, with all our mind, with all our soul, and with all our strength.
9. *Who is God?*
   The Ever Blessed Trinity. Father, Son, and Holy Ghost.
10. *If then we are to take God to be our God, what must we first have?*
    Faith. We must believe that He is, and that He is the rewarder of them that diligently seek Him (Heb. xi. 6).
11. *What must we believe that He is?*
    We must believe that He is what He has told us that He is.
12. *What has He told us that He is?*
    The Father, the Son, and the Spirit.
13. *Does truly believing in God require us to believe in Jesus?*
    Yes: Jesus says, "Ye believe in God, believe also in Me" (John xiv. 1).
14. *Can we believe in God unless we believe in Jesus Christ as His Son?*
    No: the God Who bids us have no other Gods but Himself has an only Son.
15. *Why cannot we believe in God unless we believe in His Son?*
    Because God is the Father: if, then, we do not believe in His only Son, we do not believe Him to be truly a Father.
16. *What must we believe respecting God?* That He has created us.
17. *What besides?*
    That He has preserved us, and still preserves us.
18. *What besides?*
    That He knows all things, and orders all things.

THE FIRST COMMANDMENT.   197

19. *What besides?*   That nothing is done without His permission.
20. *Does He approve of all that He permits?*
    No: He permits what is wrong, though He dislikes it.
21. *What does Christ say respecting His Father ordering all things?*
    That not a sparrow falls without His permission (Matt. x. 29).
22. *What does Christ say respecting His Father knowing all things?*
    That He numbers the hairs of our heads (Matt. x. 30).
23. *What does Christ say respecting His Father taking care of all things?*
    That He clothes the grass of the field and feeds the fowls of the air (Matt. vi. 26-30).
24. *What is this universal care which God exercises called?*
    His Providence.
25. *What, above all things, are we to believe respecting God?*
    That He sent His Son to redeem us, and raised Him from the dead after He had redeemed us by His death (Rom. iv. 24).
26. *What is the next point in our duty towards God under this commandment?*
    We must fear Him.
27. *What does Solomon say that the fear of the Lord is?*
    The beginning of Wisdom (Prov. ix. 10).
28. *In what does He say that it consists?*
    The fear of the Lord is to hate evil (Prov. viii. 13).
29. *What does our Lord say respecting the fear of God?*   Luke xii. 5.
30. *To whom does He say these solemn words?*
    To His friends ("I say unto you, my friends").
31. *What does this teach us?*
    That those in the favour of Christ must have within them the fear of God.
32. *What besides does it teach us?*
    That the greatest saints, even Apostles, have need to fear God.
33. *If we love God shall we fear Him?*
    Yes: if we love Him with a pure and holy love we shall.
34. *How must we cultivate the fear of God?*
    We must remember that we are always in His presence.
35. *How besides?*   We must remember the four last things.
36. *What are they?*   Death, Judgment, Heaven, Hell.
37. *But if we believe that God is merciful, shall we fear Him?*
    Yes: David says, "There is mercy with Thee, therefore shalt Thou be feared" (Ps. cxxx).
38. *What does this mean?*
    That the thought of our having been forgiven will make us the more fear to displease God.
39. *What is the third point in our duty towards God as taught by this commandment?*
    To love Him with all our heart, mind, soul, and strength.

40. *How are we sinful creatures to love a just and holy God?*
    By the power of His holy Spirit.
41. *Where do we learn this?*
    In the words, "the love of God is shed abroad in our hearts by the Holy Ghost, which is given unto us" (Rom. v. 5).
42. *How then are we to get this love of God into our souls?*
    By earnest prayer.
43. *Mention some prayers of the Church for the love of God to be in our hearts?*
    Almighty God, unto whom all hearts be open (Communion Service).
    O God, Who hast prepared for them that love Thee (Sixth Sunday after Trinity).
    That it may please Thee to give us an heart to love and dread Thee (Litany).
44. *What does St. John say respecting the love of God?*
    This is the love of God, that we keep His Commandments.
45. *How does our Saviour describe the man who loves Him?*
    He that hath my Commandments and keepeth them, he it is that loveth me (John xiv. 21).
46. *What is the sign that we love God?*
    When, more than anything else, we fear the displeasure and desire the approval of God.

SECTION XXXV.—THE SECOND COMMANDMENT.

1. **WHAT IS THE SECOND COMMANDMENT?**
   THOU SHALT NOT MAKE TO THYSELF ANY GRAVEN IMAGE, NOR THE LIKENESS OF ANY THING THAT IS IN HEAVEN ABOVE, OR IN THE EARTH BENEATH, OR IN THE WATER UNDER THE EARTH. THOU SHALT NOT BOW DOWN TO THEM, NOR WORSHIP THEM; FOR I THE LORD THY GOD AM A JEALOUS GOD, AND VISIT THE SINS OF THE FATHERS UPON THE CHILDREN UNTO THE THIRD AND FOURTH GENERATION OF THEM THAT HATE ME, AND SHOW MERCY UNTO THOUSANDS IN THEM THAT LOVE ME AND KEEP MY COMMANDMENTS. (1)
2. *What part of the duty towards God teaches the spiritual meaning of this second commandment?*
   My duty towards God is to . . . worship Him, to give Him thanks, to put my whole trust in Him, to call upon Him.
3. *With what has this second commandment to do?*
   With the worship of the One living and true God. (2-4)
4. *What sin does it especially forbid?*
   Idolatry, or worshipping God under the form of any creature, as well as worshipping the image of any false God. (5)
5. *Is it wrong to worship God under any form or figure?*
   Yes: God is a Spirit, whom the heaven of heavens cannot contain; and so, by worshipping Him under any form, we dishonour Him in that which should be our holiest service. (Rom. i. 25.)
6. *From what do we gather the importance of worshipping God aright?*
   From this; that because the heathen dishonoured God in their approaches to Him, God left them to the evil of their own hearts. (Rom. i. 20-32.) (6-11)
7. *With what are we to worship God?*
   We are to worship Him with the worship of both soul and body.

8. *How do we worship God, in soul or spirit?*
   By lifting up our hearts to Him in prayer.
   By abasing ourselves before Him for our sins.
   By submitting our reason to receive the mysteries of the faith.
9. *How do we worship God in body?*
   By using some lowly posture of devotion, such as bowing down to Him, or kneeling before Him. (16)
10. *Is this needful?*
    Yes; because our Blessed Saviour, God and Man, when in the garden, kneeled down and prayed (Luke xxii. 41); and not only so, but fell on His face and prayed (Matt. xxvi. 39).
    Other examples: David (Psalm xcv. 6); Daniel (Dan. vi. 10); St. Peter (Acts ix. 40); St. Paul (Acts xx. 36; xxi. 5.) (17-24)
11. *What is our next duty under this commandment, as taught us in " the duty towards God?"*
    To give God thanks (25-28)
12. *For what, above all things, should we give God thanks?*
    For our Redemption through Jesus Christ.
13. *What special service of thanksgiving is provided for this?*
    The Holy Eucharist. The word Eucharist meaning " Giving of thanks." (26-28)
14. *For what, besides Redemption, should we give thanks?*
    For everything: when we receive our food, or our wages, or when we recover from sickness, or have relief in pain. (26)
15. *What is our next duty as taught in the " duty towards God?"*
    To put our whole trust in God, especially in the Redemption which He has provided for us through Christ, in the promises of His word, and in the guiding of His Providence. (29-31)
16. *What besides are we taught by " the duty towards God?"*
    To call upon God, *i.e.*, of course, in prayer.
17. *How do you distinguish "calling upon God" from "worshipping" Him?*
    It most likely means that we are to call upon Him at all times and in all places, in every difficulty or danger, as well as to come together at stated times to worship Him. (32-34)

18. *Does this commandment forbid the worship of Saints and Angels?*
 Yes; St. Peter and St. Paul both refused even the semblance of worship (Acts x. 26; xiv. 15); and an angel refused worship from St. John, and bid him worship God. (Rev. xix. 10; xxii. 9.) (35-40)

19. *Is it lawful to make an image or picture of our Blessed Lord?*
 Yes; because our Lord was "found in fashion as a man," it is perfectly lawful to make a figure or picture of Him, provided that we do not worship it.

20. *What else is forbidden by this commandment?*
 All fortune-telling; all use of charms or amulets; all superstitious fear about (so-called) unlucky days, or numbers, or actions.
 [These are remnants of heathenism, and in some cases imply intercourse with evil spirits, or, at least, belief in such intercourse.]

21. *Why are we to keep this commandment?*
 Because God is a jealous God.

22. *With what punishment does He threaten those who break it?*
 That He visits the iniquities of the father upon the children unto the third and fourth generation of them that hate Him.

23. *Does this visiting the iniquities of the father upon the children apply to spiritual things?*
 No: we are assured by the prophet Ezekiel that it applies only to temporal judgments. (Ezek. xviii. 20.)

24. *How does St. Paul warn us that Christians can break this commandment?*
 By covetousness. "*Covetousness*, which is idolatry." (Col. iii. 5.) No "covetous man, who is an idolater." (Eph. v. 5.) (41-44)

25. *Are Christians in danger from idolatry?*
 Yes; or St. John would not have closed his first Epistle with the words, "Little children, keep yourselves from idols." (41-44)

SHORTER CATECHISM.

1. *Repeat the second commandment.*
   Thou shalt not make to thyself any graven image, nor the, &c.
2. *What is the difference between the first and second commandments?*
   In the first, God commands us to take the one true God for our God; in the second, to worship Him in a right way.
3. *Express this in other words.*
   The first orders inward devotion to God; and the second, outward worship worthy of Him.
4. *What great truth does our Lord teach us to make us worship God aright?*
   God is a Spirit, and they who worship Him must worship Him in spirit and in truth (John iv. 24).
5. *Can we make a figure or picture of such a Spirit as God?*
   No: see Deut. iv. 15: Ye saw no manner of similitude.
6. *In what then consists the especial sin of worshipping God under any form?*
   We insult God in our very worship.
7. *Does God resent this insult?* Yes.
8. *What history teaches us that He resents such an insult to His Majesty?*
   The whole history of the Jewish people.
9. *Give some instances.*
   The worship of the golden calf and its punishment (Exod. xxxii.). Baal-Peor (Num. xxv.). The Book of Judges throughout.
10. *Give two other instances.*
    The dispersion of Israel and captivity of Judah is always attributed to God's anger against this insult to His Majesty.
11. *Does this commandment only forbid a great sin?*
    No: it enjoins pure and holy worship.
12. *How is it explained in the words of the "duty towards God?"*
    My duty towards God is .... to worship Him, to give Him thanks, to put my whole trust in Him, to call upon Him.
13. *What does the word "worship" so often used in the Bible mean?*
    Bowing down to a person or thing.
14. *To what did Satan tempt our Lord in the last temptation?*
    To fall down and worship him.
15. *How did the Lord answer him?*
    Thou shalt worship the Lord thy God.
16. *Does this worship include outward worship as well as inward?*
    Yes: there can be no real inward worship without outward.

THE SECOND COMMANDMENT. 203

17. *What examples of outward worship have we?*
    Our Blessed Lord, Who kneeled down (Luke xxii. 41) and fell on His face in prayer (Matt. xxvi. 39).
18. *Give another example.* St. Peter (Acts ix. 40).
19. *Give another.* St. Paul (Acts xx. 36).
20. *Give another.* Abram (Gen. xvii. 3).
21. *Give another.* Daniel (Dan. vi. 10).
22. *Do the worshippers in Heaven outwardly worship?*
    Yes: the Seraphim veil their faces with their wings (Isaiah vi. 2), and the angels fall before the throne on their faces (Rev. vii. 11).
23. *Are we commanded by the Church to follow the examples of saints and angels in their worship?*
    Yes: the general Confession is to be said by "all kneeling" (Rubric). The Absolution is to be received by the people kneeling (Rubric). The Lord's Prayer (and all other prayers), by the minister and people kneeling.
24. *Can there be outward worship without inward?*
    Yes: men can draw near to God with their lips and their hearts be far from Him.
25. *What besides worshipping God does this commandment enjoin?*
    To give God thanks.
26. *For what are we to give God thanks?* For everything.
27. *Is there any Holy Rite of the Church, the very name of which signifies thanksgiving?*
    Yes: the Holy Eucharist.
28. *For what especially do we thank God in the Eucharist?*
    "For the redemption of the world by the death and passion of our Saviour Christ, both God and Man."
29. *What else does this commandment enjoin?*
    To put our whole trust in God.
30. *In what attribute of God must we as sinners trust above all?*
    In His mercy.
31. *For what four things especially must we put our whole trust in God?*
    For the forgiveness of our sins: for the hearing of our prayers: for the guidance of His Spirit: for the protection of His Providence.
32. *What is the fourth thing enjoined by this commandment?*
    To call upon God.
33. *At what times should we call upon God?* At all times.
34. *When especially?*
    In times of temptation, of trouble, of perplexity, of distress.
35. *What besides the worship of heathen idols is forbidden by this commandment?*
    The worship of angels and departed saints.

36. *Can you give instances of worship being offered to an an*
    Yes; in Rev. xix. 10; xxii. 9.
37. *By whom?* By St. John.
38. *What does this teach us?*
    That men of the greatest holiness may be tempted to gress in this way.
39. *Can you give any instance of worship being offered to saints*
    Yes: to St. Peter, who refused it (Acts x. 26).
40. *Did our Lord, when He lived amongst us, thus refuse wors*
    No: He said, on the contrary, that all men should hono Son even as they honour the Father (John v. 23).
41. *Whom does St. Paul call an idolater?*
    The covetous man.
42. *What Apostle warns Christians against idolatry?*
    St. John, in the words, "Little children, keep you from idols" (1 John v. 21).
43. *To what form of idolatry does he probably allude?*
    To setting up idols in our hearts.
44. *Does a word in very general use warn us of our danger this?*
    Yes: the word "idolize."

SECTION XXXVI.—THE THIRD COMMANDMENT.

1. **WHAT IS THE THIRD COMMANDMENT?**
    THOU SHALT NOT TAKE THE NAME OF THE LORD THY GOD IN VAIN, FOR THE LORD WILL NOT HOLD HIM GUILTLESS THAT TAKETH HIS NAME IN VAIN.
2. *How does the Church teach us, in the "duty towards God," that we are to keep this commandment?*
    By honouring God's holy name and His word. (1, 2)
3. *What then does this commandment especially enjoin?*
    Reverence towards God, and the things of God.
4. *In what way do men openly and directly break this commandment?*
    By false swearing or perjury; because, when we take an oath, we solemnly call God to witness that what we say is true. (3-6)
5. *Are we Christians permitted to take an oath in a Court of Justice?*
    Yes. Our Lord answered the adjuration of the High Priest when He said, "I adjure thee by (that is, I put thee on thine oath before) the living God;" which was a far stronger form of oath than any in use amongst us. (Matt. xxvi. 63.)
    St. Paul also, on several occasions, calls God to witness to the truth of his words. (Rom. i. 9; 2 Cor. i. 23.) (6-11)
6. *To what, then, does our Lord refer when He says, "Swear not at all?"*
    To all oaths used to garnish common talk, such as, among the Jews, "by heaven," "by Jerusalem," "by the temple," "by the altar;" and amongst us Christians, such ejaculations as "good God," "Lord bless us," "Lord have mercy." (12-16)
7. *How, besides, is this commandment broken?*
    By profane cursing; especially when men, on some trifling provocation, invoke upon their fellow-creatures, or upon their dumb animals, the everlasting torments which will finally overtake the utterly reprobate. (16-19)

8. *But persons who invoke this awful curse very seldom wish that it should take effect.*

That, we hope, is true: but then, the light and wanton use of so tremendous a denunciation betrays their total want of that fear of God which is the spirit of this command.

9. *In what other way is this commandment broken?*

By all jesting with holy things; by quoting Scripture, or using Scripture phrases so as to excite mirth, or by speaking lightly or disparagingly of such things as the Christian Sacraments. (20)

10. *In what other ways is this commandment broken?*

By all irreverent behaviour in Church, especially during public worship, and by letting our thoughts wander in worship without checking them. (21-23)

11. *How must you avoid such offence against God?*

By calling to mind His especial presence in the assemblies of His Church; by not allowing our eyes to wander, and by using lowly postures of devotion.

12. *What difference is there between the scope of the second and third commandments in the matter of worship?*

The second has regard to the purity of our worship; the third, to our reverence in offering that worship.

13. *How must we honour God's Holy Name?*

By making His saving name known among the heathen, and among those Christians who are living as the heathen.

14. *In what is the name of God especially glorified?*

In the worship of the Christian Church. In its unity. In the holiness of Christians. In the repentance of sinners. In their endurance of temptation. In the conversion of the heathen.

15. *What have we (according to the Catechism) to honour besides the Holy Name of God?*

His word. That is, the Scriptures. (24-31)

16. *How are you to honour the Scriptures?*

By believing that the Bible contains the last and most perfect revelation of God's will; by submitting our reason to receive the mysteries it reveals; and by reading, marking, learning, and inwardly digesting what it contains. (24-31)

17. *How do we dishonour God's holy word?*

By setting aside its plain statements when they do not suit our views, and by judging its statements by human systems, instead of by judging all human systems by its statements.*

18. *With what awful sanction is this commandment enforced?*
 "The Lord will not hold him guiltless that taketh His name in vain." (32-34)

19. *Why should the keeping of this commandment be enforced by this sanction?*
 Because there is no commandment which is more broken by thoughtlessness and want of watchfulness, and so men imagine that God thinks as lightly of their trifling with holy words and things as they do themselves. (32-34)

SHORTER CATECHISM.

1. *Repeat the third commandment.*
 Thou shalt not take the name of the Lord thy God in vain, &c.
2. *How, according to the Catechism, must we keep this commandment?*
 By honouring God's holy Name and His word.
3. *What is meant by taking God's name in vain?*
 Invoking it for a false or frivolous purpose.
4. *When do men invoke it for a false or lying purpose?*
 When they take a false oath.
5. *What do they do then?*
 They call God to witness that what they say is true when they know it to be false.
6. *Did our Lord ever allow Himself to be put upon His oath?*
 Yes: He was put on His oath by the chief priest.
7. *In what words?*
 "I adjure thee by the living God that thou tell us whether thou be the Christ" (Matt. xxvi. 63).
8. *Did our Lord answer to this?* Yes: He answered, "I am."
9. *What, by answering the High Priest's words, did He show?*
 That it is lawful for us to take oaths on solemn or proper occasions.
10. *Is there any other proof from Scripture?*
 Yes: St. Paul sometimes calls upon God to witness to the truth of what he says.

11. *Have we any other proof?*
    Yes: we read of an angel swearing by Him that liveth for ever and ever (Rev. x. 6).
12. *How besides do we break this commandment?*
    By using God's Name (or invoking it) in a light and thoughtless way.
13. *Can we break this commandment without actually pronouncing any of the names of God?*
    Yes: our Lord solemnly warns us that we can.
14. *How does He warn us?*
    When He tells the Jews that if they would keep the third commandment they must not swear by Heaven, or by the earth, or by Jerusalem (Matt. v. 34, 35).
15. *What do we infer from this?*
    That we must not use such phrases as "good gracious," "good heavens," and such like exclamations.
16. *What does our Lord say respecting all such exclamations?*
    That they come of evil. "Whatsoever is more than yea and nay cometh of evil" (Matt. v. 37).
17. *How is this commandment most commonly broken?*
    By cursing and swearing.
18. *Is this a great sin?*
    Yes: it is a very great offence against God to pray to Him to visit with His everlasting displeasure some trifling fault.
19. *What does such a sin betray?* All want of God's holy fear.
20. *To what must this third commandment be extended?*
    To every thing which has to do with the worship or service of God. To all the things of God.
21. *Mention one of these.* The public worship of God.
22. *How should we behave in Church?*
    With the greatest possible reverence. "Serve the Lord in fear, and rejoice unto Him with reverence" (Psalm ii. 11).
23. *How shall we best be able to do this?*
    By calling to mind God's especial presence there.
24. *What besides does the keeping of this commandment embrace?*
    The honouring of God's Holy word.
25. *What does the Psalmist say about this?*
    My heart standeth in awe of Thy word (Ps. cxix. 161).
26. *What does Isaiah say?*
    "To this man will I look, even to him that is poor and of a contrite spirit, and trembleth at my word" (Isaiah lxvi. 2).
27. *How are we to honour the word of God?*
    By receiving it as His word, and not the word of men (1 Thess. ii. 13).
28. *How besides?*
    By retaining it: by laying it up in our hearts.

29. *How besides?*
By believing implicitly all that it says respecting God and the salvation of God.
30. *But if there are hard things in it, are we to believe them?*
Yes, assuredly. It would not be the word of God if it did not contain things which are above us.
31. *Why?*
Because as the heavens are higher than the earth, so are His ways higher than our ways, and His thoughts than our thoughts (Isaiah lv. 9).
32. *Does God remember every oath or profane word?*
Yes: "the Lord will not hold him guiltless that taketh His Name in vain."
33. *What then should be the swearer's anxiety?*
That God, Who remembers what he has forgotten, should blot out his past sin.
34. *What should be his prayer?*
"Set a watch, O Lord, upon my mouth, and keep the door of my lips. O let not my heart be inclined to any evil thing" (Psalm cxli. 3).

SECTION XXXVII.—THE FOURTH COMMANDMENT.

1. WHAT IS THE FOURTH COMMANDMENT?
"REMEMBER THAT THOU KEEP HOLY THE SABBATH DAY: SIX DAYS SHALT THOU LABOUR, AND DO ALL THAT THOU HAST TO DO, BUT THE SEVENTH DAY IS THE SABBATH OF THE LORD THY GOD. IN IT THOU SHALT DO NO MANNER OF WORK, THOU, AND THY SON, AND THY DAUGHTER, THY MAN-SERVANT, AND THY MAID-SERVANT, THY CATTLE, AND THE STRANGER THAT IS WITHIN THY GATES. FOR IN SIX DAYS THE LORD MADE HEAVEN AND EARTH, THE SEA, AND ALL THAT IN THEM IS, AND RESTED THE SEVENTH DAY; WHEREFORE THE LORD BLESSED THE SEVENTH DAY, AND HALLOWED IT."

2. *What is the meaning or scope of this commandment?*
God in it demands that one day in seven should be especially dedicated to Himself. (2)

3. *What else does He enjoin in this commandment?*
That on six days of the week we should labour and do all that we have to do. (5-7)

4. *What then does this commandment forbid?*
It forbids all idleness on working days, as well as all unnecessary work on the Lord's day. (5-7)

5. *But if men have incomes independent of labour, are they under an obligation to work?*
Yes, all ought to have some employment for the glory of God and the good of their fellow-creatures.

6. *Does this bear on the keeping of the Lord's day?*
Yes, assuredly it does; for if men are idle on the six days, they never can dedicate the seventh to God's especial service. (6-10)

7. *What, then, is the part of our duty towards God which teaches us the duty enjoined by this commandment?*
"To serve Him truly all the days of my life." (10-12)

8. *On what special ground were the Jews to keep the seventh day?*

On the ground that on it **God** had rested from the work of creation. (10–18)

9. *How were the Jews to observe the Sabbath?*
   By resting from all unnecessary work.
   By additional sacrifices. Two lambs were offered morning and evening, instead of one, as on the other days. (Num. xxviii. 9.) (19–22).

10. *By what further typical observance was the Sabbath to be distinguished from other days?*
    By the renewal of the shew-bread. " Every Sabbath he (the priest) shall set it in order before the Lord continually." (Levit. xxiv. 6–8.) (23)

11. *But if it was the seventh day which was thus sanctified, why do we observe the first day as our weekly holyday?*
    Because, since the giving of the law, God has done an infinitely greater thing than the creation of the world, for He has redeemed it by the Sufferings and Death of His Only Begotten Son. (24–36)

12. *Is this a greater work than Creation?*
    Yes; for when God made the world He did not humble Himself; but in order to redeem us He left His throne, and came down, and humbled Himself, and became obedient unto death. (29–33)

13. *Is it reasonable then to change the day?*
    Yes; it would be most unreasonable to keep a day in memory of the lesser work, when a far greater has since been revealed to us. (32–36)

14. *But did not Christ rest in the grave on the Jewish Sabbath?*
    Yes; but we celebrate not His rest, but His triumph; for whilst He was held by death, He was in a state of humiliation; but when He rose again, He rose to glory. (37–40)

15. *Have we any warrant for changing the day, besides the reasonableness of the change?*
    Yes. Our Lord appeared to the disciples gathered together on the first day. On the first day of the next week He appeared again; and on the first day He sent down the Holy Ghost. (John xx. 19–26; Acts ii. 1.) (41–45)

16. *Have we any other warrant for changing the day?*
    Yes. On the first day the disciples met together to break bread (Acts xx. 7); and when St. John received the

visions of the Apocalypse, He was in the Spirit on the Lord's day. (Rev. i. 10.)

[The Lord's day (κυριακὴ ἡμέρα) being a day especially dedicated to the Lord Jesus, just as the Lord's Supper (κυριακὸν δεῖπνον) was. The same adjective used in both cases.]

17. *How did the early Christians mark the Lord's day?*
By the celebration of the Eucharist. (46–50)
18. *But did they not mark it by prayer, praise, and reading of Scripture?*
Yes; but all these were parts of the Eucharistic service. Every ancient Liturgy teaches us this.
19. *But did they not meet together for hearing of preaching without the Eucharist?*
We do not read that they did; but we do read that they met for the "breaking of bread." (Acts xx. 7). (48–51)
20. *Is this confirmed by the testimony of ancient writers?*
Yes. The earliest writer who gives an account of the worship of Christians particularly mentions that they came together on the first day of the week to celebrate the Eucharist. (Justin Martyr, A.D. 140.)
21. *Is it, then, our duty to mark the Lord's day by this most Holy Service?*
It is, if we are to follow the leading of Scripture, of the Apostolical Churches, and of the Prayer Book.
22. *What other acts of worship should consecrate this day?*
Psalms, hymns; such prayers as are in the Services of the Church, and the reading and exposition of the word of God.
23. *In what further way should we observe the Lord's day?*
We should abstain from all work, except what is absolutely needful. (52–59)
24. *What have you to say respecting the sin of those who work, or buy and sell, or keep open places of business on this day?*
That they not only profane the Lord's day themselves, but oblige others to profane it; for if this day is to be observed, it must be observed generally by the whole community. If any number of persons break it, all will be tempted to do so. (59, 60)
25. *Are any works lawful on the Sunday?*
Yes, works of necessity; such as lighting fires, cook-

ing food, and attending to cattle. Our Lord particularly mentions this latter : "Doth not each of you on the Sabbath loose his ox or his ass from the stall, and lead him away to watering?" (Luke xiii. 15.)

26. *What other works are lawful on this day ?*
All works of charity and mercy ; such as feeding the hungry, visiting the sick, and teaching the ignorant the truths of religion.

27. *Is this commandment one of those which our Church calls moral, or is it rather a ceremonial commandment ?*
It is founded on the obligations of morality ; for all men to whom God has made Himself known are bound to give some time to the especial service of God, and it is only by such an institution as the Sabbath, or Lord's day, that the greater part of mankind can have opportunity so to do. (62)

28. *Is there any other reason which brings this commandment among the moral precepts of the law ?*
Yes ; humanity, and due consideration for the wants of others, is a necessary part of morality ; and we cannot exercise humanity unless we give those who labour for us due time for rest and opportunity for worship. (62)

29. *Does God ever ground this commandment upon considerations of humanity ?*
Yes ; when He says, "In it thou shalt not do any work . . . . nor thy man-servant, nor thy maid-servant . . . . that thy man-servant and thy maid-servant may rest as well as thou." (Deut. v. 14.)

30. *Is there any command in the New Testament for the observance of the first day of the week as a day of rest?*
No : we observe it on the authority of the Church.

31. *Would it be lawful, as the Jewish Sabbath is superseded, to have no day of rest in the week ?*
No. Our Lord says, "The Sabbath was made for man" (Mark ii. 27) ; meaning, of course, that a certain portion of the week was set apart for his spiritual and temporal benefit.

32. *Can the principle on which we keep the Lord's day as the Festival of the Resurrection be extended to the keeping of other days ?*
Yes ; particularly to such days as Christmas Day, Good Friday, and Ascension Day. (63-65)

33. *Have these days the moral obligation of the Sunday ?*

Not in so far as the Sunday is the weekly day of rest, because, for purposes of rest, only one day in seven is required.

34. *What obligation, then, are we under to keep these days?*
We are under an Evangelical obligation. The obligation upon us to keep, by the observance of a day, the remembrance of the Resurrection of Christ must be extended to the commemoration of Christ's Birth, Crucifixion, and Ascension.

35. *Is the Sunday the only day for the celebration of Holy Communion and public worship?*
No: there is an order for Morning and Evening Prayer daily throughout the year; and special Collects, Epistles, and Gospels, that is, Communion Services, are appointed for Saints' days and some other days.

36. *If we are unable, from any just cause, to be present at Holy Communion or Public Prayer on the Sunday, what should we do?*
We should offer up to God in private, as far as possible, the same service as our brethren are offering up in Church, and so join with them in spirit, though we are absent in body.

37. *What particular care should persons who go into service exercise respecting this commandment?*
They should be careful to choose such employers or masters as will permit them to attend on the Lord's day the celebration of the Eucharist and the Public Prayers.

SHORTER CATECHISM.

1. *Repeat the fourth commandment.*
Remember that thou keep holy the Sabbath day. Six days, &c.

2. *With what has this commandment to do?*
With the consecration of our time to God.

3. *What part of our time does God consecrate to Himself?*
The seventh: one day in seven.

4. *Where is God first said to have consecrated this day?*
Gen. ii. 3. God blessed the seventh day and sanctified it, because that in it He had rested from all His work.

5. *What had God done on the six previous days?*
   He had worked in the work of creation.
6. *Is there any example for us in this?*
   Yes: God worked, so must we work: God rested, so must we rest.
7. *Does this commandment presuppose that we work?*
   Yes: six days thou shalt labour and do all that thou hast to do.
8. *What then does the fourth commandment enjoin?*
   Rest on one day.
9. *What does it forbid?* Idleness on the six days.
10. *How does our duty to God explain this commandment?*
    We are to "serve God truly all the days of our lives."
11. *How are we to do this?*
    We are to do the duties of our lawful calling on the six days, and more especially consecrate the seventh to Him.
12. *If we are not obliged to work for our living, must we still work?*
    Yes: we must always try to find some work to do for the glory of God.
13. *What does Sabbath mean?* Rest.
14. *When did God first enjoin it on the Israelites?*
    When He brought them out of Egypt.
15. *On what occasion?*
    On the sixth day, when the Israelites gathered twice as much manna as on the other days of the week.
16. *What explanation did God give of this?*
    That the next day was the Sabbath, on which there would be no manna, and no one was to go out to look for it (Exod. xvi. 29).
17. *How does this commandment begin?*
    With the word "remember," because God had bidden them to keep the Sabbath before He gave them the ten commandments.
18. *Was the Sabbath instituted before this?*
    Most probably; for if God sanctified this day (Gen. ii. 3) He would probably require man to sanctify it also, since the world was made for man.
19. *In what ways that we read of were the Jews to mark the Sabbath?*
    In three.
20. *What was the first of these?*
    They were to rest on it from all except the most necessary work.
21. *Mention one necessary work.*
    The feeding of cattle and leading them out to water.
22. *What was the second way in which the Jews were commanded to mark the Sabbath?*

By double sacrifices. Two lambs, morning and evening, instead of one (Num. xxviii. 9, 10).

23. *What was the third mark of observance?*
The renewal of the shew-bread (Levit. xxiv. 6, 8).

24. *Of what was the weekly Sabbath to remind the Jews?*
Of God their Maker: inasmuch as on this day God rested, having completed His work of Creation.

25. *Of what besides was it to remind them?*
Of their redemption from Egyptian bondage (Deut. v. 15).

26. *Have we Christians a greater thing than Creation to commemorate?*
Yes: there has been a new Creation begun in Christ Jesus.

27. *How was this new Creation begun.*
By the Incarnation, Sufferings, and Resurrection of Jesus, and by the coming of the Holy Ghost.

28. *What is the name we usually give to this work of the Son of God?*
It is our Redemption.

29. *Our redemption from what?* From sin, death, and hell.

30. *Is this a greater redemption than that of Israel out of Egypt?*
Yes: so much greater, that the one cannot be named besides the other.

31. *But were there not wonderful miracles attending the Exodus?*
Yes: but these were nothing to the Incarnation, and Sufferings, and Resurrection of Jesus.

32. *Which then was the greater work—to create or to redeem us?*
It cost God infinitely more to redeem us.

33. *In what way, then, has the Christian Church shown her sense of the infinitely greater nature of the work of Redemption?*
By changing the day of her weekly holyday from Saturday to Sunday.

34. *What day of our week corresponds to the Jewish Sabbath?*
Saturday.

35. *What day of the week do we sanctify?* Sunday, the first day.

36. *Why?*
Because on that day our Saviour rose from the dead.

37. *But did He not rest in the grave on the seventh day?*
Yes; but till He rose He was held by the grave.

38. *In what state was He till He rose again?*
In a state of humiliation.

39. *On what day did He conquer death?*
On Easter Day—the first Lord's day.

40. *What then may the Lord's day be called?*
The weekly Easter.

41. *When did the observance of the Lord's day begin?*
In the Apostolic times.

42. *What is the first notice of its observance?* Acts xx. 7.
43. *Is there any other hint given us of its observance?*
    Yes (Rev. i. 10).
44. *What is it there called?* The Lord's day.
45. *What is implied in its having such a name?*
    That it was a day especially dedicated to the Lord Jesus.
46. *If it was especially dedicated to Him, what would it commemorate?*
    His work of Redemption.
47. *Has He left us any act in which we are to commemorate His work of Redemption?*
    Yes; the Eucharist, called the Breaking of Bread.
48. *What service then would seem best to suit the day on which we commemorate Redemption?*
    The holy rite in which we especially show forth Redemption.
49. *Was this so in the beginning?*
    Yes: the only distinct New Testament notice of the keeping of Sunday is as a day on which the disciples came together to break bread (Acts xx. 7).
50. *Was there any service of prayer, and praise, and instruction, along with this breaking of bread?*
    Yes, always; but it was a part of the Communion Service.
51. *What was this service called?*
    The Liturgy, or the Holy Mysteries, or the Eucharist.
52. *Is there any distinct command in the New Testament to keep the Sunday as a day of rest?* No.
53. *But do we not require one?* No.
54. *Why?*
    Because our Lord said, "The Sabbath was made for man" (Mark ii. 27).
55. *What must this mean?*
    It must mean that it was made for his temporal and spiritual good.
56. *How for his temporal good?* Because it is a day of rest.
57. *How for his spiritual good?*
    Because it is a day of leisure on which he can attend the means of grace.
58. *If then we would preserve to ourselves and others such a blessing, what must we do?*
    We must strictly keep it as a day of rest.
59. *But cannot we work on it without making others work?*
    No: some will follow our example, others will be robbed of their day of rest by our selfishness.
60. *If then the Sunday is to be the blessing to all which Christ intends, how must it be observed?*
    It must be generally observed. It must be observed by all.

61. *Are any other creatures besides men to share in the benefit of a day of rest?*
    Yes: our cattle.
62. *On what two great principles should we observe the Lord's day.*
    On the principle of godliness or regard for the honour of God; on the principle of humanity or regard for our fellow-creatures.
63. *Should we keep any other days besides the Lord's day.*
    Yes: such days as Christmas Day, Ascension Day, and Saints' Days.
64. *Are these days to be kept as Sunday?*
    They are to be observed by Christians meeting together for Holy Communion and Prayer.
65. *Are we bound to abstain from secular occupations on them?*
    We are not bound to abstain from work on all of them, unless they are public holidays.

SECTION XXXVIII.—THE FIFTH COMMANDMENT.

1. WHAT IS THE FIFTH COMMANDMENT?
"HONOUR THY FATHER AND THY MOTHER, THAT THY DAYS MAY BE LONG IN THE LAND WHICH THE LORD THY GOD GIVETH THEE."

2. *What is there remarkable about the place of this commandment in the Decalogue?*
That it is the first commandment in the second table—the table which enforces our duty towards our neighbour, (1–7)

3. *Who is your neighbour?*
Christ teaches us by the Parable of the Good Samaritan that every man, even though he be the enemy of our Church and nation, is our neighbour. (Luke x. 36, 37.)

4. *Why then is it not said that we must love every one as ourselves?*
Because we must first exercise our love on those who have the first claim to it—our actual neighbours, our townsmen, our fellow-countrymen. (Charity begins at home.)

5. *Can our duty towards God and our duty towards our neighbour be separated?*
No : human society is the ordinance of God ; so that, in obeying the commands of the second table, we are to obey them " as to the Lord." (Eph. vi. 5, 6, 7.)

6. *What is the explanation of the fifth commandment in the duty towards our neighbour?*
"To love, honour, and succour my father and mother ; to honour and obey the Queen and all that are put in authority under her ; to submit myself to all my governors, teachers, spiritual pastors, and masters ; to order myself lowly and reverently to all my betters."

7. *Why ought we to love our parents?*
Because, under God, we owe our being to them, and they tended and nourished us when we could not support ourselves.

8. *How are we to show our love to our parents?*
   By being grateful and obliging to them.
   By making them happy by our good conduct.
   By bearing with their faults and weaknesses.
9. *How are we to honour our parents?*
   By behaving respectfully to them, and by obeying them as long as we live under their roof. (10-19)
10. *How should we succour them?*
    By supporting and comforting them in sickness and in age. (20-26)
11. *Does not God mention here the mother as well as the father?*
    Yes. "With good reason is the name of mother mentioned, that we may remember her particular claims upon our affections : with what care and solicitude she bore us in her womb : with what pain and travail she brought us forth and trained us up."
12. *How is this commandment broken?*
    By disobedience, if we are in their home; by insolence or pertness, or contemptuous demeanour. (19, 27-31)
13. *How besides?*
    By spending so much upon ourselves that we are not able to assist them when in need; and by living upon them when they are poor, and we are able to work for ourselves. (29-31)
14. *What example have we to enforce the keeping of this commandment?*
    That of our Blessed Lord, who, though "God over all," was subject to His mother and St. Joseph. (Luke ii. 51.)
15. *Does this commandment require you to honour any persons besides your parents?*
    Yes; I am to honour and obey the King (or Queen), and all that are put in authority under him (or her). (32-42)
16. *By whose authority do kings or civil magistrates bear rule?*
    By the ordinance of God. God says by Solomon : "By me kings reign." (Prov. viii. 15.) By St. Paul : "Let every soul be subject to the higher powers, for there is no power but of God; the powers that be are ordained of God." (Rom. xiii. 1.) (Also 1 Pet. ii. 13 ; Titus iii. 5.)
17. *Does this mean that the personal commands of the King, whether according to the law or not, are to be obeyed?*

No : according to the tenure on which our Sovereign holds the crown, he is bound to govern according to the laws, which can only be made by the consent of the Parliament.

18. *Has this commandment anything to do with the appointment of the Sovereign or form of government?* No.

19. *How do we break this commandment in the matter of obedience to the King or civil ruler?*

By speaking disrespectfully of the Sovereign, or of those under him.

By wilfully disobeying the law, or by evading its clear meaning and intent.

By conniving at the breaking of the law by others.

20. *Are we bound to obey a wicked King or magistrate?*

We are bound to obey the law, no matter what the personal character of the Sovereign who administers the law.

[St. Paul commanded obedience even to Nero, who was emperor when the Epistle to the Romans was written.]

21. *Why does St. Paul say that the magistrate, whosoever he be, is " the minister of God" to us "for good?"*

Because, under all circumstances, civil government is a blessing from God : and the worst tyranny is better than anarchy. (36-41)

22. *Are you to obey any other persons besides your parents and your Sovereign?*

Yes : I must submit myself to all my governors, teachers, spiritual pastors and masters. (42-45)

23. *Who are your governors, as distinguished from your teachers or masters?*

Such persons as the heads of a college, the captain of a ship, or the president of any lawful society of which I may be a member.

24. *If these societies are voluntary, are you bound to obey the governors of them?*

Yes; in all matters within their province. If I disapprove of their orders, I am bound to leave the society.

25. *Who are your teachers?*

My schoolmasters, or tutors, or my Sunday-school teacher, whilst I am in his class.

26. *Who are your spiritual pastors?*

The Bishops and Clergy, especially my Parish Minister. (49-54)

27. *In any matter in which your minister and the Bishop may differ, whose authority are you bound to respect?*
    The Bishop, because it is by his ordination and institution that the Parish Priest administers the word and Sacraments.
28. *Are you bound to follow blindly the commands of the Bishop or Parish Priest?*
    Not if they are contrary to the law of the Church; because both Bishop and Parish Priest are themselves subject to the laws of the Church.
29. *Is the authority of the Bishop the same as that of the King?*
    No. The authority of the King is from God, for the purposes of civil society; the authority of the Bishop is from Christ, as the Head of the Church.
30. *But does not the King appoint the Bishops?*
    The King, acting by the advice of his ministers, chooses the persons who are to be consecrated Bishops, but they receive all their spiritual powers at their consecration.
31. *Have the civil and spiritual authorities ever been opposed?*
    Yes; for three hundred years the civil authorities commanded men to worship false Gods, and the spiritual authorities excommunicated all who did so.
32. *If they were to be again opposed to one another, what would be our duty?*
    In spiritual matters, to obey the authorities of the Church; in temporal matters, the civil power.
33. *Can we in all cases draw the line between the respective provinces of these two authorities?*
    No: in a mixed state of things like that in which we live, in which the civil power is professedly Christian, it is impossible to do so.
34. *Who are our masters?*
    Our employers, respecting whom St. Paul says: " Servants, obey in all things your masters according to the flesh; not with eye-service, as men-pleasers; but in singleness of heart, fearing God: and whatsoever ye do, do it heartily, as to the Lord, and not unto men." (Col. iii. 22. *See* also 1 Peter ii. 18.) (55–62)
35. *How do we as servants disobey this command?*
    By impertinence or insolence; and by carelessness and idleness, as well as by disobedience.

36. *In what other respect does your duty toward your neighbour teach you to observe the fifth commandment?*
   I am to order myself lowly and reverently to all my betters: that is, to my elders and those above me in station. (63–67)
37. *What command does God give with respect to the aged?*
   "Thou shalt rise up before the hoary head, and honour the face of the old man, and fear thy God. I am the Lord." (Lev. xix. 32.) So also Rom. xiii. 7: "Render to all their dues ... fear to whom fear, honour to whom honour."
38. *How does the Holy Spirit describe a vicious social state?*
   As one in which "the child shall behave himself proudly against the ancient, and the base against the honourable." (Isaiah iii. 5.)
39. *What else does this command enjoin?*
   Courtesy and mutual submission. We are to honour all men; to submit ourselves one to another in the fear of God, and in lowliness of mind each to esteem other better than ourselves. (1 Pet. ii. 17; Eph. v. 21; Phil. ii. 3.)
40. *What beside all this is enjoined under this fifth commandment?*
   It enjoins that those to whom honour is due should act so as to be worthy of it. Parents, for instance, must rule their families well, and bring up their children in the fear of God. Kings must rule according to justice and equity. Spiritual pastors must set before themselves the example and the return to judgment of the Chief Shepherd. (1 Pet. v. 4.) Masters must carefully oversee their servants, and render to them that which is just and equal.
41. *What are the words of the promise attached to this command?*
   "That thy days may be long in the land which the Lord thy God hath given thee."
42. *How will this be fulfilled?*
   God will make good this promise, either in this world, or in the world to come.
43. *But will not all who are forgiven enter into God's rest, the true land of promise?*
   Yes; but God will particularly remember and reward the obedience of those who have kept this commandment.

SHORTER CATECHISM.

1. *Repeat the fifth commandment.*
   Honour thy father and thy mother, that thy days, &c.
2. *Into how many tables have the ten commandments been divided?*
   Into two. The first four being the first table, and the last six the second.
3. *What does the second table enforce?*
   Our duty towards our neighbour.
4. *What does our Saviour say is the second great commandment of the law?*
   Thou shalt love thy neighbour as thyself.
5. *Do we find this commandment in the Old Testament?*
   Yes: in Levit. xix. 18.
6. *In what similar precept does our Saviour sum up the Law and the Prophets?*
   "All things whatsoever ye would that men should do unto you, do ye even so to them" (Matt. vii. 12).
7. *How often is this precept, Thou shalt love thy neighbour as thyself, referred to as embracing the law?*
   Three times in the Epistles (Rom. xiii. 9; Gal. v. 14; James ii. 8).
8. *Which, then, is the first commandment of the second table?*
   The fifth.
9. *In what other way is it distinguished by St. Paul?*
   As being the first commandment with promise.
10. *How is the fifth commandment explained in "the duty towards our neighbour?"*
    First, that I am to love, honour, and succour my father and mother.
11. *How are you to honour your parents?*
    By respectful behaviour.
12. *What awful words are said of those who honour not their parents?*
    Cursed be he that setteth light by his father or his mother (Deut. xxvii. 16).
13. *In what fearful words is this curse expressed?* Prov. xxx. 17.
14. *What is he that despises his father's instruction?*
    A fool (Prov. xv. 5).
15. *How besides are you to honour your parents?*
    By submitting to their correction (Heb. xii. 9).
16. *How besides?* By bearing with their infirmities.
17. *How besides?* By concealing their faults (Shem and Japheth).
18. *What example have we in Scripture of filial obedience?*
    Isaac, who submitted to be bound for sacrifice (Gen. xxii. 9).

THE FIFTH COMMANDMENT. 225

19. *Who above all others?*
    Our Blessed Lord (Luke ii. 51).
20. *What example have we of those who would not listen to the voice of their father?*
    The sons of Eli, the priest (1 Sam. ii. 25).
21. *In what further way are you to keep this commandment?*
    I am to succour my parents.
22. *What is meant by this?*
    I am to help them when in need, and to promote their comfort by my attention.
23. *How besides?*
    If need be, I am to assist them from my earnings.
24. *Is there any special direction in Scripture respecting this?*
    Yes (1 Tim. v. 4).
25. *Who above all showed us an example of solicitude for His parents?*
    Our Lord and Saviour Jesus Christ.
26. *When?* When He was on the Cross.
27. *And how?*
    By committing His mother to the care of the beloved disciple (John xix. 26, 27).
28. *How do we break this commandment in our conduct towards our parents?*
    By rudeness and insolence.
29. *How besides?* By disobedience.
30. *How besides?*
    By selfishness. If, for instance, we spend so much upon ourselves that we have nothing left for our parents.
31. *What commandment did our Lord especially reprove the Pharisees for making void?*
    This fifth commandment.
32. *How did the Pharisees make it void?*
    By excusing children from succouring their parents under pretence of giving to God (Mark vii. 10-13).
33. *Whose authority besides that of our parents does this command enforce?*
    That of the King (or Queen), and those in authority under him.
34. *Why are you to obey the King?*
    Because a kingdom is a great family, and the sovereign is at the head of it.
35. *Does God ever command us in Scripture to obey kings and rulers?*
    Yes: very often indeed.
36. *Mention some instances.*
    Rom. xiii. 1-4; Titus iii. 1, 2; 1 Pet. ii. 13, 14, 17.
37. *What, according to St. Paul, are all kings and rulers?*
    Ministers of God to us for good

38. *Why?* Because by their power they protect us from evil men.

39. *What rule does our Lord lay down respecting obedience to the civil governor?*
"Render unto Cæsar the things which are Cæsar's, and to God the things that are God's" (Matt. xxii. 21).

40. *What does our Lord particularly enforce in these words?*
The paying of tribute or taxes.

41. *On what ground?*
On the ground that the coin was stamped with the image and superscription of Cæsar.

42. *What did this show?*
That Cæsar was the supreme governor of the country in which such coin was circulated, and must be obeyed as such.

43. *To whom besides your parents and your King are you to submit yourself?*
"To all my governors, teachers, spiritual pastors, and masters."

44. *In whose place are your governors and teachers?*
In the place of my parents.

45. *Why so?*
Because in my youth my parents commit me to their care for instruction.

46. *Is it a sin then to disobey your schoolmaster or schoolmistress?*
Yes: in so doing I sin against God, who has said, "Obey them that have the rule over you, and submit yourselves" (Heb. xiii. 17).

47. *Who are your spiritual pastors?*
The ministers of the Church.

48. *Who is the chief minister in a district (or diocese, as it is called)?*
The bishop.

49. *Why?*
Because he is the overseer of all the clergy and their flocks.

50. *Who is your spiritual pastor?*
In almost all cases my parish priest.

51. *How are you to submit yourself to him?*
By listening respectfully to his teaching.

52. *How besides?*
By upholding his authority when it is spoken against.

53. *What are we to consider the clergy to be?*
Ministers of Christ, and stewards of the mysteries (*i.e.*, of the mysterious truths and the sacraments) of God (1 Cor. iv. 1).

54. *How besides this are you to do your duty to your spiritual pastor?*
By helping him with my labours and exertions.

55. *Is there any other way in which you may be called upon to do your duty towards your spiritual pastors?*
Yes: in cases where they depend upon the offerings of their flocks, I must assist them with my alms.

THE FIFTH COMMANDMENT.

56. *To whom are servants bound by the law of God to be subject?*
    To their masters.
57. *Do the Apostles often remind them of this duty?*
    Yes ; very often indeed.
58. *Mention one place.*
    "Servants, be obedient to them that are your masters according to the flesh, with fear and trembling, in singleness of your heart, as unto Christ" (Eph. vi. 5).
59. *Why does St. Paul use the words "according to the flesh?"*
    Because he means that servants are to obey their masters, whether their masters are Christians or not.
60. *What does the Apostle mean by "singleness of heart?"*
    He means sincerity.
61. *In serving their earthly masters, whom are servants to serve?*
    Their heavenly Master, the Lord Christ.
62. *How do they do this?*
    By serving their masters faithfully, as if the eye of their Master in Heaven was upon them.
63. *Will Christ then account the service done to the earthly master as if it were done to Him?*
    St. Paul expressly says so (Eph. vi. 8 ; Col. iii. 23–25).
64. *In what other way are you to keep the fifth commandment?*
    I am to order myself lowly and reverently to all my betters.
65. *What is meant by your betters?* My elders.
66. *How does God command you to treat the aged?*
    (1 Pet. v. 5 ; Lev. xix. 32.)
67. *Who besides your elders are meant by your betters?*
    Those above me in station.
68. *What rule does St. Paul give respecting your behaviour?*
    Eph. v. 21 : "Submitting yourselves one to another in the fear of God" (also Rom. xiii. 7 : "Fear to whom fear, honour to whom honour.")

SECTION XXXIX.—THE SIXTH COMMANDMENT.

1. WHAT IS THE SIXTH COMMANDMENT?
   THOU SHALT DO NO MURDER.
2. *What is the crime of murder?*
   Taking away the life of a fellow-creature from some bad motive, such as revenge, hatred, or desire of gain.
3. *Is it necessary that there should be the deliberate intention to take away life?*
   Yes; or else the crime is that of manslaughter. (Num. xxxv. 22–28.)
4. *How is this commandment explained in the "duty towards my neighbour?"*
   "My duty towards my neighbour is to . . . hurt nobody by word nor deed . . . to bear no malice nor hatred in my heart."
5. *How is it that we are taught here that this commandment is broken when we hurt any one by word or deed?*
   Because our Blessed Lord expressly lays down that the use of all injurious and abusive language is a breach of this commandment: "Ye have heard that it was said to them of old time, Thou shalt not kill; and whosoever shall kill shall be in danger of the judgment; . . . but I say unto you . . . whosoever shall say to his brother, Raca, shall be in danger of the council; and whosoever shall say, Thou fool, shall be in danger of hell-fire." (Matt. v. 21, 22.) (12, 13)
6. *Why do we extend the scope of this commandment to the thoughts of the heart?*
   Because our Lord, in this very place, lays down that every one that is angry with his brother without a cause disobeys the spirit of this commandment; and because St. John teaches us that, "Whosoever hateth his brother is a murderer." (1 John iii. 15.) (6–11)
7. *Are there any things which, if we are true Christians, will make us righteously angry?*
   Yes; the sight of sin, and hearing the faith denied or explained away by those who are bound to profess it.

8. *If we have no feelings of indignation when we see sin committed, or when we hear the faith denied, what does it show?*
    It shows that we have no real dislike of sin, and no real love for the truth of Christ.
9. *Should we bear any ill-will against those who sin in these ways?*
    No. We should reprove the sinner, and pray for his repentance, and warn the unbeliever of his danger in rejecting the mercy of God.
10. *Who was it who, according to our Lord, first broke this commandment?*
    Satan. He was a murderer from the beginning (John viii. 44); and this because he destroyed the souls of our first parents by tempting them to sin.
11. *What learn we from this?*
    That this commandment is most foully broken when we tempt others to sin, and so destroy not their bodies, but their souls.
12. *What are our Lord's words respecting those who lead others into sin?*
    "Whosoever shall offend one of these little ones which believe in me, it were better for him that a millstone were hanged about his neck, and that he were drowned in the depths of the sea." (Matt. xviii. 6.)
13. *What is the spirit of this commandment?*
    A spirit of charity and forgiveness. (14-18)
14. *In what words of God's Holy Spirit is this spirit commended to us?*
    In such words as, "Let all bitterness, and wrath, and anger, and clamour, and evil speaking, be put away from you, with all malice; and be ye kind one to another, tender-hearted, forgiving one another, even as God for Christ's sake hath forgiven you." (Eph. iv. 31.) "Put on, therefore .... bowels of mercies, kindness, humbleness of mind, meekness, long-suffering; forbearing one another, and forgiving one another, if any man have a quarrel against any." (Col. iii. 12, 13.) (Also Tit. iii. 2, 3; I Peter iii. 8; 1 John iv. 7.) (14-18)
15. *Mention some ways in which the letter of the sixth commandment is broken.*
    By concealing, or setting free a murderer: by so doing we make ourselves accessories to his crime. By wilfully

neglecting to save a fellow-creature from death, when it is in our power to do so (as when one, who has the means of helping him, suffers a poor man to die of hunger).

By suicide, which is self-murder. We have no more right over our own lives than we have over the lives of others.

All cruelty to dumb animals is of the nature of murder.

NOTE.—In explaining the sixth commandment, the Catechist, in some parts at least of this professedly Christian country, will have to make those whom he instructs to understand that putting an end to the life of a human being, in any stage of its existence (no matter how rudimentary or imperfect), is murder.

SHORTER CATECHISM.

1. *Repeat the sixth commandment.* Thou shalt do no murder.
2. *How is this commandment otherwise expressed?*
   Thou shalt not kill.
3. *Is all killing murder?*
   No: in order to commit this crime there must be the murderous intention.
4. *If we kill our neighbour accidentally, is it murder?* No.
5. *Was there any law made by God for the protection of those who killed a fellow-creature accidentally?*
   Yes: the law of the cities of refuge (Numb. xxxv. 9-29).
6. *What evil passions lead to the crime of murder?*
   Envy, hatred, malice, and revenge.
7. *What other passions also lead men to take away the life of their fellow-creatures?*
   Covetousness and greediness.
8. *How then is this commandment first broken?*
   It is first broken in the heart.
9. *How?* By bearing malice and hatred in our hearts.
10. *Are we ever taught in Scripture that we break this commandment in the heart?*
    Yes: St. John says, "Whoso hateth his brother is a murderer" (1 John iii. 15).
11. *Does our Blessed Lord ever teach us the same truth?*
    Yes: when He says, "I say unto you, whosoever is angry with his brother without a cause shall be in danger of the judgment" (Matt. v. 22).

12. *Is this commandment ever broken by the tongue?*
    Yes: by the use of abusive and malicious words.
13. *How do you show this?*
    By the words of our blessed Lord in Matthew v. 21, 22, 23.
14. *What then does this commandment forbid?*
    All anger, hatred, envy, quarrelsomeness, and calling names.
15. *What words of the Apostle teach us this?*
    "Let all bitterness, and wrath, and anger, and clamour, and evil speaking, be put away from you, with all malice" (Eph. iv. 31).
16. *Is it sufficient for us to put away these evil things?*
    No; for the Apostle goes on to say: "Be ye kind one to another, tender-hearted, forgiving one another, even as God, for Christ's sake, hath forgiven you" (Eph. iv. 32).
17. *If people rail at us, or abuse us, are we to return it?*
    No: the Apostle says, "Not rendering evil for evil, or railing for railing: but contrariwise blessing" (1 Pet. iii. 9).
18. *How does our Blessed Saviour enforce this?*
    In the words, "Love your enemies, bless them that curse you, do good to them that hate you, and pray for them which despitefully use you, and persecute you" (Matt. v. 44).

SECTION XL.—THE SEVENTH COMMANDMENT.

1. *What is the seventh commandment?*
   Thou shalt not commit adultery.
2. *What is forbidden by this commandment?*
   Adultery, *i. e.*, unfaithfulness to the marriage vow; fornication, and all impurity, as well as everything which leads to impurity. (2-12)
3. *Against Whom do they sin who break this commandment by adultery?*
   Against God, Who has ordained marriage, and against Christ, Who has sanctified it by calling Himself the Bridegroom of His Church.
4. *By what sin besides adultery is this commandment broken?*
   By fornication.
5. *Is this a deadly sin?*
   Yes : St. Paul several times joins it with adultery, as being both of them works of the flesh which, if committed, will exclude men from the kingdom of God.
   "The works of the flesh are manifest, which are these: adultery, fornication, uncleanness, lasciviousness." (Gal. v. 19.)
   (Also, particularly, 1 Cor. vi. 9 ; Eph. v. 5.)
6. *Do not many people speak as if fornication was no great sin?*
   Yes ; but they are miserably mistaken. The word of God teaches us that all fornication or whoredom is deadly sin ; and in the Litany we pray, "From fornication and all other deadly sin . . . good Lord deliver us."
7. *What else does this commandment of God forbid?*
   Uncleanness, and every secret filthy habit which we should be ashamed for another to see.
8. *Does our Lord extend this commandment to the thoughts of the heart?*
   Yes : He says, "Ye have heard that it was said to them of old time, thou shalt not commit adultery ; but I say unto you, that whoso looketh upon a woman to lust after her hath committed adultery with her already in his heart ; and if thy right eye offend thee (that is, cause thee

to sin by lustful looks), pluck it out, and cast it from thee: for it is profitable for thee that one of thy members should perish, and not that thy whole body should be cast into hell." (Matt. v. 27–29.)

9. *How then are we to fulfil this commandment?*
We must steadfastly refuse to look at any person, or thing, as, for instance, any picture or statue, or to read any book, or listen to any conversation which may raise evil desires. (9–14)

10. *What else does this commandment forbid?*
The frequenting of all places where unchaste persons congregate, or immoral plays are acted, or where there are dances which no modest persons can look at. (15–18)

11. *What must we do if we hear immodest conversation?*
We must reprove it; and if this has no effect, we must at once leave the company of those who so offend. (20–22)

12. *Against what grace do those go contrary who break this commandment?*
Against the grace of Holy Baptism; because we were in it made members of Christ, and are bound on that account to keep pure from all sins which defile the body. (1 Cor. vi. 15–20.) (23–26)

13. *Are Christians in danger from temptation to sins forbidden by this commandment?*
St. Paul treats his converts as in need of constant watchfulness against the entrance of temptation to these sins. (1 Cor. vi. 15–20; x. 8; Gal. v. 19; Eph. v. 3–6; Col. iii. 5, 6; 1 Thess. iv. 3; Heb. xii. 16.)

14. *How must we exercise this watchfulness?*
We must watch the thoughts of our hearts, and the moment an improper thought arises we must put it away from us, and offer up a silent prayer to God, and repeat to ourselves some verse of Scripture, such as, "Thou, God, seest me," or, "Blessed are the pure in heart, for they shall see God." (5–8)

15. *What, above all, should we do in order to ward off temptation?*
We should make an act of faith in our Baptism, by saying to ourselves, I am baptized into the death of Christ that I should walk in newness of life. (Rom. vi. 4.) I am a member of Christ, and must not defile His body. (1 Cor. iii. 16, 17.) I am dedicated to God; and, as a temple dedicated to Him, I must cleanse myself from all

filthiness of flesh and spirit. (2 Cor. vi. 16, 17, 18 ; vii. 1.) (25, 26)

16. *What else should we remember?*
The judgments of God against impurity recorded in the Scriptures.
(Sins of impurity lead to other sins; as in David, they led to murder, and in Solomon, to idolatry.)

17. *What crime with awful frequency follows on the committal of this sin?*
The crime of child-murder.

18. *What is commanded in the seventh commandment?*
That husbands should love their wives, and wives their husbands; and that heads of families should take every pains to preserve the purity of their households. (Tit. ii. 2, 3, 4.)

19. *How is this commandment explained in the duty towards your neighbour?*
That it is my duty to "keep my body in temperance, soberness, and chastity."

20. *Why?*
Because gluttony and intemperance lead directly to sins against this commandment. (Ezek. xvi. 49.)

21. *What Christian exercises must be brought to bear against temptations to break the seventh commandment?*
Abstinence and fasting. (1 Cor. ix. 27.) (27–30)

22. *Mention four evil things which lead to the breach of the seventh commandment.*
Love of dress. Immodest apparel. Loose and vicious company. (Dinah: Gen. xxxiv. 1.) Idleness. (Ezek. xvi. 49.) (14, 15, 19, 31–33)

NOTE.—The Catechist should remember that the exposition of this particular commandment has been kept in the Catechetical form simply for the sake of uniformity. The Catechist must, of course, give the substance of the instruction upon this commandment more in the form of direct address. He should advert with all possible seriousness to much which has been left unsaid, or dismissed with a single word. Hard as it is to treat this matter so as to be understood, and yet not to raise the very ideas we wish to suppress, the difficulty must be faced if we are to be free from the blood of souls in the sight of God. The Scripture writers do not avoid this awful subject, and we must not. The sin is too rife amongst us to be glossed over. It will be, in two or three years—perhaps at the very time we are catechising it is beginning to be—in some of its forms, the temptation of half the young people who hear us. If we are to take the Scripture writers as our guides, then no inculcation of other truths, however precious, such as free forgiveness through Christ, or what is commonly called "the Gospel," will be sufficient. The part of the Gospel which St. Paul opposes to this sin is Baptismal truth, that our very bodies are made members of Christ, and dedicated to God; and the sins of commission must be stated so that the brand of hell may be marked upon them.

SHORTER CATECHISM.

1. *What is the seventh commandment?*
   Thou shalt not commit adultery.
2. *How are you to obey this commandment?*
   By keeping my body in temperance, soberness, and chastity.
3. *How are children to try to keep this commandment?*
   By watching their hearts, lest they think of any evil filthy things.
4. *What does our Lord say to encourage us to do this?*
   "Blessed are the pure in heart, for they shall see God" (Matt. v. 8).
5. *Do we ever pray in Church for pure and clean hearts?*
   Yes: when we pray, "O God, make clean our hearts within us."
6. *Does the Church put any other prayer like this into our lips?*
   Yes. "Cleanse the thoughts of our hearts by the inspiration of Thy Holy Spirit, that we may perfectly love Thee."
7. *What thoughts should we particularly keep out of our hearts?*
   Every thought that we should be ashamed to tell our clergyman, or our teacher, or any other person whom we honour and respect.
8. *If any evil, wicked, or filthy thoughts come into our minds, what should we do?*
   We should turn our thoughts to something else, or we should repeat to ourselves a verse of Scripture, or a verse of a hymn, or a short prayer.
9. *How besides should we try to keep this commandment?*
   By being watchful over our tongues, lest we say any filthy bad words, or even any coarse words.

10. *What words should we avoid?*
   All such words or speeches as we should be ashamed to repeat to one whom we love and respect.
11. *Should we listen to such words?*
   No: to listen to them with pleasure (or without reproof) is as bad as to repeat them.
12. *What does St. Paul say respecting the use of such language?*
   Fornication, and all uncleanness....let it not be once named among you, as becometh saints; neither filthiness, nor foolish talking, nor jesting (Eph. v. 3, 4).
13. *What rule besides this does he give?*
   Let no corrupt communication proceed out of your mouth (Eph. iv. 29).
14. *In what other way must we strive to keep this commandment?*
   By avoiding all loose and godless company.
15. *Who fell away from God, and disgraced herself by this?*
   Dinah · because she went out to see the daughters of the land, *i.e.*, idolaters (Gen. xxxiv.).
16. *In what other way are many led to break this commandment?*
   By a love of dress.
17. *Mention another way in which many are led to break this commandment.*
   By looking upon what is forbidden.
18. *What very strong words does our blessed Lord use in warning us against improper looks and sights?*
   If thy right eye offend thee, pluck it out, and cast it from thee, &c. (Matt. v. 29).
19. *What vice should we avoid if we would keep this commandment?* Idleness.
20. *When you grow up you will perhaps hear your neighbours speak lightly of sins against the seventh commandment—is this a great sin?*
   Yes: Fools (*i.e.*, wicked persons) make a mock at sin (Prov. xiv. 9).
21. *If you hear these sins spoken jestingly of, what should you do?*
   I should reprove those who so speak, and bid them remember the threatenings in God's word.
22. *What threatenings are these?*
   That these sins will lead all who commit them to hell (Prov. ii. 18; Eph. v. 4, 5; Heb. xiii. 4; Rev. xxi. 8).
23. *But are we to be kept from these sins only by remembering God's threatenings?*
   No: we are to be kept from them by remembering the grace of Holy Baptism.
24. *What were you made in Baptism?*
   I was made a member of Christ.

25. *And what should the remembrance of this make you do?*
    It should make me keep myself pure in body and in soul.
26. *To whom were you dedicated in Baptism?*   To God.
27. *What then should you remember?*
    That if I allow any evil in my heart, or on my tongue, or in my life, I defile the temple of God.
28. *What Christian habit must you exercise if you are to keep aright this commandment?*
    A habit of self-denial and abstinence. I should not eat and drink more than is necessary.
29. *In what Collect do we pray for grace to do this?*
    In the Collect for the First Sunday in Lent.
30. *How does St. Paul commend abstinence to us?*
    By his own example (1 Cor. ix. 27).
31. *What particular good quality is needful to enable us to keep this commandment?*   Modesty.
32. *Modesty in what?*   In dress and in behaviour.
33. *How must we be modest in dress and behaviour?*
    By dressing and by conducting ourselves so as not to attract the eyes of others.

SECTION XLI.—THE EIGHTH COMMANDMENT.

1. WHAT IS THE EIGHTH COMMANDMENT?
   THOU SHALT NOT STEAL.
2. *What does this commandment forbid?*
   Robbery, theft, and every kind of dishonesty.
3. *How is it explained in the duty towards our neighbour?*
   My duty towards my neighbour is to be " true and just in all my dealings .... to keep my hands from picking and stealing .... [and] to learn and labour truly to get mine own living."
4. *Why do you include this latter precept under the eighth commandment?*
   Because, unless I learn and labour truly to get mine own living, I shall probably live dishonestly on the labours of others.
5. *Mention some prevalent forms of dishonesty by which this commandment is broken.*
   This commandment is broken by those who buy, or keep, things which they have reason to believe are stolen; by all wilful misrepresentations of the value of things which we sell; by taking advantage of the ignorance of buyers, so as to get an unfair price for what we sell. (3-7)
6. *Mention some other forms of dishonesty.*
   Using short weights and scant measures; adulterating the things which we sell, so as to make them weigh more, or occupy more space than they otherwise would, and by not returning what we have borrowed or found. (8-13)
7. *In what other ways is the eighth commandment broken?*
   By those who contract debts with no sufficient prospect of being able to pay. Ps. xxxvii. 21 : " The wicked borroweth, and payeth not again." (14-19)
8. *Mention another frequent breach of this commandment.*
   It is broken by those who, in order to excite pity and obtain relief, represent themselves to be poorer and more destitute than they really are; and by those who, having the power to get their own living, yet choose to live by begging.

9. *Mention some other ways in which this commandment is broken.*

It is broken by bankrupts who conceal their property in order that they may not give it up for the liquidation of their debts. It is broken by those who do not do their best to fulfil their contracts; by those who do not faithfully administer wills, and by those who use the property of their neighbours without their consent.

10. *How is this commandment broken by servants?*

When they idle away and waste time, and neglect their work; for servants are paid for their time and labour, and if they do not honestly give this, they receive wages for that which they have not given.

11. *In what other way is this commandment broken by servants?*

When they waste, or give away, even in charity, the goods of their masters without their consent. (21-24)

12. *What is joined with stealing in the duty towards our neighbour?*

Picking. I am to keep my hands from "picking" and stealing. Unless leave is given, we are not to pick even a flower from a garden without the permission of the owner (29, 30)

13. *In what other ways is this commandment broken?*

By selling that which it is not lawful for us to sell, as our votes at an election, or our patronage, which is entrusted to us for the good of the community.

14. *What evil practices seem to be akin to the sin of dishonesty?*

Gambling, betting, and reckless speculating.

15. *Is the breach of this commandment a deadly sin?*

Yes: St. Paul writes, "Know ye not that the unrighteous shall not inherit the kingdom of God? Be not deceived...nor thieves...nor extortioners shall inherit the kingdom of God." (1 Cor. vi. 9, 10.)

[Terrible example of Judas Iscariot, who began by pilfering from the bag, and ended with selling his Divine Master to His enemies. (John xii. 6.)]

16. *If we have been dishonest and repent of it, is it enough to obtain forgiveness if we repent and believe the Gospel?*

No; we are bound to make restitution to those whom we have defrauded; and if they are dead we must seek out their representatives. Under no circumstances must we keep ill-gotten wealth. (33, 34)

17. *What two things does the Apostle St. Paul connect with honesty?*
He connects honesty with industry, and industry with almsgiving, where he says, " Let him that stole steal no more; but rather let him labour, working with his hands the thing which is good, that he may have to give to him that needeth." (Eph. iv. 28.) (36-38)

18. *Will honest-minded men give alms?*
Yes. The members of the Church of Christ have certain obligations (such as the care of the poor and the extension of the Gospel) laid upon them by Christ Himself: these duties cannot be fulfilled without the giving of our substance. They, then, who do not give according to their means, shift upon others the obligations which they themselves ought to share in bearing." (36-38)

SHORTER CATECHISM.

1. *What is the eighth commandment?* Thou shalt not steal.
2. *What is stealing?*
Taking that which belongs to another against his will, or without his leave.
3. *Can we break this commandment when we do not actually lay hands upon the goods of another?*
Yes: we break it by all manner of cheating and dishonesty.
4. *Mention some cases of dishonesty.*
When we buy or receive as a gift that which we have reason to think has been stolen.
5. *Mention another case.*
When we sell anything as sound or good knowing that it is unsound or bad, or not so good as we represent it to be.
6. *Mention a third case.*
Taking advantage of the ignorance of a buyer and asking of him a higher price than the goods are worth.
7. *Mention a fourth case.*
Taking advantage of the ignorance of one who is selling us anything, and giving him a lower price than his goods are worth

8. *How do persons in trade break this commandment?*
   By using false weights and measures.
9. *What says the Scripture respecting this?*
   Deut. xxv. 13-16 ; also Lev. xix. 35.
10. *What does the prophet call the scant measure?*
    He calls it abominable (Micah vi. 10).
11. *Does the word of God bring these transgressions under the eighth commandment?*
    Yes: where God says, "Ye shall not steal, neither deal falsely, neither lie one to another" (Lev. xix. 11).
12. *Does our Lord reckon all fraud as a breach of this commandment?*
    Yes: He says, "Thou knowest the commandments.... Do not kill, Do not steal, Do not bear false witness, *Defraud not*" (Mark x. 19).
13. *Mention another form of fraud disgracefully common.*
    Adulteration of goods, *i.e.*, mixing them with worthless things to increase their weight or measure.
14. *Mention another way of breaking this commandment.*
    By not paying our debts.
15. *What does St. Paul say respecting getting into debt?*
    "Owe no man any thing, but to love one another" (Rom. xiii. 8).
16. *Is it absolutely wrong to borrow?*
    No: but it is always the best to deny ourselves rather than to do so.
17. *When is it fraudulent to get into debt?*
    When we borrow money or order goods, and have reason to know that we shall not have means to pay for them when we are called upon to do so.
18. *What does the Psalmist call those who borrow and pay not?*
    Wicked. "The wicked borroweth and payeth not again" (Psalm xxxvii. 21).
19. *May children take what belongs to their parents?*
    No. "Whoso robbeth his father or his mother, and saith, It is no transgression, the same is the companion of a destroyer" (Prov. xxviii. 24).
20. *Are idle people, or those who neglect their work, dishonest?*
    Yes ; when they are in service.
21. *Why?* Because they are paid for their time and service.
22. *How do the poor too frequently offend against this commandment?*
    By representing themselves to be worse off than they really are in order to obtain relief.
23. *In what way can servants be dishonest?*
    By being wasteful: by not being careful about what is entrusted to them.

R

24. *May servants give food to poor persons?*
   Not unless they have their master's permission.
25. *If we find anything lying in the road or in a field, may we take it?*
   Not to keep it, for finding it does not make it ours.
26. *If we find anything that is lost, what should we do?*
   We should take pains to find the right owner and restore it to him.
27. *Is this a necessary duty?*
   Yes; if we would do to others as we would that they should do to us.
28. *What is akin to stealing, and so joined with it in the duty towards our neighbour?*
   Picking, or taking small portions from food which we are sent with, or plucking fruit or flowers in a garden without leave.
29. *Does St. Paul caution us against this particular form of sin?*
   Yes: when he bids servants not to purloin (Tit. ii. 10).
30. *Mention some things which all honest Christians will avoid.*
   Gambling, betting, bribing, receiving bribes, smuggling.
31. *Mention some virtues which all good Christians will cultivate.*
   Honesty, fidelity, uprightness, truthfulness.
32. *If in time past we have stolen anything, what must we do?*
   We must restore it.
33. *Can we truly repent if we do not?*
   No (example of Zacchæus, Luke xix. 8).
34. *What will be the portion of the dishonest hereafter?*
   1 Cor. vi. 9, 10.
35. *How, with God's blessing, can we best avoid dishonesty?*
   By learning and labouring truly to get our own living.
36. *Can the selfish, and those who give nothing, be called honest?*
   No: because they do not bear their due share of the common burdens.
37. *For what purpose does St. Paul tell us that we are to labour?*
   Eph. iv. 28.

SECTION XLII.—THE NINTH COMMANDMENT.

1. WHAT IS THE NINTH COMMANDMENT?
   THOU SHALT NOT BEAR FALSE WITNESS AGAINST THY NEIGHBOUR.
2. *What is the grossest form of the violation of this commandment?*
   The crime of perjury, when a man swears, or solemnly affirms that which is false. (4-7)
3. *Is this commandment broken by anything short of this?*
   Yes; it is broken by evil speaking, lying and slandering; as when we falsely attribute to any one some crime or weakness, or when we wilfully exaggerate the faults or failings of others. (3-10)
4. *In what other way is this commandment broken?*
   By detraction, *i.e.*, by attributing the good actions of another to some base or unworthy motive, and by denying his sincerity. (7-13)
5. *In what words does our Lord forbid all rash and censorious judgments?*
   " Judge not, that ye be not judged [condemn not, and ye shall not be condemned]. For with what judgment ye judge, ye shall be judged; and with what measure ye mete, it shall be measured to you again." (Matt. vii. 1.)
6. *Does our Lord here refer to rash and censorious judgment uttered by private persons?*
   Yes; He cannot possibly refer to the judgments of magistrates or judges, for the public administration of justice is God's ordinance.
7. *In what other way is this commandment broken?*
   By maliciously or wantonly exposing the sins or faults of others.
   " Above all things, have fervent charity among yourselves, for charity shall cover the multitude of sins," *i.e.*, it will not expose the faults of the brethren. (1 Peter iv. 8.)
8. *Can this commandment be broken by those who are silent?*
   Yes. If we hear anything said of our neighbour which we know to be untrue, and do not rebuke or expose the falsehood, we are guilty of the slander. (17)

9. *What persons are especially in danger of breaking this commandment?*
   Idle talkative persons, and busybodies.
   "We hear that there are some which walk among you disorderly, working not at all, but are busybodies. Now them that are such we command and exhort.... that with quietness they work, and eat their own bread." (2 Thess. iii. 11. Also 1 Tim. v. 13.) (26–30)

10. *Why are talkative persons especially in danger of breaking this commandment?*
    Because such persons are very seldom religious, or sensible, or well-read, and having nothing good or instructive to converse about, they naturally talk about the characters and actions of their neighbours.

11. *Is there any other temptation to such persons to break this commandment?*
    Yes: they generally desire to make their conversation amusing rather than truthful; and so they pander to the innate love of detraction and slander by exaggerating the mistakes and foibles of others.

12. *Is it sufficient simply to repent of this sin, and to rely upon the merits of Christ for pardon?*
    No: we must undo the evil which we have done, by frankly, and, if need be, publicly confessing it, and making every amends to the person we have slandered.
    [Zacchæus restoring four-fold. (Luke xix. 8.)]

13. *What will be the punishment of liars in the world to come?*
    "All liars shall have their part in the lake which burneth with fire and brimstone." (Rev. xxi. 8.) "There shall in no wise enter into it anything that .... maketh a lie." (Rev. xxi. 27.)

14. *Are religious persons under any temptation to commit the sin of slander?*
    Yes: owing to the division of Christians into parties and sects, religious persons are often desirous of upholding their party at the expense of the characters of those who do not belong to it.

15. *How is this commandment very frequently broken?*
    By attacking the religious character of others in (so-called) religious newspapers: this is a greater sin than private scandal, because its poison is more widely circulated.

16. *How are we to repress the sin of slander?*
    By refusing to listen to it when spoken, or to read it when in print.

By watching over our angry or envious feelings, and governing our tongues.

By continually putting up to God such a prayer as that of the Psalmist : " Set a watch, O Lord, before my mouth, and keep the door of my lips." (Psalm cxli. 3.)

17. *On what promise should unjustly maligned Christians rely?*

" Commit thy way unto the Lord, and put thy trust in Him, and He shall bring it to pass : He shall make thy righteousness as clear as the light, and thy just dealing as the noonday." (Ps. xxxvii. 5, 6.)

SHORTER CATECHISM.

1. *What is the ninth commandment?*
   Thou shalt not bear false witness against thy neighbour.
2. *What is the explanation of this commandment in the duty towards your neighbour?*
   I am to "keep my tongue from evil speaking, lying, and slandering."
3. *With what then has this commandment especially to do?*
   With the government of the tongue.
4. *What is the great sin against which this commandment is given?*
   Perjury.
5. *What is that?*
   It is swearing or affirming what is untrue of our neighbour.
6. *But supposing that we are not upon our oath, is it equally wrong to say what is false?*
   Yes ; it is equally a violation of this commandment?
7. *How is this commandment most commonly broken?*
   By evil speaking. By speaking falsely or maliciously of the character and conduct of our neighbour.
8. *What is this sin called?* Slander.
9. *Who are most guilty of this detestable sin?*
   Malicious persons who spread evil reports, not really believing them themselves.
10. *Are such grievous sinners?*
    Yes : "backbiters" and "inventors of evil things" are reckoned by the Apostle amongst those whom God has given up to a reprobate mind (Rom. i. 30).

11. *What other brand is put upon them?*
 They are called "revilers," and "shall not inherit the Kingdom of God" (1 Cor. vi. 10).
12. *What other common form of this sin is there?*
 Exaggerating the faults or weaknesses of others.
13. *Is this a great sin?*
 Yes: because the fact that our neighbour is known to have some fault of the kind makes the lying addition more readily believed.
14. *When we attempt to make the good qualities of our neighbour less, what is the sin called?* Detraction.
15. *What baseness of mind occasions this sin?* Envy.
16. *What baseness of mind makes us listen with pleasure to the person who attempts to lessen what is good in our neighbour?*
 The same base sin of envy.
17. *If we hear any one evil spoken of falsely, what is our duty?*
 To vindicate the character unjustly aspersed if we are able to do so with truth.
18. *Is the sin of evil speech frequently denounced in Scripture?*
 Yes; very frequently indeed.
19. *How does God denounce it by the mouth of Moses?*
 "Thou shalt not go up and down as a talebearer among thy people" (Levit. xix. 16).
20. *If any of our neighbours have done wrong, should we expose them?*
 Not unless it is our strict duty to do so.
21. *If we take pleasure in exposing the faults of another, what does it show?*
 That we have the mind of Satan.
22. *Why?*
 Because Satan both loves sin, and loves to accuse those who have fallen into it.
23. *What would charity lead us to do?*
 To think no evil, and not to rejoice in iniquity (1 Cor. xiii. 5, 6).
24. *And what besides?* To conceal a fault rather than expose it.
25. *What Apostle teaches us this?*
 St. Peter; where he says that "charity shall cover the multitude of sins" (1 Pet. iv. 8).
26. *If we are to keep this ninth commandment, over what member must we watch?*
 Over our tongues.
27. *What does St. James say of the tongue?*
 That "it is an unruly evil, full of deadly poison" (iii. 8).
28. *Who then can tame it?*
 The same Apostle says "that no man can tame it."

29. *How then is it to be tamed and brought into subjection?*
    By the grace of God.
30. *What can the grace of God do?*
    It can make us love our neighbour as ourselves.
31. *How will this make us keep our tongues from evil?*
    Because as there is nothing which we dislike more than to be evil spoken of in any way, so we shall be careful not to inflict this pain on others.
32. *What prayers have we in Scripture for grace to keep this commandment?* Ps. cxli. 3.
33. *What promise of earthly happiness seems to be connected with the keeping of this commandment?*
    "He that will love life, and see good days, let him refrain his tongue from evil, and his lips that they speak no guile" (1 Pet. iii. 10).
34. *Why is this promise particularly joined to the keeping of our tongues from evil speaking?*
    Because so much of the sorrow and uneasiness of life arises from the evil use of our tongues.

SECTION XLIII.—THE TENTH COMMANDMENT.

1. WHAT IS THE TENTH COMMANDMENT?
    THOU SHALT NOT COVET THY NEIGHBOUR'S HOUSE, THOU SHALT NOT COVET THY NEIGHBOUR'S WIFE, NOR HIS SERVANT, NOR HIS MAID, NOR HIS OX, NOR HIS ASS, NOR ANYTHING THAT IS HIS.
2. *What is the meaning of the word "covet?"*
    To lust after; to desire inordinately or sinfully.
    [When our Lord says, "Whosoever looketh upon a woman to lust after her" (Matt. v. 28), He uses the word which is translated covet in the Septuagint Translation of this commandment; and when St. Paul says, "I had not known lust except the law had said, Thou shalt not covet" (Rom. vii. 7), he uses the kindred noun (ἐπιθυμία); so that this commandment might be rendered, "Thou shalt not lust after, or wrongfully desire." (4)
3. *What is there peculiar about this commandment?*
    That it is always broken in the heart, and leads to the breach of some one of the other commandments, more particularly the sixth, seventh, and eighth. (3)
4. *How then is this commandment to be obeyed?*
    Only by earnest prayer to God for the cleansing of our hearts, and by keeping those hearts most diligently.
5. *What particularly does this commandment forbid?*
    The unlawful desire of that which belongs to another.
6. *Why do you say the "unlawful" desire?*
    Because we may lawfully desire some things which belong to our neighbour, as, for instance, his house or his field, if he is desirous of selling them, and we are willing to give a just price for them. (5–11)
7. *What, then, in such cases makes our desire unlawful?*
    When our desire would lead us to acquire that which belongs to our neighbour by some unlawful means. (5–16)
8. *What does the Holy Spirit, speaking by St. James, say of evil covetousness?*

That it is the mother of all sin. "When lust hath conceived, it bringeth forth sin." (James i. 15.)

9. *Show by some Scripture examples the truth of these words of the Apostle.*

Eve, through coveting the forbidden fruit (Gen. iii. 6), brought sin and death into the world. David, through coveting his neighbour's wife, committed the sins of adultery and murder. Judas Iscariot, through coveting what was not his own, ended with betraying his Master. (14–17)

10. *Are there any other notable examples of the evil effects of this sin?*

Yes : Balaam (2 Peter ii. 14, 15). Achan (Joshua vii.). Ahab (1 Kings xxi.). Gehazi (2 Kings v. 20–27).

11. *Is the scope of this commandment enlarged or extended under the Gospel?*

Yes. Covetousness, under the Gospel, is not only desiring that which belongs to another, but grasping tenaciously, and immoderately desiring to increase in, worldly goods, or power, or advantages. (21–24)

12. *Give a proof of this.*

When our Lord bids His people beware of covetousness, He brings forward an example of a rich man whose whole soul was bent upon holding fast and enjoying what rightly belonged to him. (Luke xii. 15–21) (23, 24)

13. *What does our Lord say will be the final portion of those who so hold their own that they can spare nothing for the relief of want?*

He says that He will say to them at the last day, "Depart, ye cursed, into everlasting fire . . . for I was an hungered, and ye gave me no meat." (Matt. xxv. 41.)

14. *Why is this character visited with such severity?*

Because it is most of all opposed to that of our Blessed Saviour, "Who being in the form of God, thought it not robbery (or a thing to be tenaciously held to) to be equal with God, but made himself of no reputation" (Phil. ii. 6); and "Who, though He was rich, yet for our sakes He became poor, that we through His poverty might be rich." (2 Cor. viii. 9.)

15. *Is then covetousness, as meaning selfishness and hard-heartedness, a deadly sin?*

Yes. St. Paul says, "No covetous man, who is an idolater, hath any inheritance in the kingdom of Christ and of God." (Eph. v. 5.) (*See* also 1 Cor. v. 11 ; vi. 10 ; Col. iii. 5 ; Heb. xiii. 5.)

16. *Is it enough that we try to root out of our souls all evil desires?*

No ; we must, by the power of God's Holy Spirit, have in our hearts good desires. (25, 26)

17. *What good gift is that which we can never too ardently desire or covet?*

The Holy Spirit and His sanctifying influence. After speaking of the gifts of the Spirit, St. Paul says, " covet earnestly the best gifts." (1 Cor. xii. 31.) (27)

SHORTER CATECHISM.

1. *What is the tenth commandment?* Thou shalt not covet, &c.
2. *How is it enforced in the duty towards our neighbour?*
   In the words, "not to covet nor desire other men's goods."
3. *What has this commandment to do with?*
   It has to do with the secret desires and inclinations of our hearts.
4. *What do you mean by coveting?*
   I mean desiring to have something which I do not now possess.
5. *What is it which you are not to covet?*
   Anything that is my neighbour's.
6. *But may not we sometimes wish to buy at a lawful price the goods of our neighbour?*
   Yes : we may, if he is willing to sell them.
7. *When then is it wrong to desire what belongs to our neighbours?*
   When the desire leads us to get it, or to wish to get it, in some wrong or sinful way.
8. *Mention an instance of this.* Ahab.
9. *What did he covet?* The vineyard of Naboth (1 Kings xxi. 2-17).
10. *Because Naboth would not sell his vineyard, what did Ahab become?*
    Discontented and envious (1 Kings xxi. 4).
11. *How at last did he succeed in getting it?*
    By perjury and murder (2 Kings xxi. 13).
12. *What other instance have we of covetousness leading to sin?*
    Gehazi (2 Kings v. 20).
13. *How did sin enter into the world?*
    Through covetousness (Gen. iii. 6).

14. *How was this?*
    Eve desired (or coveted) to eat a fruit which God had strictly forbidden her to touch.
15. *What sin occasioned the falling away of an Apostle and the betrayal of our Lord?*
    Covetousness: which led Judas to steal what was in the bag (John xii. 6).
16. *But how did this make him betray our Lord?*
    The strong desire increased with its unlawful gratification, so that he took the bribe of the chief priests.
17. *What great Old Testament saint fell into sin through unlawful desire?* David.
18. *What does our Lord say of this kind of covetousness (or evil desire)?* Matt. v. 28.
19. *What does St. Paul say of the tenth commandment?*
    That it brought him (and all men) guilty before God (Rom. vii. 7).
20. *How did it do this?*
    Because it showed him that there may be sin in the heart, though the outward conduct may be correct.
21. *Can men be covetous even though they do not desire other men's goods?*
    Yes: when they are always thinking about increasing their own goods.
22. *How besides?*
    When they think that their riches are given to them for themselves alone.
23. *What example of this does our Lord hold up for our warning?*
    The rich fool who laid up treasures for himself and was not rich toward God (Luke xii. 16-21).
24. *With what punishment will God visit those who look upon their goods as their own and do not relieve the wants of others?*
    Matt. xxv. 41.
25. *What Christian disposition will keep us from covetousness?*
    Contentment (Phil. iv. 11; 1 Tim. vi. 8; Heb. xiii. 5).
26. *But what must contentment be joined with?*
    Godliness (1 Tim. vi. 6).
27. *Is it lawful for Christians to covet anything?*
    Yes: they are to covet earnestly the best gifts of the Spirit (1 Cor. xii. 31).

SECTION XLIV.—PRAYER.

1. MY GOOD CHILD, KNOW THIS, THAT THOU ART NOT ABLE TO DO THESE THINGS OF THYSELF, NOR TO WALK IN THE COMMANDMENTS OF GOD, AND TO SERVE HIM WITHOUT HIS SPECIAL GRACE, WHICH THOU MUST LEARN AT ALL TIMES TO CALL FOR BY DILIGENT PRAYER. LET ME HEAR, THEREFORE, IF THOU CANST SAY THE LORD'S PRAYER?
OUR FATHER WHICH ART IN HEAVEN, &c.

2. *What do you mean by the special grace of God?*
I mean a particular gift of the power of God's Holy Spirit, given to each person to enable him to walk in the commandments of God, and to serve Him. (1-10)

3. *What is prayer?*
The lifting up of the heart to God, generally expressed in words of prayer and thanksgiving; but sometimes felt only in hearty desires and longings for His grace and help.

4. *Can you show that we cannot serve God without His special grace?*
Yes: our Saviour says, "Without Me ye can do nothing" (John xv. 5); and St. Paul says, "I can do all things through Christ which strengtheneth me." (Phil. iv. 13.) (11)

5. *But does not our Saviour say that God knows what we have need of before we ask Him?*
Yes; but God requires us to pray to Him for all we need, in order to testify our dependence upon Him as the Giver of all grace. (12-18)

6. *But if we cannot serve God without His special grace, is it our own fault if we do not serve Him?*
Yes; because God has promised to hear all prayer: His Son has said in His name, "Ask, and it shall be given you; seek, and ye shall find; knock, and it shall be opened unto you: for every one that asketh receiveth." (Matt. vii. 7, 8.) (12-14)

7. *How must we pray, if our prayers are to be answered?*
We must pray—

1. In the name of Christ. (John xvi. 23.)
2. With faith, *i.e.*, assuredly believing that God will keep His promise, and, if it be good for us, answer our prayer. (Mark xi. 24.)
3. With resignation to the will of God, as our Saviour Himself set us the example of doing when He prayed, "Father, if Thou be willing, remove this cup from Me; nevertheless, not my will, but Thine be done." (Luke xxii. 42.)
4. With perseverance. We cannot be sincere in our desires for grace, unless we persevere until we get an answer. (Luke xi. 5-13.) (19-24)

8. *What further condition does our Lord very emphatically lay down?*
That we must forgive others. (Mark xi. 25, 26.) (25, 26)

9. *Should we use any other words than those which the Lord has taught us?*
Yes: God invites us to make supplication to Him for everything. (Phil. iv. 6.)

10. *But does not the Lord's Prayer express everything that we can desire?*
It expresses everything that we can ask of God, but in general terms; and God invites us to mention to Him particularly all that we desire.

11. *What other prayers have Christians always used?*
The prayers in the Psalms, and other parts of Scripture. The prayers of the Church, and forms composed by holy men, and prayers expressed in our own words. (27, 28)

SHORTER CATECHISM.

1. *What things are those which you cannot do of yourself?*
The things contained in my duty towards God and my duty towards my neighbour.
2. *What must God give us to enable us to walk in His commandments and serve Him?*
His special grace.
3. *What is the one great grace which God gives to Christians?*
His Holy Spirit.

4. *What is meant by special grace?*
   A particular gift of God's Holy Spirit to each person.
5. *How are we to obtain this special grace?*
   By diligent prayer.
6. *When?* At all times.
7. *Why are we at all times to call for special grace?*
   Because at *all* times we are liable to temptation.
8. *Mention some prayer in the Prayer Book for this special grace.*
   In the Litany. "That it may please Thee to . . . . endue us with the grace of Thy Holy Spirit, to amend our lives according to Thy Holy Word."
9. *Mention another.*
   In the Absolution, the Priest thus calls upon us to pray: "Wherefore let us beseech Him to grant us true repentance and His Holy Spirit, that those things may please Him," &c.
10. *Mention a third.*
    In the Collect for Easter Day we say: "As by Thy special grace preventing us Thou dost put into our minds good desires, so by Thy continual help we may bring the same to good effect."
11. *How do we know that we cannot serve God without special grace?*
    Because our Saviour says, "Without Me ye can do nothing" (John xv. 5)
12. *If God gives us special grace, can we serve Him?*
    St. Paul says, "I can do all things through Christ which strengtheneth me" (Phil. iv. 13).
13. *If then we do not serve God, whose fault is it?* Our own fault.
14. *Why?*
    Because God, through Christ, promises to give the Holy Spirit to them that ask Him (Luke xi. 13).
15. *Was not grace given to us in Holy Baptism?*
    Yes: but we are to live in continual dependence upon God's grace.
16. *How must we show this dependence?*
    By calling for God's grace at all times.
17. *Show that we are to pray at all times.*
    St. Paul says, "In every thing by prayer and supplication with thanksgiving let your requests be made known unto God" (Phil. iv. 6).
18. *What then must we always join with prayer?* Thanksgiving.
19. *In whose Name are we to pray?*
    In the Name of Jesus (John xvi. 23).
20. *In what spirit?* In a spirit of faith.
21. *How will that appear?*
    We shall confidently believe that God will hear us according to His promises.

22. *What further grace must we have?*
    Resignation to God's will.
23. *In what words did our Lord show this resignation?*
    "Not My will but Thine be done" (Luke xxii. 42).
24. *How must we show our earnest desire for God's grace and help?*
    By our continuance in prayer; by our not ceasing (Rom xii. 12; Eph. vi. 18; 1 Thess. v. 17).
25. *To whom does our Lord confine the promises of forgiveness?*
    To those who forgive their brethren.
26. *In what words?* Matt. vi. 14, 15; Mark xi. 25, 26.
27. *In prayer to God, may we express what we want in our own words?*
    Yes; most certainly.
28. *Have we any other prayers taught us in Scripture?*
    Yes: very many in the Book of Psalms.
29. *What is the great difference between these and the Lord's Prayer?*
    We *may* use these other prayers at our discretion; we must use the Lord's Prayer.

SECTION XLV.—THE LORD'S PRAYER—OUR FATHER.

1. *When did our Lord teach us His prayer?*
   On two occasions:
   1st. In the Sermon on the Mount, where He says, "After this manner therefore pray ye" (Matt. vi. 9); and on another occasion (Luke xi. 1,2), where He says, "When ye pray, say, Our Father which art in heaven." (1–3)
2. *Has it not been said that "after this manner" means "use this as a model?"*
   Our Lord does not really say "after this manner:" He uses the word elsewhere translated "thus" (ουτως). He uses, for instance, the same word which is used in Matt. ii. 5, in giving the very words of a quotation from the Old Testament, "In Bethlehem of Judæa: for thus (*i.e.*, in these very words) it is written by the prophet, And thou Bethlehem," &c. (4–7)
3. *Is there any other reason for believing that our Lord means us to use His very words?*
   Yes; He has just been speaking against vain repetitions and much speaking; and to save us from this evil He gives us a short and concise form of words.
4. *Can you name any other reason?*
   Yes; He evidently enjoins on us the use of the very words, "And forgive us our trespasses, as we forgive them that trespass against us," for he draws attention to the form in which He had expressed this petition for forgiveness. (Matt. vi. 14.)
5. *But could not such words be used by those who use the Lord's Prayer as a model?*
   We only know this, that they who discard the use of the very words of the Lord's Prayer would be the very last to introduce any such a condition into any words of their own composing. (6)
6. *Is there any very great reason why our Lord should teach us how to pray?*
   Yes: being very God, He knows what is most in accordance with the glory of God; and being very Man, He knows what is most suitable to the needs of man.

7. *How may the Lord's Prayer be divided?*
   Into three parts :
   The address. The petitions. The doxology.
8. *What is the address?*
   Our Father which art in heaven.
9. *Why do we here call God by the name of Father?*
   Because He is the Father of one only Son, of whom we are the brethren.
   "Go to my brethren, and say unto them, I ascend unto My Father, and your Father, and to My God and your God." (John xx. 17.) (10-13)
10. *What do we learn by this, that our Lord bids us say "Our" Father?*
    That we must not be thinking of ourselves alone, even in prayer, but that we must in thought bear the whole redeemed family to the throne of grace. (14-19)
11. *Are we then to exclude the heathen from the benefit of our prayers?*
    No : God is the Father of all men by creation ; and St. Paul exhorts that prayers, supplications, intercessions and giving of thanks be made for all men ; for kings and for all that are in authority (all of whom were, in his day, heathen); for there is one God and one Mediator... who gave Himself a ransom for all. (1 Tim. ii. 1-6.) (16-19)
12. *How are the words "Our Father" explained in the answer to the question, "What desirest thou of God in this prayer?*
    I desire my Lord God, our heavenly Father, who is the Giver of all goodness, to send His grace unto me and to all people, &c.
13. *Why do we mention to God that He dwells in heaven, seeing that He is everywhere?*
    Because our Advocate, Who taught us this prayer, is there seated at His right hand. We have an Advocate WITH the Father. (1 John ii. 1.) (19-25)
14. *Does our Saviour ever set us the example of saying, "Our" Father, in His prayers to God?*
    No ; never once. He is the only-begotten of the Father, and it is His sole prerogative to say, " My Father."
15. *Do any of the Apostles ever say "My Father" in their prayers?*
    No ; they never once separate themselves from their brethren in their approaches to God.

SHORTER CATECHISM.

1. *How often did our Lord teach His disciples this Prayer?*
   Twice.
2. *What was the first of these occasions?*
   When He was delivering the sermon on the Mount.
3. *What was the second?*
   When His disciples asked Him to teach them to pray, as John also had taught his disciples (Luke xi. 1).
4. *Should we use the very words of the Lord's Prayer?*
   Yes: it is impossible to alter them for the better.
5. *How do we know this?*
   Because our Lord gave us this short and full form in order to save us from using vain repetitions.
6. *Can men make this prayer a model on which to compose other prayers?*
   No: it is impossible so to do.
   [There are paraphrases or expositions of it in abundance, but none, that I have seen, formed on it as a model.]
7. *When our Lord bids us use this prayer, does He forbid us using other words?*
   No: the Holy Spirit inspired the Apostles on many occasions to use other words (Acts iv. 24; Eph. i. 16-23; iii. 14).
8. *Should we ever use our own words?*
   Yes: unless we speak to God in our own words we cannot open our hearts to Him.
9. *Does He encourage us to tell Him all that is in our hearts?*
   Yes: in everything we are to make our requests known unto God (Phil. iv. 6).
10. *What is the first part of the Lord's Prayer called?*
    The address or invocation.
11. *How do we address God?* As our Father Who is in Heaven.
12. *Why can we call God our Father?*
    Because we have been made members of Christ.
13. *Can then only those who have been made members of Christ use this Prayer?*
    In the early Church it was only taught to the baptized.
14. *Do we say "My" Father or "Our" Father?* Our Father.
15. *What should this teach us?*
    That we are not to pray for ourselves alone.
16. *Whom besides ourselves are we to think of in our Prayers?*
    All men; but especially the Church of Christ.
17. *What word of Scripture have you for this?*
    Let us do good unto all men, especially unto them who are of the household of faith (Gal. vi. 10).

18. *Is there any other Scripture reason?*
   Yes : the living God is "the Saviour of all men, specially of those that believe" (1 Tim. iv. 10).
19. *Can you give another?* Yes (1 Tim. ii. 1-6).
20. *In invoking or addressing God, of what do we make mention?*
   Of His dwelling-place, for we say, "Our Father, *which art in Heaven.*"
21. *But does not God fill Heaven and earth?*
   Yes; but He has taught us that He especially dwells in Heaven.
22. *Why do we especially call upon God as being in Heaven?*
   Because His Son, Who is our Advocate, is there at His right hand.
23. *Does our Saviour elsewhere speak of our Father in Heaven?*
   Yes : in the very discourse in which He teaches us this prayer.
24. *When He speaks of our Father in Heaven, with whom does He compare Him?*
   With our fathers on earth.
25. *In what respect?*
   In His far greater readiness to hear the prayers of His children.
26. *What are Christ's words?*
   What man is there of you, whom if his son ask bread, will he give him a stone? . . . . If ye then, being evil, know how to give good gifts unto your children, how much more shall your Father which is in Heaven give good things to them that ask Him ? (Matt. vii. 7).

SECTION XLVI.—HALLOWED BE THY NAME.

1. *What is the first petition of the Lord's Prayer?*
   Hallowed be Thy Name.
2. *How is this petition explained in the "Desire?"*
   "I desire my Lord God, our heavenly Father .... to send His grace unto me and to all people, that we may worship Him ... as we ought to do."
3. *How do we hallow God's name?*
   By offering to Him the holy worship which is His due.
   "For from the rising of the sun even unto the going down of the same My name shall be great among the Gentiles; and in every place incense shall be offered unto My name, and a pure offering: for My name shall be great among the heathen, saith the Lord of Hosts." (Mal. i. 11.) (2–12)
4. *How has this promise of God been always interpreted by the Church?*
   As referring to that Holy Sacrament in which we especially commemorate the work of Redemption, and show forth our Lord's death till He come. (9–11)
5. *Is the hallowing of God's name ever expressly connected with our holding the faith of Christ?*
   Yes; God hath given to Christ a name that is above every name; that "at the name of Jesus every knee should bow .... and every tongue confess that Jesus Christ is Lord, to the glory of God the Father." (Phil. ii. 10).
6. *What must be inseparably connected with holy worship?*
   Hallowing God in our hearts (1 Pet. iii. 15), and in our lives and works. (Matt. v. 16; Rom. xii. 1; also Ezek. xxxvi. 20.) (13–15)
7. *What are we taught by the fact that this petition is the first petition?*
   That we should seek, and pray for, the glory of God above all things.
8. *Who set us an example of this?*
   Jesus Christ, Who could say, "I seek not mine own glory" (John viii. 50); and Who could say, "I have glorified Thee on the earth : I have finished the work which Thou gavest me to do." (John xvii. 4).

SHORTER CATECHISM.

1. *What is the next part of the Lord's Prayer?* The six petitions.
2. *What is the first of these?* Hallowed be Thy Name.
3. *What do we mean by hallowing anything?*
   Keeping it holy. Giving it the honour due to it. Keeping it from being profaned (the Lord's Day, for example).
4. *How, first of all, are we to hallow God's name?*
   By calling upon His Name in holy worship.
5. *Who set us an example of this?* Our Saviour, Christ.
6. *How did He do this?*
   By worshipping God in His temple, and by driving out of it those who profaned it.
7. *Who hallow God's Name in Heaven?*
   The cherubim and seraphim, who continually cry, "Holy, Holy, Holy."
8. *Who hallow God's Name on earth?*
   Christians, in their holy worship.
9. *What is the worship of Christians?*
   Prayer, praise, thanksgiving, supplications, intercessions.
10. *Is there any act of worship which is above all these, and comprehends them all?*
    Yes: the celebration of the Eucharist or Holy Communion.
11. *Why is this the greatest act of worship?*
    Because it is the only thing which our Lord ordained to be done in remembrance of Him—to show forth His death.
12. *Does the Church explain this petition as referring to Christian worship?*
    Yes: we desire of God grace that we may worship Him .... as we ought to do.
13. *Are we to honour God's Name with our lips only?*
    No: with our hearts and in our lives.
14. *How are we to worship Him with our hearts?*
    By worshipping Him in spirit and in truth.
15. *How with our lives?*
    By presenting our bodies living sacrifices, holy, acceptable to Him (Rom. xii. 1).

SECTION XLVII.—THY KINGDOM COME.

1. *What is the second petition?*
   Thy kingdom come.
2. *What do we ask for when we pray, "Thy kingdom come?"*
   We pray that the Church of Christ may be extended throughout the world.
3. *But as we are already living in this kingdom, since we are members of the Church, how can we pray that it may come?*
   Because we pray for all men as well as for ourselves; and we must pray for those who have not the Gospel, that God may bring them under its power.
4. *What further meanings has the term kingdom of God?*
   It means the kingdom of God in the heart.
   "The kingdom of God is not meat and drink; but righteousness, and peace, and joy in the Holy Ghost." (Rom. xiv. 17.)
   It also means the kingdom of Glory to be revealed at the second coming of Christ. (2 Tim. iv. 1.) (7–13)
5. *How do we know that we must include the coming of Christ under this petition?*
   Because the very last words of the New Testament are "Amen; even so come, Lord Jesus." (14–19)
6. *Where in the Prayer Book have we a similar petition?*
   When we pray to God in the Burial Service shortly to accomplish the number of His elect, and to hasten His Kingdom. (14–19)
7. *How is this petition explained in the "Desire?"*
   "I desire my Lord God, our heavenly Father, . . . to send His grace unto me and to all people, that we may . . . serve Him . . . as we ought to do."
8. *How ought we to serve God?*
   With the loyalty and devotion with which good soldiers and subjects serve their King.

SHORTER CATECHISM.

1. *What is the second petition?* Thy kingdom come.
2. *What does the kingdom of God mean?* It has three meanings.

3. *What is the first of these meanings?*
    It means the Church of Jesus Christ.
4. *Where in Scripture does it mean this?*
    In very many of our Lord's parables, as where He says: "The kingdom of Heaven is like unto a man which sowed good seed in his field;" and "The kingdom of Heaven is like unto a net" (Matt. xiii. 24, 47).
5. *In what way can we pray that this kingdom may come?*
    We pray that it may come to those who know it not.
6. *In what words in our Liturgy do we express the same?*
    "That Thy way may be known upon earth: Thy saving health among all nations."
7. *Is there a second sense in which we put up this petition?*
    Yes: in it we pray that God may rule in the hearts of ourselves and of all men.
8. *Is the term "kingdom of God" used in this sense in Scripture?*
    Yes, in the words: The kingdom of God is not meat and drink; but righteousness, and peace, and joy in the Holy Ghost (Rom xiv. 17).
9. *Have we any prayers for this in the Liturgy?* Yes: very many.
10. *Mention one.*
    "That all our doings may be ordered by Thy governance, to do always that is righteous in Thy sight."
11. *Mention another.*
    "O Lamb of God, that takest away the sins of the world, Grant us Thy peace;" and again, "Give unto Thy servants that peace which the world cannot give, that both our hearts may be set to obey Thy commandments."
12. *Mention another.* "Make Thy chosen people joyful."
13. *In what one word is the end of this petition expressed in the Desire?*
    That we and all men may "serve" God as we ought to do.
14. *Is there yet a third meaning of the kingdom of God?*
    Yes: it means the kingdom of glory.
15. *When will this come?* When Christ comes again.
16. *What then do we pray for when we say "Thy kingdom come?"*
    That Christ may come again and receive us to Himself.
17. *Who alone can put up such a prayer?*
    Those who are preparing themselves to meet Him.
18. *Do we pray for this in the Liturgy?*
    Yes: when we pray Him shortly to accomplish the members of His elect and to hasten His kingdom.
19. *Is there any such prayer in the New Testament?*
    Yes: Rev. xxii. 20.

SECTION XLVIII.—THY WILL BE DONE.

1. *What is the third petition?*
   Thy will be done in earth, as it is in Heaven.
2. *In how many senses may this petition be taken?*
   In two. As a prayer, or as an act of submission.
3. *Can you mention some things which are expressly declared in Scripture to be the will of God?*
   1. That we should believe in His Son, and have everlasting life by so doing. (John vi. 40.)
   2. Our Sanctification. (1 Thess. iv. 3.) (3–6)
4. *Since, then, these things are the will of God, how is it that all men do not believe in Jesus Christ, and become holy?*
   Because God, in order that He may prove men, suffers them to resist His will.
5. *Can men resist the will of an Almighty God?*
   Yes: God expressly tells us that, in a sense, they can; for He speaks of men resisting (Acts vii. 51), rebelling against (Isa. lxiii. 10), grieving (Eph. iv. 30), doing despite to (Heb. x. 29) His Holy Spirit.
6. *Why does God allow His will to be resisted?*
   Because He desires His intelligent creatures to serve Him freely and willingly; and if this be so they must be tried, and their trial would be a mockery unless they had a will free to choose the service of God or to reject His service.
7. *Mention some other things which are declared to be the will of God.*
   That in everything we give thanks. (1 Thess. v. 18.)
   That we submit to every ordinance of man for the Lord's sake. (1 Pet. ii. 13–15.)
   That we be perfect in every good work. (Heb. xiii. 21; also Col. i. 9, 10.) (7–9)
8. *But did you not say that these words of the Lord's Prayer may be taken as an act of submission as well as a prayer?*
   Yes: in them we should submit our own wills to God's

will ; so as to express our readiness to suffer all that He lays upon us, as our Saviour taught us when He said, " Not My will, but Thine be done." (Luke xxii. 42.) (10–16)

9. *How are we to do the will of God ?*
As the angels in heaven do, willingly, perfectly, continually.

SHORTER CATECHISM.

1. *What is the third petition ?*
Thy will be done in earth, as it is in Heaven.
2. *What grace do you ask for in this petition ?*
For grace to do God's will.
3. *What is the will of God ?*
That we should all believe in His Son.
4. *Where is it said that this is His will ?*
In John vi. 40. " This is the will of Him that sent Me, that every one that seeth the Son and believeth on Him, may have everlasting life."
5. *Is this declared in any other place of Scripture to be God's will ?*
Yes : God will have all men to be saved and to come unto the knowledge of the truth (1 Tim. ii. 4).
6. *Is the will of God respecting us expressed in other words ?*
Yes : that we should be holy or sanctified (1 Thess. iv. 3).
7. *Are any things besides these called the will of God ?*
Yes : " in every thing give thanks, for this is the will of God in Christ Jesus concerning you " (1 Thess. v. 18).
8. *Is the doing of God's will necessary to our attaining eternal life ?*
Yes : " Not every one that saith unto Me, Lord, Lord, shall enter into the Kingdom of Heaven, but he that doeth the will of My Father which is in Heaven " (Matt. vii. 21).
9. *What does Christ say of him who does God's will ?*
"Whosoever shall do the will of My Father which is in Heaven, the same is my brother, and sister, and mother " (Matt. xii. 50).
10. *What further grace do you ask for ?*
That I may have grace to suffer patiently all that God lays upon me.
11. *Who set us an example of thus saying " Thy will be done ?"*
Our Saviour, in the Garden of Gethsemane (Luke xxii. 42).
12. *Did our Lord desire that He might not suffer ?*
Yes : He prayed, " If it be possible, let this cup pass from Me" (Matt. xxvi. 39).

13. *Did He submit to God?*
    Yes; in the words, "not My will, but Thine be done" (Luke xxii. 42).
14. *What then are these words?*
    They are an act of submission as well as a prayer.
15. *Is it not sometimes very hard to say these words, as when God takes away from us our dear relations and friends?*
    Yes: but God in all things knows and does what is best.
16. *Can we always feel this?*
    No: sometimes we do not feel it now, but we shall know it hereafter.

SECTION XLIX.—GIVE US THIS DAY OUR DAILY BREAD.

1. *What is the fourth petition?*
Give us this day (or day by day) our daily bread.
2. *What is the explanation of this petition in the " Desire ?"*
"I pray unto God that He will send us all things that be needful, both for our souls and bodies."
3. *What then do we mean by " bread " here?*
All things needful for the sustenance and preservation of our earthly as well as our spiritual life. (3-8)
4. *Is it not our duty to labour for our daily bread?*
Yes; but it is God who gives seed to the sower, and bread to the eater (Isa. lv. 10); for it is He who gives rain and sunshine, and protects what is sown from blight. (3-8)
5. *Must those who have no need to labour for daily sustenance say this prayer?*
Yes; for God can at any time deprive them of all benefit from their stores, so that their bread will cease to nourish and support them. (13, 14)
6. *Why do we ask for " daily " bread?*
To remind us of our daily need of the provident care of God. (9, 10)
7. *What then can these words be considered?*
An act of dependence upon God; a daily committing of ourselves to His Fatherly care. (12-15)
8. *What are we taught by being bid to pray for daily " bread "?*
That we are not to desire luxuries and superfluities, remembering that such things are always spoken of in Scripture as dangerous to the soul. [So that this prayer is like in meaning to that of the wise man: "Give me neither poverty nor riches; feed me with food convenient for me." (Prov. xxx. 8.)] (11)
9. *If God has given to us more than He has given to others, what should we remember?*
That it is a mockery to put up this petition, unless we do what we can to relieve the wants of others.

10. *What is the bread of the soul?*
   The Bread of Life : Jesus Christ. (17–20)
11. *How do we receive Him as the Bread of Life?*
   In two ways :
   We receive Him in the hearing of His word ; and we receive Him Sacramentally in the devout reception of His Body and Blood in Holy Communion. (20–24)
12. *Can we receive Him as the Bread of Life in one of these ways alone, by itself?*
   Not ordinarily. They must both go together, for God has ordained both.
13. *Why do you say ordinarily?*
   Because there may be cases in which we are not able to receive the Holy Eucharist ; in which cases we hope and trust that, if we feed on the truths of God's Holy word respecting Jesus Christ with our souls, God will make up what we lose by our constrained absence from His Sacrament.
14. *For what then do we ask God, in the matter of our spiritual food, when we say this petition?*
   We ask Him, that by His grace we may labour for (John vi. 27), and obtain, Christ as the true Bread of Life ; and also that we may have opportunity and grace to receive Him in every way in which God sets Him forth to us. (20–24)

SHORTER CATECHISM.

1. *What is the fourth petition?* Give us this day our daily bread.
2. *Is there any variation of this petition?*
   Yes : in St. Luke's account we have, "Give us day by day."
3. *What is meant by "bread" here?*
   All things needful to support our lives.
4. *What things are to be reckoned amongst these?*
   Clothing, shelter, health, strength to labour, means of livelihood.
5. *Mention another needful thing.*
   Medicine and attendance when we are sick.
6. *What is there remarkable about this petition?*
   That it is the only one in which we mention the needs of the body.

7. *What bread do we ask for?* Our daily bread.
8. *What has the word daily been taken to mean?*
   Needful. Our needful necessary sustenance.
9. *What supply do we ask for?*
   Only our *daily* portion. Give us *this* day. Day by day.
10. *By teaching us to say give us "this" day, what does our Lord enjoin?*
    That we say this prayer daily, and early each day.
11. *What has been said about our Lord teaching us to pray for "bread?"*
    That He teaches us to look only for the necessaries of life, not for the luxuries.
12. *If we say this prayer from our hearts what do we show?*
    Our feeling of dependence upon God.
13. *Do the rich depend upon God?*
    Yes: God can, at any time, take away all their goods.
14. *If He does not do that, can He yet show them that they depend upon Him?*
    Yes: He can at any moment deprive them of their health, or of all worldly enjoyment.
15. *How is this prayer explained in the "Desire?"*
    I pray unto God that He will send us all things that be needful both for our souls and bodies.
16. *What needs are mentioned here?*
    Those of the soul as well as of the body.
17. *What does the soul require?* The Bread of Life.
18. *What is the Bread of Life?* Jesus Christ (John vi. 48).
19. *Who gives us this bread?* God the Son (John vi. 27).
20. *How does He give us Himself as the Bread of Life?*
    Through His Word.
21. *Is there any ordinance of His Church in which He especially offers to us Himself as the Bread of Life?*
    Yes: the Holy Communion.
22. *What does He say to us there?*
    "Take, eat, this is My body which is given for you."
23. *What then do we ask for in this petition?*
    That God would make us partakers of His Son Jesus Christ.
24. *In what way?*
    In every way in which He is pleased to do so, especially in the Holy Communion.

SECTION L.—AND FORGIVE US OUR TRESPASSES.

1. *What is the next petition?*
   And forgive us our trespasses, as we forgive them that trespass against us.
2. *What does the word " trespasses " mean in the original?*
   Debts. We owe perfect obedience to God; and everything short of that obedience, *i. e.*, all sin, is a debt which is set down against us. (2-7)
3. *In what sense, then, do we ask for forgiveness?*
   As the free remission of a debt.
4. *On what account are we forgiven?*
   On account of the full, perfect, and sufficient Sacrifice, Oblation, and Satisfaction made by our Lord upon the cross. (8, 9)
5. *Who receive this forgiveness?*
   Those who repent and believe the Gospel. (10)
6. *Is there any limitation to the grant of this forgiveness laid down by Christ Himself in this prayer?*
   Yes. Christ teaches us to ask for forgiveness for ourselves only as we forgive others. (10-16)
7. *Are we sure that He means to make this limitation?*
   Yes; because He particularly singles out the words of this condition, or limitation, and repeats their sense in other words immediately after He has taught the prayer.
   [" For if ye forgive men their trespasses, your heavenly Father will also forgive you; but if ye forgive not men their trespasses, neither will your Father forgive your trespasses." (Matt. vi. 14, 15.) So also in Mark xi. 26 ; " If ye do not forgive, neither will your Father which is in heaven forgive your trespasses." And He also gives us the Parable of the Unmerciful Servant (Matt. xviii. 23-35), who was cast out of his state of forgiveness, and had all his sins imputed afresh to him, because he did not forgive his fellow-servant.] (10-16)
8. *If he whom we have offended, or who has offended us, will not be reconciled, what must we do?*
   We must determine in our hearts to bear no malice

against him, and we must pray to God for him that God may give him a better mind. [Pray for them which despitefully use you, and persecute you. (Matt. v. 44).]

9. *What must be the limit of our forgiveness of others?*
"Lord, how oft shall my brother sin against me, and I forgive him? till seven times? Jesus saith unto him, I say not unto thee, Until seven times : but, until seventy times seven." (Matt. xviii. 21, 22.)

SHORTER CATECHISM.

1. *What is the fifth petition?*
And forgive us our trespasses as we forgive them that trespass against us.
2. *How is this expressed in the sermon on the Mount?*
And forgive us our debts, as we forgive our debtors.
3. *And how in the Gospel of St. Luke?*
And forgive us our sins, for we also forgive every one that is indebted to us.
4. *Does our Lord teach us what these debts are?*
Yes : He teaches us that they are sins or trespasses ; for He says, If ye forgive men their trespasses, your Heavenly Father will also forgive you (Matt. vi. 14).
5. *How is it that sins can be called debts?*
Because we owe obedience to God in all things, and if we do not obey we do not pay what is due from us, and so are in debt.
6. *Can we pay in the future what we owe from the past?*
No : future obedience cannot make up for past transgressions.
7. *Why?* Because we owe all possible obedience for the future.
8. *How then can we be forgiven?*
Through the merits and mediation of Jesus Christ.
9. *How is this expressed in the Scriptures?*
In such words as—In whom (Jesus Christ) we have redemption through His blood, the forgiveness of sins (Col. i. 14).
10. *Will all be forgiven?*
No : only those who repent and believe the Gospel.
11. *To whom is this forgiveness limited?*
To those who forgive their brethren.
12. *Who has set this limit?* Jesus Christ our Saviour.
13. *How often?* Many times. Five times at least.
14. *What is the first of these?*
When He teaches us to pray in this very prayer : "And

forgive us our trespasses, as we forgive them that trespass against us."

15. *In what further words does He limit forgiveness to those who forgive?*
   If ye forgive men, &c. (Matt. vi. 14: also Mark xi. 26; Luke xi. 4).

16. *By what parable does our Lord enforce the same truth?*
   By that of the Unmerciful Servant (Matt. xviii. 23-35).

17. *What will make us ready to forgive?*
   Striving by God's help to follow the example of Christ.

18. *What besides?*
   The remembrance of how much we ourselves need forgiveness (Matt. xviii. 32, 33).

SECTION LI.—AND LEAD US NOT INTO TEMPTATION.

1. *What is the last petition of the Lord's Prayer?*
And lead us not into temptation, but deliver us from evil.

2. *Have we here two petitions, or one only?*
It is explained by some of the best expositors, ancient and modern, as if it were one. We pray not to be exempted from temptation; for, as long as we are in a state of probation or trial, we must be proved or tried by temptation; but we pray to be delivered from falling into sin under temptation: that is, from evil. (1–6)

3. *How then would you express the meaning of this petition in other words?*
Suffer us not to be led into any temptation unless Thou be with us to save us from falling into sin.

4. *Does God lead men into temptation?*
He may be said to do so when by His providence men are exposed to temptation. (Matt. iv. 1.)

5. *Does God tempt men to sin?*
No: St. James tells us that God cannot be tempted with evil, neither tempteth He any man. (James i. 13.) (15–17.)

6. *Are we all exposed to temptation from within?*
Yes; our original sin issues in some propensity to evil; some are tempted by anger or passion, some by lust, some by covetousness, some by sloth, some by pride or vainglory. (5–12)

7. *Are we exposed to temptations from without?*
Yes: the word of God teaches us that we are surrounded by wicked spirits, who have the power to suggest to our hearts things which lead us to fall from God. (Eph. vi. 12.) (11–14)

8. *Are we ever safe from the suggestions of these evil spirits?*
No: we read that Adam and Eve were tempted when in a state of innocence; and Satan entered into Judas when he was in the immediate presence of Christ Himself. (John xiii. 27.)

9. *Are the "people of God," and "believers," in danger from temptations?*

Yes. St. Paul cites the example of the Israelites repeatedly falling from God as a warning to baptized believers (1 Cor. x. 1-10); and our Lord speaks of those who "for a while believe, and in time of temptation fall away." (Luke viii. 13.)

10. *Can you show in the words of the Catechism that we do not pray to be exempted from trial, but that we may be upheld under the trial?*

Yes. We pray God to save and defend us not *from* all danger, but, *in* all dangers, ghostly and bodily. (2-8, (15-18)

11. *Give an example of God saving a man not from, but in, a ghostly danger.*

Joseph: by the providence of God he was exposed to temptation, but by the grace of God he was preserved from sin. (Gen. xxxix.)

12. *Give an example of one saved, not from, but in bodily danger.*

St. Paul; who was shipwrecked, beaten with rods, stoned, persecuted, and yet upheld to persevere under all. (2 Cor. xi. 23-27.)

13. *Would it have been well if the providence of God had kept these men from trial or danger?*

No: in the one case the Church would have lost a bright example of faith realizing the presence of God; in the other, of love "enduring all things."

14. *Is it enough for us to pray that we may not be led into temptation?*

No; we must "watch and pray," and we must keep out of the way of temptation.

15. *What besides these things must we do?*

We must remember that God's eye is upon us, and make an act of faith in His presence; as, for instance, "Thou God seest me."

16. *What besides this must we do?*

We must remember that our Saviour said respecting certain evil spirits, "This kind goeth not out but by prayer and fasting" (Matt. xvii. 21); and that St. Paul said, "I keep under my body, and bring it into subjection." (1 Cor. ix. 27.)

17. *What, above all, must we remember?*

That we are redeemed with the Blood of Christ. "They overcame him (Satan) by the Blood of the Lamb." (Rev. xii. 11.)

18. *What is the latter part of this petition?*
But deliver us from evil.

19. *How is this explained in the " desire?"*
"And that he will keep us from all sin and wickedness, and from our ghostly enemy, and from everlasting death." (26–30)

20. *In saying this petition, do we pray to be delivered from such evils as sickness, or poverty, or distress?*
Not absolutely; because any of these things may be the means, by God's blessing, of leading us to seek God.

21. *What, then, are the only real evils?*
Sin and its consequences. (28–32)

22. *But do we not pray to be delivered from " our ghostly enemy," that is, from Satan?*
Satan himself has no power to hurt us except through our yielding to sin.

23. *What is the last and irremediable evil?*
Everlasting death. (Mark ix. 43–48.) (31, 32)

24. *Does the Lord's Prayer end here?*
In all the oldest copies of the word of God it ends with the words "But deliver us from evil."

25. *Is it right, then, to append to it the doxology: "For thine is the kingdom, the power, and the glory, for ever and ever?"*
At times it is; for whatsoever good thing we receive from God, we receive it by His appointment as the King (Thine is the Kingdom); by His power as the Almighty (and the Power); and to His glory as the Maker and Upholder of all things (and the Glory). (33–38)

26. *What does "Amen" mean?*
So be it. May it be so. May God, our Father, grant us all these things.

SHORTER CATECHISM.

1. *What is the sixth petition?*
And lead us not into temptation, but deliver us from evil.

2. *Do we pray here that we may never be tempted or tried?*
   No: as long as we are in this world we are on our trial.
3. *But do we not express a desire not to be tempted or tried?*
   Yes: knowing our own weakness, we must desire not to be tempted or tried.
4. *What then do we mean by praying not to be tried when life is full of trials or temptations?*
   Because we earnestly desire and pray to be sustained under any trial or temptation.
5. *What is temptation?*
   Being drawn away by our own lusts and enticed.
6. *How is it that we are liable to be enticed by our own lusts?*
   Because we are born in sin.
7. *Are all men subject to temptations?* Yes: all.
8. *Have all men the same temptations?*
   No: almost all have different temptations.
9. *Mention some common temptations.*
   Temptations to strong drink, to dishonesty, to greediness, to lying, to swearing.
10. *What leads us to do these evil things?*
    The evil desires of our hearts.
11. *Is there anything else which tempts us to sin?*
    Yes: evil spirits (Eph. vi. 12).
12. *Mention one who was tempted through an evil spirit.* Eve.
13. *Mention another.* Judas Iscariot (John xiii. 2).
14. *Mention one whom Satan was suffered to tempt by pain and distress.* Job (Job i. 12; ii. 7).
15. *Why does God allow us to be tempted?*
    In order to see whether we will serve Him or not.
16. *What is our present state here on earth called?*
    A state of probation.
17. *What is probation?* It is our being tried or proved.
18. *Can we of ourselves resist temptation?* No.
19. *Is it then our own fault if we fall into sin?*
    Yes: because God has promised to uphold us if we call upon Him.
20. *Where has He promised this?*
    In many places; especially Psalm l. 15.
21. *Are any temptations so strong that we must yield to them whether we call upon God or not?*
    No: St. Paul says, "God is faithful, who will not suffer you to be tempted above that ye are able" (1 Cor. x. 13).
22. *Must we do something in addition to praying if we would conquer temptation?* Yes: we must "watch" as well as pray.
23. *What must we watch against?*
    The very first beginnings of any evil wish or desire.

24. *What must we remember?* That God's eye is always upon us.
25. *What, above all things, must we remember?*
 That we belong to Christ, and are bought with His blood.
26. *What is the last thing which we ask for in this prayer?*
 That our Father would "deliver us from evil."
27. *How is this explained in the desire?*
 That He will keep us . . . . from everlasting death.
28. *What is the one evil?* Sin.
29. *Why do you call this the one evil?*
 Because if it were not for sin the devil could not hurt us nor everlasting death overtake us.
30. *When you pray to be kept from all sin and wickedness, mention some things that you pray to be kept from.*
 From profaning God's Holy Name, from lying, stealing, disobedience to parents, dishonesty, impurity, malice, pride, contention, quarrelling, selfishness.
31. *What will be the end of these and such-like things if unrepented of and unforsaken?*
 Everlasting death.
32. *In what words does our most merciful Saviour bid us avoid everlasting death?*
 Mark ix. 43-48.
33. *What words are often added to the Lord's Prayer?*
 The Doxology.
34. *What is a Doxology?* A form of giving glory to God.
35. *What are the words of the Doxology?*
 For Thine is the kingdom, and the power, and the glory, for ever and ever.
36. *Why do we say, " For Thine is the kingdom?"*
 Because all the blessings we pray for are given by God's appointment as our King.
37. *Why do we say (For Thine is) the power?*
 Because all we receive and hope for is given through His power as the Almighty.
38. *Why do we say (For Thine) is the glory?*
 Because all we receive is given us to use for His glory.

SECTION LII.—THE NATURE OF THE SACRAMENTS.

1. HOW MANY SACRAMENTS HATH CHRIST ORDAINED IN HIS CHURCH?
   TWO ONLY, AS GENERALLY NECESSARY TO SALVATION, THAT IS TO SAY, BAPTISM, AND THE SUPPER OF THE LORD.
2. WHAT MEANEST THOU BY THIS WORD SACRAMENT?
   I MEAN AN OUTWARD AND VISIBLE SIGN OF AN INWARD AND SPIRITUAL GRACE GIVEN UNTO US, ORDAINED BY CHRIST HIMSELF, AS A MEANS WHEREBY WE RECEIVE THE SAME, AND A PLEDGE TO ASSURE US THEREOF.
3. *Why are we first asked the number of the Sacraments?*
   To distinguish the two Sacraments ordained by Christ Himself from all other rites, such as Confirmation, or Ordination, which have the nature of Sacraments. (2–5)
4. *How are they distinguished?*
   As being generally (*i.e.*, universally) necessary to salvation; because in the one our union with the Church or Body of Christ is begun, and in the other it is continued. (5–8)
5. *Is there any other reason why the attention of the Catechumen should be fixed on these two Sacraments?*
   Yes: the Catechism is designed to prepare those who have received the Sacrament of Baptism for Confirmation, as a preliminary to their receiving the Sacrament of the Lord's Supper.
6. *What is the original meaning of the word Sacrament?*
   It originally meant anything (as an oath) by which a person solemnly bound himself.
7. *Does it appear in the New Testament?*
   Yes. In the earliest Latin translations, the Greek word mystery (μυστήριον) was sometimes translated by the word sacramentum. [Thus 1 Tim. iii. 16: "Great is the mystery of godliness," is rendered, "Magnum est pietatis sacramentum."]
8. *How is the word used in early Christian writers?*
   As some sacred thing which lies concealed under an outward form, either of words or of material things.

[Thus Tertullian speaks of our Lord being anointed with the Holy Ghost as " Sacramentum unctionis ;" and St. Cyprian speaks of the many Sacraments, meaning sacred truths, which lie hid in the Lord's Prayer. (Bp. Browne on Articles, p. 177.)]

9. *How is the word used in later writers?*
To denote certain visible rites in which God conveys to us certain invisible graces or blessings.

10. *Has our Church given any other definition of a Sacrament similar to that in the Catechism?*
Yes. " Sacraments ordained of Christ be...certain sure witnesses, and effectual signs of grace and God's good will towards us, by the which He doth work invisibly in us." (Article xxv.) (12-22)

11. *But if the Christian be a spiritual religion, how is it that Christ ordained in it certain outward signs as channels of His grace?*
Because we are not mere spirits, but have an outward frame or body, as well as an inward spiritual essence.
["If thou hadst been incorporeal, He would have delivered thee the incorporeal gifts bare ; but because the soul hath been locked up in a body, He delivers thee the things that the mind perceives, in things sensible." (Chrysostom on Matthew xxvi. ; Hom. lxxxii.)]

12. *But are not outward rites out of place in so spiritual a dispensation?*
All merely outward rites would be ; but the Sacraments are not merely outward rites, but outward visible means whereby we receive spiritual grace.

13. *But is not the Christian system a system of purely spiritual truth?*
No ; by no means. The very first thing in the Christian revelation is that the Eternal Word was made flesh ; and then this Word "dwells amongst us " in a body of *flesh;* which *flesh* He gives for the life of the world, and in the body of His *flesh* He ascends into heaven, and will at last raise up to eternal life not our souls only, but our bodies.

14. *What state of things did Christ ordain?*
He ordained a state of things which corresponded to His own compound nature, and the compound nature of those whom He came to save. (33-38)

15. *Show this more fully.*

Christ ordained an outward organization or body of men, to be under an outward government exercised by their fellow-men, and distinguished from all other bodies or societies by certain outward ordinances, so that, though not of this world, this organization, or body, should take its place amongst the things of time and sense.

16. *But the Christian state is not outward only?*
No: it is an outward and visible kingdom, inhabited by an invisible Spirit, which Spirit pervades all its parts, and works in, and by, all its ordinances : by which Spirit, too, it is united to Christ as its Head. (33–38)

17. *Under what circumstances did Christ ordain Baptism and the Lord's Supper?*
Under the most solemn possible. He ordained Baptism just as He was leaving the world to go to the Father ; and He ordained the Holy Eucharist on the night before He offered Himself for sin. (28–32)

18. *What do we gather from the fact that the Eternal Son of God ordained these Sacraments at such times as these?*
We cannot but gather that they must be necessary to salvation in all cases where they may be had ; for it is impossible to imagine that our Lord would have ordained, on such occasions, anything which might safely be dispensed with. (28–32)

19. HOW MANY PARTS ARE THERE IN A SACRAMENT?
TWO: THE OUTWARD VISIBLE SIGN, AND THE INWARD SPIRITUAL GRACE.

20. *Of what is the inward and spiritual grace a part?*
It is a part of the whole Sacrament, for Christ ordained the use of the outward sign as the means of conveying it to us.

21. *How are the two parts of the Sacrament connected?*
That is a very deep mystery, only known to Almighty God. (38–48)

SHORTER CATECHISM.

1. *How many Sacraments hath Christ ordained in His Church?*
Two only, as generally necessary to salvation, &c.
2. *What Sacraments hath Christ Himself ordained?*
Baptism and the Lord's Supper.

3. *To what end did He ordain these two Sacraments?*
   That they should be "generally necessary to salvation."
4. *What do you mean by "generally?"*
   In all cases where they may be had (or obtained).
5. *In what body of men hath Christ ordained these two Sacraments?*
   In His Church.
6. *What does that mean?*
   That they are to be given in His Church, by its ministers, for its benefit.
7. *How especially does Baptism benefit the Church?*
   Because by it the Church is continued in existence, by having fresh members engrafted into it (born again into the body of Christ).
8. *How does the Lord's Supper benefit the Church?*
   Because in it the members of the Church are fed by the Living Bread, and so abide in Christ, and continue members of His body.
9. *Explain to me what a Sacrament is.*
   It is "an outward and visible sign of an inward and spiritual grace given unto us, ordained by Christ Himself, as a means whereby we receive the same, and a pledge to assure us thereof."
10. *Because, then, Baptism is a Sacrament, what is it?*
    It is "an outward visible sign of an inward spiritual grace given to us, ordained by Christ Himself, as a means," &c.
11. *Because the Lord's Supper is a Sacrament, what is it?*
    It is "an outward visible sign of an inward spiritual grace given unto us, ordained by Christ Himself, as a means," &c.
12. *What do you mean by an "outward" sign?*
    A sign that I can feel, or touch, or taste.
13. *What by a visible sign?* One that I can see.
14. *What is a sign?*
    A thing intended to remind us of some other thing.
15. *Mention some "signs" mentioned in Scripture.*
    Our Lord's miracles, and especially His Resurrection.
16. *What were these signs to teach or remind men of?*
    To remind men that He came from God, or was the Son of God.
17. *Mention another sign.* The rainbow.
18. *Of what did it remind men?*
    Of the covenant that God made with them that He would never again drown the world (Gen. ix. 13).
19. *What must the sign in a Sacrament be?*
    It must be outward and visible.
20. *Who ordained the outward and visible sign in each Sacrament?*
    Christ Himself (John iii. 5 [water]; 1 Cor. xi. 24, 25 [bread and wine]).
21. *Of what did Christ ordain the outward thing to be the sign?*
    Of an inward and spiritual grace given unto us.

22. *Why do you say " given unto us ?"*
   Because this inward and spiritual grace is given to us when we duly receive the outward sign.
23. *Is the outward and visible sign the sign of an inward and spiritual grace which we have received before ?*
   No: it is the sign of a grace which God intends us to receive when we receive the Sacrament.
24. *How do you know that this is the meaning of the Catechism ?*
   Because we are told in the Catechism that the outward and visible sign is ordained by Christ "as a means whereby we receive the same."
25. *Receive the same what ?* The same inward and spiritual grace.
26. *And does anything make us still more sure that this is the meaning of the Catechism ?*
   Yes: we are told that it was ordained by Christ Himself "as a pledge to assure us thereof."
27. *What do you mean by " a pledge to assure us thereof ?"*
   A pledge to assure us that we do receive that of which Christ has ordained the outward sign to be a sign.
28. *Who ordained the Sacraments ?* Jesus Christ Himself.
29. *Who is He ?* He is both God and Man.
30. *If one who is at once God and Man ordained them, what must they be ?* They must be very necessary for us to receive.
31. *But might not our Lord at times ordain things of small moment ?*
   No: we cannot imagine that at such times as those in which He ordained the Sacraments He would ordain things of little importance.
32. *When did He ordain the Sacraments ?*
   He ordained Baptism just as He was leaving this world, and He ordained the Lord's Supper at His last meal with His Apostles, before He gave Himself for our sins.
33. *Why may we suppose that He ordained outward signs for conveying inward grace ?*
   Because both He Himself and we ourselves have an outward part or body as well as an inward part or soul.
34. *What then are the two Sacraments of Baptism and the Lord's Supper ?*
   They are means of supernatural connection between Christ and us.
35. *Why do we need to be supernaturally joined to Christ ?*
   Because we are naturally connected with the first Adam, and receive evil from him.
36. *From what part of Adam do we receive evil—from his soul only ?*
   No: from his whole person.
37. *From what in Christ, then, must we receive grace ?*
   From His whole Person.

38. *But is not this very mysterious?*
   Not more mysterious than that our Lord is both God and man, and that we receive sin and death from our first parent Adam.
39. *How many parts are there in a Sacrament?*
   Two: the outward visible sign, and the inward spiritual grace.
40. *What do these two parts together make?*
   They make one Sacrament.
41. *Who has joined together these two parts?*
   Our Lord and Saviour Jesus Christ.
42. *Do we know how they are joined?* No.
43. *If two things of the most opposite natures are joined together, and we canot tell how, what do we call such a connection?*
   A mysterious one.
44. *What were the Sacraments usually called in very ancient times?*
   Mysteries.
45. *Why are we sure that the Sacraments are very mysterious in their nature?*
   Because our Lord, when ordaining them or speaking of them, used the most mysterious words to be found in the whole Bible.
46. *In what mysterious terms does He speak of Baptism?*
   John iii. 5.
47. *In what mysterious words does He speak of the Lord's Supper?*
   John vi. 47–71.
48. *Are there any words like these in the Bible?*
   No: there are no words like these in connecting what is inward and spiritual with what is outward and visible.

SECTION LIII.—BAPTISM. THE OUTWARD SIGN.

1 WHAT IS THE OUTWARD VISIBLE SIGN OR FORM IN BAPTISM?
WATER; WHEREIN THE PERSON IS BAPTIZED IN THE NAME OF THE FATHER, AND OF THE SON, AND OF THE HOLY GHOST.

2. *Are there any things in the Old Testament which would prepare men to expect grace in Christian Baptism?*
Yes: the salvation of Noah in the ark, and the passage of the Red Sea, are both types of Christian Baptism. (1 Peter iii. 21; 1 Cor. x. 1-10.) There was also a laver or font in the temple itself, in which the priests who sacrified were to wash, lest they should die (Exod. xxx. 21); and God healed Naaman when he submitted to wash seven times in Jordan. (2 Kings v. 14.) (2-12)

3. *How did God prepare the Jews in our Lord's time to receive the Baptism of Christ?*
He sent John the Baptist to prepare the way of Christ, by baptizing in water as well as by preaching of repentance; and to this Baptism even Christ Himself submitted. (13-18)

4. *Why is water the outward visible sign in Baptism?*
Because Christ so ordained when He said, "Except a man be born of water and of the Spirit, he cannot enter into the kingdom of God." (John iii. 5.) (19-30)

5. *How do you know that by "water" here our Lord means the water of Baptism?*
Because when the kingdom of God was actually set up, on the day of Pentecost, men were admitted into it by a Baptism in water. (Acts ii. 38-41.) (23)

6. *Is there any other reason for believing that our Lord here alluded to Baptism?*
Yes; in many other places of Scripture salvation is more or less connected with the right reception of Baptism in water (Mark xvi. 16; Acts xxii. 16; Rom. vi. 1-4; Gal. iii. 27; Eph. v. 26; 1 Pet. iii. 21); so that if in this passage (John iii. 5) there be no reference to the Sacrament of Baptism, our Lord's words seem gratuitously calculated to mislead. (27-30)

7. *Why do you say "gratuitously" calculated to mislead?*
Because if our Lord had desired to express to Nicodemus the need of some spiritual change unconnected with Baptism, He only obscured His meaning by bringing in the word " water," seeing that by His own appointment water has a religious use, with which is connected the reception of grace from God.

[This reference to water has, from the first age of the Church, led her to connect Regeneration with Baptism. Writers as old as Hermas, Justin Martyr, and Tertullian all see an allusion to Baptism in these words of Christ.]

8. *Why is it said water "wherein" the person is baptized?*
Because in Baptism the person baptized is, or is assumed to be, in, or under, the water.

[The rubric for the Baptism of persons of riper years is: " Then shall the priest... dip him in the water, or pour water upon him ;" that for the Baptism of infants runs : " He shall dip it in the water discreetly and warily." " But if they certify that the child is weak, it shall suffice to pour water upon it," &c.] (31-33)

9. *On what warrant then do we substitute "pouring on water" for dipping in water?*
In such a climate as this, on the warrant of the words, "I will have mercy, and not sacrifice." (Matt. xii. 7.) (31-33)

10. *Is it probable that all the persons whose baptisms are mentioned in the New Testament were immersed?*
No : such a thing is very improbable. The Baptism of three thousand in one day, and the Baptism of the Philippian jailor at night, seem to imply rather a pouring on of water than a total immersion in the water.

[In all probability, the most common form of the administration of this Sacrament would be that represented in many old pictures—the person baptized standing in the water, and the baptizer on the bank pouring water on him.]

11. *What error do they hold who teach that total immersion is necessary?*
The error of supposing that the *quantity* of water, and not its application in the name of the Trinity, is of the essence of the Sacrament.

12. *Is there any place in the New Testament where the word Baptism is used in the sense of "washing," and cannot imply "immersion?"*

Yes ; when it is said of the Pharisees and all the Jews, that " When they come from the market, they eat not except they wash " (ἐὰν μὴ βαπτίσωνται, unless they be baptized). Also, in the same verse, the washing of tables (or couches) (κλινῶν) is in the original the "baptism" of tables, not meaning, of course, the total immersion of tables or couches. (Mark vii. 4).

13. *Is the mere application of water without the use of any words sufficient?*

No : according to Christ's commandment we baptize in the name of the Father, and of the Son, and of the Holy Ghost. (34, 35)

14. *What does the use of such words imply?*

They imply a real appropriation of the person baptized to the Holy Trinity ; a transfer of him from the kingdom of Satan into the family of the God Whose name of Father, Son, and Holy Ghost is then named upon him.

15. *Does such an invocation imply that God makes us partakers of grace in Baptism?*

Nothing less than this can be believed by any one who believes in the greatness of the Name of the Ever-blessed Trinity, and in the Divine power of Him Who ordained the use of such words. (36)

SHORTER CATECHISM.

1. *What is the outward visible sign or form in Baptism?*
Water ; wherein the person is baptized in the Name, &c.

2. *Are there any types in the Old Testament of a Baptism in water as a means of grace?*
Yes : the writers of the New Testament mention two.

3. *What is the first of these?* The salvation of Noah in the ark.

4. *By whom is this quoted as a type of Holy Baptism?*
By St. Peter, where he says : " Few, that is, eight souls were saved by water : the like figure whereunto (or antitype of it) even Baptism doth also now save us, not the putting away of the filth of the flesh, but the answer of a good conscience towards God " (1 Pet. iii. 21).

5. *Put in other words what St. Peter means by this.*
He means that as the waters of the flood saved Noah by bearing up the ark, so Baptism now saves those who sincerely and faithfully receive it.

6. *What does the use of such language show?*
   The exceeding importance of Christian Baptism.
7. *What other event in the Old Testament is referred to in the New as a type of Baptism?*
   The deliverance of the children of Israel in the waters of the Red Sea.
8. *By whom is this quoted as a type of Baptism?*
   By St. Paul, in 1 Cor x. 1-10.
9. *For what purpose does he quote it?*
   To show that as all the Israelites passed through the Red Sea and yet came not into the promised land, so all Christians baptized into Christ must see to it that they perish not as the Israelites did.
10. *What does this place also show?*
    The great importance of Baptism.
11. *How?*
    Because the deliverance of Christians by Baptism is shadowed out by no less a thing than the deliverance of God's people from Egypt by their passage through the Red Sea.
12. *Did God confer any blessing on one who submitted to wash in water in obedience to the command of a prophet?*
    Yes: on Naaman (2 Kings v. 14).
13. *Who prepared the way of our Lord?* John the Baptist.
14. *How?* By baptizing as well as by preaching.
15. *Who submitted to receive the Baptism of John?*
    Our blessed Lord Himself.
16. *Did He need to receive it?*
    No: for He was without stain of sin.
17. *Why did He then receive it?*
    In order that He might "fulfil all righteousness" (Matt. iii. 15)
18. *What does His submission to such a thing teach us?*
    That if He thought so highly of the Baptism of His servant, much more ought we to regard the Baptism ordained by our Lord and Master, the Eternal Son of God.
19. *Who ordained water as the outward sign of Baptism?*
    Christ Himself.
20. *In what words?*
    In the words, "Except a man be born of water and of the Spirit" (John iii. 5).
21. *In what other words?* Matt. xxviii. 19, and Mark xvi. 16.
22. *How do you know that our Lord alludes to Baptism in John iii. 5?*
    Because at no other time than at that of our Baptism can we be born of water as well as of the Spirit.
23. *Is there any other reason?*
    Yes: from the day of Pentecost men were added to the Church by Baptism.

24. *Does our branch of the Church lay down that this place refers to Baptism?*
　　Yes: in the office of " Baptism of such as are of riper years."
25. *In what words?*
　　"Beloved, ye hear in this Gospel the express words of our Saviour Christ, that except a man be born of water and of the Spirit, he cannot enter into the kingdom of God."
26. *And what does she gather from this?*
　　"The great necessity of this Sacrament, where it may be had."
27. *Do the declarations of the rest of Scripture confirm this interpretation of the Church?*
　　Yes: in almost every place where Baptism is mentioned, it is connected with grace from God.
28. *Mention one or two of these places.*
　　Eph. v. 26; Col. ii. 12; Titus iii. 5; Heb. x. 22; 1 Peter iii. 20, 21.
29. *Has the Church always interpreted this place of Baptism?*
　　Yes: from the very first.
30. *Must our Lord have foreseen this?*
　　Yes: being God, and knowing all things, He must have foreseen it.
31. *How are we baptized?*
　　Either by being dipped in the water, or by having water poured upon us.
32. *Does our Church recognise both these modes?* Yes.
33. *Why do we almost universally baptize children by pouring water upon them?*
　　Because, owing to the coldness of our climate, immersion would in many cases endanger life.
34. *Is there anything else besides water required for Baptism?*
　　Yes: the water must be applied "in the name of the Father, and of the Son, and of the Holy Ghost."
35. *By whose command do we use these words?*
　　By the command of Christ.
36. *What does the use of such words lead us to expect?*
　　That what is done by Christ's command, and in the name of the Trinity, is accompanied by the grace of the Trinity.

SECTION LIV.—BAPTISM: ITS INWARD AND SPIRITUAL GRACE.

1. WHAT [*then*] IS THE INWARD AND SPIRITUAL GRACE?
A DEATH UNTO SIN, AND A NEW BIRTH UNTO RIGHTEOUSNESS; FOR BEING BY NATURE BORN IN SIN, AND THE CHILDREN OF WRATH, WE ARE HEREBY MADE THE CHILDREN OF GRACE.
2. *What is the latter part of this answer?*
An explanation of the first part. The death unto sin, and the new birth unto righteousness consists in this: that we, who are "by nature born in sin, and the children of wrath, are hereby made the children of grace."
3. *What name is given by the Catholic Church to this "death unto sin," and "new birth unto righteousness?"*
Regeneration: in accordance with the words of St. Paul, "By His mercy He saved us, by the washing (or bath, or font, or laver, λουτροῦ) of regeneration." (Titus iii. 5.)
4. *Why do we need a new birth, or Regeneration?*
Because we are "born in sin," partakers of the sinful nature of the first Adam. (3-9)
5. *What then is the grace of Regeneration?*
It must be the grace opposite to, and the remedy for, original sin: as original sin is the reception of evil from Adam, so Regeneration must be the reception of some counteracting benefit from Christ. (11-19)
6. *From what in Adam do we receive an evil nature?*
From his whole nature of flesh and spirit, which we partake of through our conception and birth of human parents. (14-18)
7. *From what, then, in Christ must we receive a better nature [and counteracting benefit]?*
From His whole human nature. (14-18)
8. *Is it through our own personal act that we receive an evil nature?*
No; we inherit it from our parents, as they do from theirs.

U

9. *Is there anything corresponding to this in the way in which we receive Regeneration?*
   Yes: we receive it of free grace, through no personal merits of our own, or of our parents.
10. *In what state do we always receive original sin [or the evil nature of the first Adam]?*
    In a state in which we are passive and unconscious of the evil which we receive; for we receive original sin in a state of infancy.
11. *Is there anything corresponding to this in the reception of Regeneration?*
    Yes; there is, if we are baptized in a state of infancy, for we then receive the inward and spiritual grace from Christ in the same state of unconsciousness in which we have received the infection of nature from Adam.
12. *What authority in Scripture have we for connecting a death to sin with Holy Baptism?*
    The express authority of St. Paul, where he asks (Rom. vi. 2), "How shall we, who have died to sin, live any longer therein?" and then he proceeds to say, "We were buried with Christ by Baptism into death [or rather it should be rendered, "we were buried with Him through our Baptism into His death"]: that like as Christ was raised up from the dead by the glory of the Father, even so we also should walk in newness of life." (22–28)
13. *Can this be true of all the baptized?*
    St. Paul expressly asserts that it is, when he says, ";Know ye not that so many of us as were baptized into Jesus Christ were baptized into His death?" (37)
14. *For what purpose does the Apostle write such remarkable and unusual words?*
    To convince baptized Christians that they are not to continue in sin, but to "walk in newness of life." (Rom. vi. 2, 4.) (24–38)
15. *By what power alone can the Christian walk in newness of life?*
    By the power of Christ's new, or risen Life.
16. *When does the Apostle imply that some of this power is made over to us?*
    When we were "buried with Christ in Baptism:" that "like as He was raised from the dead," so we also should "walk in newness of life." (34–38)
17. *How are we sure that such is his meaning?*

Because a little further on he assumes that all the baptized have a portion in this risen Life of Christ when he says, " In that Christ died, He died unto sin once ; but in that He liveth, He liveth unto God. Likewise reckon ye also yourselves to be dead indeed unto sin, but alive unto God through Jesus Christ our Lord." (30–40)

18. *Can you put into other words what the Apostle means ?*
Yes : he means that when baptized Christians are tempted to commit sin, they must call to mind their Baptism into the body of that Saviour Who died to sin in order that He might free us from its guilt and power ; they must plead with God that He may continue and increase His grace in them, so that they may mortify sin by resisting and denying it. (30–40)

19. *In writing this remarkable passage respecting Baptism as a means of union with a Crucified and Risen Saviour, what must the Apostle have had in his mind?*
He must have had in his mind the parallel between the two Adams ; the one bringing in evil, the other bringing in good to counteract that evil.

20. *Are we sure that the Apostle had this in his mind?*
Yes ; because he had just been drawing out this comparison between Adam as the source of death to all in him, and Christ as the source of life to all in Him. (Rom. v. 12–21)

21. *When the Apostle speaks of Christians having died to sin in Baptism, does he mean that they cannot sin any more, just as a dead man cannot sin ?*
No ; on the contrary, he assumes that those once dead to sin may again fall into it, and writes to warn them against such a fall. (35–39)

22. *What, then, is this death to sin ?*
It is a sacramental or mystical death, and it consists in our being accounted by God as dead, buried, and risen with His Son in Baptism, after such a sort that the virtue of Christ's Death and Resurrection are made over to us.

23. *But is not all this too great a thing to depend on our receiving so simple a rite as Baptism ?*
We shall not consider it so if we remember Who instituted Holy Baptism, and in Whose Name He commands us to be baptized.

24. *What, then, will keep us from low thoughts of such a Sacrament ?*

The thought that He Who ordained it was the Eternal Word made flesh, and dwelling amongst us.

25. *Hitherto you have spoken rather of the death to sin, than of the new birth to righteousness: is this latter connected with Baptism?*

Yes: by our Blessed Saviour Himself, when He says, "Except a man be born of water and of the Spirit, he cannot enter into the kingdom of God." (John iii. 5.) (40–42)

26. *But was Christian Baptism then instituted?*

No; but almost all that our Lord said and did had reference to the kingdom which He would set up after His Ascension rather than to the state of things which existed during His sojourn upon earth.

27. *Mention an instance.*

In this very discourse our Lord speaks of a future "looking to Him" after He was crucified, when He says, "As Moses lifted up the serpent in the wilderness, even so must the Son of Man be lifted up; that whosoever believeth in Him should not perish." (John iii. 14.)

28. *Can you give another?*

Yes: Christ said, "If any man thirst, let him come to Me and drink." And yet the Evangelist tells us, "This spake He of the Spirit, which they that believe on Him should receive [not then, but afterwards; for the Evangelist proceeds to say], for the Spirit was not yet given, because that Jesus was not yet glorified." (John vii. 37, 39.)

29. *What is this New Birth?*

It is an engrafting into Christ the Second Adam, and through this the reception of a principle of good from Him, in order to counteract and destroy the evil we have received by our first or natural birth in the first Adam.

30. *What is the idea always suggested by a birth?*

Entrance into a state or family: we, being born of the family of Adam, must be new born into the family of God.

31. *Our Lord says, "Except a man be born of water and of the Spirit:" does the "water" contribute anything to our new birth?*

Not, of course, of itself. The application of water, in the Name of the Ever Blessed Trinity, is the time at which the Holy Spirit (and He alone) transfers a human being out of Adam into Christ.

32. *Is this ever asserted elsewhere in Scripture?*

Yes. By St. Paul, in the words, "By one Spirit are we all baptized into one body." (1 Cor. xii. 13.)

33. *But does not St. Paul speak here of spiritual Christians?*

No: on the contrary, he is speaking to a Church the members of which He calls "carnal," and some among them He rebukes as being gross sinners.

34. *But can such a term as "new birth" be applied to designate the entrance into such a society as the Church?*

Yes, if the Church is the mystical body of One now at the Right Hand of God, and if each member of it has an invisible relationship to Him as its Head.

35. *May not our Lord, by the term "born of water and of the Spirit," allude to a conscious spiritual change in the soul (as a change from sin to holiness), seldom, if ever, joined with Baptism?*

No: if our Lord alluded to any such change as conversion or repentance He would certainly have expressed it in far more simple and direct terms than as "a birth of water and of the Spirit."

36. *But may not our Lord here allude to a birth of water in Baptism, and a birth of the Spirit at some future time of conversion?*

No. A birth is *one* thing, occurring at *one* time. If our Lord (which He does) explains the *one* thing being "born again," by the being "born of water and of the Spirit," this latter must also be *one* thing, occurring at one time, as the former is.

37. *What makes it impossible for a Churchman, well instructed in his Bible, to explain this place without reference to Baptism?*

The fact that in many other places of Scripture the reception of Baptism is connected with the reception of spiritual blessings or benefits. (43–51)

38. *Mention some of these places.*

In three places Baptism is directly connected with the reception of Salvation:

1. Mark xvi. 16; where our Lord says, "He that believeth and is baptized shall be saved."

2. Acts ii. 37, 38; where St. Peter, in answer to the question of those who asked what they were to do to be saved, said, "Repent, and be baptized every one of you in the name of Jesus Christ for the remission of sins, and ye shall receive the gift of the Holy Ghost."

3. Titus iii. 5; where St. Paul says, "By His mercy He saved us by the washing (or rather bath, or font) of Regeneration."

4. 1 Pet. iii. 21; where St. Peter, having said that eight souls were at the time of the flood saved by water, proceeds to say, "The like figure whereunto even Baptism doth also now save us (not the putting away of the filth of the flesh, but the answer of a good conscience towards God), by the Resurrection of Jesus Christ." (43–51)

39. *How can such a simple rite convey salvation to those who repent and believe?*

Because it is the ordained means whereby we are engrafted into Him in Whom is salvation, or rather, Who is Himself our Salvation.

40. *Are there any other places in which spiritual benefits are said to be made over to us in Baptism?*

Yes. In two places it is said to be the means whereby we receive the remission of sins, and in two others we are said to be "buried" and "raised again" with Christ in it.

Acts xxii. 16. "Arise, and be baptized, and wash away thy sins."
Eph. v. 26. "That He might sanctify and cleanse His church with the washing of water by the word." Also Rom. vi. 1—4; Col. ii. 12.

41. *How do these places bear upon the true interpretation of our Lord's words respecting the New Birth?*

They compel the well-instructed Christian to attach such a meaning to the term "New Birth" as will enable him to regard it as a work of the Spirit, connected with the application of water in the name of the Ever-Blessed Trinity.

SHORTER CATECHISM.

1. *How many parts are there in a Sacrament?*
   Two: the outward, &c.

2. *You have said that a dipping in, or pouring on, of water in the Name of the Trinity, is the outward visible sign in Baptism: what is the inward and spiritual grace?*
   "A death unto sin, and a new birth unto righteousness, for being by nature born in sin, and the children of wrath, we are hereby made the children of grace."

3. *Why do all men require to receive a death unto sin and a new birth unto righteousness?*
   Because all men are by nature born in sin.

4. *If men are born in sin, what are they?*
    The children of wrath.
5. *What does that mean?*
    They belong to a family or race which is at enmity with God.
6. *How came they to be in this state?*
    They came into it by nature, *i.e.*, by their natural birth.
7. *How must the evil of their natural birth be remedied?*
    They must be brought into a new family.
8. *What is this family?* The Church of God.
9. *Who is the Head of this new family?* Jesus Christ.
10. *If He be the Head of the new family, what can we say of all the members of the family?*
    That they are all reckoned under Him as the Head of the family of God.
11. *Anything more?*
    They all receive life from Him, just as the members of the human body have life by being joined to its head.
12. *When are we brought into this new family?*
    At the time of our receiving Holy Baptism.
13. *Does the Catechism teach this?*
    Yes: for we say, "Being by nature born in sin, and the children of wrath, we are hereby made [*i.e.*, by Baptism] the children of grace."
14. *Can Baptism of itself make us the children of grace?*
    No: but it is the time at which, and the means by which, God brings us into His family.
15. *In whom are all men born naturally?* In Adam.
16. *What do they receive at their birth?*
    They receive an evil nature (sin and death).
17. *Is there any means of counteracting or remedying this?*
    Yes: God has provided a Second Adam—Jesus Christ.
18. *If Jesus Christ be the Second Adam, what must we receive from Him?*
    We must receive grace and life to remedy the sin and death we received at our birth from the first Adam.
19. *What is the most fitting word to express this better thing we receive from Christ?*
    A new birth.
20. *Of what does our Saviour say we must be born?*
    Of water and of the Spirit (John iii. 5).
21. *What does He mean by this?*
    He means that by Holy Baptism we must be engrafted into Him.
22. *And what do we receive from Him?*
    Something to remedy the evils we have received from the first Adam.

23. *But does not the Catechism say that we receive "a death unto sin" in Baptism?*
   Yes: for St. Paul teaches us that we do.
24. *What are his words?*
   "How shall we, who are dead to sin, live any longer therein? Know ye not that so many of us as were baptized into Jesus Christ were baptized into His death?" (Rom. vi. 2, 3).
25. *What does St. Paul mean by such remarkable words?*
   He means that we have a part in Christ's Death and Resurrection made over to us in Baptism.
26. *If we have a part in Christ's Death made over to us, what must we receive?*
   We must receive a share in the benefit of His Atonement.
27. *Why?* Because He died for our sins, *i.e.*, to atone for them.
28. *If we have a share in Christ's Resurrection made over to us, what must we receive?*
   We must receive some life from Him.
29. *Do we know from Scripture that this is so?*
   Yes: St. Paul says that we who are baptized must reckon ourselves dead indeed unto sin but alive unto God through Jesus Christ (Rom. vi. 11).
30. *How must we do such a thing as reckon ourselves dead unto sin?*
   When we are tempted to do wrong we must believe that we have grace from God through Christ to resist the temptation.
31. *What was Christ's intention in ordaining Holy Baptism?*
   That they who have received it should walk in newness of life, *i.e.*, in righteousness and holiness.
32. *Can they who have received Baptism do this of themselves?* No.
33. *How then can they do it?*
   By falling back upon and stirring up the grace they have received.
34. *What chapter of the Bible teaches us all this?* Rom. vi.
35. *What is this chapter about?*
   A death to sin in Holy Baptism.
36. *Can those who have died to sin in Baptism sin again?*
   Yes: if they forget Whose members they are made in Baptism.
37. *Do we actually die with Christ in Baptism (by a natural death)?*
   No: we die sacramentally or mystically.
38. *Do all thus die to sin in Baptism?*
   St. Paul says that all who have been baptized into Christ have been baptized into His death (Rom. vi. 3).
39. *And for what purpose?*
   That all those so baptized might walk in newness of life (Rom. vi. 4).

40. *If Christ ordained Holy Baptism in order that all the baptized might walk in newness of life, what does He give us in Baptism?*
   Grace to walk in newness of life.
41. *Repeat, then, what the inward and spiritual grace of Baptism is.*
   A death to sin and a new birth unto righteousness.
42. *What Scripture ground have we for connecting a "new birth unto righteousness" with Baptism?*
   Our Lord's words: "Except a man be born of water and of the Spirit, He cannot enter into the kingdom of God."
43. *Why must our Lord here refer to a change wrought by the Spirit in Baptism?*
   Because He speaks of being born of "water" as well as of the Spirit.
44. *But must our Lord mean here the "water" used in Baptism?*
   Yes: because unless He alludes to the water of Baptism, His words must mislead us.
45. *How is this?*
   Because in so many other places of God's Holy Word our salvation is connected with Baptism in water.
46. *Mention one.*
   Our Lord says, in His last commission to His Apostles, "Go ye into all the world, and preach the Gospel to every creature, He that believeth and is baptized shall be saved" (Mark xvi. 15, 16).
47. *Does He mention Baptism on another equally important occasion?*
   Yes: when He says: "Go ye and teach all nations, baptizing them in the name of the Father, and of the Son," &c. (Matt. xxviii. 19).
48. *Mention a third place.*
   Remission of sins is connected with Baptism by St. Peter, when he says, "Repent, and be baptized every one of you in the name of Jesus Christ for the remission of sins." (Acts ii. 38).
49. *Mention two other places in which remission of sin is connected with Baptism.*
   Acts xxii. 16, where it is said to St. Paul, "Arise, and be baptized, and wash away thy sins:" and Eph. v. 26, where St. Paul says that Christ cleanses His Church "with the washing of water by the word."
50. *Mention two other places.*
   St. Peter speaks of Baptism, when received in sincerity, as saving us, and St. Paul says that, By His mercy He saved us, by the washing, or bath, of regeneration (1 Pet. iii. 21; Tit. iii. 5).
51. *Are any other remarkable words used to describe the grace of Baptism?*
   Yes: in two places it is called a Burial and a Resurrection with Christ (Rom. vi. 1-4; Col. ii. 12).

52. *By whose inspiration are all these things said of Holy Baptism?*
   By the inspiration of God's Holy Spirit.
53. *Can Baptism save of itself?*
   No one ever supposed that it could.
54. *Why, then, are such wonderful things said of its grace?*
   Because it is the will of God that men should humble themselves to receive an inward grace through an outward sign.
55. *What does the belief that we must receive grace through outward signs do for us?*
   It humbles the pride of our natural heart.
56. *Is there any natural connection between the outward sign and the inward grace?*
   No : the connection is above nature, and brought about by the will of God.
57. *What is that which leads so many men to reject the plain teaching of the Bible respecting Baptism?*
   The natural pride of our hearts, which leads us to reject all that is not according to the usual course of things (*i.e.*, according to the course of what men call nature).

SECTION LV.—REQUIREMENTS OF THE BAPTIZED.

1. *Would an impenitent and unbelieving person receive any benefit in Baptism?*
   No : in the case of such an one, the benefit would be suspended till he was in a fitting state of heart to receive it.
2. WHAT IS REQUIRED OF PERSONS TO BE BAPTIZED?
   REPENTANCE, WHEREBY THEY FORSAKE SIN ; AND FAITH, WHEREBY THEY STEADFASTLY BELIEVE THE PROMISES OF GOD MADE TO THEM IN THAT SACRAMENT. (2-5)
3. *You say that faith is required of persons to be baptized: is this faith a general faith in the person and work of Christ?*
   No : it must be not only this, but also a particular faith in the promises of God made to us in that Sacrament, *i. e.*, in Holy Baptism.
4. *But if persons repent and believe, are they not already regenerate?*
   Not in the view of the Scripture writers. They are in a condition to receive regeneration, or an engrafting into Christ, but they do not receive it till they receive Baptism into the mystical Body of Christ. (7-10)
5. *Can Regeneration then be properly described as a change of heart, or a change of views respecting the work or righteousness of Jesus Christ?*
   No : a change of heart of the deepest character is implied in the possession of repentance and faith, both which a person must have before he comes to Baptism. (7-13)
6. *But does not St. John say, " Whosoever is born of God does not commit sin," and " whatsoever is born of God overcometh the world?"*
   Yes ; for Regeneration is an engrafting into the Body of Christ, *i. e.*, into the Body of One Who knew no sin and overcame the world ; and if we abide in Him, we deny sin and overcome the world.
7. *How comes it then to pass that such vast numbers of the baptized live in sin, and are overcome by the world?*

Because they do not abide in Him into Whom they were once engrafted. (18–23)

8. *But may it not be because God withheld His grace from them?*

No: the Scripture writers invariably teach that if a baptized man commits sin, it is because he resists grace, not because God has withheld grace. (20–23)

9. *But does not this make the state of the Church very awful because all its members are so near to Christ?*

Yes, it does: and God intended it to be so, in order that we should live in the constant sense of the greatness of the state into which His mercy has brought us, and in constant watchfulness lest we should fall from it.

SHORTER CATECHISM.

1. *How many things are required of the person who comes to be baptized?* Two.
2. *What is the first?* Repentance.
3. *What is the sign that repentance is sincere?*
   When it leads us to forsake sin.
4. *Why, at our Baptism, must we forsake sin?*
   Because we are baptized into the death of a Saviour Who came to deliver us from sin.
5. *What is the second thing required?* Faith.
6. *What is the sign that this faith is genuine?*
   When by it we steadfastly believe the promises of God made to us in that Sacrament.
7. *Why is it needful to have faith in the promises made to us in Baptism?*
   Because it is insulting to God to come to an ordinance which He has ordained as a means of grace, and not to believe that He will give us grace in it.
8. *What are we taught by repentance and faith being required of those to be baptized?*
   That regeneration is something besides repentance and faith.
9. *What is repentance?* A change of heart.
10. *What, then, must regeneration be?*
    Something besides a change of heart
11. *What is faith?*
    Christian faith is a true belief in all which God reveals.

REQUIREMENTS OF THE BAPTIZED.

12. *What then must regeneration, or the new birth to righteousness in Baptism, be?*
    Something more than believing in God and Christ.
13. *What is that "something" more?*
    It is being grafted into the Body of Christ, or being made a member of Christ.
14. *Were holy men who lived before Christ came, regenerate?* No.
15. *But did they not repent of sin and believe in God?*
    Yes : but there was then no Body of Christ of which they might be made members.
16. *Is regeneration ever mentioned in the Old Testament?*
    No : not once.
17. *Why is it not mentioned in the Old Testament?*
    Because, in the times of the Old Testament, Christ had not become Incarnate, so that men could not partake of Him as the Second Adam.
18. *What should the baptized ever remember?*
    The words of St. John, that if the holy seed remain in them, they do not commit sin (1 John iii. 9).
19. *If they are sinful or worldly, what is it owing to?*
    To their forgetting or sinning against the grace they have received.
20. *Do baptized persons sin because God has withheld grace from them?* No.
21. *For what does God hold all the baptized to be answerable?*
    For grace received in Holy Baptism.
22. *Can there be any danger in our believing that we received grace in Baptism?*
    No : the danger lies in our not believing it.
23. *Why so?*
    Because, unless we believe it, we are in danger of forgetting that we belong to God, and are bound to love and serve Him.

SECTION LVI.—INFANT BAPTISM.

1. *You said that repentance and faith are required of persons to be baptized.* WHY THEN ARE INFANTS BAPTIZED, WHEN BY REASON OF THEIR TENDER AGE THEY CANNOT PERFORM THEM?

    BECAUSE THEY PROMISE THEM BOTH BY THEIR SURETIES, WHICH PROMISE, WHEN THEY COME TO AGE, THEMSELVES ARE BOUND TO PERFORM.

2. *Is this answer intended to give a full and sufficient reason for the Baptism of infants?*

    No: it is only given to explain how it is that in their case the profession of repentance and faith can be dispensed with. (1–5)

3. *How is the profession of repentance and faith dispensed with?*

    By the employment of sponsors, who answer in the child's name, and also undertake to see that "the infant be taught so soon as he shall be able to learn what a solemn vow, promise, and profession he hath made by them." (6–9)

4. *Does it seem reasonable that infants should receive such a grace as that promised in Baptism in a state in which they are not able to repent and believe?*

    Yes; it is most reasonable; for in a similar state (*i. e.*, in a state in which they could not repent and believe) they received that infection of nature which Regeneration is designed to remedy. (4)

5. *But are not repentance and faith necessary to make us worthy recipients of Baptism?*

    No: none of us are, or possibly can be, worthy recipients of such a grace as that of union with the Second Adam.

6. *Why, then, are repentance and faith required in persons of riper years who come to Baptism?*

    Because repentance and faith show the willingness of him who is baptized to receive grace from God; and because God does not thrust His grace on those who are unwilling to receive it.

7. *On what ground do all, whether infants or adults, receive the grace of Baptism?*
On the ground that God desires all men to be saved, and that Christ has by His Death made an Atonement for the sin of all men. (10-12)

8. *To what, then, is the regeneration of infants in Holy Baptism a witness?*
It is a witness to the perfect freedom of God's grace, inasmuch as He imparts grace to the infant before that infant can possibly have done anything to merit grace. (12-13)

9. *But is not one who repents and believes in a fitter state than an infant to receive grace?*
No; on the contrary, our Lord assures us that the man who would receive the kingdom of God must receive it as a little child. (Luke xviii. 17.)

10. *What does He mean by this?*
He means that, in the matter of receiving the grace of His kingdom, the man of full age must be conformed to the likeness of the infant, rather than the infant to the likeness of the man of full age.

11. *To what, then, does the Church testify by her requirement of sureties or sponsors to promise repentance and faith in the name of the child?*
She testifies to the exceeding need of repentance and faith in all who are capable of exercising them, seeing that she will not ordinarily allow even an infant to be baptized unless she receives from him as personal a pledge as she can possibly exact that he will, when he comes of age, repent and believe.

[For the Scripture reasons for Infant Baptism, *see* Section IV., page 14.]

SHORTER CATECHISM.

1. *What did you say was required of persons who come to receive Holy Baptism?*
Repentance and faith.

2. *Do all who are baptized exercise repentance and faith?*
No: in Christian countries persons are mostly baptized in a state of infancy.

3. *But can infants be brought into the Church or kingdom of God?*
   Our Saviour, Christ, says, "Of such is the kingdom of God."
4. *Why should they who, at such a tender age, cannot repent and believe, be baptized?*
   Because at such a tender age they have already received an evil nature of which the grace of Baptism is intended to be the remedy.
5. *Will they ever have to repent and believe?*
   Yes: when they come of age they must repent of sin, and believe the Gospel.
6. *Is there any security required by the Church that they should know this?*
   Yes: the greatest possible.
7. *What is this?*
   The Church requires that at their Baptism their godparents should promise repentance and faith in their name.
8. *Does the duty of the godparents end here?*
   No: it is their "duty to see that the infant be taught so soon as he shall be able to learn what a solemn vow, promise, and profession, he hath made by them."
9. *What does all this show?*
   The great anxiety of the Church that when the child comes of age he himself should repent and believe.
10. *Is a child baptized because his sureties promise anything in his name?*
    No: he is baptized because he is redeemed by the Blood of Christ.
11. *Is there any other reason?*
    Yes: because being born in sin of the first Adam, he needs a new birth unto righteousness in the Second Adam.
12. *But because he needs it, are we sure that he is permitted to receive it?*
    Yes: St. Paul expressly says, "If through the offence of one many be dead, *much more* the grace of God, and the gift by grace, which is by one man, Jesus Christ, hath abounded unto many" (Rom. v. 15).
13. *Can an infant deserve to be grafted into the Second Adam?*
    No: no one, infant or person of full age, can possibly deserve such grace.

NOTE.—With much that is written on Baptism in the foregoing pages many good men who use the Catechism as a manual of Christian instruction will probably disagree. They may differ from me respecting the nature and extent of the grace which God confers therein. Now I would earnestly ask both those who agree with what I have written here and elsewhere on this subject, and those who differ from it, to consider two short statements respecting the nature and extent of the benefit which a child receives, written by two men of very different schools in the Church, and I would ask them whether the benefits set forth in these two statements are not absolutely the same.

Dr. J. H. Newman describes the benefits of the Second Birth in Baptism in these words: "Original sin is washed away, and such influences of grace given and promised as make it a child's own fault if he, in the event, fails of receiving an eternal inheritance of blessedness in God's presence."—*Newman's Paroch. Sermons*, vol. iii. Sermon xx.

The late Rev. H. V. Elliott, of Brighton, certainly one of the foremost, if not the foremost, in point of ability and thoughtfulness, among the Evangelical party, describes the benefits of the same Sacrament thus: "Christian Baptism confers on the infant baptized, for Christ's sake (Who is the only satisfaction for sin), and by His appointment, a change of spiritual state or condition towards God, containing these things: 1. The remission of the guilt, though not the extinction of the infection of original sin: that remaineth 'even in the regenerate.' 2. The transfer of the infant born in sin, and a child of wrath, from that fearful state of nature into the family of God; so that it may, as soon as it is able to pray to God as a Father, cry "Abba Father," and use the Lord's Prayer: while nevertheless it remains to be seen whether it will grow up as an obedient and dutiful child, or a rebellious child. 3. I conceive that with the remission of the guilt of original sin, and adoption into the family or Church of God, there will be vouchsafed to the child spiritual influences, disposing it to listen to the word of God, and to obey the rules of the Father's house into which it has been received; that is, with the adoption there will be bestowed a measure of the Spirit of Adoption."—*Bateman's "Life of H. V. Elliott."*

If High Churchmen, in dealing with mixed congregations (some of whom are miserably prejudiced against the truth), would express their meaning in the guarded terms of such a man as Dr. Newman; and if Evangelicals would express themselves in the equally well-chosen terms of this great ornament of their school, they would much sooner bring their respective hearers to a practical understanding respecting a Sacrament which Christ has ordained to enable Christians to walk in newness of life; and surely this should be no secondary matter with those who have at heart the honour of Christ.

SECTION LVII.—THE LORD'S SUPPER. THE MEMORIAL.

1. WHY WAS THE SACRAMENT OF THE LORD'S SUPPER ORDAINED?
   FOR THE CONTINUAL REMEMBRANCE OF THE SACRIFICE OF THE DEATH OF CHRIST, AND OF THE BENEFITS WHICH WE RECEIVE THEREBY.
2. *By Whom was the Sacrament of the Lord's Supper ordained?*
   By the Eternal Son of God, the Word made flesh.
3. *When was the Sacrament of the Lord's Supper ordained?*
   It was ordained by the Son of God on the night on which He was betrayed ; *i. e.*, on the night before the day on which His Body was broken and His Blood shed for the remission of sins. (3–5)
4. *In what words did the Son of God ordain this Sacrament?*
   In the words, " Take, eat : this is My Body, which is broken for you : this do in remembrance of Me." " This cup is the New Testament in My Blood [or this is My Blood of the New Testament]. This do ye, as oft as ye drink it, in remembrance of Me." (1 Cor. xi. 24–26.) (6–10)
5. *What do you mean by the " continual remembrance of the Sacrifice of the death of Christ"?*
   I mean a memorial or commemoration of the Death of Christ, to be perpetually celebrated by His Church till He come (8–13, 16, 17)
6. *Before whom, more especially, does the Church make the memorial?*
   Before God the Father. (13–15)
7. *But is not Holy Communion intended to enable us to profess our individual faith in the Death of Christ?*
   No : it was ordained to be a memorial or showing forth of the Sacrifice of the Death of Christ ; not of our belief in it.
8. *Why are we sure that our Lord ordained this Sacrament, not to enable us to exercise an act of the memory,*

but to enable the Church to make before God a public commemoration of His Death?

Because our Lord, in speaking of "remembrance," employs the word anamnesis (ἀνάμνησις), which is elsewhere only used as betokening such a public memorial as the Church has ever held the Eucharist to be.

9. *In what other place does this word occur in the New Testament?*

Only in Hebrews x. 3 : "In these sacrifices there is a remembrance (ἀνάμνησις) made of sins every year;" where the remembrance was evidently the solemn sacrificial recognition before God, on the great day of atonement, of the sins of the people.

10. *Is this word ever used in the Old Testament?*

Yes, in two places; in each one of which it signifies a memorial before God.

11. *Mention these places.*

(1.) The shew-bread, with the frankincense upon it, is said to be a memorial [or anamnesis] before God. (Levit. xxiv. 7.) (21–26)

(2.) The burnt offerings and peace offerings are said to be an "anamnesis," or memorial, before God. (Num. x. 10.) (18–21)

12. *What, then, is the remembrance which Christ ordained?*

It is the most solemn possible mode of pleading before God, and showing forth before the Church, the meritorious Death of the Eternal Son of God. (27)

13. *To what, then, does the Eucharist correspond?*

To the sacrifices which were offered under the law: as these sacrifices prefigured the Death which was to atone, so the Eucharist shows forth the Death which has atoned, and applies its virtue. (27–32)

14. *Why must the Holy Communion be a commemoration before God, rather than a means whereby we remind ourselves that Christ died for us?*

Because it is an infinitely higher thing to show forth the Death of Christ before God and the Church than merely to remind one another of its benefits. (31–34)

15. *Why must you, of necessity, assign the highest meaning?*

I cannot help doing so, when I consider the exceeding greatness of the Person Who ordained this Sacrament, and the exceeding solemnity of the occasion on which He ordained it. (31–34)

16. *If, then, the Holy Eucharist be a commemoration of the Lord's Death, as the Jewish sacrifices were prefigurements of the same Death, is it a sacrifice?*
   The Church of Christ has always held it to be a sacrifice. (35, 36)
17. *What reasons from Scripture has she for so doing?*
   First of all, the Jewish prophets, in foretelling the pure worship of the times of Christ, always apply to it language of a sacrificial nature. (37-42)
18. *Give an instance.*
   We read in Malachi the words, "From the rising of the sun to the going down of the same my name shall be great among the Gentiles; and in every place incense shall be offered unto my name, and a pure offering" [or a pure mincha, *i.e.*, an offering of fine flour or cakes of bread]. (Mal. i. 11.) (37-40)
   Also, He [*i. e.*, Christ] shall purify the sons of Levi . . . that they may offer unto the Lord an offering in righteousness. (Mal. iii. 3.)
19. *Show how this applies to Christian worship.*
   Christ never purified the literal sons of Levi to offer legal sacrifices; but when He came He ordained a ministry which, from the first, has celebrated a service which the Church has always held to be sacrificial.
20. *Are there any other similar prophecies?*
   Yes. Isaiah [lvi. 6, 7], prophesying of the times of the Messiah, says, "Also the sons of the stranger, that join themselves to the Lord, to serve Him, and to love the name of the Lord . . . even them will I bring to my holy mountain, and make them joyful in my house of prayer: their burnt offerings and their sacrifices shall be accepted upon mine altar; for mine house shall be called an house of prayer for all people."
   [Jeremiah also (xxxiii. 15-22) speaks of the pure worship of the times of the Messiah in the strongest sacrificial language.] (41-43)
21. *Is this sacrificial language adopted by our Lord and His Apostles?*
   Yes; our blessed Saviour supposes that His followers will bring their gifts to the altar (Matt. v. 23); and St. Paul (Heb. xiii. 10) says that "we have an altar whereof they have no right to eat who serve the tabernacle." (44-50)

22. *But were not our Lord's words spoken to Jews rather than to Christians?*
No: they are a part of that discourse from which the Church of Christ learns the best of all prayers, and the most precious precepts of holiness.

[Our Lord, too, being God, and so foreseeing the sacrificial terms which His Church would always apply to her most solemn act of worship, would not have used language calculated to uphold erroneous views of such a matter.]

23. *How do you know that St. Paul alludes to the Lord's table, when he says, " We have an altar?"*
Because he speaks of an altar whereof men *eat;* and it is through eating of the Lord's table that we partake of the One Sacrifice. (47–50)

24. *What do these places, taken together, show?*
They show that we are bound to understand the words, "Do this in remembrance of Me," as teaching that in them our Lord ordained a public sacrificial memorial, or re-presentation, of His Death before God.

25. *Have you another Scripture reason for applying sacrificial terms to the Eucharist?*
Yes. The book of Psalms has, on the authority of Apostles (1 Cor. xiv. 26; Eph. v. 19; James v. 13), always formed a leading part in the service of God amongst Christians; and this book is full of sacrificial allusions which have now their counterpart only in Eucharistic worship.

26. *Give a few instances.*
"I will wash mine hands in innocency, O Lord: and so will I go to thine altar." (Psalm xxvi. 6.)
"That I may go unto the altar of God, even unto the God of my joy and gladness." (xliii. 4.)
(Also xx. 3; xxvii. 7; lxvi. 13; cxvi. 13, 14, 17.)

27. *But may not all these expressions be understood of acts of praise and prayer?*
If in a lower and more indirect sense they *may* be understood of simple prayer and praise, much more *must* they be applied to that service in which we set forth before God Christ's Body sacrificially broken, and His Blood sacrificially shed.

28. *Do the ancient Liturgies uphold this view of the Eucharist as a sacrifice?*
Yes; all, without exception, are founded upon it.

29. *In saying that the Eucharist is a sacrifice, do you mean*

that Christ in any way suffers again when the bread is broken?
No; Christ hath once suffered for sins, the just for the unjust. (1 Peter iii. 18.)

30. *In saying that the Eucharist is a sacrifice, do you mean that the Sacrifice on the Cross is not all-sufficient?*
No: the Sacrifice on the Cross was a complete and finished sacrifice, containing in itself all-atoning virtue. (51–54)

31. *Why then do you call the Eucharist a Sacrifice?*
Because as, by God's appointment, the One all-sufficient Sacrifice was set forth before God in the typical representations of the old Law, so, equally by God's appointment, the same all-atoning Sacrifice requires to be commemorated in the memorial re-presentation of the New Law.

32. *Is it needful that we should look upon the Eucharist as thus a Sacrifice?*
Yes; for, unless we do so, we shall not regard it as the most solemn "bounden duty and service" of religious worship; but merely as one means, amongst many, of enabling us to exercise an act of memory.

33. *Did the Priesthood of Christ cease when He offered up Himself upon the cross?*
No: He is "a Priest for ever after the order of Melchizedec." (Psalm cx. 4.) (68–74)

34. *If He is a Priest, must He not have somewhat to offer?*
Yes; and so He offers Himself in that Body which is yet marked with the wounds He received (The Lamb as it had been slain, Rev. v. 6); and in offering Himself, He offers His Church, of which He is the Head. (72–82)

35. *Can the sacrificial memorial in the Eucharist be disjoined from this presentation of Himself by our Lord?*
No; on the contrary, it is inseparably joined with it.

36. *Can you show this from Scripture?*
Yes: in the words of St. Paul: "The cup of blessing which we bless, is it not the Communion of the Blood of Christ? The Bread which we break, is it not the Communion of the Body of Christ? For we being many are one bread, and one body; for we are all partakers of that one Bread." (1 Cor. x. 16, 17.) (69–72)

37. *How does this passage bear upon the point?*
In this way: Christ, in presenting Himself to God, presents us in Himself, for, by partaking of that one

bread, we are made one body in Him, and so are included in this presentation of Himself. (See Note B, page 318.) (73-82)

38. *In what part of the Eucharistic service does the Sacrifice consist?*

It consists in observing the whole of what Christ has instituted: for our Lord took bread, gave thanks, brake it, and gave it to His disciples, saying, "Take, eat; this is my body;" and then said, "Do this in remembrance of me." And St. Paul adds, "As oft as ye eat this bread, and drink this cup, ye do show the Lord's death till He come."

39. *In what words is the Eucharistic Sacrifice recognised in our service?*

In the words, "Did institute, and in His Holy Gospel command us to continue a perpetual memory of that His precious death, until His coming again." Also, "We, Thy humble servants, entirely desire Thy fatherly goodness mercifully to accept this our sacrifice of praise and thanksgiving." And also, "Although we be unworthy to offer unto Thee any sacrifice, yet we beseech Thee to accept this our bounden duty and service."

40. *Does the Sacrifice of praise and thanksgiving consist in the Hymns and words of praise and thanksgiving which are in the office?*

No. It consists in the exhibition before God of the Sufferings and Death of His dear Son (together with the acknowledgment of the benefits which we receive thereby), which is inherent in the whole sacramental act. (53-63)

41. *But does God need to be reminded of the Sacrifice of the Death of His Son?*

He *needs* not to be reminded, but He has willed that we should so remind Him; just as He needs not to be reminded of the Name of His Son in our daily prayers, and yet He has bidden us to ask for all things in the Name of His Son.

42. *Does the Sacrifice consist in the offering up of ourselves?*

No: the offering up of ourselves is in connection with the sacrificial memorial of Christ; so that we offer up ourselves not alone, as it were, but in Christ, because in communion with that Body of which He is the Head. (65-68)

SHORTER CATECHISM.

1. *Why was the Sacrament of the Lord's Supper ordained?*
   For the continual remembrance of the sacrifice of the Death, &c.
2. *If the Lord's Supper be a "Sacrament of the Gospel," by Whom must it have been ordained?*
   By Christ Himself.
3. *When did our Lord ordain this Sacrament?*
   On the night on which He last ate the Passover.
4. *What took place on that night?*
   He was betrayed to be crucified.
5. *If the Son of God ordained it on the night when He was betrayed, how should we regard it?*
   We should regard it as most solemn, and most necessary for us to receive.
6. *What did our Lord do when He ordained the Sacrament?*
   "He took bread, and when He had given thanks, He brake it, and said, Take, eat; this is My body which is broken for you" (1 Cor. xi. 23, 24).
7. *Did He tell His disciples why they were to "do this"?*
   Yes: He said, "Do this in remembrance of Me."
8. *What besides this did He do?*
   After the same manner, also, He took the cup when He had supped, saying, "This cup is the New Testament in My blood. This do ye, as oft as ye drink it, in remembrance of Me" (1 Cor. xi. 25).
9. *In doing this, then, what did He ordain?*
   A continual remembrance of the Sacrifice of His Death.
10. *Why do you say of the "Sacrifice" of His Death?*
    Because His Death was a sacrifice or offering for sin, and we have to make a remembrance of this above all.
11. *What does the word "remembrance" mean?*
    It means a commemoration or solemn public memorial.
12. *Can it mean that the Holy Communion is intended merely to remind us of Christ's Death?*
    No: it must mean much more.
13. *What more does it mean?*
    It means that we are to make a celebration or re-presentation before God of the Death of Christ.
14. *How is the Holy Communion this?*
    Because the bread broken and wine poured forth represent the broken Body and shed Blood of Christ.
15. *Before Whom do we re-present them?*
    Before God and before the Church.

16. *Is this to be a frequent act?*
    Yes: it is for the "continual" remembrance or memorial.
17. *What words of the Holy Spirit teach us this?*
    "As oft as ye eat this bread and drink this cup, ye do shew the Lord's death till He come" (1 Cor. xi. 26).
18. *Is there anything in Scripture which explains to us the way in which we make a memorial before God?*
    Yes: the Jewish sacrifices, especially those offered by the high priest on the great day of atonement.
19. *How do these explain the way in which we make the memorial?*
    Because as in these sacrifices there was a showing forth of a future Death, so in Holy Communion there is a showing forth of a past Death.
20. *Before whom did the Jewish sacrifices show forth the future death?*
    Of course, before God.
21. *Before Whom, then, must our Holy Communion set forth the death of Christ?*
    Before God and before the Church; but more especially before God.
22. *Had the Jews any bread set before God in solemn worship?*
    Yes: they had the shew bread.
23. *What was the shew bread?*
    Twelve loaves, with frankincense upon them, set before God as a memorial (Lev. xxiv. 7).
24. *A memorial of what?*
    Of the twelve tribes of the people of God.
25. *Is our memorial like this?*
    No: it is part of one loaf, to signify that the people of God now are "one bread and one body" (1 Cor. x. 17).
26. *What else of a typical nature has it which the shew bread had not?*
    It is broken before God to signify the breaking of the Body of Christ as our Sacrifice.
27. *Why must we show forth this Death before God?*
    In order to plead the merits of it.
28. *How were the Jews ordered to plead the Sacrifice of Christ before He came?*
    By the sacrifices which they offered up upon their altar.
29. *Had these sacrifices any virtue or grace in themselves?*
    No: they only pointed to the Sacrifice of Christ.
30. *Have our Eucharists any virtue of themselves?*
    Not apart from that One Sacrifice which they set forth and apply.
31. *Which sets forth most fully the sacrifice of Christ, the Jewish sacrifices, or the Eucharist?*
    The Eucharist.

32. *Why?*
   Because our Lord says, respecting the bread, "This is My body;" and respecting the wine, "This is My blood."
33. *Was anything like this said by God respecting any Jewish sacrifice?*
   No: such words would have been unmeaning before the Incarnation and Birth of the Son of God.
34. *What then must that memorial be which is made with things which Christ called by such names?*
   It must be beyond everything great and efficacious.
35. *On account of all this, what has the Church always called it?*
   A Sacrifice.
36. *Is it a Sacrifice apart from the Sacrifice of Christ?*
   No: it is only a Sacrifice because it sets forth, and pleads and applies, the One Sacrifice of Christ.
37. *Are there any prophecies of the Eucharist as a Sacrifice?*
   Yes: one particularly in Malachi i. 11.
38. *What are the words of the prophet?*
   "In every place incense shall be offered unto my name, and a pure offering."
39. *What is the word used for offering in this place?*
   The same word (mincha) which is used for the offering of bread or flour in Leviticus ii.
40. *Has this always been understood of the Eucharist?*
   Yes: the earliest writers in the purest ages of the Church always understand it of the Eucharist.
41. *Are there any other prophecies which teach us that Christians would have a sacrificial worship?* Yes: Jeremiah xxxiii. 15-22.
42. *Any other?* Yes: Isaiah lvi. 6, 7.
43. *But these places speak of "burnt offerings," and Christians have no such rites or ordinances.*
   No: but they have an ordinance which is far more significant of Christ and of His Death than all these Jewish rites put together.
44. *Does our Lord ever use words which teach that His followers will, in some sense, offer a sacrifice?*
   Yes: He speaks of our bringing our gift to the altar (Matt. v. 23).
45. *Did our Lord, when He said such words, foresee that His Church would always call the Holy Table an altar?*
   Yes: being God Himself, and being full of the Spirit of God, He must have foreseen it.
46. *What, then, do we learn from this?*
   That it is right for us to call the Lord's table an altar, and that of which we there partake a heavenly and spiritual Sacrifice.
47. *Does any servant of Christ use similar words?*
   Yes: St. Paul says, "We have an altar whereof they have no right to eat who serve the tabernacle" (Heb. xiii. 10).

48. *By Whose Inspiration did St. Paul speak?* By the Spirit of God.
49. *Why must St. Paul here mean the Lord's table?*
    Because he speaks of an altar of which men are to eat.
50. *But may not the Apostle allude to the offering up of prayers and hymns only?*
    No: he speaks of an altar of which men eat, not of prayers and hymns, which have no special connection with an altar.
51. *How many atoning sacrifices have there been?*
    There has been but One.
52. *What is that?*
    The Sacrifice of Jesus Christ on the cross.
53. *But has not that one Sacrifice made all other sacrifices unlawful?*
    No: on the contrary, it has made other sacrifices necessary.
54. *What other sacrifices has it made necessary?*
    The sacrifice of praise and thanksgiving.
55. *Any others?* Yes; the sacrifice of ourselves.
56. *Can we offer up our praises and thanksgivings apart from the Sacrifice of Christ?*
    No: "By Him let us offer the sacrifice of praise to God continually, that is, the fruit of our lips giving thanks to His Name" (Heb. xiii. 15).
57. *What, then, is the Christian's great offering of praise and thanksgiving?*
    The Holy Communion.
58. *Why?*
    Because in it we exhibit before God by His Son's appointment the tokens of His Son's Passion.
59. *Do any acts of praise and thanksgiving accompany this?*
    Yes: the deepest and greatest we offer to God.
50. *Mention one of these?*
    The Hymn of the Seraphim, "Holy, Holy, Holy."
51. *Mention another.*
    The Gloria in Excelsis (Glory be to God on high, and on earth peace, &c.).
52. *Are these the things which make the Holy Communion to be a sacrifice?* No.
53. *Why, then, do we offer them up at the time of Holy Communion?*
    In order to connect them as closely as we can with the Sacrifice of our Blessed Lord.
54. *What name is given to Holy Communion because it is a sacrifice of praise and thanksgiving?*
    The Eucharist (which word means thanksgiving).
55. *Do we offer up any other sacrifice in the service?*
    Yes: the sacrifice of ourselves.
56. *In what particular words?*
    "Here we offer and present unto Thee, O Lord, ourselves,

our souls, and bodies, to be a reasonable, holy, and lively sacrifice unto Thee."

67. *Do we offer up this alone, as it were, separate from the Sacrifice of Christ?*
   No: we here offer it in connection with the setting forth of the Sacrifice of Christ.

68. *When we celebrate and partake of Holy Communion in earth, with what do we join ourselves?*
   With the offering of Christ in Heaven.

69. *How can we do this?*
   Because by Holy Communion we are one with Christ as the Head of His Church.

70. *What passage of Scripture teaches us this?*
   "We being many are one bread, and one body: for we are all partakers of that one bread" (1 Cor. x. 17).

71. *Does Christ offer anything in Heaven?*
   Yes: if He be a priest, He must have somewhat to offer (Heb. viii. 3).

72. *What does He offer?*
   He presents Himself before God as the Lamb once slain.

73. *How besides?*
   As the Head of His Church, or mystical Body.

74. *What is the name given to all this?*
   The Intercession of Christ.

75. *Do we understand how Christ intercedes for us?*
   No: it is one of the deepest things of God.

76. *Do we believe it?* Yes: most firmly.

77. *On what Scripture grounds?*
   On the ground that our Lord is "a priest for ever, after the order of Melchizedec" (Heb. vii. 21).

78. *What is His work as a Priest?* The work of Intercession.

79. *Does He offer Himself often?* Not as a sufferer.

80. *What, then, is the ground of His Intercession?*
   His past sufferings.

81. *Is there any memorial of these past sufferings in Heaven.*
   St. John saw in Heaven a Lamb, as it had been slain (Rev. v. 6).

82. *Is there any memorial on earth?*
   Yes: our Lord says, This is My body which is given: This is My blood which is shed: Do this in remembrance of Me.

83. *What then, does the Holy Communion enable us to do?*
   To join with our Lord in His Heavenly act of Intercession.

NOTE A.—As much difference of opinion exists as to whether, and as to how far, the Holy Eucharist is a sacrifice, it might bring some of us, at least, to a better understanding among ourselves if those who *deny* it to be a sacrifice would consider what is contained in the following short extracts from men of undoubted Protestantism ; and also, if those who *assert* it to be a sacrifice would use no stronger language than that which is contained in the succeeding extracts from the writings of men of equally undoubted Catholicity.

"That in the sacred supper there is a Sacrifice (in that sense wherein the Fathers spoke) none of us ever doubted. . . . As Augustine interprets it, a memorial of Christ's passion celebrated in the Church, and from this sweet commemoration of our redemption THERE ARISES ANOTHER SACRIFICE, the sacrifice of praise ; and from thence a true peace offering of the Christian soul."—*Bishop Hall:* " *No Peace with Rome,*" xix.

"By this sacred rite of bread and wine we present and inculcate His Blessed Passion to His Father. We put Him in mind thereof by setting the monuments thereof before Him."—*Mede:* " *The Christian Sacrifice.*"

"The mystery of which rite they (the Fathers) took to be this, that as Christ, by presenting His death and satisfaction to His Father, continually intercedes for us in Heaven, so the Church on earth semblably approaches the throne of grace by representing Christ to His Father in these Holy Mysteries of His Death and Passion."—*Mede:* " *The Christian Sacrifice.*"

> "With solemn faith we offer up,
> And spread before Thy glorious eyes,
> That only ground of all our hope,
> That precious bleeding Sacrifice,
> Which brings Thy grace on sinners down,
> And perfects all our souls in one."
> *Wesley: from "Hymns on the Lord's Supper,"* by *J. and C. Wesley,* Hymn cxxv.

"As the bread is justly called Christ's Body, as signifying it, so the action was of old called a sacrifice, as representing and commemorating it. And it is no more improper than calling our bodies, and our alms, and our prayers, sacrifices. And the naming of the table an altar, as related to the representative sacrifice, is no more improper than the other. 'We have an altar whereof they have no right to eat' (Heb. xiii. 10), seems plainly to mean the Sacramental Communion."—*Baxter's* " *Christian Institutes,*" i. p. 304.

"What are the principal differences between the sacrifice of the Holy Eucharist now and that of our Lord upon the cross?

"The one real, and the other only commemorative. The one meritorious in itself, the other deriving its merit from the first.

"The one of our Lord's mortal and passible body, the other of His immortal body."—*Dr. Neale:* " *Catechetical Notes,*" p. 131.

"Thus the sacrificial rite of the earthly church represents and typifies that act of love of which it is the appointed memorial."—*Döllinger: "First Age of the Church."*

'The memorial of His accomplished atonement, celebrated by those who need constantly fresh forgiveness, is necessarily a constant renewal of the Reconciliation."—*Döllinger: "First Age of the Church."*

"A memorial of His own broken Body and His shed Blood, once sacrificed, now perpetually pleaded, and by such continual commemoration effectually applying the propitiation which He made for the sins of the world upon the cross."—*Carter's "Doctrine of Holy Eucharist,"* p. 13.

"A sacrifice, not by way of a new death, but by way of a standing memorial of His death; a daily celebration and representation of His death to God, and an application to our souls of the fruits of it."—*"Garden of the Soul."*

Note B.—St. Augustine, in his "City of God," Book x. Ch. vi., defines a true sacrifice to be "every act which is performed with the purpose of joining us to God in a holy bond of union." He then proceeds to show that nothing which we can do, not even the pity or charity by which we assist others, can be called a sacrifice unless it be done with reference to God (si propter Deum non fit). And then, at the conclusion of this chapter, in commenting on Romans xii. 5, he says, "*This is the sacrifice of Christians: 'we, being many, are one body in Christ;' which thing also the Church continually celebrates in that Sacrament of the altar which the faithful well know, wherein it is shown that, included in the thing which she offers, she offers herself.*"

In a subsequent chapter of the same book (x. 20), St. Augustine says that our Blessed Lord is both the priest, inasmuch as He Himself makes the offering, and is also Himself the oblation. "*Of which thing He has willed the sacrifice of the Church to be the daily sacramental sign, which* [Church], *since she is the body of which He Himself is the Head, learns to offer herself through Him.*"

SECTION LVIII.—THE SACRAMENTAL MYSTERY.

1. *Is the Holy Communion anything besides a commemoration or memorial of the death of Christ?*
   Yes: it is a Sacrament; and so it is the outward visible sign of an inward spiritual grace given unto us. (1–7)
2. *If, then, the Holy Communion be thus a Sacrament, how many parts must there be in it?*
   Two; the outward visible sign, and the Inward Spiritual Grace. (8–9)
3. WHAT IS THE OUTWARD PART OR SIGN OF THE LORD'S SUPPER?
   BREAD AND WINE, WHICH THE LORD HATH COMMANDED TO BE RECEIVED.
4. *Show from the words of Scripture that the Lord commanded bread and wine to be received.*
   As they were eating, Jesus took bread, and blessed it, and brake it, and gave it to the disciples, and said, "Take, eat; this is My Body. And He took the cup, and gave thanks, and gave it to them, saying, Drink ye all of it. For this is My Blood of the New Testament, which is shed for many for the remission of sins." (Matt. xxvi. 26–28.) (11–19)
5. *If our Lord commands both bread and wine to be received, is it competent to any Church to give the Holy Communion only in the bread?*
   No: under such a way of communicating, the laity cannot be assured that they receive that which Christ promises when He says, "He that eateth my flesh, *and drinketh my blood*, dwelleth in me, and I in him." (John vi. 56).
6. *Are there any reasons for depriving the laity of the cup?*
   There are no reasons which had the smallest weight with the Church for the first twelve hundred years of her existence.
   [A pope of the fifth century (Gelasius) says with reference to this very point, "The division of one and the same mystery cannot take place without great sacrilege."]

7. *What, then, in the words of the Catechism, are this bread and wine?*
   They are the outward part or sign. (11–19)
8. *If this Communion be a Sacrament, what must there be besides this "outward part or sign" of bread and wine?*
   There must be an Inward Part which corresponds to the outward part, a Thing Signified which corresponds to the sign.
9. *When you say that bread and wine is the outward part or sign, of what is the outward part the sign?*
   The outward part is the sign which evidences the presence of the Thing Signified. (20–22)
10. *Why do you say, the "presence" of the Thing Signified?*
    Because there are two parts in a sacrament. We see the outward part, which is a visible sign; but the Inward Part is not discernible by the senses, and requires the outward sign to assure us that we receive it. (24–31)
11. WHAT IS THE INWARD PART OR THING SIGNIFIED?
    THE BODY AND BLOOD OF CHRIST, WHICH ARE VERILY AND INDEED TAKEN, AND RECEIVED BY THE FAITHFUL IN THE LORD'S SUPPER.
12. *Why do you say that the outward part or sign of bread and wine is the sign of the presence of the Inward Part or Thing Signified?*
    Because our Blessed Lord, God and Man, called the outward part by the name of the Inward Part when He said, "Take, eat; this is My Body." "Drink ye all of it, for this is My Blood." (20, 21, 29–37)
13. *Is there any other Scripture reason?*
    Yes. The Holy Ghost says by the mouth of St. Paul, "The cup of blessing which we bless, is it not the communion [or participation] of the Blood of Christ? The bread which we break, is it not the communion of the Body of Christ?" (1 Cor. x. 16.) (31)
14. *Have we any other Scripture reason?*
    Yes. St. Paul says that "He who eats and drinks unworthily," is "guilty of the Body and Blood of the Lord," and "eateth and drinketh condemnation to himself, not discerning the Lord's Body." (1 Cor. xi. 27–29.)
15. *If our Blessed Lord, Who is the Truth, and Whose words are spirit and life, gave men the outward part as*

His Body and Blood, can there be a doubt about our receiving Them?

No. The Body and Blood of Christ must be "verily and indeed taken and received by the faithful in the Lord's Supper." (32–37)

16. *Do these words "verily and indeed" explain the mode in which the Body and Blood are present?*

No: they only assert that, no matter what the secret and mysterious nature of the Presence, it is a real Presence.

17. *After what manner is the Body and Blood of Christ so present as to be "given, taken, and eaten" in the Lord's Supper?*

After a heavenly and spiritual manner: *i.e.*, they are present by the power and working of God's Holy Spirit, and for the highest spiritual ends.

18. *Can we explain the way in which the Body and Blood of Christ become the Inward Part of the Lord's Supper?*

No: it is a mystery known only to Almighty God, and is pronounced to be a mystery by the Church.

["He hath instituted and ordained Holy Mysteries:" "we who have duly received these Holy Mysteries."] (32–37)

19. *Are the bread and wine so changed into the Body and Blood of Christ that the truth and reality of the outward parts no longer exist?*

No. The Church of England denies such a gross, local, and physical mode of presence, and asserts that the outward part or sign never loses its truth and reality.

20. *What does the Church of England say of this opinion?*

That it overthrows the nature of a Sacrament, because they who hold it deny that there is really and truly any outward part.

21. *Is the outward part merely a sign of the Body and Blood of Christ really absent?*

No: if such were the case, the nature of a Sacrament would be equally overthrown, for it would really have no Inward Part.

22. *Is the Presence a Presence only in the heart of the receiver?*

No. The Body and Blood of Christ are "*given*," as well as "taken and eaten" (as our Article says), all which things are done that the Presence of Christ may *ultimately* be in the faithful receiver.

23. *Can the words of Christ respecting eating His Flesh (or*

Y

the words of Institution) be interpreted as meaning that we must love Him, or believe in His Atonement?

No : we cannot suppose that our Lord would have used such mysterious terms to express such simple truths as that we must love Him and believe in His Atonement.

24. *But is it not said that His Presence is through faith, or that He is present to our faith?*

Faith is " the evidence of things not seen " (Heb. xi. 1) ; not the cause of their existence. Our Lord ordained this Sacrament as the Communion of His Body and Blood ; and faith enables us to believe His word, and to discern the Inward Part.

25. *What then must be our faith?*

It must be a faith by which we " steadfastly believe the promises of God made to us in this Sacrament." (38, 39)

26. *What are these promises?*

They are that, if we eat and drink in penitence and faith, we shall " spiritually eat the Flesh of Christ and drink His Blood ; we shall dwell in Christ, and Christ in us ; we shall be one with Christ, and Christ with us."

27. *Where, in the Scriptures, are we encouraged to look for such wonderful benefits?*

In the words of our Blessed Lord Himself : " Verily, verily, I say unto you, except ye eat the Flesh of the Son of Man, and drink His Blood, ye have no life in you. Whoso eateth My Flesh, and drinketh My Blood, hath eternal life ; and I will raise him up at the last day. For My Flesh is meat indeed, and My Blood is drink indeed. He that eateth My Flesh, and drinketh My Blood, dwelleth in Me, and I in him." (John vi. 53–56.) (39–44)

28. *But do not some say that these words do not refer to the Blessed Sacrament?*

If the Holy Communion be only the outward part or sign, and have no Inward Part, of course our Lord does not refer to it ; but if the Holy Communion have an Inward Part, which is His own blessed Body and Blood, then He must refer to it. (44–47)

29. *How are we sure of this?*

Because our Lord promises certain extraordinary benefits to those who eat His Flesh and drink His Blood ; and in the Holy Eucharist alone does He offer to us His Body and His Blood. (46–49)

. *Are then such terms as eating the Body of Christ, and drinking the Blood of Christ, never used except in connection with the Eucharist?*

They are never used by our Lord, or by His Apostles, except when they are speaking of the Holy Eucharist. (49–52)

. *But is it not often said that in this discourse there can be no reference to the Eucharist, because when it was spoken the Eucharist was not yet instituted?*

On the contrary, we cannot suppose that our Lord would have ordained the Eucharist in words so unique and remarkable, unless He had previously given some teaching or promises by which the Apostles might see what love and grace He was then offering to them; and the only teaching recorded is that which is contained in the discourse in John vi.

. WHAT, THEN (*in the words of the Catechism*), ARE THE BENEFITS WHEREOF WE ARE PARTAKERS THEREBY?

THE STRENGTHENING AND REFRESHING OF OUR SOULS BY THE BODY AND BLOOD OF CHRIST, AS OUR BODIES ARE BY THE BREAD AND WINE.

. *Why is this the peculiar benefit of the Lord's Supper?*

Because of the Body and Blood of Christ, which are in it verily and indeed taken and received by the faithful in the Lord's Supper. (65–68)

. *Why do we need the strengthening and refreshing of our souls?*

Because of the weakness of our mortal nature, which we have inherited through the flesh and blood of the first Adam. (69–73)

. *If then we are to be strengthened and refreshed, what must we have?*

We must have within us the presence of Christ, the Second Adam; and so our Lord says, "He that eateth My Flesh, and drinketh My Blood, dwelleth in Me, and I in Him." (John vi. 56.) (69–73)

. *What then do these wonderful words of our Lord imply?*

They must imply some mysterious communication to us of His Human Nature as the Second Adam, in order to undo the evil which we have received from the flesh and blood (*i. e.*, the human nature) of the first Adam, and to sustain the life which we have received from Him.

. *Does this short answer of the Catechism (The strengthen-*

ing, &c.) express all the benefits which the faithful receive in Holy Communion?

No. One short sentence cannot possibly express all the benefits of this Sacrament.

38. *Mention some other benefits recognised in our Communion office.*

We pray that "our sinful bodies may be made clean by Christ's body, and our souls washed through His most precious blood." "That we may receive remission of our sins, and all other benefits of His Passion ;" and we thank God that "He doth assure us thereby that we are very members incorporate in the mystical body of His Son."

39. *Has the body any share in the benefits of Christ's Body and Blood?*

Our Lord says, "He that eateth my flesh, and drinketh my blood, hath eternal life, and I will raise him up at the last day;" and so the minister communicates the people in the words, "The Body of our Lord Jesus Christ, which was given for thee, preserve thy *body* and soul unto everlasting life." (63, 64)

40. *Do "the wicked, and such as be void of a lively faith," receive the Body and Blood of Christ?*

The Church of England has ruled that, "The wicked, and such as be void of a lively faith, although they do carnally and visibly press with their teeth (as St. Augustine saith) the Sacrament of the Body and Blood of Christ, yet in no wise are they partakers of Christ ; but rather to their condemnation do eat and drink the sign or Sacrament of so great a thing." (Article xxix.) (53-58)

41. *Does this overthrow in any way the truth that the Inward Part is always a real part of the one Sacrament?*

No : it is so expressed as to enable us to hold to the words of Christ : "He that eateth my flesh, and drinketh my blood, dwelleth in me, and I in him" (which, of course, the wicked cannot do) ; and yet fully to accept the awful fact revealed by the Holy Spirit through St. Paul, that the Body and Blood are so present as to make the wicked guilty of their profanation. "Whosoever shall eat of this bread, and drink of this cup of the Lord unworthily, shall be guilty of the body and blood of the Lord," and "eateth and drinketh condemnation to himself, not discerning the Lord's body." (1 Cor. xi. 27-29.) (53-58, 77)

42. *Can the Body and Blood of Christ be only received in Holy Communion?*
Our Blessed Lord has laid upon us that we are to receive His Body and Blood, and has given us, on the night of His betrayal, a means in the faithful use of which we are to receive them to our salvation. If, then, we neglect or despise the only means set forth in Scripture, we cannot hope that God will give us these blessings apart from such means. (59, 60, 66)

43. *But supposing that God has, in His providence, withheld from us the use of the outward means?*
The Church of England has ruled that, "if by reason of such extremity of sickness ... or any other just impediment, a man do not receive the Sacrament of Christ's Body and Blood, the curate shall instruct him, that if he do truly repent him of his sins, and steadfastly believe that Jesus Christ hath suffered death upon the Cross for him, and shed His Blood for his redemption, earnestly remembering the benefits he hath thereby, and giving Him hearty thanks therefore, he doth eat and drink the Body and Blood of our Saviour Christ profitably to his soul's health, although he do not receive the Sacrament with his mouth."—*Communion of the Sick.*

44. *How is the union between the outward part or sign, and the Inward Part, or Thing Signified, brought about?*
By the Bishop or Priest, who, as the minister of Christ and of the Church, gives thanks, blesses and breaks the bread, and blesses the cup; that is, consecrates the elements.

45. *Are we assured of this by Scripture?*
Yes. St. Paul says, "The cup of blessing which we bless, is it not the communion of the Blood of Christ? the bread which we break, is it not the communion of the Body of Christ?" (1 Cor. x. 16.) The Apostle evidently makes the communion to depend upon the outward action (the blessing and breaking), in which the Bishop or Priest performs the act which Christ enjoined.

SHORTER CATECHISM.

1. *Did our Saviour ordain the Holy Communion only as a memo rial?*
   No: He ordained it as a Sacrament.
2. *What is a Sacrament?*
   The outward visible sign of an inward spiritual grace give unto us.
3. *Why did Christ ordain Sacraments?*
   He ordained them that by partaking of the outward sign w might receive the Inward Spiritual Grace.
4. *Is there any difference between a Sacrament and a Memorial?*
   Yes: we ourselves make a memorial or commemoration t God, but in a Sacrament we receive from God.
5. *Are these two things joined in the Lord's Supper?*
   Yes: so joined that man cannot put them asunder.
6. *In what words of Christ is the Sacrament set forth?*
   In the words, "Take, eat, this is My Body." "Drink y all of it, for this is My Blood."
7. *In what words is the memorial set forth?*
   "As oft as ye eat this bread, and drink this cup, ye do shov the Lord's death till He come."
8. *How many parts are there in the Sacrament of the Lord' Supper?* Two.
9. *What is the first of these called in the Catechism?*
   The outward part or sign.
10. *What is the other part called?*
    The Inward Part, or Thing Signified.
11. *What is the outward part or sign of the Lord's Supper?*
    Bread and wine.
12. *Why are bread and wine the outward sign of the Lord's Supper?*
    Because the Lord commanded them both to be received.
13. *Where are we told that He commanded them to be received?*
    In St. Matthew's Gospel, xxvi. 26-28.
14. *Where else?* In St. Mark's Gospel, xiv. 22-24.
15. *In any other place?* Yes; in St. Luke's Gospel, xxii. 19, 20.
16. *Is there yet another account?* Yes, in 1 Cor. xi. 23-26.
17. *From whom did St. Paul receive the account which he ha given us?*
    From our blessed Lord Himself.
18. *What do we gather from all these accounts?*
    That our Lord took bread, blessed it, brake it, and gave it

and that our Lord took a cup of wine, blessed it, and gave it to His disciples.

19. *What then did He give them?*
   The outward part or sign.
20. *Did He give them only the outward part?*
   No: He gave them, along with it, the Inward Part.
21. *How do you know this?*
   Because when He gave them the bread, He said, This is My Body; and when He gave them the cup, He said, This is My Blood.
22. *By what name, then, did He call the outward part or sign?*
   By the name of the Inward Part.
23. *What, then, must the Inward Part be?*
   The Body and Blood of Christ.
24. *Of what must the Inward Part be a part?*
   Of the one Sacrament.
25. *If, then, the Inward Part be a part of the one Sacrament, what do we receive?*
   With the outward part, the bread and wine, we receive the Inward Part.
26. *Why?*
   Because the outward part is ordained by no other than Christ Himself, as a means whereby we receive the Inward Part.
27. *By what other name is the inward part called?*
   It is called the Thing Signified.
28. *The thing signified by what?*
   By the outward sign.
29. *Why did our Lord ordain an outward sign?*
   As a pledge to assure us that we receive the Thing Signified.
30. *Where, then, must the Inward Part be?*
   It must be given, taken, and received in the outward sign.
31. *What express word of Scripture have we for this?*
   "The cup of blessing which we bless, is it not the communion of the Blood of Christ? the bread which we break, is it not the communion of the Body of Christ?" (1 Cor. x. 16).
32. *Can we understand the way in which the outward and Inward Parts are joined?*
   No: it is a very deep mystery.
33. *Is it necessary that we should understand how, when we receive the bread and wine, we receive Christ's Body and Blood?* No.
34. *Is it necessary that we should believe it?* Yes.
35. *Why?*
   Because, if we do not, we cannot look upon this Sacrament as it is set forth in Scripture.
36. *How is it set forth in Scripture?*
   As the Body and Blood of Christ.

37. *By whom?*
   By our blessed Lord Himself, and by the Holy Spirit, speaking by St. Paul.
38. *For what other reason must we believe that in Holy Communion we receive the Body and Blood of Christ?*
   In order that we may steadfastly believe the promises of God made to us in this Sacrament.
39. *What are the promises of God made to us in this Sacrament?*
   The promises which Christ has made to those who eat His Flesh and drink His Blood.
40. *What is the first of these promises?*
   "Whoso eateth My flesh, and drinketh My blood, hath eternal life, and I will raise him up at the last day" (John vi. 54).
41. *Name another?*
   "He that eateth My flesh, and drinketh My blood, dwelleth in Me, and I in Him" (John vi. 56).
42. *Does God fulfil to us these promises in Holy Communion?*
   Yes: our Lord offers to us His Flesh and Blood only in Holy Communion.
43. *By which part of the Holy Communion do we receive these promises?*
   By the Inward Part.
44. *Does then the Lord, in saying these things, refer to the mere reception of an ordinance?*
   No: He refers to the Divine Gift, of which He has ordained the ordinance to be the channel.
45. *But was the Sacrament of the Lord's Supper ordained when Christ said these words?*
   No: and therefore, before our Lord ordained it, He wished to prepare men's minds for it.
46. *How, then, did He prepare them for it?*
   By leading them to expect extraordinary blessings through receiving His Body (or Flesh) and Blood.
47. *Would He have offered to them His Body and His Blood unless He had in some measure led them to expect some great gift by it?*
   We cannot believe that He would have done so.
48. *What means did our Lord ordain in order that we might receive His Body and His Blood?*
   The Holy Communion.
49. *Is this the only means?*
   It is the only means mentioned in the Scriptures.
50. *Does St. Paul ever speak of eating our Lord's Body and drinking His Blood?*
   Yes: St. Paul speaks of our doing this when he speaks of the Holy Communion.
51. *What are his words?*

THE SACRAMENTAL MYSTERY.

The cup of blessing which we bless, is it not the communion of the Blood of Christ? the bread which we break, is it not the communion of the Body of Christ? (1 Cor. x. 16).

52. *But does not St. Paul use such terms as eating our Lord's Flesh when he speaks of believing in Christ's merits?*
   No: He never speaks of eating Christ's Body except when he is speaking of the Sacrament of His Body.

53. *What does St. Paul say of those who come to the Holy Communion unworthily?*
   That they discern not the Lord's Body (1 Cor. xi. 29).

54. *And of what does he say that they are guilty?*
   They are guilty of the Body and Blood of the Lord (1 Cor. xi. 27).

55. *And what is the fearful consequence of this profanation?*
   They eat and drink judgment (or condemnation) to themselves.

56. *Why do the wicked incur such guilt and judgment?*
   Because they discern not the Lord's Body.

57. *How is it that they do not discern the Lord's Body?*
   Because they have no desire to receive what Christ offers to us in this Sacrament.

58. *Why have they no such desire?*
   Because Christ offers to us His Body and Blood that we may partake of His Life, and the wicked desire to continue in the death of sin.

59. *Is it then a safer thing to stay away from Holy Communion than to receive it?*
   No: because if we do not receive it, we can have no hope that God will give us the benefits of His Son's Body and Blood.

60. *But cannot He give us these blessings in other ways?*
   He is not likely to do so if we neglect the dying command of His Dear Son.

61. *Express, in the words of Scripture, the great present benefit of receiving the Body and Blood of Christ.*
   He that eateth My flesh, and drinketh My blood, dwelleth in Me, and I in him (John vi. 56).

62. *Is this benefit recognised in our service?*
   Yes: we pray that we may "so eat the flesh of the Son of Man, and drink His blood, that . . . . we may evermore dwell in Him, and He in us."

63. *Express, in the words of Scripture, the great future benefit of receiving the Body and Blood of Christ.*
   Whoso eateth My flesh, and drinketh My blood, hath eternal life, and I will raise him up at the last day (John vi. 54).

64. *Is this benefit also set before us in our Service?*
   Yes: when the minister gives the bread, He is directed to say

"The body of our Lord Jesus Christ, which was given for thee, preserve thy *body* and soul unto everlasting life."

65. *What benefits of Holy Communion are particularly mentioned in the Catechism?*
    The strengthening and refreshing of our souls by the Body and Blood of Christ as our bodies are by the bread and wine.
66. *But are we not strengthened by God's Holy Spirit?*
    Yes: but we cannot expect to be so strengthened unless we receive what Christ offers to us.
67. *By what does the Spirit strengthen us in Holy Communion?*
    By the Body and Blood of Christ, *i.e.*, by the Inward Part.
68. *Has God permitted us to see why we are to receive these blessings through the Body and Blood of Christ rather than through His Spirit alone?*
    Yes: because Christ is the Second Adam.
69. *If Christ be the Second Adam, what must He be to us?*
    He must be to us for life and salvation what the first Adam is for sin and condemnation.
70. *Why do we receive sin and condemnation from the first Adam?*
    Because we inherit (or partake of) the flesh and blood of the first Adam.
71. *What must we receive from the Second Adam?*
    We must receive life through partaking of His Flesh and Blood.
72. *What else do we receive from the first Adam?*
    We receive spiritual weakness.
73. *What must we have to remedy this?*
    We must have spiritual strength from the Second Adam.
74. *What has God given to man to strengthen him?* Bread.
75. *Who is the bread of life?*
    Christ says, "I am the bread of life."
76. *But cannot we eat this bread by merely reading His word?*
    Christ says, "The bread that I will give is my flesh," and He has given to us in this Sacrament the means of eating His Flesh.
77. *Do all who come to the Holy Communion receive Christ as the bread of life?*
    No: the wicked, and such as have not a lively faith, are in no wise partakers of Christ.

SECTION LIX.—THE LORD'S SUPPER: WHAT IS REQUIRED OF THEM WHO COME.

1. *Is there, then, no place for our faith?*
   Yes; unless we have faith we eat and drink unworthily, and are guilty of the Body and Blood of the Lord; and eat and drink our own condemnation, not discerning the Lord's Body. (1 Cor. xi. 27, 29.)
2. WHAT (THEN) IS REQUIRED OF THEM WHO COME TO THE LORD'S SUPPER?
   TO EXAMINE THEMSELVES, WHETHER THEY REPENT THEM TRULY OF THEIR FORMER SINS, STEADFASTLY PURPOSING TO LEAD A NEW LIFE; HAVE A LIVELY FAITH IN GOD'S MERCY THROUGH CHRIST, WITH A THANKFUL REMEMBRANCE OF HIS DEATH; AND BE IN CHARITY WITH ALL MEN.
3. *Can you express in one word what is required?*
   Yes: in the word "Self-examination." (2–6)
4. *Why is this the one requirement laid down?*
   No doubt because the only direction given by St. Paul is, "Let a man examine himself, and so let him eat of that bread, and drink of that cup." (1 Cor. xi. 28.) (2–6)
5. *Upon what points must we examine ourselves?*
   Upon three. Our repentance, our faith, and our love, or charity.
6. *How must we examine ourselves as to our repentance?*
   We are to examine ourselves as to whether we "repent us truly of our former sins, steadfastly purposing to lead a new life." (13–17)
7. *What is repentance?*
   It is a change of heart and mind with regard to sin, so that we are sorry and ashamed of it, and long to be delivered from it, and to have grace to subdue it.
8. *Why must our repentance be joined with "steadfastly purposing to lead a new life?"*
   Because there can be no repentance without it.
9. *Why is such repentance especially required before we receive Holy Communion?*
   Because all strength from God which we receive in Holy Communion is strength to hate and avoid sin, and to love and please God, and do His will: and it would be

a mockery to come professedly to receive strength against sin whilst we are determined to go on in sin.

10. *What is the next point on which we must examine ourselves?*

As to whether we have "a lively faith in God's mercy through Christ, with a thankful remembrance of His death." (18-21)

11. *Why must we have this?*

Because the Holy Communion is a remembrance or showing forth of the infinite mercy of God to mankind in the atoning Death of Christ; and we cannot join in showing forth before God the memorial of His Son's death unless we believe in the grace and love which it exhibits.

12. *Why are we especially to remember "God's" mercies; i. e., the mercies of God the Father?*

Because it was God Who gave His only Begotten Son, and Who sent His Son into the world, and it is God Who gives us the true Bread from heaven, and it is God the Father before Whom especially we make the Sacramental Memorial.

13. *In what especial mercies of God should we have a lively faith?*

In the mercies especially joined with the devout reception of Holy Communion, such as the partaking of the Body and Blood of Christ to eternal life of body and soul, and the assurance that "thereby we are very members incorporate in the mystical Body of God's Son." (20-22)

14. *What is the third and last point on which we should examine ourselves?*

As to whether we are in charity with all men. (25-28)

15. *Why?*

Because we cannot acceptably approach God in a service which, above all others, sets forth reconciliation between God and man, if we have within us the spirit of enmity and uncharitableness; for our Lord says, "If thou bring thy gift to the altar, and there rememberest that thy brother hath ought against thee, leave there thy gift before the altar, and go thy way: first be reconciled to thy brother, and then come and offer thy gift." (Matt. v. 23.)

16. *Is there any other reason?*

Yes. St. Paul says, "We, being many, are one bread and one body, for we are all partakers of that one bread."

We cannot have any true faith in Holy Communion, as the means of keeping us all "one in Christ," if we have no desire to be one in soul and spirit with our brethren.

17. *Do any other words of the Spirit express the mind in which we should partake?*

Yes: the words, "Christ our passover is sacrificed for us: therefore let us keep the feast, not with the old leaven, nor with the leaven of malice and wickedness, but with the unleavened bread of sincerity and truth." (1 Cor. v. 7.)

SHORTER CATECHISM.

1. *If, then, we are to receive the promises of God, what must we do?*

We must examine ourselves as to whether we repent us truly of our former sins, steadfastly purposing to lead a new life, have a lively faith in God's mercy, through Christ, with a thankful remembrance of His death, and be in charity with all men.

2. *In what words of Scripture are we told that we must examine ourselves?*

In the words of St. Paul. Let a man examine himself, and so let him eat of that bread and drink of that cup (1 Cor. xi. 28).

3. *As to what are we to examine ourselves?*

As to the state of our hearts and lives.

4. *In what words of our service is this self-examination enjoined?*

In the words, "Judge, therefore, yourselves, brethren, that ye be not judged of the Lord."

5. *Why are we so earnestly bidden to examine ourselves, and to judge ourselves?*

Because "as the benefit is great, if, with a true penitent heart and lively faith, we receive that holy Sacrament. . . . so is the danger great if we receive the same unworthily," &c.

6. *Can you express the reason for this searching self-examination in other words?*

Yes: "Because of the dignity of that holy mystery, and the great peril of the unworthy receiving thereof."

7. *What is meant by "unworthy" receiving?*

Receiving without thought, or prayer, or earnest desire, for God's grace and help.

8. *What is meant by "worthy" receiving?*

Receiving with the hope and earnest desire of obtaining the blessing God has promised in this Communion.

9. *Can we ever be really worthy?*
   No: we can never be of ourselves worthy to receive the Inward Part, *i.e.*, the Body and Blood of the Son of God.
10. *In what sense can we never be worthy?*
    We can never be worthy, in the sense of meriting, or deserving to receive the Body and Blood of the Eternal Son.
11. *In what sense can we be worthy?*
    Only in the sense of being among the number of those who desire the grace of this Sacrament, and in whom it can be effectual to salvation.
12. *In what words do we express our own unworthiness?*
    In the words, "We do not presume to come to this, Thy table, O merciful Lord, trusting in our own righteousness, but in Thy manifold and great mercies. We are not worthy so much as to gather up the crumbs under Thy table."
13. *How must we begin our self-examination?*
    We must begin by seeing to our repentance, whether it be true and real.
14. *When is our repentance true and sincere?*
    When we are sorry and ashamed of ourselves, and pray earnestly for pardon for the past, and for grace to forsake sin.
15. *What, if our repentance be real, will always be joined with it?*
    A steadfast purpose to lead a new life.
16. *What purpose must this be?* A steadfast purpose.
17. *Can there be any repentance if this is wanting?* No.
18. *Upon what, besides repentance, must we examine ourselves?*
    Upon our faith, as to whether we have a lively faith in God's mercy through Christ.
19. *What must we believe respecting the mercy of God in Christ?*
    That He hath "given His Son, our Saviour, Jesus Christ, not only to die for us, but also to be our spiritual food and sustenance in this Holy Sacrament."
20. *Why must we believe that God gave His Son to die for us?*
    Because this Sacrament is the "perpetual memory of Christ's precious Death," and the perpetual application of the benefits of that Death.
21. *Why must we see to our belief in God giving His Son to be "our spiritual food and sustenance in this Holy Sacrament?"*
    Because God gives us Christ as the true Bread from Heaven, and Christ offers Himself to us in this Sacrament to be eaten as the Bread of Heaven.
22. *But is it not enough to believe in Christ as our atonement or our righteousness?*
    No: Christ especially offers Himself to us in this Sacrament as our "Living Bread," and we must come particularly believing in this if we would receive Him as our Living Bread.

WHAT IS REQUIRED OF THEM WHO COME. 335

23. *What must be joined with this faith?*
    A thankful remembrance of His Death.
24. *Who are those who will thankfully remember Christ's D*.
    Those who feel their need of it.
25. *As to what besides must we examine ourselves?*
    As to whether we be in charity with all men.
26. *If we are at enmity with any one, what must we do?*
    We must seek reconciliation.
27. *If we have wronged any one, what must we do?*
    We must make amends.
28. *Why must we see to our love and charity before we come to Holy Communion?*
    Because we come to receive the pledges of God's love to us, and of the forgiveness of our own sins.

APPENDIX.

ON CONFIRMATION.

1. *What is Confirmation?*
   The Laying on of hands upon those that are baptized [and are come to years of discretion]. (1–4)
2. *Where in the Prayer Book does the order for Confirmation come?*
   After the Baptismal services and the Catechism.
3. *Why?*
   Because Confirmation is a rite only for baptized Christians, and because the Catechism is "an instruction to be learned of every person, before he be brought to be confirmed by the Bishop."
4. *Does the Church tell us what she means by the term "come to years of discretion?"*
   She directs that "none shall be confirmed but such as can say the Creed, the Lord's Prayer, and the Ten Commandments, and can also answer to such other questions as in the short Catechism are contained." (5, 6)
5. *Who lays his hands upon those that are to be confirmed?*
   The Bishop. (2)
6. *For what purpose?*
   That they may be strengthened with the Holy Ghost. (11)
7. *Is there any other purpose for which he lays his hands upon baptized persons?*
   Yes: "to certify them, by this sign, of God's favour and gracious goodness towards them."
8. *Why does the Church retain this holy custom?*
   Because she has received it from the Apostles of Christ. ["We make our humble supplications unto thee for these thy servants, upon whom (after the example of thy Holy Apostles) we have now laid our hands."]
9. *From what places of Scripture do we learn this?*
   First, from Acts viii. 14–20.
   "When the Apostles which were in Jerusalem heard that Samaria had received the word of God, they sent unto them Peter and John: who, when they were come down, prayed for them, that they might receive the Holy Ghost: (for as yet he was fallen upon none of them: only they were baptized in the name of the Lord Jesus.) Then laid they their hands on them, and they received the Holy Ghost." (13)

10. *What do you gather from this passage?*
   I gather first that there was in the Apostolic Church a sacramental rite or holy custom of " Laying on of hands." (14, 19)
11. *What besides?*
   That this rite was celebrated by the principal ministers of the Church, for the Apostles sent two of their number to give to these Samaritan converts what Philip the deacon or inferior minister could not supply. (17-19)
12. *What besides do you gather?*
   I gather that the hands of the Apostles were laid upon those who had been baptized. (17)
13. *What besides?* That the gift which God gave through the Laying on of the Apostles' hands was the Holy Spirit. (15)
14. *Is there any other instance recorded of the administration of this " Laying on of hands?"*
   Yes : in Acts xix. 1-6.

   "And it came to pass that Paul . . came to Ephesus, and finding certain disciples, he said unto them, Have ye received the Holy Ghost since ye believed? And they said unto him, We have not so much as heard whether there be any Holy Ghost. And he said unto them, Unto what were ye baptized? And they said, Unto John's Baptism. Then said Paul, John verily baptized with the Baptism of repentance, saying to the people that they should believe on him that should come after him, that is, on Christ Jesus. When they heard this they were baptized in the name of the Lord Jesus. And when Paul had laid his hands upon them the Holy Ghost came on them, and they spake with tongues and prophesied." (20)

15. *What do you gather from this account?*
   The same four things which I gathered from the first account. 1. That there was in the Apostolic Church a rite of " Laying on of hands." 2. That the chief pastors of the Church (in this case the Apostle Paul) administered it. 3. That it was ordained in order that men might receive the gift of the Holy Ghost ; and, 4. That it was performed on those who had been baptized. (21-25)
16. *But is it not said that these men spake with tongues and prophesied?*
   Yes. (26)
17. *What gifts of the Spirit are these called?*
   The extraordinary gifts. (30)
18. *Have these gifts ceased to accompany the laying on of hands?* They seem to have ceased. (27)
19. *Is it right then that the rulers of the Church should now lay their hands on the baptized, although they no longer confer such gifts?*

z

Yes: it is right. For the Holy Spirit is the same now as then; and though these extraordinary manifestations of His presence have ceased, yet His ordinary gifts are yet vouchsafed to us. (28)

20. *Were these extraordinary gifts of the Spirit given only through this " Laying on of hands ?"*

No: they were by no means confined to it. In Acts viii. 6-13, they seem to have preceded it. In the case of Cornelius and his household (Acts x. 44-46) they preceded Baptism. Our blessed Lord laid His hands upon infants, without, of course, conferring on them such gifts, but only, as is supposed, ordinary spiritual grace adapted to their years.

21. *Which are the most important, the extraordinary or the ordinary gifts of the Spirit?*

His ordinary gifts; for if we do not receive these we do not receive Him at all. (32, 33)

22. *What gifts do we all require for our salvation, or for the perfection of our Christian life?*

Those which the Bishop, before he confirms us, prays that we may receive. "The spirit of wisdom and understanding, the spirit of counsel and ghostly (spiritual) strength, the spirit of knowledge and true godliness, and the spirit of God's holy fear." (34-36)

23. *What passage of Scripture clearly proves the perpetual obligation of this " Laying on of hands ?"*

Hebrews vi. 1, 2.

"Therefore leaving the principles of the doctrine of Christ, let us go on unto perfection: not laying again the foundation of repentance from dead works, and of faith toward God, of the doctrine of Baptisms, and of laying on of hands, and of resurrection of the dead, and of eternal judgment." (37)

24. *What do you gather from this passage?*

I gather that a " Laying on of hands " is one of the principles or foundations of the doctrine of Christ, and so that all Christians must receive it. (38-40)

25. *How does this passage show that all Christians are bound to receive it?*

Because this " Laying on of hands " is reckoned by the Apostle as a principle or foundation along with matters of such universal obligation as Repentance, Faith, and Baptism. (4~, 41)

26. *Show this further.*

As we acknowledge that all men must exercise Repentance and Faith, and receive Baptism, and look for the Resurrection of the dead, so (if we are to be guided by this Scripture) they must all receive this "Laying on of hands," whatever it be. (43, 44)

27. *But is there any other "laying on of hands" practised in the Church of Christ?*
Yes. In Ordination : in which, men, by the imposition of hands, are set apart for the work of the ministry. (45)

28. *Is it likely that this latter is meant in this place?*
No ; because the Apostle is enumerating certain things which all must have or receive, and the Laying on of hands in Ordination pertains to a very few Christians ; whereas such Laying on of hands as is mentioned in the book of the Acts and in ancient Church history was administered to all. (46)

29. *What then does this last passage* (Heb. vi. 1, 2) *teach us respecting Confirmation?*
That being of general obligation it is intended, not for the age of the Apostles only, but for all ages of the Church. (47, 48)

30. *Show how it teaches this.*
Here are six principles or foundations : five of these are, by common consent, considered necessary for all Christians at all periods of the existence of the Church. Why should we make a difference in respect of the sixth, and say that it was only for Apostolic times ? (47, 48)

31. *Express this more plainly.*
All persons must repent of "dead works," and believe in God, and be baptized into the body of Christ ; that is, they must realize the first three principles: must they not also now, just as much as then, receive the strengthening grace conferred in " Laying on of hands," which is the fourth ? (41–48)

32. *What practical view of Confirmation do we get from this last passage?* (Heb. vi. 1, 2.)
If it be classed along with repentance, and the resurrection, as a first principle, it must be of very great importance, and so it must be a very serious thing indeed either to receive it or to reject it.

33. *What then do we gather from these three Scripture references to the " Laying on of hands ?"*
We gather from the two first that God has ordained a rite of " Laying on of hands," in order that, in its due re-

ception, His people may receive the increase of His Holy Spirit: we gather also that it should be administered by the chief Pastors of His Church: we gather from the third passage that it is a principle or foundation of our holy religion; and so can neither be rejected on the one hand, nor received carelessly on the other, without very great sin.

34. *If all this be so, how should you come to such an ordinance?*
I should come to it in faith and with prayer.

35. *In what faith should you come?*
In the faith that God is as ready to bless me in this Holy Rite, with His Holy Spirit, as He was to bless those who received it in the times of the Apostles.

36. *On what grounds can you believe this?*
On the ground that the Church is the same now as it was in the Apostles' time, and that Christ, its Head, is "the same yesterday, to-day, and for ever." (Heb. xiii. 8.)

37. *But is there now a ministry which can give it?*
Yes: Christ said to the Apostles, "Lo, I am with you alway, even unto the end of the world," though before fifty years after He thus spake almost every Apostle had been removed by death. (51–53)

38. *How does this apply to Confirmation?*
Since the end of the world is not yet come and yet the Apostles have been long dead, these words must have been spoken to the Apostles as representing a ministry which was to last till Christ comes again. So that Christ is just as present with those who now lay on hands in His Name as He was with those who did so in the Apostolic age.

39. *But are not Bishops now very far behind the Apostles in grace and labours?*
They may be, and, if so, all the more reason have we to believe that it is an ever present Christ Who confirms by their hands.

40. *Do the Apostles make the efficacy of their acts to depend upon anything personal in themselves?*
No. St. Paul expressly disclaims such a thing where he says, "We have this treasure in earthen vessels, that the excellency of the power may be of God, and not of us." (11 Cor. iv. 7.)

41. *Was there any essential difference between Apostles and other men?*

No. An Apostle says to the Heathen, "We are men of like passions with you." (Acts xiv. 15.)

42. *But is it not hard to believe that any man can, by the laying on of hands, make his fellow man a partaker of the Spirit of God?*

Not harder than to believe that one man can graft another into Christ by Baptism, and that one man can, in a heavenly way, make another a partaker of the Body and Blood of Him Who is now at the right hand of God.

43. *What will assist us to believe in such great things?*

We must realize that it is not man who works these things, but Christ Who works them by the hands of man. (56)

44. *What use should we make of those passages of Scripture which teach us that Confirmation is a first principle, and that through "Laying on of hands" the Holy Ghost was given? Should we use these mainly to defend the truth against opponents?*

No, certainly not. We should read, mark, and learn them, to stir up our faith in the ever present power of Christ to make all the ordinances of His Church effectual. (57)

45. *What effect should the belief that God will give us grace in Confirmation have upon us?*

It should make us pray very earnestly that we may receive God's Holy Spirit when the hands of His servant are laid upon us. (54–56)

46. *Can we hope to receive a blessing without earnest prayer on our own part?* No, assuredly not. (55)

47. *But have we not received a gift of God's Spirit when we could not ourselves pray, as when we were baptized in early infancy?*

Yes; but they who come to Confirmation are no longer infants. They are at least of an age to know what was promised in their name at their Baptism, and "with their own mouth and consent to ratify and confirm the same."

48. *But if Confirmation be so precious a means of grace, how is it that so many seem to receive no grace in it?*

Because they do not expect God's grace in it, or desire it, and so do not pray for it; or because they come without repentance for past sin, or without faith in the promises of God.

49. *Can there be any other reason?* No.

50. *But do not many say that because they believe in Christ, they have no need of Confirmation, and can be saved without it?*

We have nothing to do with what the "many" say. If God has led us to expect a blessing from Himself in the use of any means of grace, if we are faithful, we shall thankfully use such means.

51. *Hitherto we have been considering Confirmation as a means of grace. What, in addition to this, has the Church of England connected with it?*

She has connected with it the ratification of the promises and vows made in our name at our Baptism. (63)

52. *How will you be enabled to ratify the solemn promises and vows made in your name?*

The Bishop will say to all that are to be confirmed, "Do ye here, in the presence of God and of this congregation, renew the solemn promise and vow that was made in your name at your Baptism; ratifying and confirming the same in your own persons, and acknowledging yourselves bound to believe, and to do, all those things which your godfathers and godmothers then undertook for you? (64-67)

53. *What answer do you return to this?*

The answer "I do." [And every one shall audibly answer, I do.]

54. *What mean you by the words "I do?"*

I mean that, "I do here, in the presence of God and of this congregation, renew the solemn promise and vow that was made in my name at my Baptism: I do ratify and confirm the same in my own person: I do acknowledge myself bound to believe and to do all those things which my godfathers and godmother then undertook for me." (69, 70)

55. *Repeat in the words of the Catechism what your godfathers and godmother then undertook for you.*

"They did promise and vow three things in my name: first, that I should renounce the devil and all his works ... secondly, that I should believe all, &c. ... thirdly, that I should keep God's Holy will and commandments," &c. &c. (68)

56. *Express then, in the words of the Catechism, the full meaning of your answer to the Bishop.*

When I say, "I do," I mean that "I do acknowledge

myself bound to renounce the devil and all his works, the pomps and vanity of this wicked world, and all the sinful lusts of the flesh. I do acknowledge myself bound to believe all the Articles of the Christian faith : I do acknowledge myself bound to keep God's Holy will and commandments, and to walk in the same all the days of my life." (68–70)

57. *Is this confirming of our vows any part of the original ordinance of Confirmation ?*
   No. It is added to the original rite of " Laying on of hands " by our branch of the Catholic Church. (76)

58. *Is it not reasonable that there should be a stated time for acknowledging before the Church that we are bound to believe and to do what was promised for us ?*
   Yes. We are baptized as infants before we know what we are bound to believe and to do by our receiving Holy Baptism, and it is most reasonable that there should be a time appointed for us to acknowledge our Baptismal obligations. (74–77)

59. *Supposing that you were baptized without god-parents, are you equally bound to believe and to do the same things ?*
   Yes. If we are dedicated to God, and made members of Christ, we must renounce the enemies of God and of Christ, and we must believe in the faith in which we are baptized, and we must determine to serve and please God.

60. *Are we bound by Confirmation to believe or to do anything more than we are bound to do because we are Baptized ?*
   No. By our Baptism we are bound to walk in newness of life (Rom. vi. 4), and we cannot do more.

61. *How is it with those who refuse or neglect to receive Confirmation ?*
   They reject a means of grace which God has ordained to strengthen us to fulfil His Holy will.

62. *What else do they lose ?*
   They lose the opportunity of confessing before the Church their obligations to the God who made them and has caused them to be baptized into the Church of His Dear Son.

SHORTER CATECHISM.

1. *What is Confirmation?* The Laying on of hands.
2. *By whom?* By the Bishop.
3. *Upon whom?* Upon those who have been baptized.
4. *Does he lay his hands upon the baptized immediately after their Baptism?*
    Not in our branch of the Church.
5. *What baptized persons then are confirmed?*
    Those that have come to years of discretion.
6. *What knowledge does the Church require in them to prove that they are come to years of discretion?*
    That those confirmed can say the Creed, the Lord's Prayer, and the Ten Commandments, and be further instructed in the Catechism.
7. *Does this imply anything else?*
    Yes; that they should understand the meaning of the answers which they give.
8. *Is there any other qualification necessary?*
    Yes: sincerity of heart.
9. *Why are these qualifications necessary?*
    Because each child will at his Confirmation renew before God the solemn promise and vow made in his name.
10. *Is any other qualification needful in those who wish to be confirmed?*
    Yes: a sincere desire and hope to receive God's Holy Spirit.
11. *Why?* Because God ordained Confirmation, that in it Christians should receive the Holy Spirit.
12. *But will they receive God's Spirit if they do not pray for and desire His help?*
    They have no right to expect Him unless they pray for Him.
13. *How do you prove that God ordained Confirmation for the bestowing upon us of His Holy Spirit?*
    I prove it from the Scriptures. Especially from Acts viii. 14–20.
14. *What do you read there?*
    That SS. Peter and John laid their hands on certain baptized persons.
15. *And what did those persons receive?* The Holy Ghost.
16. *Did the Apostles themselves give them the Holy Ghost?*
    No: God gave it to them when the Apostles laid their hands on them.
17. *Had these persons been baptized?*
    Yes: by Philip, one of the seven deacons.
18. *Why then did not Philip lay his hands upon them?*
    Because this power appears to have been exercised only by the Apostles.

19. *Did the Apostles deem this Laying on of hands of importance?*
    Yes: they sent two of their number some distance in a time of persecution, that they might administer it.
20. *Can you prove the "Laying on of hands" from any other example?*
    Yes: from the practice of St. Paul.
21. *Do we read of St. Paul laying his hands on baptized Christians?*
    Yes: he laid his hands on twelve disciples at Ephesus.
22. *For what purpose?*
    That they might receive the Holy Ghost.
23. *Did St. Paul himself baptize these persons?*
    No, probably not (Acts xix. 5 compared with 1 Cor. i. 14, 15).
24. *Did he himself lay his hands on them?*
    It is expressly said that he did.
25. *What do you gather from this?*
    I gather from this place also that it was reserved to the chief ministers to lay on hands.
26. *Was there any outward sign that these persons had received the Spirit?* They spake with tongues.
27. *Is this sign given in Confirmation now?* No.
28. *If, then, these signs have ceased, ought men to be confirmed?*
    Yes: in Confirmation we hope and pray to receive the Spirit Himself.
29. *Are His gifts always the same?*
    No: they are very different in different persons (1 Cor. xii. 8).
30. *What are such gifts as prophecy, miracles, and speaking with tongues called?*
    The extraordinary gifts of the Spirit.
31. *What are such gifts as faith, love, peace, knowledge, called?*
    The ordinary gifts of the Spirit.
32. *Which are the most important?* The ordinary gifts, by far.
33. *Why?*
    Because we may be saved without miracles and the gift of tongues; but we cannot be saved without faith and love.
34. *What does St. Paul consider the best gift of the Spirit?*
    Undoubtedly love or charity (1 Cor. xii. 31; xiii. 1, 13).
35. *What gifts does the Bishop pray that we may receive?*
    The gifts needful for all.
36. *What are they?* Wisdom, understanding, counsel, ghostly strength, knowledge, godliness, holy fear.
37. *Is there any other place which teaches the necessity of Confirmation?*
    Yes: Heb. vi. 1, 2.
38. *What is Confirmation there called?* The Laying on of hands.
39. *Amongst what does St. Paul reckon it?*
    He reckons it amongst the principles or foundations of the Gospel.

40. *How many principles does he enumerate?*
   Six.
41. *What are they?*
   1. Repentance. 2. Faith. 3. The doctrine of Baptism. 4. That of Laying on of hands. 5. The Resurrection. 6. The Judgment.
42. *What must this " Laying on of hands" mean?*
   It must mean that which the Apostles gave.
43. *To whom did they give it?*
   Apparently to all baptized Christians.
44. *Is there any other "Laying on of hands" conferred on all the baptized?* No.
45. *What other laying on of hands is there in the Christian religion?*
   "Laying on of hands" in Ordination.
46. *Is this given to all?*
   No: only to the few Christians who become ordained ministers.
47. *Are any of the other five principles (repentance, faith, &c.) only to be realized by a few?*
   No: all must repent, all believe, and all be baptized; all must look for the resurrection, and all prepare for judgment.
48. *What do we learn from this?*
   That the Laying on of hands is necessary for all, just as the other five principles are.
49. *But is not this too much to say of Confirmation?*
   We do not say it. It is not *we* who have inserted it into this list of principles, but the Holy Spirit.
50. *Is there any other reason for believing that this Laying on of hands is Confirmation?*
   Yes: it follows on the "doctrine of Baptisms," as a thing would naturally do which, like Confirmation, succeeds Baptism.
51. *What minister of the Church now lays his hands on the baptized?*
   The Bishop.
52. *Why?*
   Because Bishops succeed the Apostles.
53. *On what ground do we reserve this power to the Bishops of the Church?*
   Because we find that the Apostles ministered Confirmation to those who had received Baptism from other ministers (Acts viii. 17; xix. 6).
54. *If God has ordained this Laying on of hands, that we may receive His Holy Spirit, what should we do?*
   We should pray earnestly, that we may receive His blessing in it.
55. *Can we hope to receive any benefit in it without prayer?* No.
56. *If we are to pray earnestly, what must we have?*
   We must have faith.
57. *In what will this faith consist?*

In a strong belief that God will be present to give us His blessing.
58. *In order that we may have this belief, what must we remember?*
The promises of God to give us of His Spirit.
59. *Mention one of these promises.*
"I will pour my Spirit upon thy seed, and my blessing upon thine offspring" (Isaiah xliv. 3).
60. *Mention a second.*
"Your Heavenly Father will give the Holy Spirit to them that ask Him" (Luke xi. 13).
61. *But will God give the Holy Spirit only in Confirmation?*
No; but He has led us to expect that He *will* give His Spirit in Confirmation.
62. *Have we, then, any right to expect grace from Him if we refuse Confirmation?*
No: for in such a case we should not submit to God's dispensations.
63. *Is there anything in our Order of Confirmation besides the Laying on of hands and the Bishop's prayers?*
Yes: the renewing of our baptismal promises and vows.
64. *Before whom do we renew those promises and vows?*
Before God and the congregation.
65. *Who ought to be amongst the congregation?*
Every one shall have a godfather or a godmother as a witness of their Confirmation (Rubric at the end of the Catechism).
66. *Who will solemnly ask you to renew your promise and vow?*
The Bishop.
67. *In what words?*
Do ye here, in the presence of God and of this congregation, &c.
68. *Have you learned what your godfathers and godmothers promised for you in Baptism?*
Yes: I learned all this when I learned the Catechism.
69. *What, then, is now your duty?*
"I must myself, with my own mouth and consent, openly before the Church, ratify and confirm the same."
70. *And what besides?*
"I must also promise that, by the grace of God, I will evermore endeavour myself faithfully to observe them."
71. *Who confirms you?* The Bishop.
72. *How?* By laying his hands on me.
73. *In whose name and power does he do this?*
In God's name, and relying only on His power.
74. *Do you confirm anything?*
Yes: I ratify and *confirm* in my own person what was promised in my name.

75. *Is there any difference between the Bishop's confirming and your confirming?*
    Yes: the greatest possible difference.
76. *What is the Bishop's confirming?*
    It is strengthening—God giving me strength by the Laying on of hands.
77. *What is your confirming?*
    It is renewing in my own person my baptismal vows.
78. *What must you have if you are to benefit by the Bishop's confirming you?*
    I must have a sincere desire to receive the grace of God.
79. *How will this desire show itself?* In earnest prayer.
80. *What must you have to make you confirm aright your baptismal vows?*
    I must have a sincere resolution to serve and please God.

PRAYERS FOR CANDIDATES.

[One of the following, or some other suitable prayer, should be reprinted or written out, and a copy given to each candidate, to be used night and morning during the time of preparation, and the whole class, or each member privately, should be frequently urged to use it.]

O MOST merciful God, I thank Thee that Thou hast called me to the knowledge of Thy grace and faith in Thee. Increase this knowledge, and confirm this faith in me evermore. Give me Thy help now that I am preparing to draw near to Thee in Confirmation, cleanse me from all the sins of my past life, and give me a true sorrow for them. Help me to know how sinful and weak I am, that I may learn to trust only in Jesus Christ for pardon and strength. Grant that when the hand of Thy servant the Bishop is laid upon me I may receive such an increase of the gift of Thy Holy Spirit that I may conquer all the temptations of the world, the flesh, and the devil (especially . . . .), and continue in Thy faith and love unto my life's end. Prepare me to receive with a true penitent heart and lively faith the Holy Sacrament of the Body and Blood of Christ, and grant that I may never fall from Thee, but be at last received into Thine heavenly Kingdom, for Jesus Christ's sake. *Amen.* (*Altered and adapted from a prayer in "The Narrow Way."*)

O GOD, by whose merciful Providence the Holy Church continueth to observe the laying on of hands, we beseech Thee to be with Thy servant, our Bishop, when, after the example of Thy Holy Apostles, he shall administer in this place the Holy Rite of Confirmation. Grant me, I beseech Thee, Thy heavenly grace, that I may partake of it with an undefiled body, a watchful mind, and a pure heart; that being strengthened with might by Thy Spirit in the inner man, I may never be ashamed to confess the faith of Christ crucified, but manfully fight under His banner against sin, the world, and the devil, and continue His faithful soldier unto my life's end : through the same Jesus Christ our Lord. *Amen.* (*Altered and adapted from a Prayer by Bishop Doane.*)

O LORD God, who hast sent Thy Holy Spirit into the world to comfort us and to lead us into all truth, I pray Thee that I, believing in Thy promises and trusting in Thy love, may be so prepared by Thee to receive the grace of Confirmation, that I may come with faith and a penitent heart unto that Holy Mystery, and may obtain the fulness of those gifts which Thou dost promise, so that I may have strength to resist all sin and grace to persevere unto the end : through Jesus Christ our Lord. *Amen.* (*Altered and adapted from a Prayer in a Catechism on Confirmation by a Committee of Clergy.*)

THE END.

LONDON:
PRINTED BY W. CLOWES AND SONS, STAMFORD STREET
AND CHARING CROSS.

WORKS BY THE REV. M. F. SADLER.

PARISH SERMONS.
Vol. I. ADVENT TO TRINITY. *Second Edition.* 6s.
Vol. II. TRINITY TO ADVENT. *Second Edition.* 6s.
Vol. III. PLAIN SPEAKING ON DEEP TRUTHS. *Second Edition.* 6s.
Vol. IV. ABUNDANT LIFE. 6s.

CHURCH DOCTRINE—BIBLE TRUTH. *Fourth Edition.*
Tenth Thousand. Fcap. 8vo. 5s.

This Work contains a full discussion of the so-called Damnatory Clauses of the Athanasian Creed. The New Edition has additional Notes on Transubstantiation and Apostolical Succession.

"Some writers have the gift of speaking the right word at the right time, and the Rev. M. F. Sadler is pre-eminently one of them. 'Church Doctrine—Bible Truth' is full of wholesome truths fit for these times. . . . He has the power of putting his meaning in a forcible and intelligible way, which will, we trust, enable his valuable work to effect that which it is well calculated to effect, viz., to meet with an appropriate and crushing reply one of the most dangerous misbeliefs of the time."—*Guardian.*

THE SECOND ADAM AND THE NEW BIRTH; or, the
Doctrine of Baptism as contained in Holy Scripture. *Fourth Edition,* greatly enlarged. Fcap. 8vo. 4s. 6d.

"The most striking peculiarity of this useful little work is that its author argues almost exclusively from the Bible. We commend it most earnestly to clergy and laity, as containing in a small compass, and at a trifling cost, a body of sound and Scriptural doctrine, respecting the New Birth, which cannot be too widely circulated."—*Guardian.*

THE SACRAMENT OF RESPONSIBILITY; or, Testimony of the Scripture to the teaching of the Church on Holy Baptism, with especial reference to the Cases of Infants; and Answers to Objections. *Sixth Edition.* 6d.

————— With the addition of an Introduction, in which the religious speculations of the last twenty years are considered in their bearings on the Church doctrine of Holy Baptism, and an Appendix giving the testimony of writers of all ages and schools of thought in the Church. On fine paper, and neatly bound in cloth. 2s. 6d.

LONDON: BELL AND DALDY, YORK STREET, COVENT GARDEN.

www.ingramcontent.com/pod-product-compliance
Lightning Source LLC
Chambersburg PA
CBHW031427230426
43668CB00007B/465